Eco-restructuring: Implications for sustainable development

Robert U. Ayres, Editor
Paul M. Weaver, Assistant Editor

With the editorial support of
Gilberto Gallopín, Walther Manshard,
R. Socolow, Mikoto Usui

**United Nations
University Press**

TOKYO · NEW YORK · PARIS

D1367951

United Nations University Press
The United Nations University, 53-70, Jingumae 5-chome,
Shibuya-ku, Tokyo 150, Japan
Tel: (03) 3499-2811   Fax: (03) 3406-7345
E-mail: mbox@hq.unu.edu

UNU Office in North America
2 United Nations Plaza, Room DC2-1462-70, New York, NY 10017
Tel: (212) 963-6387   Fax: (212) 371-9454   Telex: 422311 UN UI

United Nations University Press is the publishing division of the United Nations University.

Cover design by Kerkhoven Associates, London

Printed in the United States of America

UNUP-984
ISBN 92-808-0984-9

Library of Congress Cataloging-in-Publication Data

Eco-restructuring : implications for sustainable development /
Robert U. Ayres, editor ; Paul M. Weaver, assistant editor ; with
the editorial support of Gilberto Gallopin . . . [et al.].
    p.   cm.
  Includes bibliographical references and index.
  ISBN 92-808-0984-9 (pbk.)
  1. Sustainable development. 2. Environmental policy. I. Ayres,
Robert U. II. Weaver, Paul M. (Paul Michael). 1956-
  HC79.E5 E217   1998
  333.7—ddc21

                                                            98-8938
                                                              CIP

Contents

1   Eco-restructuring: The transition to an
ecologically sustainable economy   1
Robert U. Ayres

Part I: Restructuring resource use

2   The biophysical basis of eco-restructuring: An
overview of current relations between human
economic activities and the global system   55
Walther Manshard

3   Ecological process engineering: The potential of
bioprocessing   77
Anton Moser

4   Materials futures: Pollution prevention, recycling,
and improved functionality   109
*Pradeep Rohatgi, Kalpana Rohatgi, and
Robert U. Ayres*

v

Contents

5 Global energy futures: The long-term perspective for eco-restructuring   149
Hans-Holger Rogner

6 Fuel decarbonization for fuel cell applications and sequestration of the separated CO_2 180
Robert H. Williams

7 Photovoltaics   223
Paolo Frankl

Part II: Restructuring sectors and the sectoral balance of the economy

8 Global eco-restructuring and technological change in the twenty-first century   259
Faye Duchin

9 Agro-eco-restructuring: Potential for sustainability   276
Heinrich Wohlmeyer

10 The restructuring of tropical land-use systems   311
Gilberto C. Gallopín

11 The restructuring of transport, logistics, trade, and industrial space use   338
Paul M. Weaver

12 National and international policy instruments and institutions for eco-restructuring   364
Mikoto Usui

Contributors   408

Index   410

1

Eco-restructuring: The transition to an ecologically sustainable economy

Robert U. Ayres

The paper that follows was originally prepared for the United Nations University (UNU) as a background "white" paper in support of the development of UNU's long-term research programme (in fact, the UNU version was based on an earlier version that I prepared for a workshop held at IIASA in January 1991). As such, it was also the main background paper for the UNU Eco-Restructuring Conference held in Tokyo in July 1993, at which most of the papers in this book were first presented.

For various reasons, the preparation of this book from those conference papers has been an unusually long and difficult process. The review and revision process has been very slow. A few of the original papers had to be dropped because the authors were too busy to undertake necessary revisions and submit revised versions. Some that were topical at the time have become a little dated. To fill gaps (some of which were evident from the start) several additional papers have been solicited and included. But because these authors were not present at the conference they lacked the common background and required more than the usual amount of "editorial guidance." I think, however, that the final result is useful and interesting, if not the "last word" on the subject (which, in any case, will never be written).

1

The objective of the 1993 Tokyo conference was to explore the technical and economic feasibility of long-term sustainability. The conference did not totally neglect the political and institutional issues, but they were deliberately given secondary status. Social and cultural issues were set aside altogether, as being outside our collective ken. The overarching issue of population control was discussed only in my background paper, which follows, and only in terms of generalities. The bulk of the book deals with technological issues. Economics should have been given more attention than it was, but few economists are prepared to take on the practical aspects of long-range restructuring. This remains an open subject for future research.

Because of the background sketched above, I have since revised the paper only moderately to respond to reviewers' comments, while retaining much of its original logical structure. I recognize that the structure is not ideal for the intended audience of the book. (It is probably not ideal for any audience). But, as I say, the paper was essentially the "terms of reference" for all the other authors. To change it fundamentally would be a little unfair.

It must be acknowledged that, in many ways, the terms of the discussion have changed since the paper was written. In some ways, as on the problem of global climate change, there has been clear progress. One can only applaud this fact. On the other hand, thanks to the too vague definition offered in the Brundtland Commission Report *Our Common Future*, the term "sustainability" has been popularized and made virtually meaningless in recent years. It has been consistently misused, in particular, by the World Bank and other economic development agencies. These institutions are inclined to interpret "sustainable development" as "perpetual growth," which is an extreme perversion of the original sense of the phrase. But sustainability is also now an icon of generalized political correctness, where it is carelessly applied to a variety of attributes from culture to democracy.

Holding to the original sense of the word, this chapter seeks to sort out the questions about sustainability on which there is substantial scientific agreement from those unresolved questions that are still subject to considerable controversy. In this context, several testable theses are proposed. The first thesis is that there *are* limits to the capacity of the natural environment to accommodate anthropogenic disturbances. The earth is finite. Second, there are also limits to the substitutability of conventional market goods and services for environmental services. Third, there are limits to the extent to which technology can repair or replace environmental resources that are irreversibly damaged. For instance, only the most naive technological optimist can imagine undertaking to substitute positive engineering control systems, designed by humans, for natural means of climate control and stabilization.

With respect to some controversial questions we cannot expect firm answers. For instance, there is a possibility that nature may be exceedingly adaptable, resilient, and resistant to anthropogenic disturbance. Or nature may not be so resilient. It is conceivable, too, that human ingenuity could invent engineering alternatives to natural processes being threatened, or that technology could offer means of "adaptation" to ecological and climatic stress. However, the argument is that these possibilities are not probabilities. The limits of resilience are probably not very distant, and it is very difficult to justify a high degree of confidence that "business as usual" can continue without risk for even a few more decades.

In brief, the underlying problem is that many current demographic, economic, and industrial trends currently seem to point unmistakably in the wrong direction, i.e. away from sustainability. To achieve sustainability, and to minimize ecological risk, it will be necessary to reverse most of these trends. Indeed, some aggregated measures of material and energy use may have to be reduced by large factors (four to ten). Such a reversal will entail very fundamental changes in the economic system. The directions and magnitudes of these changes are assessed briefly, and various approaches to their implementation are analysed.

Introduction: On sustainability

Before the beginning of the industrial revolution, some two centuries ago, human activities – on the average – were not really incompatible with a healthy and sustainable biosphere. The vast majority of humans lived and worked on farms. Land was the primary source of wealth. Horses and other animals, supplemented by windmills, sails, and waterwheels, provided virtually all power for ploughing, milling, mining, and transport. The sun, either directly or through products of photosynthesis, provided virtually all energy except in a few coal-mining regions. Metals were mined and smelted (primarily by means of charcoal), but their uses were almost exclusively metallic rather than chemical. Recycling was normal. Precisely because wealth was derived exclusively from the land, Thomas Malthus worried at the end of the eighteenth century about the propensity of human population to grow exponentially, in view of the limited amount of potentially arable land available for human cultivation.

As we approach the end of the twentieth century, humans are far more numerous and also wealthier (on average) than they were two centuries ago when Malthus wrote. In particular, those countries that industrialized first are now comparatively rich. In the rich countries most people live in cities. Land is no longer the primary source of wealth. Energy (except food) is largely derived from the combustion of fossil fuels (coal, oil, gas). Power for machines is obtained mainly from engines driven by heat from (internal or external) combustion of fossil fuels. (Nuclear and hydroelectric power, together, account for a relatively small percentage of the total.) However, one key attribute of this recent rise to wealth is critical for the future of humankind: what we have achieved so far has been done by exploiting an endowment of natural capital, especially topsoil and minerals. For some material resources technology can offer viable substitutes. For other resources in the natural endowment – notably the biosphere and its functions – no substitute is likely.

The report of the United Nations' World Commission on Environment and Development (WCED) – known as the Brundtland Commission – was published in 1987 under the title *Our Common Future*. This triggered the Global Environmental Summit at Rio de Janeiro in June 1992 and its major product, *Agenda 21*. Since that time it has been widely recognized that there is a very real conflict between meeting the needs and desires of the 5 billion people now alive and the possibility of satisfying the 10 billion or so people expected by the middle of the twenty-first century. It will be exceedingly difficult simultaneously to satisfy the objectives of environmental preservation, on the one hand, and accelerated economic development of the third world, based on current population trends and energy/material-intensive technologies, on the other. The implications of this conflict have been delineated eloquently in the Commission's report (Brundtland 1987; McNeill 1989). They need not be spelled out in detail again here.

Experts can and do disagree on the probabilities and timing of environmental threats relative to other problems facing the human race. Some ideologues have even argued that the threats are figments of the fevered imaginations of the "Greens." I think not. Arguments on these matters will probably continue for some time to come. But there is increasing evidence to suggest that major changes in the global economic and industrial system may be needed if the world is to achieve a sustainable state before the middle of the twenty-first century. Even though there is not yet a scientific consensus on the extent of the needed changes, it is clear that they will involve significant technological elements, as well as major investments.

The population problem comes to mind first, especially in the context of the 1994 Cairo Conference on Population and the Status of Women. It is unlikely that the other problems of the global environment can be solved if the world's population is not stabilized. Experts now generally agree that education and the status of women are central issues here. This implies that a world of relatively stable population must be one in which social patterns are significantly different from those now encountered in many parts of the world.

The kinds of techno-economic changes envisaged as necessary conditions for long-term sustainability also include a sharp reduction in the use of fossil fuels (especially coal) to minimize the danger of global "greenhouse warming." Alternatives to increasing use of fossil fuels include a return to nuclear power, large-scale use of photo-voltaics, intensive biomass cultivation, large-scale hydroelectric projects (in some regions), and major changes in patterns of energy consumption and conservation. Again, there are disputes over which of these energy alternatives is the most (least) desirable, feasible, etc. However, the future of energy, from both the supply (technology) and the demand perspective, is a critical topic (to which several chapters of this book are devoted).

Again, the broad question addressed in this book is how to shift from a techno-economic "trajectory" based on exploiting natural resources – soil, water, biodiversity, climate – that, once lost, can never be replaced, to one that could lead to a future society that preserves and conserves these resources. To facilitate this search, this chapter approaches the problem in three stages. First, it attempts to identify the most pressing questions, especially with regard to the severity of the threat and the technical feasibility of solutions. Next, it attempts to distinguish those questions on which there is little or no scientific disagreement from those on which the evidence itself is disputed. Thirdly, it raises the most fundamental question of all: how to get from "where we are" to "where we need to be."

However, before plunging into the argument, some subsidiary topics are worthy of brief mention. These are discussed in the next two sections.

The need for holistic systems analysis

Since the early 1970s, the environmental movement has become increasingly professionalized and bureaucratized. As a consequence, largely, of the latter development, the "environment" is seen no longer in a holistic sense but in terms of a number of specific, essentially independent issues. Nowadays, the "causes" of pollution are attributed, for the most part, to narrowly defined actions (or failures to act) of equally narrowly defined "polluters." The responsibilities for abatement or clean-up are correspondingly narrow. Solid wastes, hazardous or toxic wastes, liquid wastes, and airborne wastes are likely to be allocated to different government departments, ranging from public health agencies to water/sewerage authorities, whose regulatory powers are controlled by different kinds of legislation framed in different circumstances, sometimes based on quite different regulatory philosophies. "The right hand does not know what the left hand is doing," and vice versa.

Activities of different arms of the same agency can interfere with each other. For instance, incineration can reduce the solid waste disposal problem, and even produce useful energy as a by-product, but it creates an air pollution problem. On the other hand, to reduce the emissions of particulates and sulphur oxides from power plants creates solid wastes that must be disposed of somewhere on land. There is nobody with a global view of the problem to mediate among the parochial interests. There is nobody with the responsibility or the authority to induce competing offices, departments, and bureaux to cooperate.

Yet the environment is, by its very nature, unsuited to incremental control strategies. It is equally unsuited for reductionist "bottom–up" modes of analysis. The problem is that scientific insights are now, and will continue to be, insufficient for predicting the detailed environmental consequences of any change or perturbation. To take a concrete instance, nobody can predict the exact physiological effects of ingesting any chemical from knowledge of its structure. Still less can the genetic or ecological consequences of its dispersion be predicted. This uncertainty is multiplied by the enormous number of different chemicals, materials, and mixtures simultaneously manufactured and used by man (natural and synthetic alike), not to mention the variety (type and intensity) of possible reaction modes and interaction effects.

Setting aside carcinogens and highly toxic or radioactive substances,[1] only one important environmental problem has as yet been predicted in advance from the creation or displacement of any particular material stream. This single exception was Rowland's chance recognition of the reactive potential of chlorofluorocarbons (CFCs) in the stratosphere, and the resulting possibility of stratospheric ozone depletion. This potential hazard, derided by chemical industry spokesmen in the 1970s as "speculative," has turned out to be real.

In speaking of the environment it is literally true that "everything depends upon everything else." A holistic "top–down" perspective is essential to identifying the most important underlying factors and relationships. It is equally important to adopt a very broad perspective for seeking and – it is hoped – finding effective global strategies to save the planet.

Environmental threats and (un)sustainability indicators

There has been a good deal of academic debate in recent years on the exact meaning that should be ascribed to the term "sustainability." For instance, Repetto states that "current decisions should not impair the prospects for maintaining or improving future living standards" (Repetto 1985, p. 16). The WCED paraphrased the same general idea; sustainable development "meets the needs of the present without compromising the ability of future generations to meet their own needs" (Brundtland 1987). Tietenberg phrases it in utility terms, and defines sustainability as non-declining utility (Tietenberg 1984, p. 33). Pezzey goes further and insists that it is the discounted present value of utility that should not decline (Pezzey 1989). Mainstream economists have concerned themselves with replacing depleted natural resource stocks. For instance, Nobel Laureate Robert Solow proposed that "an appropriate stock of capital – including the initial endowment of resources – [be] maintained intact" (Solow 1986). More recently Solow has said: "If 'sustainability' is anything more than a slogan or an expression of emotion, it must amount to an injunction to preserve productive capacity for the indefinite future. That is compatible with the use of non-renewable resources only if society as a whole replaces used-up resources with something else" (Solow 1992).

All of these definitions (and others) essentially agree on a single economic measure of welfare (GNP). They fundamentally assume unlimited substitutability between conventional economic goods and services that are traded in the market-place and unpriced environmental services, from stratospheric ozone to the carbon cycle. However, virtually all environmentalists and an increasing number of economists explicitly reject the unlimited substitutability view as simplistic (e.g. Boulding 1966; Ayres and Kneese 1971; Ayres 1978; Daly 1990). Similar critiques have been articulated by David Pearce and his colleagues (Pearce 1988; Pearce et al. 1989).

The "ecological" criterion for sustainability admits the likelihood that some of the important functions of the natural world cannot be replaced within any realistic time-frame – if ever – by human technology, however sophisticated. The need for arable land, water, and a benign climate for agriculture is an example; the role of reducing bacteria in recycling nutrient elements in the biosphere is another; the ozone layer of the stratosphere is a third. The ecological criterion for long-run sustainability implicitly allows for some technological intervention: for example, methods of artificially accelerating tree growth may compensate for some net decrease in the area devoted to forests. But, absent any plausible technological "fixes," this definition does *not* admit the acceptability of major climate changes, widespread desertification, deforestation of the tropics, accumulation of toxic heavy metals and non-biodegradable halogenated organics in soils and sediments, or sharp reductions in biodiversity, for instance.

Having said this, it is obviously easier to find indicators of unsustainability than of sustainability. In work for the Advisory Council for Research on Nature and the Environment (Netherlands), preparing for the UNCED Conference in Rio de Janeiro, 1992, Dutch researchers proposed a taxonomy of sustainability indicators (Weterings and Opschoor 1992). Their taxonomy has three dimensions:

1. Pollution of natural systems with xenobiotic substances or natural substances in unnatural concentrations. The results include acidification and "toxification" of the environment.
2. Depletion of natural resources: renewable, non-renewable, and semi-renewable. In fact, biodiversity can be regarded as a depletable resource, though not one that is commonly thought of as such. Of course, it also differs from other depletable resources that are exchanged in (and priced by) well-developed markets. There is no such market for biodiversity, or for its complement, genetic information. Nevertheless, I regard this as a market failure and argue that loss of biodiversity is an aspect of depletion.
3. Encroachment (human intervention) affecting natural systems, e.g. loss of groundwater or soil erosion.

8

Based on this taxonomy, Weterings and Opschoor prepared the summary table of quantifiable sustainability indicators shown in table 1.1. The notion of "sustainable level" in regard to pollution, toxification, acidification, greenhouse gas build-up, and so on is predicated on the idea that natural processes will compensate for some of the damage. For instance, natural weathering of rocks generates some alkaline materials that can neutralize acid. (Increased acidity will, however, increase the rate of weathering.) Similarly, it is assumed that some of the excess carbon dioxide produced by combustion processes may be absorbed in the oceans or taken up by accelerated photosynthetic activity in northern forests (this process is called "CO_2 fertilization").

Regarding depletion, it is assumed that some minerals (such as aluminium) can be mined more or less indefinitely, even though the highest-quality ores will be exhausted first. Other depletable ores could in effect be exhausted, in the sense that recovery from minable ores would be too expensive to be worthwhile except for very specialized and limited uses. Copper might be an example of this kind (though many geologists are more optimistic than Weterings and Opschoor). As regards renewable resources such as fisheries and groundwater, it has long been known that there is a level of exploitation that can be sustained indefinitely by scientific management, but that beyond that level harvesting pressures can drive populations down to the point where recovery may take decades, or may never occur at all. Many fisheries appear to be in this situation at present, notwithstanding the fact that sustainable levels are not very precisely known. Granted some uncertainty, it is nevertheless clear that, in all three dimensions, "sustainability" would require significant reductions in current levels of impact.

In recognition of the fact that both soil erosion and groundwater loss overlap considerably with the "depletion" category, the later version of their work substituted "loss of naturalness," namely loss of integrity, diversity, absence of disturbance (Weterings and Opschoor 1994). What remains in category (3) is the notion of "disturbance of natural systems" as such. Most environmentalists think of "systems" in terms of ecosystems and biomes. The sum total of such disturbances is indeed a significant environmental problem, though individual cases tend to be geographically localized. However there are also global systems that are being dangerously disturbed by anthropogenic activity. Examples of global systems include the hydro-

Table 1.1 **Sustainable vs. expected level of environmental impact for selected indicators**

Dimension/indicator of environmental impact	Sustainable level	Expected level, 2040	Desired reduction	Scale
Depletion of fossil fuels:				
Oil	Stock for 50 years	Stock exhausted	**85%**	Global
Natural gas	Stock for 50 years	Stock exhausted	**70%**	Global
Coal	Stock for 50 years	Stock exhausted	**20%**	Global
Depletion of metals:				
Aluminium	Stock for 50 years	Stock for >50 years	**None**	Global
Copper	Stock for 50 years	Stock exhausted	**80%**	Global
Uranium	Stock for 50 years	Depends on use of nuclear energy	Not quantifiable	Global
Depletion of renewable resources:				
Biomass	20% terr. animal biomass	50% terr. animal bio-mass	**60%**	Global
	20% terr. primary production	50% terr. primary production	**60%**	Global
Diversity of species	Extinction of 5 species/year	365–65,000 species/year	**99%**	Global
Pollution:				
Emission of CO_2	2.6 gigatonnes carbon/year	13.0 gigatonnes carbon/year	**80%**	Global
Acid deposition	400 acid eq./hectare/year	2400–3600 acid eq.	**85%**	Continental

10

Deposition of nutrients	P: 30 kg/hectare/year	No quantitative data	Not quantifiable	National
	N: 267 kg/hectare/year	No quantitative data	Not quantifiable	National
Deposition of metals:				
Cadmium	2 tonnes/year	50 tonnes/year	**95%**	National
Copper	70 tonnes/year	830 tonnes/year	**90%**	National
Lead	58 tonnes/year	700 tonnes/year	**90%**	National
Zinc	215 tonnes/year	5190 tonnes/year	**95%**	National
Encroachment:				
Impairment through dehydration	Reference year 1950	No quantitative data	Not quantifiable	National
Soil loss through erosion	9.3 billion tonnes/year	45–60 million tonnes/ year	**85%**	Global

Source: Weterings and Opschoor (1992), table 6, p. 25.

logical cycle, ocean currents, the climate, the global radiation balance (including the ozone layer that protects the earth's surface from lethal ultraviolet radiation), the carbon/oxygen cycle, the nitrogen cycle, and the sulphur cycle.[2] This problem is discussed in detail later.

Holistic analysis presupposes that it is possible to classify variables by degree of importance and derive significant and defensible results by judicious simplification. A universal measure to estimate and compare the relative environmental impact of different activities, goods, services, and regulatory policies would be of great value.

Such a measure should satisfy the following conditions:
- it should be based on measurable quantities;
- it should relate to the most significant environmental impact potentials of human activities;
- it should allow transparent, cost-efficient, and reproducible estimates of the environmental impact potentials of all kinds of plans, processes, goods, and services;
- it must be applicable on the global level as well as regional and local levels.

Choosing a single indicator to compare the environmental impact intensities of all kinds of present and future processes, goods, and services might seem to be a daring step, precisely because it constitutes a vast reduction of complexity. Simplification cannot be proven to be "correct" in scientific terms.[3] Only its plausibility in a variety of circumstances can be established.

For several reasons it can be argued that aggregate *resource productivity,* the ratio of GNP (or a better unit of economic welfare) to an index of total renewable-but-unrenewed or non-renewable resource inputs, in physical units, might be a plausible measure of sustainability. At least the two are correlated: the greater the resource productivity, the nearer to long-term sustainability. Obviously, the inverse of resource productivity – non-renewable or non-renewed resource use per unit of welfare output – is a measure of unsustainability.

Regrettably, neither this measure nor anything similar is currently computed at the national level by statistical agencies, and the required data are not readily available even to them, still less to non-government organizations. However, note that the corresponding measure can be computed in principle for a sector (industry), a firm, a region with well-defined boundaries, or even a single product. Something like the inverse of resource productivity, *materials intensity per unit service* (MIPS), has been calculated for a number of specific cases at the Wuppertal Institute.[4]

Sharpening the debate

It is important now to confront three basic questions:

(1) Is continued economic growth (appropriately defined) compatible *in principle* with long-run ecological sustainability?

(2) If so, is our current mix of technologies and economic instruments consistent *in practice* with this goal?

(3) If not, what is the "least-cost" (and "least-pain") political/ institutional path from where we are now to a sustainable world economy? Will it be very expensive, as claimed by many conservatives, or are there enough opportunities for energy and material savings by intelligent use of "clean technology" to compensate for many of the costs?

This trio of central questions, as stated, currently elicits passionately opposed positions. Fortunately, several of these questions can be restated in a way that leads toward an answer. The first question above can be restated:

(1′) Bearing in mind that most economists have been trained to believe that substitution of capital and/or technology for natural resources is virtually always possible, one can ask: is there any class of environmental assets or services *both* that is essential to human life (or to the biosphere) and for which there are no plausible substitutes?

If substitutability (e.g. of capital for environmental resources) is more or less without limit, or if the limits are very remote, then it can be argued that present trends are sustainable, or could become sustainable (depending on one's exact definition of sustainability) with a few marginal changes in policy.

A majority of business and political leaders appear to assume that only minor changes in current technology and/or regulatory policy would suffice to overcome any environmental threat. In fact, even most so-called "environmentalists" appear to believe that the most serious environmental threats we face are direct threats to human health (contaminated water or food, skin cancer) or loss of amenity (forest die-back, oil spills, dirty beaches, litter, haze, bad smells, etc.) No doubt ex-president Bush truly saw himself as an "environmentalist" because of his long-standing love of hunting, boating, and fishing. It has to be said, at the outset, that the problems that appear on most lists of "priority concerns" are localized, not global, problems. Even the rising public concern about loss of "endangered species" is limited to birds, fish, whales, and mammals – especially large mammals such as pandas and tigers. These are *not* the environmental problems of greatest concern from the standpoint of long-term survival of the earth as a habitable planet.

The second question can also be restated:

(2′) If there are environmental assets and services that are both essential and non-substitutable (i.e. the answer to the first question is "yes") – as I believe – a second question follows: are any of these environmental assets or services now threatened by irreversible and/or irreparable damage? Is there a credible – not necessarily probable – threat to the long-term survival of life on this planet?

The answer to this question is obviously critical for what follows. It can be further broken down into several subsidiary questions, for example:

(2.1) Is continued global population growth compatible with long-run eco-sustainability? Can the most densely populated countries (China, India, Indonesia, Bangladesh) continue to feed themselves as their numbers increase? If not, what is the relationship between demographic variables and economic growth potential in various regions (notably China, India, and Africa)?

(2.2) Do industrial activity and its associated demand for raw materials and depletion of high-quality deposits of natural mineral or other environmental resources constitute a major constraint on continued environmentally sustainable economic growth? If so, how and why?

(2.3) Do waste and pollution (including acidification and environmental accumulation of toxic elements) constitute a direct threat to human welfare or to the habitability of the planet? For example, do they constitute a constraint on food production? If so, do they constitute a constraint on economic growth? If so, how and why?

(2.4) Does anthropogenic disturbance of balanced environmental systems (including ecosystems) constitute a major threat in the above sense? If so, how and why?

A brief digression is appropriate in connection with (2.4): the earth system depends on several balanced, biologically controlled recycling systems for nutrient elements that are required by living organisms in forms or amounts greater than would be found in the earth's crust or the prebiotic atmosphere or hydrosphere. Nitrogen, for instance, constitutes the major part of the atmosphere, but molecular nitrogen (N_2) is so stable that it is virtually unusable by plants or animals. It is only when this strong nitrogen bond is split by some external agency (yielding nitrogen compounds such as ammonia, ammonium, nitrates, or nitrogen oxides) that the nitrogen becomes a nutrient element. Free oxygen would not exist at all without living organisms; it would all be combined with other elements as water, carbonates, silicates, sulphates, etc. Carbon, too, would be tied up (mostly as insoluble carbonates) and unavailable. Thus, a truly "dead" planet (such as Mars or Venus) is literally uninhabitable.

Destruction of the earth's nutrient recycling systems would probably be the surest way of destroying all life on earth. To be sure, human intervention at present can better be characterized as "eutrophication", in the sense of sharply increasing the availability of these nutrients. Yet eutrophication in a lake or stream can be disastrous if it leads to an unbalanced and explosive growth of a few species, which exhaust the supply of some other nutrient (e.g. oxygen) resulting in a "crash" that destroys the whole food web. What we do not (and probably cannot) predict is the probability or imminence of such a threat at the global level. (I do suspect that it is more likely than being struck by a comet!)

Turning to the third major question, which concerns strategies for change and their cost, here too a breakdown into subsidiary questions is helpful. For example:

(3.1) Are there any feasible strategies, and implementable means, of bringing population growth to an end without government coercion, war, or epidemic? Which of them would involve the least economic cost and/or the least conflict with deeply held religious beliefs?

(3.2) Is there any fundamental technological limit (other than the second law of thermodynamics) to the energy and materials productivities that can be achieved in the long run? Is there any fundamental limit to the long-run efficiency of materials recycling? To put it another way, is there a plausible set of technological "fixes"? We seek, in effect, an "existence proof" that solutions are possible.

(3.3) Among the technological "fixes" postulated above, is there one (or more) that is inexpensive, even profitable? Can the needed technology be harnessed at modest, or even negative, cost? From the macroeconomic perspective, the question is: can continued economic growth be achieved simultaneously with environmental improvement by increasing resource productivity – thereby reducing the need for resource inputs and the generation of

15

wastes – *without* significantly decreasing labour and capital productivity? To put it another way, is it feasible to find ways to increase *all* factor productivities simultaneously, i.e. without substituting energy or material resources for labour? In simpler words, is there a mother-lode of "win–win" possibilities – "free lunches" – for reducing pollution and increasing the value of output at the same time?

It is interesting to note that affirmative answers to (3.2) and, especially, (3.3) – the existence of possible technological "fixes" at low (or no) cost – imply a high degree of technological optimism. Curiously, most economists adopt an extremely optimistic stance in regard to questions of resource availability (2.2) but become pessimists when it comes to eliminating or repairing damage caused by pollution (3.3). It would seem logical that a Malthusian pessimist would be entitled to be pessimistic about the existence of "win–win" opportunities, but an opponent of the neo-Malthusian position should also be optimistic with regard to finding low-cost or profitable solutions to the growth problem. Simple consistency would seem to require that both question (2.2) – resource substitutability – and question (3.3) – technological "fixes" – be answered the same way: either "yes" to both or "no" to both.

Non-controversial issues: Population, resources, and technology

There has been, and still is, great controversy as regards the essentiality (non-substitutability) of certain environmental resources. However, the controversy is largely over definitions and details, not fundamentals. Possibly this confusion has arisen because the issues were not formulated sharply enough, until recently. I think there is a reasonable consensus among experts on the fact that some environmental services are essential to long-run human survival on this planet. The existence of "critical" environmental resources is not seriously doubted by most people. The doubters are mostly conservative libertarians with a deep faith in the ability of markets to allocate scarce resources and to call forth technological (or other) substitutes in response to any perceived scarcity.

The weakness of this position is that markets for environmental services are virtually non-existent. Markets must function through price signals. Clearly we need food, sunshine, clean air, and fresh water. We also need the waste disposal services of bacteria, fungi, and insects. All are, at bottom, gifts of nature. Because they are not "commodities" that can be owned and possessed or physically exchanged, they have no prices. Moreover, since these services are not produced by human activity, price signals could not induce an increase in the supply. What is still doubted by many scientists, on the other hand, is the answer to the second half of the question: whether or not these essential environmental resources are truly vulnerable to human interference and possibly subject to irreversible damage.

One example of an essential environmental resource that appears to be subject to irreversible damage is the ozone layer of the stratosphere. The cause of damage, it is now agreed, is atomic chlorine, which originates from the inert chlorofluorocarbons (CFCs) that do not break down in the lower atmosphere and gradually diffuse into the stratosphere where they are broken up by high-energy ultraviolet radiation (UV-B). The chlorine atoms, in turn, react with and destroy ozone molecules, thus depleting the protective ozone layer. This phenomenon was very controversial 20 years ago, but the controversy has largely subsided, thanks to the discovery of annual "ozone holes" in the polar stratosphere, which were first seen in the mid-1980s.

Another example of increasing consensus concerns climate change. The climate is certainly an environmental resource. Even a decade ago there were still a number of scientists expressing serious doubts about whether the problem was "real." The major source of doubt had to do with the reliability of the large-scale general circulation models of the atmosphere that had to be used to forecast the temperature effects of a build-up of greenhouse gases (e.g. carbon dioxide, methane, nitrous oxide, CFCs). Since then, the models have been improved significantly and it has been established fairly definitely that climate warming has been "masked" up to now by a parallel build-up in the atmosphere of sulphate aerosol particles (due to sulphur dioxide emissions), which reflect solar heat and cool the earth. The two effects have tended to compensate for each other. However, the greenhouse gases are accumulating (they have long lifetimes) whereas the sulphate aerosols are quickly washed out by rain. In other words, the greenhouse gas concentration will continue to increase geometrically, whereas the sulphate problem may increase only arithmetically or not at all (if sulphur dioxide emissions are controlled). In any case, the Intergovernmental Panel on Climate Change (IPCC) has now agreed that the greenhouse problem is indeed "real." The controversy continues, however, with regard to likely economic damage and optimal policy responses.

There is already a near-consensus among experts that continued human population growth is not consistent with long-run sustainability (question 2.1) and that some natural resources must eventually be depleted (question 2.2). On the other hand, there is less agreement about whether or not increasing waste and pollution would constitute a limit on growth (question 2.3) or whether or not the balanced natural systems such as the carbon, nitrogen, and sulphur cycles are at risk (question 2.4).

The unacceptability of continued population growth (question 2.1) is a matter on which there is reasonably wide consensus. Malthus foresaw that population growth would eventually outrun the carrying capacity of the earth. Colonization of new lands in the western hemisphere, together with dramatic improvements in agricultural technology, forestalled the crisis for two centuries. Some conservative economists regard this as sufficient evidence that "Malthus was wrong" and that today's neo-Malthusians are unnecessarily alarmist. Nevertheless, the alarm has been raised once again, perhaps on better grounds: there are no more "new lands" waiting for cultivation, and the potential increases in yield available from fertilizers and plant-breeding have already been largely exhausted.

Technological optimists – notably Herman Kahn and his colleagues (Kahn et al. 1976) – have unhesitatingly projected that early twentieth-century rates of increase in agricultural productivity can and will continue into the indefinite future. However, agricultural experts are much less sanguine. The potential gains from further uses of chemicals by traditional methods are definitely limited. Groundwater is already becoming seriously depleted and/or contaminated in many regions of the United States and Western Europe, where intensive irrigation cum chemical agriculture have been practised for a few decades. Such problems are now also becoming acute in places such as northern China. Over a decade ago Bernard Gilland wrote:

Since the onset of the rapid rise in the world population growth rate over 30 years ago, there has been speculation on the human carrying capacity of the planet. Most writers on the problem either hold, on technological grounds, that the Earth can support several (or even many) times its present population, or warn, on ecological grounds, that the Earth is already overpopulated and that human numbers should be reduced. I shall try to show that neither of these views is realistic, and that a plausible assessment of carrying capacity leads to the view that the world is not yet overpopulated but will be so in the second decade of the twenty-first century, when the population will be 60 percent larger than at present. (Gilland 1983, p. 203)

Gilland went on to conclude:

Estimates for global carrying capacity and long-range demographic projections are admittedly subject to wide margins of error, but the consequences of relying on an excessively optimistic assessment of the future population–food supply balance would be so serious that a conservative assessment is justified. (Ibid., p. 209)

Admittedly, Gilland's assessment was based on conventional agriculture using land now classified as "arable." Julian Simon argued that this is not a fixed quantity, and that so-called arable land had actually been increasing at a rate of about 0.7 per cent per annum (from 1960 to 1974) (Simon 1980, p. 1432). This is one of the reasons food shortages projected earlier did not occur. But most of the "new" cropland was formerly tropical forest (the rest was grassland, such as, for instance, the vast and ill-conceived "new lands" projects of Soviet central Asia). Deforestation has now become an acute problem throughout the tropics, and most tropical forest soils are not very fertile to begin with and are rapidly exhausted of their nutrients by cropping. There is no basis for supposing that the amount of arable land can continue to increase much longer, if indeed it has not begun to decrease already for the reasons noted above. In any case, erosion and salination are taking a constant toll of the lands already in production.

With regard to the possibility of continuing to increase the productivity (yield) of existing arable land, there is a continuing push to develop improved varieties and higher photosynthetic efficiencies. Biotechnology is now beginning to be harnessed to increase food production. There is optimistic talk of a "second green revolution." For some years past, global grain production per capita has actually been declining. Thus, incremental improvements will be needed just to keep up with population growth.

Gilland also did not take into account several theoretical possibilities, including such "high-tech" schemes as genetically engineered bacteria capable of digestion of cellulose or crude oil, large-scale hydroponics, and massive irrigation of tropical deserts such as the Sahara using desalinated sea water. Certainly, these possibilities must be taken seriously, and some of them may play an important role before the end of the twenty-first century. On the other hand, there is no chance that any of them could make a difference within the next 20 or 30 years. In short, there are strong indications that agricultural technology cannot continue to outpace population growth in the third world for more than another few decades. For these reasons, the majority of demographers, and most economists, now take it for granted that population growth must be brought to an end as soon as possible if sustainability is to be achieved (e.g. Keyfitz 1990, 1991).

As regards concerns about resource exhaustion (question 2.2), the "neo-Malthusian" position was taken very seriously by some alarmists, such as Paul Ehrlich, in the 1970s. The argument was made that economic growth is inherently restricted by the limited availability of exhaustible natural resources (e.g. Meadows et al. 1972). However, it is now widely agreed among both economists and physical scientists that energy or mineral resource scarcity is *not* likely to be a growth-limiting factor, at least for the next half-century or so. The Malthusian "limits to growth" position adopted by some environmentalists in the 1960s and 1970s has been largely discredited, both by empirical research (e.g. Barnett and Morse 1962; Barnett 1979) and by many theorists. The main reason for the change of perspective is that the neo-Malthusian view was naive in two respects.

First, the neo-Malthusians neglected the fact (well known to the fuel and mineral industries) that there is no incentive for a mining or drilling enterprise to search for new resources as long as it has reserves for 30 years or so. This is a simple consequence of discounting behaviour. It explains why "known reserves" of many resources tend to hover around 20–30 years of current demand, despite continuously rising demand. Secondly, they gave too little credit to the power of market-driven economies to call forth technological alternatives to emergent scarcities (e.g. Cole et al. 1973; Goeller and Weinberg 1976).[5] However, as it turns out, it is overused "renewable" resources, such as arable land, fish, fresh water, forests, biodiversity, and climate, that are more likely to be limiting factors.

The existence of feasible strategies to achieve population stability (question 3.1) is now generally accepted. The subsidiary question of the most appropriate *means* remains murky. This optimism is based partly on evidence of a slow-down in global population growth in recent decades. However it is admittedly unclear whether the observed slow-down (mostly in China, so far) can be extrapolated to other countries, particularly in the Muslim world. Still, the majority of experts seem to believe that the required "demographic transition" is economically and institutionally feasible, in principle. Here the central problem is seen to be to achieve near-universal literacy, equal rights and legal standing for women, a social security net for the poor, and real economic growth to finance all of this, at a rate fast enough to reach that "middle-class" standard within a few generations.[6]

Demographers and social scientists generally agree that these are the preconditions for radically reduced birth rates. A few years ago Jessica Matthews of the World Resources Institute (WRI) had the following comment:

The answer *is* emphatically that there is a realistic path to global population control. The demographers measure what they call unmet needs for contraceptives. That's the place where action has to begin – with women and couples who express a desire to use contraceptives, but who currently have no access to them. The cost is about $10 per couple per year. The need is several times world spending on contraception – a trivial, almost infinitesimal sum, compared to defense spending. I dare say it would probably be covered by the cost of one B-2 bomber, about $500 million.... The second most important realistic, feasible, direct intervention is through women's education. For reasons that are not entirely understood, even primary school education makes a huge difference in women's fertility rates. Therefore education of women in developing countries, and expansion of that opportunity, will have a huge effect. (Matthews 1990, pp. 27–28)

The 1994 Cairo Conference on Population and the Status of Women echoed most of Matthews' themes. Although there were passionate objections to the conference itself, and to the manifesto signed by most attendees, they scarcely challenged the cause–effect relationships set forth by Matthews. On these issues, there is a wide consensus among experts. The most passionate debates with regard to population policy centre on moral (and, of course, political) questions of methods of birth control and, especially, the legitimacy of abortion. These arguments are *not* within the realm of science or scientific debate.

Controversial issues: Pollution, productivity, and biospheric stability

The existence of plausible threats to biospheric stability, even survival (questions 2.3 and 2.4 above), is by no means obvious. The question about whether or not pollution constitutes a possible limiting factor for economic growth (question 2.3) is perhaps the one most debated at present. It is highly controversial. If there is any consensus on this issue it is merely that "toxification" – in the sense of "toxic wastes anywhere near my neighbourhood" – is unacceptable (i.e. must be prohibited regardless of cost). The next section discusses this further. But the extent to which pollution constitutes a limitation on growth itself, or on the welfare generated by economic activity, remains an open question.

The problem of climate warming has been extensively studied and debated (as mentioned above), though there are still significant areas of disagreement among experts with regard to economic damage and the appropriate response strategies. On the other hand, the issue of environmental acidification and/or toxification has never been considered seriously as a global threat to human survival. However, concerns are beginning to arise, especially in regard to cancer and human reproductive capacity. The link between various chemical agents and biological impacts none the less remains largely speculative, and is likely to remain so for many years. Damage mechanisms and thresholds are known in some cases, but not in others. However, it is fairly easy to construct a simple catalogue of measures of materials flux and consequent waste generation that self-evidently cannot continue to increase indefinitely.

The issue of whether or not there is a threat to biospheric stability itself (question 2.4) is rather deep. There are two aspects: the first has to do with phenomenology; the second has to do with the essential indeterminacy of the risk. Not only is there no consensus on either of these points, there has been almost no discussion up to now. I return to this question at greater length below.

As regards the third main question, concerning the least-cost (or "least-pain") transition to a sustainable trajectory, the problem of slowing population growth (question 3.1) has already been mentioned. The existence of plausible technological "fixes" (question 3.2) and the possible existence of large numbers of "win–win" opportunities or "free lunches" (question 3.3) are much more controversial. There is also no consensus as yet. These questions are discussed after the two digressions – on toxicity and on biospheric stability.

On toxicity

There is no doubt that widespread fear of exposure to toxic chemicals is one of the major driving forces behind the environmental movement. The near-hysterical media coverage of the "Love Canal" episode and the proliferation of "Superfund" sites certainly support this contention. Yet, as a basis for discussing environmental threats half a century hence, one needs a different kind of evidence. Unfortunately, methodological problems proliferate even faster than superfund sites.

First, the number of industrial chemicals produced in annual quantities greater than 1 metric ton is estimated at 60,000. The number grows by thousands each year. Only a tiny percentage of these has been tested for the whole range of toxic effects. In fact, it could be argued that none has, since new effects are being discovered all the time, often by accident or from epidemiological evidence long after the fact. For instance, mercury was not known to be harmful in the environment until the mysterious outbreak of "Minamata disease," a severe and sometimes lethal neurological disorder among cats, seabirds, and fishermen living near Minamata Bay, in Japan. It took several years before public health workers were able to trace the problem to organic mercury compounds (mainly methyl mercury) in fish from the bay. The ultimate source turned out to be inorganic mercury from spent catalysts discharged by a nearby chemical plant. The toxic effects of cadmium ("itai-itai disease") were discovered in a similar way.

Second, quantitative production and consumption data for chemicals are not published consistently even on a national basis, still less on a worldwide basis. Data can be obtained only with great difficulty, from indirect sources (such as market studies), and for only the top 200 or so chemicals. In the United States and virtually all countries with a central statistical office (or census), production and shipments data are collected, but the data are withheld for "proprietary" reasons if the number of producers is three or fewer. In Europe, the largest producer of most chemicals, all quantitative production and trade data are suppressed. Data are published in terms only of "ranges" so wide (e.g. 100–10,000 tonnes) that the official published numbers are useless for analysis.

Data on toxic chemical emissions are extremely scarce. The US Environmental Protection Agency's Office of Toxic Wastes is the only official primary source of such data in the world, and its major tool is the so-called Toxic Release Inventory (TRI), which is an annual survey that has been in effect since 1987. The survey must be filled out by US manufacturing firms (Standard Industrial Classification 20–39) with 10 or more employees and that produce, import, process, or use more than a threshold amount of any of 300 listed chemicals. The reporting threshold as regards production or processing for each chemical was initially (1987) 75,000 lb; since 1989 it has been 25,000 lb (roughly 12 metric tons), while for use the reporting threshold is now set at 10,000 lb (roughly 4.5 metric tons) per year. Releases are reported by medium (air, water, land) and transfers for disposal purposes to other sites are also reported. There is serious doubt about both the completeness and the accuracy of the TRI reports, because published data are very difficult to reconcile with materials balance estimates, as discussed elsewhere (Ayres and Ayres 1996).

Third, a large number of manufactured chemicals – probably the vast majority in terms of numbers, if not tonnages – are produced not because they are really needed as such, but because they are available as by-products of other chemical processes. This is particularly true of products of chlorination and ammonylation reactions, which require repeated separation (e.g. distillation) and recycling stages to obtain reasonably pure final products. For instance, it has been estimated that 400 chlorinated compounds are used for their own sake, but at least 4,000 are listed in the directories (Braungart, personal communication, 1992). This is because it is easier to treat them as "products" than as wastes. Many such chemicals are found in products such as pesticides, paint thinners and paint removers, dry-cleaning agents, and plasticizing agents.

Fourth, many of the most dangerous toxic chemicals are known to be produced by side reactions in the manufacturing process, or "downstream" reactions in the environment. Perhaps the most infamous toxic/carcinogenic chemicals are the so-called "dioxins," which are not produced for their own sake but appear to be minor contaminants of some chlorinated benzene compounds that are used for herbicide manufacturing. Thus dioxins were accidental contaminants in the well-known herbicide 2-4-D, which became known as "Agent Orange" during the Viet Nam war. They are also probably produced by incinerators and other non-industrial combustion processes, depending on what is burned. As regards downstream processes, the example of methyl mercury – produced by anaerobic bacteria in sediments – was mentioned earlier. Exactly the same problem arises in the case of dimethyl and trimethyl arsine, extremely toxic volatile compounds that are generated by bacterial action on arsenical pesticide (or other) residues left in the soil. Still other examples would be the dangerous carcinogens such as Benz(a)pyrene (BAP) and peracyl nitrate (PAN) produced by reactions between unburned hydrocarbons, especially aromatics, nitrogen oxides (NOx), and ozone. (This occurs in Los Angeles "smog", for instance.) In fact, oxides of nitrogen are themselves toxic. NOx is produced not only by most high-temperature combustion processes but also by atmospheric electrical discharges.

An even more indirect downstream effect is exemplified by the *Waldsterben* (forest die-back) in central Europe. The conifer trees of the Black Forest and much of the Alps are now being weakened and many are dying. This appears to be the result of a complex sequence of effects starting with increased acidity of the soil. As the pH drops below 6 there is a sharply increased mobilization of aluminium ions, which are toxic to plants. There is also an increased mobilization of heavy metals hitherto fixed in insoluble complexes with clay particles. Many toxic heavy metals – from pesticides, or from deposition of fly ash from coal burning – have long been immobilized by adherence to clay particles at relatively high pH levels (thanks, in part, to liming of agricultural soils). However, as the topsoil erodes as a result of intensive agriculture, it is being washed into streams and rivers and, eventually, into estuaries, bays such as the Chesapeake, or enclosed seas (such as the Baltic, the Adriatic, the Aegean, or the Black Sea), where it accumulates.

This sedimentary material is "relatively" harmless as long as the local environment is anaerobic, except for the localized risk of bacterial methylation of mercury, arsenic, and cadmium mentioned earlier. But this accumulated sedimentary stock of heavy metals (and other persistent toxic chemicals too) would become much more dangerous in the event of a sudden exposure to oxygen. For instance, sediments dredged from rivers and harbours may be rapidly acidified and could become "toxic time bombs" (Stigliani 1988).

Fifth, many toxic compounds are produced naturally by plants and animals, largely as protection against predators or as means of immobilizing prey. Nicotine, rotenone (from pyrethrum), heroin and morphine (from opium), cocaine, curare, digitalis, belladonna, and other alkaloids are well-known examples from the plant world. Recent research suggests that natural (i.e. biologically produced) compounds have about the same probability of being toxic or carcinogenic as synthetic compounds. The widespread idea that "natural" products are *ipso facto* safer than synthetic ones is apparently false. In fact, Bruce Ames (inventor of the "Ames test") has argued with considerable force that the use of synthetic pesticides is less dangerous, to humans, than reliance on "non-chemical" methods of agricultural production, because plants produce greater quantities of natural toxins when they are under stress. However, probably even less is known about the range of toxic effects from natural chemicals than from industrial chemicals.

In fact, there is no general theory of toxicity. It comes in many colours and varieties. The notion includes mutagenic effects visible only after generations, effects on the reproductive cycle, and carcinogenic effects (e.g. asbestos, dioxins, vinyl chloride), or chronic but minor degradation of physiological function. At the other extreme are acute effects resulting in rapid or even instantaneous death. Methyl isocyanate (MIC), the cause of the Bhopal disaster, is an example of the latter. Chlorinated pesticides and polychlorinated biphenyls (PCBs) were not even thought to be dangerous to humans until long after they had been in widespread use. It was belatedly discovered that these chemicals tend to accumulate in fatty animal tissues and to be concentrated as they move higher in the food chain. Eagles, falcons, and ospreys were nearly wiped out in some areas by DDT because their eggshells were weakened to the point of non-viability.

As noted above, soil acidification resulting from anthropogenic emissions of SO_2 and NOx to the atmosphere is also releasing toxic metals (and other compounds) that were formerly immobilized in the soil. Large accumulations of toxic metals reside in the soils and sediments in some areas. For many decades lead arsenate was used as an insecticide, especially in apple orchards. Copper sulphate and mercury compounds (among others) were widely used to control fungal diseases of plants. Mercury was also used to prevent felt hats from being attacked by decay organisms. Chromium was, and still is, used for the same purpose to protect leather from decay. Copper, lead, nickel, and zinc ores were roasted in air to drive off the sulphur (and the arsenic and cadmium). Lead paint was used for more than a century, for both exterior and interior surfaces. For half a century tetraethyl lead and tetramethyl lead were used as gasoline octane additives (they still are so used in much of the world). Soft coal has been burned profusely in urban areas; usually the bottom ash was used as landfill for airports and roads. Coal ash contains trace quantities of virtually every toxic metal, from arsenic to mercury to vanadium. For decades, phosphate fertilizers have been spread on farmland without removing the cadmium contaminants. In all of these cases, increasing acidity means increased mobilization of toxic metals. These metals eventually enter the human food chain, via crops or cows' milk.

It is clear that toxicity is not simply a problem associated with the production and use of industrial chemicals or heavy metals. It is intimately linked to a number of other anthropogenic processes, not least of which is global acidification. To take another example, it is well known that CFCs emitted to the atmosphere are responsible for depleting the ozone layer in the stratosphere. The major consequence on the earth's surface is an increase in the intensity of harmful UV radiation reaching the surface. Spawning zooplankton and fish in shallow surface waters are likely to be adversely affected. This is, in effect, a form of eco-toxicity.

Is there any common factor among all these types of toxicity? It can be argued that all human toxins are, in effect, causes of physiological disturbance. All interfere with some biological process. Mutagens interfere with the replication of the DNA molecule itself. Carcinogens interfere with the immune system; neurotoxins (e.g. cyanide) interfere with the ability of the nerves to convey messages. Many toxins cause problems for the organism because they closely resemble other compounds that perform an essential function. Thus carbon monoxide causes suffocation because it binds to the haemoglobin in the blood, as oxygen does. But, when the haemoglobin carrier arrives at a cell in need of oxygen, the potential recipient "sees" only a carbon atom where an oxygen atom should be.

The point of this example is that *toxicity*, to an organism, is just another word for *imbalance* or *disturbance*. A toxin is an agent that causes some metabolic or biological process to go awry. Every organism has a metabolism. Metabolic processes are cyclic self-organizing systems far away from thermodynamic equilibrium. The same statement can be made of the metabolic processes – the "grand nutrient cycles" such as the carbon and nitrogen cycles – that regulate the whole biosphere. Any disturbance to the biosphere is "toxic," in principle.

The stability of the biosphere: The impossibility of computing the odds

The fundamental question about whether or not the stability of the biosphere is at risk was deferred. This is a very deep question indeed.

First, a quick review of the case for believing there may be a real threat to survival. Most people who have never thought deeply about the matter tend to assume that life is a passive "free rider" on the earth. In other words, most people suppose (or were taught) that life exists on earth simply because earth happened to offer a suitable environment for life to evolve. They imagine that earth was much like it is now (except for more volcanic activity) before life came along, and that if life were to be snuffed out by some cosmic accident – say a massive solar flare – the animals and plants would disappear but the inanimate rivers, lakes, oceans, and oxygen–nitrogen atmosphere would remain much as they are today.

The above quasi-biblical vision is not in accord with the scientific evidence. It is true that life probably originated on earth (though some scientists speculate that the basic chemical components of all living systems may actually have originated in a cold interstellar cloud – Hoyle and Wickramasinghe 1978). Life certainly evolved on earth. The earliest living organisms appear to have been capable of metabolizing organic compounds (such as sugars) by fermentation, to yield energy and waste products such as alcohols. The organic (but non-living) "food" for these simple organisms was created by still-unknown processes in a reducing environment. The composition of the atmosphere of the early earth cannot be reconstructed with great accuracy, but it undoubtedly contained ammonia, hydrogen sulphide, and carbon dioxide, plus water vapour. There was certainly no free oxygen. It is less certain, but possible, that no free nitrogen was present. Life would have disappeared as soon as the supply of "food" was exhausted, if it had not been for the evolutionary "invention" of photosynthesis.[7]

The first photosynthetic organisms converted carbon dioxide and water vapour into sugars, thus replenishing the food supply. But they also generated free oxygen as a waste product. For a billion years or so, the free oxygen produced by photosynthesis was immediately combined with soluble ferrous iron ions dissolved in the oceans, yielding insoluble ferric iron. Similarly hydrogen sulphide and soluble sulphites were oxidized to insoluble sulphates. These were deposited on the ocean floors. Thanks to tectonic activity, some of them eventually rose above sealevel and became land. (Virtually all commercial iron ores and gypsum now being mined by humans are of biological origin.) When the dissolved oxygen acceptors were used up, oxygen began to build up in the atmosphere. As a metabolic waste product, oxygen was toxic to the anaerobic organisms that produced it. Again, there was a threat of self-extinction.

Once again, an evolutionary "invention" came to the rescue. This was the advent of aerobic respiration, which utilized the former waste product (oxygen) and also increased the efficiency of energy production sevenfold over the earlier fermentation process. Aerobic photosynthesis followed, thus closing the carbon cycle (more or less) for the first time. This occurred less than 1 billion years ago, though life has existed on the earth for at least 3.5 billion years. But the carbon cycle and the earth's atmosphere did not stabilize for several hundred million more years. The free oxygen in the atmosphere exists only because large quantities of carbon, with which it was originally combined, have been *sequestered* in two forms: (1) as calcium carbonate, in the shells of tiny marine organisms (which later reappear as chalk, diatomaceous earth, or limestone), or (2) as coal or shale. The carbon sequestering process took place over several hundred million years – a period culminating in the so-called carboniferous era – during which the carbon dioxide content of the atmosphere declined to its present very low level. In addition, sulphur has been sequestered, primarily as sulphates. Similarly, though somewhat less certainly, the free nitrogen in the earth's atmosphere was probably originally combined with hydrogen, in the form of ammonia of volcanic origin. Whereas the carbon has mostly been buried, the missing hydrogen has probably recombined with oxygen as water vapour.

The early atmosphere and hydrosphere of the earth were quite alkaline compared with the present, because of the ammonia. The hydrogen-rich *reducing* atmosphere of the early earth has been replaced by an *oxygenating* atmosphere; the hydrosphere is correspondingly more acid than it once was before life appeared. The biosphere has stabilized the atmosphere (and the climate), at least for the last several hundred million years. If all life disappeared suddenly today, the oxygen in the atmosphere would gradually but inexorably recombine with atmospheric nitrogen and buried hydrocarbons and sulphides (converting them eventually to carbon dioxide, nitric acid, nitrates, sulphuric acid, and sulphates). Water would be mostly bound into solid minerals, such as gypsum (hydrated calcium sulphate). This oxygenation process would also further increase the acidity of the environment.

Suppose all possible chemical reactions among carbon, nitrogen, and sulphur compounds – including those currently sequestered in sediments and sedimentary rocks – proceed to thermodynamic equilibrium. The atmosphere would consist mainly of carbon dioxide. The final state of thermodynamic equilibrium would be totally inhospitable to life. (For one thing, the temperature would rise to around 300°C.) Once dead, the planet could never be revived (Lovelock 1979). Table 1.2 displays some of these "ideal" effects.

The point of the capsule history of the earth shown in table 1.2 is that our planet is, in reality, an extraordinarily complex interactive system in which the biosphere is not just a passive passenger but

Table 1.2 **The stabilizing influence of the biosphere (Gaia)**

Reservoir	Substance	Actual world	Ideal world I	Ideal world II
Atmosphere	Nitrogen	78%	0%	1.9%
	Oxygen	21%	0%	trace
	CO_2	0.03%	99%	98%
	Argon	1%	1%	0.1%
Hydrosphere	Water	96%	85%	? Not much water
	NaCl	3.4%	13%	?
	$NaNO_3$	–	1.7%	?
Temperature	°C	13	290 ± 50	290 ± 50
Pressure	Atmospheres	1	60	60

Source: Lovelock (1972).
Note: Life is impossible if the average temperature is too high for liquid water, or if salinity exceeds 6 per cent.

an active element. It is important to establish that the earth (atmosphere, hydrosphere, geosphere, biosphere) is a *self-organizing system* (in the sense popularized by Prigogine and his colleagues, e.g. Prigogine and Stengers 1984) in a stable state far from thermodynamic equilibrium. This system maintains its orderly character by capturing and utilizing a stream of high-quality radiant energy from the sun. Living organisms perform this function, along with other essential functions such as the closure of the carbon cycle and the nitrogen cycle (Schlesinger 1991).

Complex systems stabilized by feedback loops are essentially non-linear. An important characteristic of the dynamic behaviour of some non-linear systems is the phenomenon known as *chaos*. Such systems are characterized by trajectories that move unpredictably around regions of phase-space known as *strange attractors*. "Stability" for such a system means that the trajectory tends to remain within a relatively well-defined envelope. However, a further characteristic of non-linear multi-stable dynamic systems is that they can "jump" – also unpredictably – from one attractor to another. (Such jumps have been called "catastrophes" by the French mathematician René Thom, who has classified the various theoretical possibilities for continuous systems.) The *resilience* of a non-linear dynamic system – its tendency to remain within the domain of its original attractor – is not determinable by any known scientific theory or measurement. In fact, since the motion of a non-linear system along its trajectory is inherently unpredictable (though deterministic), the resilience of the earth system is probably unknowable with any degree of confidence. It is like a rubber band whose strength and elasticity we have no way of measuring.

The climate of the earth, with its feedback linkages to the biosphere, is a non-linear complex system. It has been stable for a long time. However, there is no scientific way to predict just how far the system can be driven away from its stable quasi-equilibrium by anthropogenic perturbing forces before it will jump suddenly to another stable quasi-equilibrium. Nor is there any way to predict how far the equilibrium will move if it does jump. The earth's climate, and the environment as a whole, may indeed be very resilient and capable of absorbing a lot of punishment. Then again, they may not.

What can be gained by more research? Probably we can learn a lot about the nature of the earth–climate–biosphere interaction. We will learn a lot about the specific mechanisms. We will learn how to model the behaviour of the system, at least in simplified form. We will learn something about the stability of the models. We may, or may not, learn something definitive about the stability of the real system. The real system is too complex, and too non-linear, for exact calculations. There is no prospect at all of "knowing the odds" and making a rational calculation of risk. The problem we face is that the odds cannot be calculated, even in principle. In the circumstances, prudence would seem to dictate buying some insurance. The question on which reasonable people can still differ is: how much insurance is it worthwhile to buy? The answer depends, in part, on the technological alternatives.

Technical preconditions for sustainability

Given the previous discussion, one can identify the following hypothetical necessary (but not sufficient) conditions for long-term sustainability:
- no increase in the atmospheric concentration of "greenhouse gases" (beyond some limit yet to be determined);
- no increase in environmental acidification (hydrogen ion concentration) in surface waters and soils (beyond some limit);
- no increase in toxic heavy metal concentrations in soils and sediments (beyond some limit);
- no further topsoil erosion, beyond the rate of natural soil formation;

- no further degradation of groundwater with nitrates and nitrites; no further draw-down of "fossil" (non-replaceable) groundwater;
- preservation of (most of) the remaining tropical rain forests, estuarine zones, coral reefs, and other ecologically important habitats; no further disappearance of species.

A shorter list that is substantially equivalent to the above has been set forth by Holmberg, Robèrt, and Erikkson (Holmberg et al. 1995). Their list (paraphrased) is as follows:

- no accumulation of substances taken from the earth's crust in "nature," i.e. the biosphere or its supporting physical systems (atmosphere, oceans, topsoil);
- no accumulation of synthetic materials produced by man in natural systems;
- no interference by man in the conditions for biospheric diversity and stability;
- natural resources should be utilized as efficiently as possible.

To satisfy these conditions, several straightforward implications can be drawn. Among them are the following:

1. use of fossil fuels must stop increasing and must drop to very low (and declining) levels by the middle of the twenty-first century;
2. agricultural, forestry, and fishery practices must be radically overhauled and improved, with much less dependence on chemicals and mechanization;
3. net emissions to the environment of long-lived toxic chemical compounds (especially compounds of the toxic heavy metals and halogenated organics) must drop to near zero levels by the middle of the twenty-first century, or so.

To simplify even further, one can argue that the average materials intensity per unit of service (MIPS) must be decreased radically for society as a whole (Schmidt-Bleek 1992, 1994). Putting it another way, which is perhaps more acceptable to economists, I think that sustainability in the long run requires a very sharp increase – by at least a factor of 4 and perhaps a factor of 10 – in the *materials productivity* of our society.[8] Although such a radical productivity increase may seem utopian at first, it is well to recall that labour productivity in the Western world has increased by much larger factors, perhaps a hundredfold or more, since the beginning of the industrial revolution, largely by substituting capital goods and energy from fossil fuels for human and animal labour. What I am suggesting now amounts to a minor (but necessary) reversal of that historical substitution trend. In short, the time has come to substitute a modest additional amount of human labour to achieve a radical decrease in the extraction, mobilization, and discard of physical materials and fuels.

Do technically feasible solutions exist?

Question 3.2 was: is there a range of plausible technological possibilities that would be compatible with long-run eco-sustainability? Paraphrased in less abstract language, the question is whether sustainability is *technically feasible* for a stable population of 10–12 billion people living with "middle-class" (or higher) standards of living in the very long run (say, by the end of the twenty-first century)? This question, as such, is hardly new. The negative position has been strongly and somewhat dogmatically asserted in the past by some environmentalists of the "no growth" school, notably Paul Ehrlich (Ehrlich 1968; Ehrlich and Ehrlich 1970) and Barry Commoner (Commoner 1971, 1976). Most economists, however, did not and do not subscribe to this view, at least in its original (somewhat simplistic) form.

The main counter-argument adduced by economists such as Beckerman, Nordhaus, and Solow against the neo-Malthusians (e.g. Meadows et al.) was, and is, that, given the right incentives – prices – and time enough, technology is capable of finding a way to avoid essentially *any* physical resource bottleneck, as long as the product or service in question is produced and exchanged within the competitive market system. However, this answer is much too theoretical to be satisfying. It really avoids the question; it does not answer it.

To attempt an "existence proof" of at least one plausible long-run solution (setting aside the question of cost for the moment), the technical implications of eco-sustainability must be spelled out more precisely. As noted already, agricultural and industrial activity today is almost entirely dependent on fossil fuels (and also on dissipative uses of toxic chemicals and heavy metals) whose extraction and use harm the environment. This pattern is clearly incompatible with long-term sustainability.

It is obviously not possible to describe, in detail, technology based on discoveries and inventions that still lie in the future, perhaps a century hence. However, the constraints imposed by the definition of sustainability limit the range of possibilities worth exploring considerably. In addition, it is possible to carry out a major part of the analysis in terms of macro-scale indicators of technological performance that could be achieved in many different ways.

For example, it is clear that sustainability requires much more efficient use of energy in the future than we observe today. Some improvement will occur as a direct consequence of the fact that electricity is displacing other energy carriers, because of its convenience and cleanliness at the point of use. Electric space heating can be quite economical (using heat pumps), especially in properly insulated buildings. (However, effective means of recycling refrigerant fluids will be necessary.) Microwave cooking is so much faster and more efficient than its competitors (gas or electric cooking) that it is rapidly spreading anyhow.

Substitution of electric power for other fuels for space heating, hot water, and cooking can and will occur more or less quickly, assuming appropriate price incentives. There are no technological barriers. Most energy needs, except for transportation, can be supplied by electricity. Very long distance high voltage lines – or possibly super-conducting lines – could distribute power around the globe, and even under the sea. Orbiting solar satellites or lunar photovoltaic (PV) farms transmitting energy to earth via satellite are a possible variant.

Of course, there is little or no environmental advantage in using electricity if it is generated by burning fossil fuels. Fortunately, there are viable long-term alternatives on the supply side, including biomass and wind (near term), PV-electric and PV-hydrogen (longer term). Chapters 5, 6, and 7 in this book go into detail. Also, efficiency gains can reduce the need for more energy. Nuclear power (fission or fusion) cannot be ruled out of consideration. However both variants involve long-term storage of radioactive wastes, not to mention other major costs that continue to escalate. Thus, nuclear options are less attractive in the very long run than the solar option.

Most mobile power sources at present (except for the few electric trams or trains) depend on liquid fuels derived from hydrocarbons. Up until the present time, centrally generated and wire-distributed electric power has not been economically attractive for mobile power, although it is technically feasible for local deliveries and commuting. Middle East petroleum will finally approach exhaustion around the middle of the twenty-first century (or sooner). It seems probable that electric vehicles (for short distances) will finally become economically competitive with any coal-based synthetic fuel, especially if coal is made to bear anything like its real environmental costs. There seems little doubt today that, sooner or later, the electric car will play a bigger role.

The fact that gasoline-burning vehicles are becoming increasingly intolerable in large cities suggests a plausible mechanism for this to come about: large cities plagued by traffic congestion, noise, and smoggy air may begin to create "car-free" zones in their centres, permitting only small electric cars (as some lakes already permit only electric boats). At first, the electric cars will be found largely in these zones. But, these same central zones will also be accessed by high-speed electric (probably "mag-lev") intercity trains, which will finally begin to reverse the auto-induced suburban sprawl of recent decades. As time passes, the electric vehicles will get better and cheaper, the "electric" zones will spread to the suburbs, and eventually gasoline (or synfuel) powered ground vehicles will be essentially limited to rural use. By the second half of the twenty-first century electric vehicles may be able to extend their range by using automated mag-lev pallets along major intercity routes.

Electrification is only part of the solution. As suggested above, sustainability implies reliance mainly – if not entirely – on renewable sources of energy. In principle, the energy could easily be supplied by the sun, as combustible biomass, as direct heat for buildings, as heat to operate engines, or via photovoltaic cells. The latter, in turn, could generate hydrogen by electrolysis. (There are other possibilities too, including geothermal heat and nuclear fusion.) The most likely solution seems to be a combination of wind power for irrigation water pumps, direct solar heating or "district heat-pumping" using waste heat from high-temperature industrial processes to supply warm water for many buildings, and electrolytic hydrogen as a fuel for aircraft.

To reduce waste and pollution by converting them into raw materials is another technological and economic challenge of the next half-century. To accomplish this structural change we need to create a whole new class of economic activities – the equivalent of decay organisms in an ecosystem – to capture useful components, compounds, and elements and re-use them. In other words, the linear raw material–process–product chains characteristic of the present system must ultimately (within the next century or so) be converted into closed cycles analogous to the nutrient cycles in the biosphere (Ayres 1989; Frosch and Gallopoulos 1989). This new class of activities, called "industrial ecology," will gradually replace some of the extractive activities and associated waste disposal activities that are characteristic of the current system.[9]

The existence question can also be addressed theoretically by putting it in the negative sense: are there any fixed minimum materials/energy requirements to produce useful goods and services for humans? Or are there fundamental limits to the amount of service (or welfare) that can be generated from a given energy and/or material input? If there is no such limit, then energy intensities and materials intensities can be reduced indefinitely; there can be no fixed relationship between primary energy or materials requirements and GNP.

In fact, if this condition is met there is, in principle, *no* theoretical maximum to the quantity of final services – i.e. economic welfare in the traditional sense – that can be produced within the market framework from a given physical resource input (Ayres and Kneese 1989). It follows, too, that, there is *no* physical limit (except that imposed by the second law of thermodynamics) to the theoretical potential for energy conservation and materials recycling.

This restatement is actually critical to the fundamental case for optimism today. However, it is not a "mainstream" view among engineers and "men of affairs," or even economists, at present. In common with the World Commission on Environment and Development (WCED), virtually all economists would regard continuing economic growth as both necessary and possible. However, the implication that economic growth can and must be permanently "delinked" from energy and materials use is far from universally accepted. (In short, most economists and business leaders have not thought through the consequences of their assumptions.) In fact, something like an "existence proof" is needed, to demonstrate that there are feasible technologies that, if adopted, could end our current dependence on fossil fuels and substantially close the materials cycle.

This is still an area of sharp disagreement. The politically powerful extractive industry argues strongly for linkage:

No doubt about it, we all need to be careful of the amount of energy we use. But as long as this nation's economy needs to grow, we are going to need energy to fuel that growth. ... For the foreseeable future, there are no viable alternatives to petroleum as the major source of energy ... Simply put, America is going to need more energy for all its people. (Mobil Corp "Public Service" advertisement in the *New York Times*, April 1991)

In other words, the conventional position is that economic growth cannot occur without more energy – i.e. a fixed relationship *does* exist.

In principle, any such fixed relationship between energy/materials use and economic activity would be quite inconsistent with fundamental axioms of economic theory, which assume general substitutability of all factors of production. Economists who are quick to attack neo-Malthusians for unjustified worry about natural resource scarcity should be equally optimistic about the potential for energy savings by increased conservation. Unfortunately, this is not the case, for reasons discussed later.

Optimism in regard to the potential for energy/materials conservation – or increasing energy/materials productivity – is also justified by recent history. The energy/GNP ratio has been declining more or less continuously for many decades in the case of the advanced industrialized countries (fig. 1.1). Past experience suggests that this ratio tends to increase for countries that are in the early stages of industrialization, only to decrease later; this is the so-called "inverted U" phenomenon (World Bank 1992). Moreover, countries industrializing later have lower peaks than countries that industrialized earlier. Lower energy intensity reflects the shift from heavy industry to "high tech" and services. The trend would almost certainly continue in any case. It can probably be accelerated significantly by appropriate policy changes.

The energy/GNP ratio is closely related to the thermodynamic efficiency with which the economy uses energy. For this purpose, it is convenient to define the so-called "second-law" efficiency – or, in European parlance, the "exergy efficiency" – with which energy is converted from primary sources to final services.[10] Electricity is currently generated and delivered to homes with an overall efficiency of about 34 per cent in the United States. This figure has increased only slightly in recent years. Efficiency in less developed countries (LDCs) is significantly lower, implying greater room for improvement. Energy experts generally agree that by the year 2050 efficiency might increase to something like 55–60 per cent for steam-electric plants, taking advantage of higher temperature (ceramic) turbines, combined cycles, co-generation, etc.

Energy is currently used very inefficiently to create final services, as compared with the first stage of energy conversion and distribution. The problem is that energy is lost and wasted at each step of the chain of successive conversions, from crude fuels to intermediates, to finished goods, to final services. For instance, incandescent lights (converting electricity to white light) are only 7 per cent efficient (fluorescent lights are better). Moreover, lighting fixtures are typically deployed very inefficiently (c.10 per cent) so that the final service (illumination where it is actually needed) is probably less than

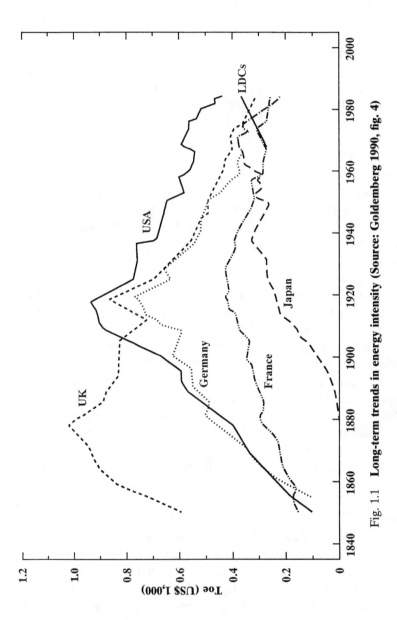

Fig. 1.1 **Long-term trends in energy intensity (Source: Goldemberg 1990, fig. 4)**

1 per cent. Electricity may be used less wastefully than fuel, although this is doubtful because many end-uses of electricity are extremely inefficient from a second-law perspective.

Second-law (exergy) end-use efficiency has been estimated at 2.5 per cent for the United States as a whole (Ayres 1989). This means that, in principle, the same final services (heat, light, transport, cooking, entertainment, etc.) could have been obtained by the expenditure of only 1/40 as much energy as was actually used. Western Europe and Japan are significantly more efficient (in the second-law sense defined above) than the United States. Both regions are in the 4 per cent range, while Eastern Europe, the former Soviet Union, and the rest of the world are even less efficient than the United States – perhaps 1.5–2.0 per cent (Schipper 1989; Nakicenovic et al. 1990; Nakicenovic et al. 1996).[11] For the world as a whole, it is likely that the overall efficiency with which fuel energy is used is currently no greater than 3.0–3.5 per cent. But there is no fundamental technical reason why end-use efficiency could not be increased by several-fold (perhaps as much as a factor of 5) in the course of the next half-century or so.

Finding the least-cost (least-pain) path

To summarize, there are three technical elements to a programme leading to long-term sustainability. The first is to reduce, and eventually eliminate, inherently dissipative uses of non-biodegradable materials, especially toxic ones (such as heavy metals). This involves process change and what has come to be known as "clean technology." The second is to design products for easier disassembly and re-use, and for reduced environmental impact, known as "design for environment" (DFE). The third is to develop much more efficient technologies for recycling consumption waste materials, so as to eliminate the need to extract "virgin" materials that only make the problem worse in time.

There is also an important socio-economic and political dimension to the problem that we do not address sufficiently in this book. To state it very briefly, the strategies that maximize profits for an individual firm in the manufacturing sector of our competitive economic system tend to be the ones that exploit economies of scale and do so by maximizing sales and production. The downstream consequences, in terms of energy consumption, pollution, and final disposal of worn out goods, are not the responsibility of the producer and are, therefore, not taken account of in either product design or pricing. Thus, competitive markets, as they currently function, tend to over-produce both goods and pollution, while simultaneously over-consuming natural resources. In short, there is an inherent dissonance – economists call it an externality – in the economic system that must be eliminated or compensated.

It does not follow that the resolution of this fundamental dissonance is to be found in public ownership. That "solution" clearly does not work. The next most obvious solution seems to be regulation. But the regulatory approach works well only when the regulations are simple and easy to enforce. It has worked well mainly in the case of outright bans on the production of certain products, such as DDT, PCBs, and tetraethyl lead. But this strategy is also limited. It does not work well, for instance, when applied to widely used consumer products such as cigarettes, liquor, drugs, hand-guns, or pornographic literature. "Green" taxes on resource consumption, or on pollution *per se*, are another possibility. But, there are at least two major drawbacks. One is that taxes on resource consumption – or pollution – tend to be regressive (hitting low-income consumers most heavily). The other drawback is that they would be complex to administer, because of the need to provide exceptions and exemptions, e.g. for farmers, health workers, exporters, et al. In practice, green taxes are probably not feasible at the national level. There would have to be major efforts at cross-border "harmonization" in order to maintain international competitiveness. Still other approaches are currently being explored, such as tradable permits and quotas. However, there is very little experience of actual implementation for these newer ideas.

But, having said this much, the fundamental issue of compensating for externalities in the economic system is not addressed further in this or the following chapters.

It is not easy to discern a long-term trend toward increasing recycling/re-use. Indeed, anecdotal evidence would suggest the contrary: poor societies recycle and re-use far more efficiently than rich ones do. Also, the increasing complexity of both materials and products has made recycling and re-use more difficult in many cases. For instance, old wool clothes were once routinely collected by rag-merchants and recycled (after a complicated process of washing, unpicking, bleaching, re-spinning, re-weaving, and re-dyeing) into blankets and pea jackets. Today, because of the prevalence of blends of natural and synthetic fibres, recycling is almost impossible. Much the same problem occurs in many other cases. To increase re-use and recycling, it may be necessary to induce manufacturers to sell services, rather than products, and/or to take back products they have previously made.

Remanufacturing avoids many of the problems of recycling. It is not an important economic activity at present. However, it may grow, especially as the shortage of landfill sites induces municipal authorities (or, perhaps, original equipment manufacturers forced by law to accept trade-ins) to offer subsidies. Remanufactured refrigerators, cars (or engines), and other large appliances can offer a good low-priced alternative to low-income workers in the rich countries, or they could fill an important economic niche in the developing countries. Actually, since remanufacturing will always be more labour intensive than original equipment manufacturing, it is inherently a suitable activity for border regions such as Mexico, Eastern Europe, or North Africa. (As these countries develop, of course, the "border regions" will shift too.)

In the case of municipal waste (mostly paper products and containers), recycling is already increasing in importance. Again, the shortage of land for disposal is mainly responsible. More efficient technologies for separating materials will certainly be developed in coming decades. In any case, there is no technical reason why the recycling/re-use rate for most types of materials should not be dramatically increased from the low levels of today. This will happen, eventually, when material prices better reflect the true environmental costs of both extraction and use.

It is not really necessary to know in detail how this will be accomplished. It is sufficient to know that it is technically and economically feasible. (It remains, still, for policy makers to create the appropriate incentives to harness market forces. But this is a separate topic.) Of course, specific "scenarios" might be helpful in making such a conclusion more credible to doubters. However this would serve a communications purpose rather than an analytic one.

Assuming the existence of a collection of potential technological "fixes," the last question follows: is there a *feasible political/ institutional pathway* to get from "here" to "there"? What, in particular, is the role of economics? This question can be rephrased to make the underlying problem clearer. Assuming technical and economic feasibility, it is reasonable to assume political feasibility if (and only if) there exists a painless (or near-painless) development trajectory, such that each incremental socio-economic change leaves every politically powerful interested party better off – or at least no worse off – than before. Along such a path there must be very few or no losers. Everybody gets richer more or less automatically. This is called a "win–win" strategy, in the language of game theory. In more literary terms, it might be termed a "Panglossian" path.

To restate the question then: is there a Panglossian path? The fundamental problem is that an affirmative answer (i.e. that low-cost "win–win" solutions, or "free lunches," do exist) is essentially inconsistent with most economists' fundamental belief in profit-maximizing behaviour and perfect information. Given these assumptions, the economy would always be in (or close to) equilibrium and this equilibrium would reflect the most efficient (i.e. least-cost) choices of technology. If this were true, energy and natural resource conservation should cost a lot more money ("there is no free lunch"). This view seems to be supported by econometric data, based on historical responses of energy demand to price changes. These data indicate that higher prices encourage lower consumption, and vice versa. Reduced physical consumption is commonly interpreted by economists as "anti-growth."

It happens to be convenient to incorporate this set of assumptions in long-term forecasting models based on the assumption of a quasi-general equilibrium varying slowly along an optimal path over time (e.g. Edmonds and Reilly 1985; Manne and Richels 1990, 1992; Jorgenson and Wilcoxen 1990a,b; Nordhaus 1994).[12] However, such models do not – and cannot – reflect the endogenous nature of technological change. How can an optimal path be determined that takes into account unpredictable technological change? Nor do these models reflect the distortions due to institutional barriers and "wrong" prices.

To explain the dilemma in non-economic terms, if a lot of "win–win" opportunities really do exist, then somehow these opportunities must have been overlooked by entrepreneurs. Assuming entrepreneurs always do what is in their own best (economic) interest, any real opportunities to make profits would be instantly snapped up; consequently no more such opportunities can exist.

The obvious flaw in this reasoning is that entrepreneurs are constantly finding opportunities for making extraordinary profits. If no profitable opportunities existed, there would be no entrepreneurs. Since there are many entrepreneurs, it follows logically that many more such profit opportunities must exist. In recent years, since environmental concerns have become more pressing, surprisingly many profitable opportunities have been found to reduce environmental pollution. To explain this, it must be assumed that industry and consumers have *not* always chosen the optimal energy technologies, even at present (too low) prices. Entrenched oligopolies or monopolies, established regulatory bodies, institutional separation between technological decision makers and final consumers who pay the costs, and lack of technical information are the most likely reasons (see, for instance, Sant 1979; Lovins et al. 1981; Goldemberg et al. 1987; Ayres 1990, 1994; Mills et al. 1991). Inappropriately low prices due to subsidies (e.g. to coal mining and nuclear power) compound the problem.

Fortunately, there is a potential link between increasing resource productivity and reducing unemployment. Unemployment is becoming a very serious political issue in Europe. Conservative (business-oriented) economists tend to blame the problem equally on high wages and benefits and "labour market rigidity" (i.e. the network of taxpayer-supported measures known as the "social safety net"). But there is growing recognition that the tax system itself may be more to blame than the size of the public sector. The problem is that the "safety net" in Europe is financed almost exclusively by taxes on labour, whereas the use of energy and materials by industry is virtually untaxed (except for motor fuel) and, in many countries, fossil energy is heavily subsidized.[13]

Up to now, environmentalists have approached the issue of environmental protection largely as a regulatory problem. Regulations in this field are now numerous, burdensome, and – in many cases – inefficient. As an alternative, environmental economists have recommended schemes such as effluent taxes, but this approach has not been strongly supported by the business community (which, surprisingly, is less opposed to regulation than its rhetoric would suggest). Environmental economists argue that revenue from effluent taxes and resource-based taxes could be used to reduce other unpopular taxes, such as taxes on savings or investment. Conservatives fear that "revenue neutrality" would not be adhered to in practice, and that any increase in government revenue would be used to finance more "spending."

In recent years another scheme ("tradable permits") has received some support. The idea here is that "rights to pollute" would be issued, but in limited amounts corresponding to the total target level for a given pollutant. The initial allocation system could be either "free" to current polluters or based on an auction (as with offshore oil rights). Once allocated, these rights would be tradable. Those firms able to reduce their emissions below their entitlements could sell the excess entitlement. This possibility would induce firms to innovate. The revenues would remain in the private sector and government revenues (after the initial auction, at least) would not be increased by such a system.

The tradable permit is opposed by many environmentalists on moral grounds. It is argued that there should be no "right to pollute," and certainly it is repugnant that such a right should be purchased for money. But, to some extent, this issue is a matter of perception. For instance, consumers now have an implicit "right" to pollute by virtue of the fact that they have a right to consume. Thus, the right to consume gasoline, for instance, could be rationed equally. Those able and willing to consume less than their "share" could be allowed to sell the excess. This would actually provide a kind of minimum income for the poor and elderly (if they do not drive cars) and could serve as a partial substitute for existing and increasingly unaffordable social services provided by the government from taxes.

The main alternative to regulation is to use emission-based or resource-based taxes or exchangeable permits as a method of internalization of environmental damage costs. For both regulation or standard-setting and for the use of emissions taxes or permits, there is still a problem of enforcement and a role for government. On the one hand, bureaucrats must determine the standards; on the other hand, they must set the scale of fees or fix the allocation of permits, and regulate the operation of the market mechanism to minimize opportunities for fraud. In any case, government must also monitor the effects of the policy.

Unfortunately, a "win–win" path is not necessarily painless. Those now receiving subsidies will experience pain. Those who cannot reduce their pollution levels by innovation will have to pay more. This being acknowledged, the obvious implication is that a truly painless pathway to an ecologically sustainable future may *not* exist! If a painless path does not exist, or cannot be found, it means that to get from our present techno-economic state to one capable of permanent sustainability – even by the "least-pain" route – significant short-term adjustment costs must eventually be borne by some groups or institutions. This means, in turn, that some very hard decisions will have to be taken, and soon. Unfortunately, experience suggests reason to doubt that our chaotic world of nearly 200 sovereign nation-states can make such a transition successfully. Nevertheless, if the human race is to have a long-term future, we must make the attempt.

Notwithstanding the difficulties, I think there is a "win–win" path to sustainability, or at least a policy that could take us a good part of the way in the right direction. I have noted that, if a single "objective function" for societal sustainability were to be selected, it would probably have to be something like the following: *sharply to increase the productivity of natural resources, especially non-renewables.* The reason this could turn out to be a "win–win" strategy is that increasing resource productivity implies decreasing the use of natural resources as a substitute for human labour. This, in turn, implies increasing employment! Since high unemployment (together with increasing associated costs of social security) is one of the most persistent socio-economic problems in the West, it seems only logical to explore possibilities for solving both the sustainability problem and the unemployment problem with a single common policy approach. It may not be too much to hope that this approach will also be beneficial to the less developed countries and the developing countries.

At first glance, increasing employment seems to imply decreasing labour productivity, which is *not* consistent with continuing economic growth. In the short run, some measures to increase resource productivity – especially by using less energy – may temporarily have this effect. Recycling tends to be more labour intensive than manufacturing with virgin materials, for instance. However, in the longer run, the object is to increase *total factor productivity* while using a lot fewer resources and a little more labour. This can be done, I believe, by reducing the cost of labour and increasing the cost of material resources while encouraging technological innovation and the development of new (but not resource-intensive) services.

At any rate, it seems clear that there are some promising possibilities to be explored. This exploration is critically important. Some will say that society must seek pathways to long-run eco-sustainability regardless of what the cost in conventional economic terms turns out to be, whether high or negative (i.e. profitable). If the latter turns out to be the case, so much the better. However, society will be much slower to adopt a high-cost path than a profitable one. Indeed, there is good reason to fear that, if the cost (or pain) appears too high, the difficult decisions will be delayed too long – perhaps until it is too late.

Concluding comments

For pessimists (or, by their own estimation, "realists"), the deeper question lying behind all of the foregoing is this: should we defer taking actions that might have economic costs (at least to some sectors) in the hope that further research will reveal that the threat is overstated or non-existent? Needless to say, those likely to be affected adversely by restructuring changes – especially the extractive industries – will tend to argue vociferously for delaying any serious action until more research is done. Scientists, too, are usually in favour of more research. Both these groups are influential. Hence, the argument for delay is likely to prevail indefinitely, or until there is "indisputable" evidence of the seriousness of the problems.

A case in point: the scientific predictions of ozone depletion between 1974 and 1984 were countered by protracted arguments for delay by the affected industries. It was only after the discovery of the "ozone hole" that the resistance crumbled and the Montreal Protocol was adopted.

Unfortunately, in some cases indisputable evidence may not be available until it is too late to reverse, or prevent, major damage. Indeed, the damage itself may *be* the only convincing evidence. For example, the sceptics about climate warming may not be convinced until the average temperature of the earth has risen by half a degree or so (with accompanying sealevel rise). By that time, hundreds of thousands of hectares of low-lying land may have become unproductive or uninhabitable, and hundreds of thousands of peasants in Bangladesh or Indonesia may have been killed by floods. Thus it is particularly important to state clearly the case for not waiting until the evidence is "indisputable." It is also important to develop clear and defensible criteria for (1) when looking is better than leaping, and (2) when it is time to stop looking and to leap, even into the dark.

It need hardly be said that most elected officials in most countries are committed (at least in public) not only to the existence of such a painless development trajectory but to the idea that we are already moving along it, thanks to the "invisible hand" of the free market. According to this comforting view (which, it must be said, is supported by many mainstream economists), market forces left to operate with minimal government intervention will automatically induce the necessary technological responses. These "techno-fixes" (it is assumed) will compensate for gradual resource exhaustion and environmental degradation.

I believe that the optimistic view that the free market will take care of the problem is false and unwarranted. The present path is one in which virtually all of the trends are clearly in the wrong direction, as I have taken some pains to explain above. Energy use, exhaustible resource use, erosion, toxic pollution, and waste are all increasing globally.

It is not enough to establish a plausible case that technical solutions do exist. The institutional framework of society, as it is structured today, is not likely to allow these solutions to emerge spontaneously. If unregulated competitive markets were going to solve these problems, there should be some indication of it; the trends, at least, should be in the right direction. There is no such indication. The fact we must face is that competitive "free" markets are imperfect. Market forces do not function in some of the critical areas. Alternative approaches are going to be needed. Governments must intervene on several fronts. They must increase the level of R&D support in critical areas (notwithstanding the usual criticism that governments should not attempt to "pick winners").

Governments must also intervene to eliminate or compensate for externalities. Regulation is only part of the answer. "Green" taxes may be another part. The encouragement of voluntary agreements may be a part, also. Tradable pollution permits or tradable consumption permits may be a part of the answer in the future. But all of these interventions will have the effect, separately and cumulatively, of increasing the cost of resources *vis-à-vis* labour and capital. This is the negative view. It has led many economists to conclude (with the assistance of so-called computable general equilibrium, or CGE, models) that environmental regulation, by driving up costs, must inevitably reduce the rate of growth of the economy.

The other side of this coin is that rising resource costs imply *ipso facto* that labour and some kinds of capital (especially knowledge-based capital) will be relatively less expensive, *vis-à-vis* resource inputs. The argument can be turned on its head. When one factor of production becomes less expensive than another, that factor will be more utilized. The factor that is to become less expensive is labour. This implies – or seems to imply – that the demand for labour can be expected to increase. In other words, costlier material resource inputs ⇒ more jobs and less unemployment.

Actually, this outcome would be a kind of "double dividend," if it can be achieved. But theory is one thing, practice is another. The service sectors are growing, to be sure. If the costs of physical materials were to increase (to compensate for externalities) this trend should accelerate. But the "growing tip" of the service sector is "high tech." It is health services, biotechnologies, telecommunications, and information technologies. Unemployed factory workers or miners cannot easily convert themselves into medical technologists or network systems managers. Since older, uneducated people are very difficult to retrain, the transition is limited by the rate at which skilled and educated young people can enter the labour force.

This, again, is an area requiring government intervention. In brief, governments must invest much more in human capital. This will be increasingly difficult in the environment of extreme budgetary stringency that will have to be faced by virtually every industrialized Western country in coming decades.

But the socio-economic and political dimensions of eco-restructuring are far more complex than even the last few paragraphs have suggested. As noted earlier, the socio-economic and political aspects of the "eco-restructuring" problem deserve – and must ultimately get – much more attention than they have yet received. Indeed, it is a subject for another book.

Notes

1. Toxins and carcinogens are considered dangerous from a human health point of view and are therefore commonly placed under strict control, irrespective of whether ecological consequences are likely or not.
2. Phosphorus is the other nutrient element that is required in amounts greater than the earth's crust normally contains. It is not recycled biologically, however, but accumulates on the ocean floors where it is recycled by ocean currents and by tectonic action. If the earth ever ceased to be tectonically active, the land surface would eventually run out of phosphorus.
3. Agreeing on the common use of simple and crude measures is nothing new. The gross domestic product (GDP) has been used for decades as a measure of "welfare," despite serious doubts that it really measures any such thing. It omits important sectors, including subsistence agriculture and unpaid household work (mostly by women), and it omits environmental services. On the other hand, it includes dubious items, such as "defensive measures" to protect health and safety, despite the fact that the health and safety hazards result from human activity in the first place. Clearly, defensive expenditures make no contribution to net social welfare. Nevertheless, GDP is still being used by macroeconomists, almost universally, without any of the adjustments or corrections that numerous critics have advocated.
4. The Wuppertal calculations of mass moved, or mass disturbed, generally include more than material "inputs" in the strict sense. The difference may be quite significant in some cases.
5. For a more complete review of this controversy, see Ayres (1993).
6. It is unclear what should be meant by "middle class." To put a specific monetary equivalent on it seems futile. A more functional suggestion might be that the relevant criterion of middle-class-ness is that children do not contribute to the family income, but rather constitute a financial obligation.

7. Some scientists argue that organic synthesis of a sort may have been going on in the reducing atmosphere of the early earth by mechanisms as yet unknown.
8. The argument for "factor 4" is set forth in German by von Weizsäcker et al. (1995); the argument for "factor 10" is summarized in Schmidt-Bleek (1994).
9. The phrase "closed cycle" should not be taken literally. Closure with respect to materials is possible, but the cycle cannot be closed with respect to exergy.
10. The "second-law" efficiency of any process is defined as the ratio of the minimum amount of energy theoretically needed for the process to the energy actually used. It can be defined consistently, in principle, for any process (given a suitable convention on the treatment of co-inputs and by-products), although actual numerical determination can be difficult in some cases. It must be pointed out that there is another widely used definition of efficiency, namely the ratio of "useful" energy outputs to total energy inputs. In some cases, such as electric power generation, the two definitions are equivalent. However in other cases (such as heating units) there is a very big difference. Gas furnaces are often advertised as having "efficiencies" up to 90 per cent, which merely means that 90 per cent of the heat is "useful" and only 10 per cent is lost with the combustion products. However, it often happens that the same amount of final heating effect could have been achieved with much less energy expenditure (e.g. by means of a "heat pump"). In this sense, most heating systems are actually very inefficient.
11. Note that efficiency of use is quite independent of the amount of use. The United States uses far more energy per capita than India, for instance, because it receives more energy services. But many energy-using activities in India, from electric power generation to cooking, nevertheless tend to be considerably less efficient than their Western counterparts.
12. For a more detailed review of this literature, see Ayres (1994).
13. This issue was highlighted in the 1994 White Paper, *Growth, Competitiveness, Employment – The Challenges and Ways Forward into the 21st Century*, issued by Jacques Delors, then Chairman of the European Commission (EC 1994).

References

Ayres, Robert U. (1978) *Resources, Environment and Economics: Applications of the Materials/Energy Balance Principle*. New York: Wiley.

—— (1989) Technological transformations and long waves. *Journal of Technological Forecasting and Social Change* **36**(3).

—— (1990) Energy conservation in the industrial sector. In: N. A. Ferrari, J. W. Tester and D. O. Woods (eds.), *Energy and the Environment in the 21st Century*. Cambridge, MA: MIT Press.

—— (1993) Commentary: Cowboys, cornucopians and long-run sustainability. *Ecological Economics* **8**: 189–207.

—— (1994) On economic disequilibrium and free lunch. *Environmental and Resource Economics* **4**: 435–454.

Ayres, Robert U. and Leslie W. Ayres (1996) *Industrial Ecology: Closing the Materials Cycle*. Aldershot, UK: Edward Elgar.

Ayres, Robert U. and Allen V. Kneese (1971) Economic and ecological effects of a stationary economy. *Annual Review of Ecology and Systematics* **2**, April.

—— (1989) Externalities: Economics and thermodynamics. In: F. Archibugi and P. Nijkamp (eds.), *Economy and Ecology: Towards Sustainable Development*. Netherlands: Kluwer Academic Publishers.

Barnett, Harold J. (1979) Scarcity and growth revisited. In: V. K. Smith (ed.), *Scarcity and Growth Reconsidered*, pp. 163–217. Baltimore and London: Johns Hopkins University Press for Resources for the Future.

Barnett, Harold J. and Chandler Morse (1962) *Scarcity and Growth: The Economics of Resource Scarcity*. Baltimore, MD: Johns Hopkins University Press.

Boulding, Kenneth E. (1966) Environmental quality in a growing economy. In: H. Jarrett (ed.), *Essays from the Sixth RFF Forum*. Baltimore, MD: Johns Hopkins University Press.

Brundtland, G. H. (ed.) (1987) *Our Common Future*. New York: Oxford University Press.

Cole, H. S. D. et al. (eds.) (1973) *Models of Doom: A Critique of the Limits to Growth*. New York: Universe Books.

Commoner, Barry (1971) *The Closing Circle*. New York: Alfred Knopf.

——— (1976) *The Poverty of Power*. New York: Bantam Books.

Daly, Herman E. (1990) Toward some operational principles of sustainable development. *Ecological Economics* **2**: 1–6.

EC (European Commission) (1994) *Growth, Competitiveness, Employment – The Challenges and Ways Forward into the 21st Century*. White Paper. Luxembourg: Office for Official Publications of the European Communities.

Edmonds, Jae A. and J. M. Reilly (1985) *Global Energy – Assessing the Future*. New York: Oxford University Press.

Ehrlich, Paul (1968) *Population Bomb*. New York: Ballantine.

Ehrlich, P. H. and A. H. Ehrlich (1970) *Population, Resources, Environment: Issues in Human Ecology*. San Francisco: W. H. Freeman.

Frosch, Robert A. and Nicholas E. Gallopoulos (1989) Strategies for manufacturing. *Scientific American* **261**(3): 94–102.

Gilland, Bernard (1983) Considerations on world population and food supply. *Population and Development Review* **9**, July: 203–211.

Goeller, H. and Alvin Weinberg (1976) The age of substitutability. *Science* **191**, February.

Goldemberg, Jose (1990) Energy and environmental policies in developed and developing countries. In: N. A. Ferrari, J. W. Tester, and D. O. Woods (eds.), *Energy and the Environment in the 21st Century*. Cambridge, MA: MIT Press.

Goldemberg, Jose et al. (1987) *Energy for Development*. Research Report, Washington, D.C.: World Resources Institute, September.

Holmberg, John, Karl-Henrik Robèrt, and Karl-Erik Eriksson (1995) Socio-ecological principles for a sustainable society: Scientific background and Swedish experience. In: J. Holmberg (ed.), *Socio-Ecological Principles and Indicators for Sustainability*. Göteborg: Institute of Physical Resource Theory.

Hoyle, Fred and N. Chaudra Wickramasinghe (1978) *Life Cloud*. New York: Harper & Row.

Jorgenson, Dale W. and Peter J. Wilcoxen (1990a) Intertemporal general equilibrium modeling of U.S. environmental regulation. *Journal of Policy Modeling* **12**, Winter: 715–755.

——— (1990b) Environmental regulation and U.S. economic growth. *RAND Journal of Economics* **21**, Summer: 314–340.

Kahn, Herman, William Brown, and L. Martel (1976) *The Next 200 Years – A Scenario for America and the World*. New York: William Morrow.

Keyfitz, Nathan (1990) Population growth can prevent the development that would slow population growth. In: J. Matthews (ed.), *Preserving the Global Environment: The Challenge of Shared Leadership*, pp. 39–77. New York: W. W. Norton.

––––– (1991) Population and development within the ecosphere: One view of the literature. *Population Index* **57**(1): 5–22.

Lovelock, James E. (1972) Gaia as seen through the atmosphere. *Atmospheric Environment* **6**: 579–580.

––––– (1979) *Gaia: A New Look at Life on Earth*. London: Oxford University Press.

Lovins, Amory B. et al. (1981) *Least-Cost Energy: Solving the CO_2 Problem*. Andover, MA: Brickhouse Publication.

McNeill, James (1989) Strategies for sustainable economic development. *Scientific American* **261**(3).

Manne, Alan S. and Richard G. Richels (1990) CO_2 emission limits: An economic cost analysis for the USA. *The Energy Journal* **11**(2): 51–74.

––––– (1992) *Buying Greenhouse Insurance*. Cambridge, MA: MIT Press.

Matthews, Jessica (1990) The great debate I: The world environmental crisis. *Futures Research Quarterly* **6**(1).

Meadows, Dennis et al. (1972) *The Limits to Growth: A Report for the Club of Rome's Project on the Predicament of Mankind*. New York: Universe Books.

Mills, Evan, Deborah Wilson, and Thomas B. Johansson (1991) Getting started: No regrets strategies for reducing greenhouse gas emissions. *Energy Policy*, June.

Nakicenovic, Nebojsa, Luigi Bodda, Arnulf Grubler, and Paul V. Gilli. (1990) *Technological Progress, Structural Change and Efficient Energy Use: Trends Worldwide and in Austria*. Laxenburg, Austria: International Institute for Applied Systems Analysis. Also published in German in Schriftenreihe der Forschungsinitiative des Verbundkonzerns, vol. 6, Vienna, 1990.

Nakicenovic, Nebojsa, Paul V. Gilli, and Rainer Kurz (1996) Regional and global exergy and energy efficiencies. *Energy* **21**.

Nordhaus, William (1994) *Managing the Global Commons: The Economics of Climate Change*. Cambridge, MA: MIT Press.

Pearce, David W. (1988) Economics, equity and sustainable development. *Futures* **20**, December: 598–605.

Pearce, David W., Anil Markandya, and Edward Barbier (1989) *Blueprint for a Green Economy*. London: Earthscan.

Pezzey, John (1989) *Sustainability, Intergenerational Equity and Environmental Policy*. Discussion Paper in Economics 89-7. Boulder, CO: Department of Economics, University of Colorado, Fall.

Prigogine, Ilya and Stengers, I. (1984) *Order out of Chaos: Man's New Dialogue with Nature*. London: Bantam Books.

Repetto, Robert (1985) Natural resource accounting in a resource based economy: An Indonesian case study. Paper presented at the 3rd Environmental Accounting Workshop, sponsored by UNEP and the World Bank, Paris, October.

Sant, R. W. (1979) *The Least-Cost Energy Strategy: Minimizing Consumer Costs through Competition*. Report 55. Virginia: Mellon Institute Energy Productivity Center.

Schipper, Lee (1989) Energy efficiency in an era of apparent energy stability: Progress, plateau, or passé? In: *International Energy Workshop*. Laxenburg, Austria: International Institute for Applied Systems Analysis, June.

Schlesinger, William H. (1991) *Biogeochemistry: An Analysis of Global Change*. New York: Academic Press.

Schmidt-Bleek, Friedrich B. (1992) Eco-restructuring economies: Operationalizing the sustainability concept. *Fresenius Environmental Bulletin* **1**(46).

—— (1994) *Carnoules Declaration*. Wuppertal, Germany: Factor Ten Club, October.

Simon, Julian (1980) Resources, population, environment: An oversupply of false bad news. *Science* **208**, 27 June: 1431–1437.

Solow, Robert (1986) On the intergenerational allocation of natural resources. *Scandinavian Journal of Economics* **88**: 141–149.

—— (1992) An almost practical step towards sustainability. *Invited Lecture on the Occasion of the 40th Anniversary of Resources for the Future*. Washington, D.C.: Resources for the Future, 8 October.

Stigliani, William D. (1988) Changes in valued "capacities" of soils and sediments as indicators of non-linear and time-delayed environmental effects. *Environmental Monitoring and Assessment* **10**: 245–307.

Tietenberg, Tom (1984) *Environmental and Natural Resource Economics*. Glenview, IL: Scott, Foresman.

Weizsäcker, Ernst Ulrich von, Amory B. Lovins, and L. Hunter Lovins (1995) *Faktor Vier*. Munich: Droemer Knaur.

Weterings, R. and J. B. Opschoor (1992) *The Ecocapacity as a Challenge to Technological Development*. Rijswijk, Netherlands: Advisory Council for Research on Nature and Environment, Publication RMNO 74a, April.

—— (1994) *Towards Environmental Performance Indicators Based on the Notion of Environmental Space*. Rijswijk, Netherlands: Advisory Council for Research on Nature and Environment, Publication RMNO 96, March.

World Bank (1992) *World Development Report*. New York: Oxford University Press.

Part I
Restructuring resource use

2

The biophysical basis of eco-restructuring: An overview of current relations between human economic activities and the global system

Walther Manshard

Introduction

Eco-restructuring cuts across almost all scientific subjects and covers nearly all chapters of Agenda 21. But, for the purposes of this chapter, two focal points in the global debate are emphasized: namely the UNCED conventions on climatic change and biological diversity. Broad interdisciplinary research themes, such as industrial metabolism, industrial ecology, landscape analysis, and "eco-restructuring," are now emerging. It is to be hoped that they will contribute to better understanding of the interactions between human activities and the biosphere. It is helpful to look at the environment as an exhaustible resource and at the earth as a self-organizing system. This overview attempts to point out some useful principles for steering the processes of "eco-transition." It is based on lessons taken from cases – including climatic change, biodiversity, and African development – to highlight problems and approaches.

In this context it is useful to focus attention on a few of the more fragile subsystems such as fresh water, soils, and aspects of relief and surface development. These biophysical elements belong both to the natural environment and to the economic system. Human driving forces, especially industrial development, have an impact on environment, especially on natural resource depletion and land-use and land-cover transformation. Similarly, climatic and biogeochemical systems have an influence on the pace and scope of eco-restructuring.

The chapter concludes with a regional thumbnail sketch on a sub-continental scale, focusing on one of the world's least developed regions (West Africa). Because of the lack of hard empirical data, this discussion must largely remain on a descriptive level, primarily by making use of geographical information. It stresses the problems of sustainability and vulnerability of the African continent. There is still a lot of research to be done to find out how Africa contributes to the global situation.

The earth system

The total earth system consists of the geosphere and the biosphere. The geosphere is conventionally defined as the lithosphere (rocks), the hydrosphere (oceans, rivers, and lakes), and the atmosphere, together with the pedosphere (soils) and the cryosphere (ice). It constitutes the substrate for the biosphere, which is the earth's integrated life support system.

On the other hand, the biosphere can also be subdivided into terrestrial and marine subsystems, with living organisms further subdivided into animal and vegetable species (plus bacteria). The animal world consists of humans, other mammals, birds, fish, insects, and a number of other orders, phyla, and families. The human section (which dominates the rest) is sometimes called the anthroposystem (Husar 1993). This can be further broken down into the sociosphere and the "technosphere." The latter, in particular, influences the other different natural systems of the geosphere, and is in turn influenced by them.

The human impact on the other components of the earth system has now reached a level comparable to – and in some respects greater than – that of natural processes. Anthropogenic activities include the extraction of raw materials, their physical and chemical separation and refining, as well as their conversion and distribution. Manufacturing represents only a small fraction of these activities. Indeed, from some environmental standpoints it is not necessarily the most important. Extractive industries, including agriculture and forestry, and also "final" consumption (including personal transportation) often generate more harmful waste materials and residues than cutting, or shaping, or forming, or assembly. In spite of the adoption of waste-minimization policies, the continued use of new "virgin" materials and fossil fuels still imposes a heavy burden on the bio-physical environment. This can be overcome only in time by more appropriate research and development strategies, including informa-tion systems that facilitate the optimization of the exchanges between industry and nature (Ayres et al. 1992). An interesting and different approach is offered by the concept of "landscape ecology." This has developed out of a kind of merger between traditional geography and ecology. A "landscape" is, by definition, a kind of shorthand for the complex spatial interaction patterns of natural and human systems. Widespread landscape transformations have now become a pressing global problem. There are no landscapes, except perhaps in Antarc-tica, free from human influence. The industrial type of landscape in particular reflects a very high level of technological and environmen-tal interference by humans.

The climate system and climatic change

The basic objective of the Framework Convention on Climate Change (1992; further discussed by the Berlin Conference in 1995) was to further a political process leading to "stabilization of green-house gas concentrations in the atmosphere at a level that would prevent anthropogenic interference with the climate system" (Article 2) and to do so in such a manner as to allow ecosystems to adapt naturally, and so as not to interfere with food production and economic development. Needless to say, it is also important to understand better the processes that are influenced by the earth's atmosphere on a global, regional, and local level. These include biophysical, geochemical, hydrological-oceanic, and socio-economic processes. This calls for an improved understanding of the socio-economic consequences of climatic change and for further investiga-tions of the response mechanisms to mitigate such changes.

The climate system is mainly driven by solar radiation. The major engine of global atmospheric circulation is the so-called hydrological cycle. Solar heating of the ocean surface causes evaporation of water. The moist air rises until it cools to condensation point. The water vapour condenses and returns to the earth, partly over land. The condensation process releases heat in the atmosphere. Water from precipitation then flows from the land back to the sea, carrying nutrient elements (and causing salinity gradients). Thermal imbal-ances between high and low latitudes drive both winds and ocean currents, redistributing energy and matter within the atmosphere and the hydrosphere.

As a result of the interactions between solar radiation and the geo/biosphere, the climate system changes continually. This has occurred throughout the history of our planet. However, in the recent past a new factor has appeared: increased emission of "greenhouse gases" or GHGs (e.g. carbon dioxide, methane, nitrous oxide, chlorofluorocarbons). These emissions are strongly linked to human activities, especially the combustion of fossil fuels and high-intensity agriculture. The build-up of these gases in the atmosphere has made it act somewhat like a mirror for heat radiation. This has led to a marked global warming process, whose magnitude and rate are still under discussion.

The task of determining likely "winners" and "losers" resulting from this ongoing climatic change is extremely difficult. It will affect mainly agriculture. Among the industrialized countries, agriculture accounts for only a very small part of the economy. This has led some economists (mainly in the United States) to conclude that climate warming is not a great concern and that major efforts to counteract it would not be economically justified. Yet it is undeniable that agriculture is essential for human survival and that it counts for a much larger part of the economies of poorer developing countries. The Intergovernmental Panel on Climate Change (IPCC 1990) projects that the results of global warming, such as increased precipitation and longer frost-free periods, could bring about rather limited immediate benefits to some regions, located mainly in the northern hemisphere. In the South, however, where food supplies are regionally more limited, difficulties related to food security problems may increase. Since climate warming would also be accompanied by sealevel rise, it is of even more immediate concern to small low-lying island nations and countries such as Bangladesh with large populations heavily concentrated in estuarine zones.

One of the most significant results of climate change is likely to be the shifting of agro-climatic zones, although the spatial distribution of such shifts is still difficult to predict. Also sealevel rise affecting low-lying coastal areas by flooding will influence industrial planning and development. The establishment of international funds to counter the adverse consequences of climatic change and the creation of an International Insurance Pool (IIP) to provide insurance against the consequences of sealevel rise are under discussion.

An important implication of the IPCC's work is that uncertainty is itself costly. In other words, it is important to find out (and quantify) the real costs of action (or inaction) in the area of climatic change and to establish economic incentives or disincentives for achieving the stabilization and eventual reduction of greenhouse gas emissions. In this respect, a narrow application of the "polluter-pays" principle would adversely affect economic development in some countries (notably China and India) that are heavily committed to the use of coal. Hence, there is increasing interest in "joint implementation" and such devices as tradable permits (see chap. 12 in this volume).

Other important aspects of human activities on the global level include stratospheric ozone depletion and its potential biospheric effects, as well as the processes involved with acid deposition. Both can be directly linked to industrial emissions of gaseous pollutants. Stratospheric ozone is important for the biosphere because of its absorption of ultraviolet (UV) radiation, which is harmful to humans, animals, and plants. But long-lived chlorinated fluorocarbons (CFCs), which gradually diffuse from the lower atmosphere into the stratosphere, are broken up by UV radiation, releasing atomic chlorine (Cl) atoms. These, in turn, react with ozone (O_3) molecules, which are converted back into ordinary molecular oxygen and atomic oxygen, leaving the chlorine atoms free to attack more ozone. Each chlorine atom can destroy hundreds of thousands of ozone molecules. Hence, CFCs are literally capable of destroying the ozone layer. Thanks to the Montreal Protocol (1987) and the subsequent London revision (1990), CFCs are being phased out of production, at least in the industrial world. But, because so many CFCs are already in the atmosphere, their environmental impacts are likely still increasing and will not disappear for many decades.

Acid deposition is caused by the emission of chemicals such as nitrogen oxides (NOx) and sulphur dioxide (SO_2) to the atmosphere, mainly from combustion processes. Nitrogen oxides are produced in high-temperature flames when there is excess air. This happens mainly in coal-burning electric power generating plants and internal combustion engines. The nitrogen in the air itself is oxidized. Sulphur dioxides are produced when coal, containing a small percentage of sulphur, is burned or from the smelting of sulphide ores of copper, nickel, lead, or zinc. These gaseous oxides are further oxidized in the air or on the surfaces of small particles, which act as catalysts. These oxides, reacting with and dissolved in water, become nitric and sulphuric acids, respectively. They may travel hundreds of miles through the atmosphere and descend in the form of rain, fog, and snow or even in dry form. These acids are eventually deposited by rain on the surface of the earth or on the surfaces of trees and other vegetation.

This acid deposition has had great effects on aquatic ecosystems by increasing the acidity of rivers and lakes. This has negatively affected both the flora and fauna. It also has a marked direct impact on terrestrial vegetation, mainly because of its effects on soils. The acidification of forest soils releases and mobilizes metal ions (especially aluminium) that were formerly bound to clay particles. Some of these metals are toxic to trees. The ongoing discussion of the complex causes of "*Waldsterben*" (forest die-back) is largely related to acidification.

An interesting integrated approach to climatic impact assessment that takes into account the primary, secondary, and tertiary sectors of the economy has been proposed by Parry et al. (1988). This interaction concept not only focuses on climatic parameters but also includes social factors such as poverty, war, or hunger as necessary for a useful evaluation of the effects of climatic change. In addition to policy implications, this allows for feedbacks regulating and enhancing possible change effects. For instance, a change in climate may lead to a change in natural vegetation belts, which itself will influence the climate through changes in fluxes of gases or through changes in surface reflectivity. This integrated approach will allow a more comprehensive treatment of interactions between climate and society.

Climatic change and vulnerability

The concept of vulnerability is central to any research into climatic change. The World Meteorological Organization (WMO) has defined the objective of its climate programme as "determining the characteristics of human societies at different levels of development which make them either specially vulnerable or specially resilient to climatic variability and change." Vulnerability can be seen as "the degree to which a system may react adversely to the occurrence of a hazardous event" (Timmerman 1981). This concept has often been used in relation to climatic and global change research (Kates et al. 1985; Liverman 1991), being linked to terms such as resilience, marginality, susceptibility, adaptability, fragility, and criticality.

In the tropics especially, a wide-ranging integrative approach encompassing all aspects of vulnerability is needed. This includes biophysical monitoring, modelling, and studies on the transformation of the physical environment. In this respect, only an improved understanding of the socio-economic, cultural, and demographic factors will provide the necessary insight into the situation of social groups at risk. In the regional case-study on Africa, below, further reference is made to this.

Biological diversity

The Convention on Biological Diversity (UNEP 1992) and also Chapter 15 of Agenda 21 (UNCED 1992), on the conservation of biological diversity, call for the development of national, regional, and global strategies for an improved sustainable use of biological resources. A closer integration of these strategies into the respective development plans and concepts is advocated. This would include a broader promotion of international cooperation and a furthering of the scientific and economic understanding of biodiversity in the functioning of ecological and human-use systems.

Biodiversity describes the abundant variety and variability of living organisms, which, in the context of different ecosystems, have evolved over the past 3 billion years. The biological evolution responded to unstable situations (open cycles) by "inventing" new processes to stabilize the system by closing the cycles (Ayres 1994). This self-organizing capability has been called "Gaia" (Margulis and Lovelock 1976; Lovelock 1987).

In the latest stage of evolution, humans, as the dominant species, have been responsible for major habitat changes. For instance, land-use changes resulting in deforestation and desertification have often brought about a loss of biodiversity, both at the level of ecosystems and also within ecosystems, leading to a loss of genetic and species diversity. This loss has many wide-ranging potential and real effects on both man-made and natural ecosystems and the human populations depending on them.

In return, humans have also, over thousands of years, exploited and manipulated the genetic wealth of biodiversity by selecting and breeding crops and animals. It could perhaps be argued that the effects of climatic change upon agricultural crops would be negligible, because of their great variability. However, one of the main problems is the trend towards great genetic and ecological uniformity. This has occurred through the introduction of commercial seeds that have good yields under optimal conditions but that produce very little in less favourable environments. Therefore the conservation of indigenous varieties, bred and specialized to local conditions for centuries, is potentially advantageous (Ezcurra et al. 1991). The recent global warming trend has the consequence that these localized specialized varieties with limited distribution will disappear sooner than the more uniform commercial crops. This underlines the vulnerability of agro-ecosystems and the general importance of an increased emphasis on preserving biological and genetic diversity.

The consequences of intentional or unintentional "invasions" of living organisms, through export or exchange between different ecosystems, should also be increasingly considered. This has long been a problem associated with human commerce and colonization. Many desirable crops – including maize, potatoes, and tobacco – were brought to Europe from the Americas, for instance. Pineapples were taken to Hawaii from South America. Rubber trees were taken to Malaya and Indo-China from the Amazon valley. But pest species also migrate. The rabbit plague in Australia, Dutch Elm disease, the starling, the grey squirrel, the Norway rat, the water hyacinth, and dozens of other examples could be cited. Meanwhile, in many cases other competing species were eliminated by the interlopers.

As another response to this biological "erosion," various forms of biotechnology have emerged, ranging from traditional fermentation techniques to modern breakthroughs in genetic engineering and recombinant DNA technology (see chap. 3 in this volume). Biotechnology can offer new possibilities for food production, medicine, and energy supply, including special chemicals for improved environmental management. In addition to the protection and conservation of the biosphere, the international Convention on Biological Diversity (UNEP 1992) advocated better handling of biotechnology and improved distribution of its benefits as key elements for successful economic development.

Fresh water

Fresh water supply is a key factor for the maintenance of terrestrial ecosystems. A good example is the hydrology and water balance of the tropical forests, which has also become important for its impact on human land use (Douglas 1990). Estimates for the Amazon Basin suggest that a complete replacement of the rain forest by grassland (if it were possible) would increase soil and surface temperatures by 1–3°C, with rainfall and evapo-transpiration declining by 26 per cent and 30 per cent, respectively (Salati et al. 1990).

The main global water uses are for irrigation, electric power generation, and industry. Municipal uses, for washing, cooking, drinking, and sewage disposal, are comparatively minor at the global level, though locally important – especially in dry regions.

Concerning water consumption, there are important differences between the industrialized countries ("North") and the developing countries ("South"). In Europe, for instance, industrial use (including electric power) is dominant, with only 37 per cent for all other human uses, including agriculture. In Africa and Asia in the 1980s, by contrast, withdrawals for human use and agriculture were over 90 per cent of the total (Tolba and El-Kholy 1992).

In industry, much water is recycled several times before it is finally discarded as waste water. (In the United States, the petroleum refineries use water – mostly for cooling – nine times before it is discarded.) On the other hand, industrial waste water is often toxic. If it is discharged into surface water or groundwater without treatment it creates serious environmental problems. During the past 20 years (since the 1977 Mar del Plata Conference) some progress has been made in water resources management. However, recent experiences in Eastern Europe have shown that problems of water quality in the former communist countries are much more serious than it was previously thought.

It is estimated that agricultural use of water for irrigation in the South will decline further, at least in many areas such as northern China, owing to falling water tables. The share of industrial water use will rise and it is expected that an adequate supply of fresh water will constitute the most critical resource "bottleneck" at the turn of the twenty-first century.

Soils

Topsoil is a fragile and elusive interface between the biosphere and the lithosphere. The soils (i.e. the pedosphere) have been deeply affected, and even (in some cases) created, by human action. No analysis of vegetation, land cover, and land use can be undertaken without a comprehensive knowledge of the soils, their nutrient status, and their stability.

Because of the great variety and variability of soil development, in both time and space, a sharp distinction between natural and anthropogenic changes is quite difficult to make. Human-induced changes are mainly caused by agricultural land use (crops and livestock), and by transportation and settlements. Roads and settlements have decreased the total area of productive soils (especially fertile top-soils) in all urbanized societies. This process is of great concern now in Asia, where most of the population still live on farms but migration to cities is accelerating.

In a number of studies of the relation of agricultural production and the population carrying capacity, the importance of soil constraints within the biophysical framework has been stressed. Several soil zones have been identified where present food demand exceeds the agricultural production potential. These are designated as critical zones of food insecurity.

Climatic and soil data have also increasingly been used to assess vulnerability. This has been done on a global scale by emphasizing biophysical driving forces. It has also been done at the local and regional scale by associating vulnerability with changes in crop yields, harvest failures, and agro-ecological potential. In this connection the ecotoxic impacts of industrial wastes and agricultural chemical usage on the biosphere have not been treated adequately.

The solid earth (lithosphere)

Global change processes involving the lithosphere are often ignored. However, as the main supplier of mineral raw materials, this part of the geosphere plays a leading role in relation to important biogeochemical and nutrient cycles. With the exceptions of carbon and oxygen, the anthropogenic mobilization of most nutrients and trace metals by industrial activities can already be compared with the natural rate. In many cases, the anthropogenic mobilization is considerably greater than the natural flux. This applies, for instance, to most heavy metals.

Processes of erosion, deposition/sedimentation, tectonic movement, and volcanic eruption can deeply affect human use-patterns, especially of the soils. Earlier assumptions about the humid tropics have increasingly been questioned. These include the assumption that weathering and chemical denudation proceeded there much faster than elsewhere and the idea that tropical rivers were only "passive conveyors" without eroding their own bed. New work on quaternary climatic changes and tectonic diversity has contributed significantly to our knowledge of the stability (and instability) of tropical landscapes (Douglas 1990).

Of course, geomorphological factors can influence technological development. An interesting example is the construction of multi-purpose dams for both irrigation and power-generating purposes in the subtropical zone of excessive "planation" (or retarded valley formation). Most tropical dry savanna regions belong to this zone, which is also sometimes referred to as the savanna planation zone. These land forms are basically related to climatic factors such as sheetflow on sloping surfaces with extreme peaks of river discharge. Although it is generally perceived that big rivers cut deep gashes into the bedrock, in the semi-humid and semi-arid tropics reality is somewhat different. Here most rivers flow in shallow river beds. On tectonically stable blocks, planation surfaces are dominant even at altitudes over 1,000 m. The geomorphological term for this type of valley is "trough valley" (Young 1972) or "*Flachmuldental*" (Louis 1964). In these geomorphic circumstances it is quite difficult to find suitable sites for irrigation or power dams. Large technological and financial investments for this purpose can be much less profitable than in other tropical regions. It must be recognized, therefore, that the seasonally wet and dry outer tropics suffer from persisting constraints caused by land forms and river discharges which also affect the economic development of this very important climatic zone. Aside from Africa, many examples can be cited from the Deccan Plateau in India and the Planaltos on the Brazilian Shield (Weischet and Caviedes 1993).

Land-cover and land-use changes

Land-cover and land-use changes have become global in scale. For the better understanding of these changes, more work on the linkages between biophysical and human-induced driving forces is essential. Generally speaking, land cover refers to attributes of parts of the earth surface including vegetation, soil, groundwater, and topographical features. Broad categories would include, for instance, the boreal forest, tropical savanna, cropland, wetland, or settlements. On the other hand, land use refers to the purpose for which land cover is exploited. These uses can be as varied as agriculture, industry, recreation, or even wild life conservation.

Looking at it globally, at the scale of the earth system land-cover changes over the past three centuries can be described briefly as follows: considerable net loss of forest, a marked gain of arable cropland, partly former forest and partly from wetlands, and considerable loss of wetlands that have been partially or completely cultivated or otherwise drained and changed.

The direct impacts of these changes on the biogeochemical budget are not yet clear. But the following can be assumed:

- The conversion from natural to human-induced systems over the past 150 years has resulted in a net flux of CO_2 that is almost equal to the net release by fossil fuel burning over the same period.
- The present release of CO_2 from land-cover changes amounts to about one-third of that from fossil fuel consumption.
- Land-use and land-cover changes represent the largest source of N_2O emissions, which contribute to greenhouse warming and (possibly) also to stratospheric ozone depletion.
- The two largest land uses in spatial terms are crop cultivation (14–15 million km^2) and livestock production (with pastures and rangelands, about 70 million km^2). Settlements with industries cover only a small percentage of the world's land area (Turner et al. 1993).

Among the main driving forces of land-use changes, population growth, socio-economic and cultural organization, and technology play leading roles. Technological development changes the use of and demand for land resources. Other societal factors related to political and economic structures and to change in attitudes and value systems add a new dimension to environmental change, which will be illustrated by some regional examples from Africa (below).

Human impacts and industrial metabolism

Human economic activities have now reached an order of magnitude where their influence on the natural earth systems is quite significant. If we accept the analogy between biological and industrial metabolism, the latter can be defined as "the whole integrated collection of physical processes that convert raw materials and energy, plus labor, into finished products and wastes ... with the economic system as the metabolic regulatory mechanism" (Ayres 1994). The firm (factory/plant) as a basic unit of the economic system can be compared to living organisms in biology. This analogy, taken a step further, leads into the notion of "industrial ecology."

Similarly, the "cycle" concept of the geo-scientists (e.g. the hydrological, carbon/oxygen, nitrogen, or sulphur cycles) can be adopted as "materials cycles" of the industrial system, starting with raw materials from the earth and returning them to nature as wastes (Ayres

1994). Industry converts primary resources into products useful for humans. In the course of these transformations, large amounts of waste are generated. It is important to measure these fluxes and processes. A number of measures of industrial metabolism have been proposed, which also require a sound knowledge of the biophysical basis. They include measurements of dissipative losses, of recycled materials, and also of the economic output per unit of material input, which can be called material productivity. Clearly, more exact measurements based on geophysical and geochemical data are desirable. This is because, collected at a sectoral level, they would allow improved analyses of the entire process of industrial metabolism. The establishment of an information system on industrial metabolism has been proposed (Fischer-Kowalski et al. 1993).

One attempt to introduce a universal measure for ecological disturbances is "materials intensity per unit of service" (Schmidt-Bleek 1992). The underlying idea is that the potential for disturbance is closely related to the mass of materials moved or processed in the whole chain of processes beginning with extraction and ending with disposal or recycling. The difference between the mass of the product itself and the total mass moved indirectly in the chain has been given the evocative term "rucksack." The size of the rucksack of a material product is a rough measure of the potential for disturbance resulting from its production and use.

The case of West Africa

In order to get a clearer picture of the biophysical base and the human impacts on it, including brief comments on associated economic activities, it is helpful to "go down" in scale from a global to a continental or even to a subcontinental or regional scale. For a first overview one could adopt the zonal classification of "landscape belts" (*Landschaftsgürtel*), which can be used as an expression of the existing combined attributes of climate, vegetation, soil, and land use.

In West Africa, this sequence of "landscape zones" extends from the rain forest to the desert in a fairly regular fashion. An analysis linking this major biophysical pattern with corresponding patterns of land use and economic development poses some interesting questions. Political boundaries have cut right across this ecological zonation, usually encompassing several landscape belts within each state. Development of land use, including industry, has been strongly influenced by history, i.e. mainly by events in the pre-colonial, colonial, and post-colonial periods. Within this biophysical zonation, agricultural activities and mining industries play a more dominant role than manufacturing. Similarly, rapid urbanization has influenced the patterns of development.

West Africa belongs, broadly speaking, to the group of less and least developed countries, although some states such as oil-rich Nigeria or the resources-rich Gabon and Côte d'Ivoire have been (erratically) nearing the level of the newly industrialized economies (NIEs). In many African countries, economic development has been assisted by foreign aid programmes. Much of the rest has been driven by natural resource development projects controlled by large foreign-based oil and/or mining companies. There is no history or deep-rooted tradition of political democracy. Ethnic and tribal identities are stronger than national loyalties. "Checks and balances" are weak. Government, when based on parliamentary forms, is likely to be single party in practice. The alternative is military dictatorship. Owing to the political situation (in Liberia, the Sudan, Angola, Mozambique, Rwanda, Somalia, etc.), so far only very limited chances for any eco-restructuring exist.

In a few of the better-functioning African economies, industrial activities cover the whole chain of production from the extraction of raw materials to materials processing and manufacturing and final waste disposal. Industrial enterprises are the main consumers of renewable and non-renewable natural resources, including mineral ores, energy, and agricultural products in all forms. Industrial processes often produce toxic wastes, gases, and other effluents. Furthermore, many goods imported from the North cannot be recycled and become difficult or even hazardous wastes.

Land resources and land use in West Africa

For many West African nations, access to land resources is important for sustainable development. Land resources provide the basis of most human activities, including the management of soil, water, and energy. In urban areas, in particular, access to land is becoming difficult because of growing conflicts between industry, housing, transportation, and recreational needs. But in rural areas too the increasing use of fragile, marginal land calls for improved planning and management of land resources. As a first step to combat unsustainable practices, a sound land-use policy, with improved land tenure structures, possibly even introducing a more efficient land registry system, will be important.

Population growth in Africa is generally correlated strongly with the expansion and intensification of agricultural land use. Often this results in deforestation, if not desertification. On the other hand, studies (e.g. Zaba 1991) have shown that population density and growth may rank well below economic factors causing environmental degradation. However, these relationships are by no means clear. They often depend on rather complex local circumstances and require further situational assessments of considerable subtlety.

Whereas there are a number of very well-documented studies on the Amazonian forests (e.g. Dickinson 1987; Fearnside 1990), we know very little about the corresponding African situation. One of the marked differences is the much more limited impact (or even absence) of livestock farming or ranching in the cleared forests. This is mainly because of the adverse effects of the tsetse fly, carrier of "sleeping sickness" (trypanosomiasis) in tropical Africa.

So far, only very few comparative aggregate studies have researched the role of environmental driving forces in Africa on a statistical/empirical basis. Most micro-type studies have been of a more descriptive nature, often in relation to population carrying capacity and landscape transformation. Perhaps the UNU project on Population Growth, Land Transformation and Environmental Change (PLEC) and also UNU's Research and Training Centre on Natural Resources in Africa (INRA) will provide some further insights into regional and local dynamics of environmental land-use/ land-cover changes leading in many cases to land degradation.

Some environmental aspects

Only a small number of African problems can be mentioned explicitly here.

Air pollution

In many urban areas, air pollution resulting from electric power generation, transportation, local industries, and domestic cooking is already a major problem. In addition to the normal sources, atmospheric pollution is also the result of widespread forest-clearing operations, especially forest burning by smallholding farmers and bigger agricultural enterprises.

Another source is the large-scale transportation and deposition of dust by desert winds. Estimates of the quantities of dust moved are quite large: 13 million tonnes per season, mainly from the Saharan and Sahelian zones, are deposited on land all the way across the Atlantic. This material not only "fertilizes" the Latin American and Caribbean forest belt; it also provides trace nutrients (including phosphorus) that permit the growth of oceanic plankton (Morales 1979).

Water pollution
Through clearing of vegetation and the transformation and intensification of land use, both for ploughing and for the accumulation of "bricks and mortar" (urbanization), surface runoff has increased and a number of river beds have become significantly silted. In the bigger urban centres the industrial impact on the hydrological cycle is quite marked. The dumping of liquid and solid wastes of all kinds has polluted the urban water supply almost everywhere. Water-borne wastes include industrial waste water from timber and paper-pulp mills, mercury pollution from gold mining, pollution from leather tanning, and pollution from cellulose-based industries. There are presumably significant saline water wastes from oil drilling and pumping operations in Angola and Nigeria.

Solid waste
Data on solid waste are very scanty. Pollution by solid waste is generally high in countries with major mining operations (e.g. iron ore in Liberia and Mauritania, tin/columbite mining in Nigeria, gold mining in Ghana, or bauxite mining in Guinea and Cameroon). These operations cause major potential environmental hazards but they also often constitute the only source of hard currency – along with cocoa or coffee – for the national economies.

Manufacturing waste is far less voluminous than mining or agricultural waste. Municipal waste is an increasing problem, however. In many urban agglomerations, "waste economies" are an important part of the informal sector. Special situations arise when social groups live on (and from) waste dumps, as for instance in Cairo.

Industrialization and urbanization
In West Africa, industrialization is still in a very early stage. So far, West Africa is suffering many of the disadvantages and enjoying

only a few of the benefits of industrialization. Local small-scale industries often concentrate on repairing and renovating industrial products.

Urbanization has fuelled industrialization. Energy supply, transportation facilities, public infrastructure, and proximity to political power (because of security and influence considerations) are important locational factors for the siting of industries in the big cities. Metallurgical and chemical industries exist on a very limited scale, if at all. The same applies to electronics industries. There is, however, a certain growth of small-scale industries in rural areas and in smaller regional centres.

The main resource-based industries such as mining, quarrying, and agricultural enterprises are generally not closely linked to urban centres. The socio-political influence of the transnational corporations has declined in Africa in recent years. These enterprises often operate in isolated "enclaves," such as mining or plantation areas, with minimum interaction with the larger society.

Pollution control and other regulatory measures, including recycling and cleaner forms of production, are in a very initial phase. In most African countries environmental control mechanisms exist only "on paper." For instance, Nigeria has its Environmental Protection Law of 1986, but, as in most developing countries, actual enforcement remains difficult.

Social impacts
Besides demographic growth (generally around 3 per cent per annun or more), African development is strongly influenced by the situation of the political economy and the access of countries to resources. Critics of a one-sided climatic explanation of hazards and disasters often quote the Sahel crisis of the 1970s as an example to prove the dominant role of socio-political parameters in coping with a famine initiated by drought. However, it seems clear that only consideration of both biophysical and socio-economic and cultural factors can explain the vulnerability of the "political ecology" within this zone. If one looks at it spatially, one finds that the most vulnerable groups do not necessarily live in the most vulnerable locations. It is the combination and overlap of the two that leads to the most problematic cases of marginality and sensitivity.

In this respect the impact of technology may vary. Irrigation, for instance, may reduce biophysical vulnerability. On the other hand, irrigation practices may lead to salinization and waterlogging. The heated controversy over the consequences of the "Green Revolution," with its technology packages (improved water supply, seed selection, chemical fertilizers, etc.), for resulting development is typical of this debate.

Structural adjustment programmes

Structural adjustment programmes (SAPs) have been adopted by more than 30 countries in sub-Saharan Africa, more especially in the 1980s, although African states were already affected by World Bank and IMF policies in the 1960s. Because world recession problems had to be overcome, African governments cooperated with the Bank and the IMF in various ways. Sometimes "shock treatments" were implemented in less than two years to resolve a crisis. In other cases more gradual reforms were spread over longer periods, also affecting the industrial sector. It was claimed that the beneficiaries of SAPs were the rural poor, because they were protected in relation to the urban poor by the stimulation of exports and an increase in farm incomes, offsetting in part the decline in wages. However, it seems unsafe to argue on the basis of the rural–urban dichotomy alone. What, for instance, is happening to rural incomes that are often dependent on remittances from urban and industrial workers (Morgan 1994, 1996)?

On the whole, and in most parts of the world, one of the most generally recognized impacts of SAPs has been increased social differentiation, including the rural poor. Although this process seems to have been stronger in Latin America and Asia than in Africa, even the World Bank initiated special policies directed at the poor to complement the existing SAPs.

It is interesting to note that environmental problems, such as, for instance, the dependence of economic productivity on the conservation of the endowment of natural resources, have so far hardly been considered in the design of SAPs.

Although it can be reasonably argued that in some cases SAPs have been a success (e.g. the Economic Recovery Programme in Ghana), on the whole sub-Saharan Africa has had a long history of poverty, war, and famine extending over millennia: "vulnerability, inequality and threats to the social fabric in Africa are not a product of the 1970's and 1980's, much less of Fund and Bank prescriptions for stabilization and adjustment. Nor are they purely imported colonial phenomena" (Green 1989).

Africa's economic and financial problems were made worse by a combination of:

1. an investment in growth and development that failed to earn the expected rewards;
2. the international debt crisis, oil price hikes, and rising interest rates, plus the inadequacy of the aid programmes that were meant to provide relief;
3. repeated drought, crop failure, and widespread famine;
4. the failure of agricultural production to contribute significantly to growth and the increased dependence on imported food. (Morgan 1996: 48)

Poverty, which contributes so much to the environmental degradation of Africa, can in the long run be overcome only by improving economic sustainability, which will be achieved not only through economic reforms but by more appropriate investments, including industrial activities and expanding trade.

Outlook

It has become clear that many of our conventional models of development and the policy framework now in place have to be challenged. Much has been learned about how ecosystems at various scales function. We now have to translate that understanding into actions that will help us to integrate the technosphere and the sociosphere with the biosphere.

This growing understanding has led to the emergence of concepts such as vulnerability, resilience, flexibility, thresholds, and non-linearities. These are important guides in the management of our interactions with the biosphere. Equally, we are beginning to take lessons from nature that are applicable both in the parametrization of management tasks and in respect to specific aspects of interaction (see Kasperson et al. 1995).

With respect to parametrization, for example, we have to question our established notions about competition (leading to a debate over the roles of and the balance between competition and collaboration as modes of interaction). We also have to look into the need for institutional arrangements at the global level that will facilitate rather than preclude sustainable solutions at local and regional scales. The search for such a framework leads us to question existing institutional arrangements. This could lead toward defining an agenda for international negotiations over setting in place appropriate governance structures. With regard to the specifics of humans' direct interaction with the biosphere, one can think of the lessons we have learned about capturing solar energy, using it efficiently, increasing materials productivities, developing multi-functional materials, closing the materials cycle, etc. This is the rationale for exploring technological options as represented by biotechnology, photovoltaics, and so on.

In conclusion: on a per capita basis the world's growing number of inhabitants expect year after year a growing share both of the finite non-renewable resources as well as of the only slowly growing renewable resources. An increasing conflict between these expectations and the ability of the biophysical environment to fulfil them is obvious. Although science can try to find some answers for this predicament, the final solutions must be political.

Bibliography

Adedeji, A. (1993) *Africa and Orthodox Structural Adjustment Programmes: Perception, Policy and Politics.* Tokyo: United Nations University.

Ayres, R. U. (1989) Industrial metabolism and global change. *ISSC Journal* **121**: 363–374.

——— (1994) Industrial metabolism, theory and policy. In: R. U. Ayres and U. E. Simonis (eds.), *Industrial Metabolism. Restructuring for Sustainable Development.* Tokyo: United Nations University Press.

Ayres, R. U., H. L. Beckers, and R. Y. Quassim (1992) Industry and waste. In: ICSU, *An Agenda of Science for Environment and Development into the 21st Century.* Cambridge: Cambridge University Press.

Biswas, A. (1979) World models, resources and environment. *Environmental Conservation* **6**: 3–11.

Blaikie, P. M. and H. C. Brookfield (1987) *Land Degradation and Society.* London: Methuen.

Bohle, H. G. (ed.) (1993) *Worlds of Pain and Hunger.* Freiburg Studies in Development Geography. Saarbrücken: Breitenbach.

Daly, H. (1991) The case that the world has reached limits. In: R. Goodland, H. Daly, E. S. Serafy, and B. von Droste *Environmentally Sustainable Economomic Development: Building on Brundtland.* Paris: UNESCO.

Dickinson, R. E. (ed.) (1987) *The Geophysiology of Amazonia – Vegetation and Climate Interactions.* New York: Wiley.

Douglas, I. (1990) Sediment transfer and siltation. In: B. L. Turner et al. (eds.), *The Earth as Transformed by Human Action,* pp. 215–234. Cambridge: Cambridge University Press.

Ezcurra, E. et al. (1991) Vulnerability to global change in natural ecosystems and rural areas: A question of latitude? Draft. Worcester, MA: Clark University.

Fearnside, P. M. (1990) Deforestation in Brazilian Amazonia. In: G. M. Woodwell (ed.), *The Earth in Transition: Patterns and Processes of Biotic Impoverishment.* Cambridge: Cambridge University Press.

Fischer-Kowalski, M., H. Haberl, and H. Payer (1993) A paradise for paradigms. In:

R. U. Ayres and U. E. Simonis (eds.), *Industrial Metabolism. Restructuring for Sustainable Development*. Tokyo: United Nations University Press.

Green, R. H. (1989) The broken pot: The social fabric, economic disaster and structural adjustment in Africa. In: B. Onimode (ed.), *The IMF, the World Bank and the African Debt. Vol. 2. The Social and Political Impact*, pp. 31–55. London: Zed Books.

Husar, R. B. (1993) Ecosphere and the biosphere. Metaphors for human-induced material flows. In: R. U. Ayres and U. E. Simonis (eds.), *Industrial Metabolism. Restructuring for Sustainable Development*. Tokyo: United Nations University Press.

IGBP (1988–1994) *Global Change Reports*. Stockholm.

IPCC (1990) *Climate Change: The IPCC Scientific Assessment*. Cambridge: Cambridge University Press.

Jacobson, H. K. and M. F. Price (1990) *A Framework for Research for the Human Dimension of Global Environmental Change*. Paris: ISSC–UNESCO.

Kasperson, R., J. X. Kasperson, and B. L. Turner (1995) *Understanding Global Environmental Changes – The Contribution of Risk Analysis and Management*. Tokyo: United Nations University.

Kates, R. W., J. H. Ausubel, and M. Berberian (1985) *Climate Impact Assessment*. New York: Wiley.

Lele, U. (1989) *Agricultural Growth, Domestic Policies, the External Environment and Assistance to Africa*. Washington D.C.: World Bank.

Liverman, D. M. (1986) The sensitivity of global food systems to climatic change. *Journal of Climatology* **6**: 355–373.

———— (1991) Vulnerability to global environmental change. Worcester, MA: Clark University.

Louis, H. (1964) Über Rumpfflächen- und Talbildung in den wechselfeuchten Tropen. *Zeitschrift für Geomorphologie*, New Series, Special Issue.

Lovelock, J. E. (1987) Geophysiology: A new look at earth science. In: R. E. Dickinson (ed.), *The Geophysiology of Amazonia – Vegetation and Climate Interactions*. New York: Wiley.

Manshard, W. (1974) *Tropical Agriculture*. London: Longman.

———— (1982) *Ressourcen, Umwelt und Entwicklung*. Paderborn: Schöningh.

———— (1984) *Entwicklungsprobleme in den Agarräumen des Tropischen Afrika*. Darmstadt: Wiss. Buchgesellschaft.

Manshard, W. and E. Ehlers (1994) Symposium on human dimension of global change. Frankfurt, Manuscript.

Manshard, W. and R. Mäckel (1995) *Umwelt und Entwicklung in den Tropen – Naturpotential und Landnutzung*. Darmstadt: Wiss. Buchgesellschaft.

Margulis, L. and J. E. Lovelock (1976) Is Mars a spaceship, too? *Natural History*, June/July: 90–96.

Morales, C. (1979) *Saharan Dust*. Scope Report No. 14. New York: Wiley.

Morgan, W. B. (1994) Agricultural crisis in sub-Saharan Africa: Development constraints and policy problems. *Geographical Journal* **160**: 57–73.

———— (1996) Poverty, vulnerability and rural development. In: G. Benneh, W. B. Morgan, and J. I. Uitto (eds.), *Sustaining the Future*, pp. 17–51. Tokyo: United Nations Univeristy Press.

Okigbo, B. N. (1996) Towards sustainable environmental and resource management futures in Sub-Saharan Africa. In: G. Benneh, W. B. Morgan, and J. I. Uitto (eds.), *Sustaining the Future*, pp. 123–164. Tokyo: United Nations University Press.

Parry, M. L., T. R. Carter, and N. T. Konjin (eds.) (1988) *The Impact of Climatic Variations on Agriculture*, 2 vols. Dordrecht: Kluwer.

Ruddle, K. and W. Manshard (1981) *Renewable Natural Resources and the Environment. Pressing Problems in the Developing World*. Dublin: Tycooly.

Salati, E. et al. (1990) Amazonia. In: B. L. Turner et al. (eds.), *The Earth as Transformed by Human Action*, pp. 479–493. Cambridge: Cambridge University Press.

Schmidt-Bleek, F. (1992) Toward universal ecology disturbance measures. Position Paper, Wuppertal Institute.

Sen, A. K. (1984) *Resources, Values and Development*. Oxford: Blackwell.

Simonis, U. E. (1989) Ecological modernization of industrial society. Three strategic elements. *ISSC Journal* **121**: 347–363.

Simonis, U. E. and E. U. von Weizsäcker (1989) Globale Umweltprobleme. In: *The Crisis of Global Environment – Demands for Global Politics*. Interdependenz 3, Bonn.

Timmerman, P. (1981) *Vulnerability, Resilience and the Collapse of Society*. Environmental Monographs No. 1. Institute of Environmental Studies, University of Toronto.

Tolba, M. K. and O. A. El-Kholy (eds.) (1992) *The World Environment 1972–1992. Two Decades of Challenge*. London: Chapman & Hall.

Turner, B. L. et al. (eds.) (1990) *The Earth as Transformed by Human Action*. Cambridge: Cambridge University Press.

Turner, B. L. and W. B. Meyer (1991) Land use and land cover in global environmental change: Considerations for study. *ISSC Journal* **130**: 669–680.

Turner, B. L., R. H. Moss, and D. L. Skole (1993) *Relating Land Use and Global Land-Cover Change*. IGBP Report No. 24, HDP Report No. 5. Stockholm.

UNCED (1992) *Agenda 21*. Conches, Switzerland.

UNDP and World Bank (1992) *African Development Indicators*. Washington D.C.: World Bank.

UNEP (1988) *Industry and Environment*. Environmental Brief No. 7. Nairobi: UNEP.

——— (1992) *Convention on Biological Diversity*. Environmental Law and Institutions Programme Centre. Nairobi: UNEP.

UNESCO (1986) *Perceptions and Analyses of World Problems*. Paris: UNESCO.

Watts, M. (1983) *Silent Violence: Food, Famine and the Peasantry in Northern Nigeria*. Berkeley: University of California Press.

Weischet, W. and C. N. Caviedes (1993) *The Persisting Ecological Constraints of Tropical Agriculture*. London: Longman.

Weizsäcker, E. U. von (1991) *Erdpolitik*, Darmstadt: Wiss. Buchgesellschaft.

World Bank (1981) *Accelerated Development in Sub-Saharan Africa: An Agenda for Action*. Washington D.C.: World Bank.

——— (1989) *Sub-Saharan Africa: From Crisis to Sustainable Growth*. Washington D.C.: World Bank.

World Commision on Environment and Development (1987) *Our Common Future*. Oxford: Oxford University Press.

World Resources Institute/IIED (1986–1991) *World Resources Reports*. New York: Basic Books.

Young, A. (1972) *Slopes*. Edinburgh: Oliver & Boyd.

Zaba, B. (1991) Population, resources and environment in sub-Saharan Africa: Looking for linkages. Paper, Royal Swedish Academy, Stockholm.

3

Ecological process engineering: The potential of bioprocessing

Anton Moser

Editor's note

The best introduction to this chapter is a book written over 20 years ago by Lewis Thomas (1974). Thomas, writing about medicine, makes the important point that current medical technologies are either "non-technologies" or "half-way technologies" (1974, p. 32). In the medical case, Thomas defines "non-technologies" as supportive therapy, or "caring for" a person with a disease whose underlying causes and mechanisms are not really understood. As examples, he mentions cancer, rheumatoid arthritis, multiple sclerosis, stroke, and advanced cirrhosis. Today one would certainly add AIDS and Alzheimer's disease to that list. Although most of the diseases on his list are now better understood than when Thomas wrote, it is doubtful that any of them, except some types of cancer, have moved even to the next (half-way) level.

It is fairly natural to suggest that other technologies can be characterized along the same axis as medical technologies. A non-technology in the production sphere is perhaps one in which nature does essentially all the work. The current technologies of forestry, ranching, and dairy farming (for instance) are virtually non-technologies. Nature does everything. The human contribution is largely limited to culling and harvesting (with a bit of tree planting, animal breeding, and veterinary medicine).

"Half-way technologies" are the ones that dominate current practice. In the medical sphere, Thomas defines them as "the kinds of things that must be done after the fact, in efforts to compensate for the incapacitating effects of certain diseases that one is unable to do very much about" (1974, p. 33). His examples include organ transplants, most types of surgery, wheelchairs, and the "iron lung" that was used to assist victims of infantile paralysis to breathe. Technologies that assist detection and diagnosis (but not cure) are also surely in this category.

Conventional agriculture may be characterized as a half-way technology. In the case of agriculture, the state of conventional technology can be summarized as breeding, tilling, fertilizing, seeding, weeding, and harvesting. Machines utilizing fossil fuels have been developed to do a lot of the tilling, seeding, weeding, and harvesting, while chemicals (also based largely on fossil fuels) do the fertilizing and pest control. Yet this combination is wasteful, harmful to wildlife and soil, and unsustainable in the long run. This would seem to be "half-way" technology. Moser argues that knowledge-based biotechnologies can potentially do a lot more, reducing the need for machines and chemicals on the one hand, and reducing harmful side-effects on the other.

The third type of medical technology, according to Thomas, is "the kind that is so effective that it attracts the least public notice; it has come to be taken for granted." Vaccines, antibiotics, and hormone treatments of endocrine disorders are examples. The ability to clone and grow replacement organs *in vitro* would be a big step forward over the current techniques, but the ability to regrow organs *in vivo* would, of course, be the ultimate substitute for surgical transplants. The discovery of the Salk vaccine, which essentially made "iron lungs" obsolete and eliminated infantile paralysis as a threat (and forced the "March of Dimes" to find another target for fund-raising), perfectly exemplifies the transition from "half-way" technology to truly advanced technology. An important and perceptive observation by Thomas is that what we often think of as "high-tech" medicine is, more often than not, actually the expensive and complicated "half-way" variety rather than the truly effective variety.

Indeed, most other conventional production technologies are undoubtedly very primitive when compared with the technologies utilized by nature. Is there any fundamental reason why complex metal, ceramic, or plastic structures could not be "grown" as an organism grows? In the very long run, I see no fundamental barrier. In fact, current developments in semi-conductor manufacturing and advanced ceramics technology seem to point in that direction.

Moser's principal contribution, in this chapter, is to lay out some of the next intermediate steps in this possible evolutionary development. His notion of "eco-technology" corresponds to a considerably more advanced stage of this possible evolution, but one that can be plausibly envisioned in general terms – at least by a technological optimist – within the next half-century.

I have to say, here, that Moser's original paper contained a great deal of interesting material, including a considerable discussion of measures of and criteria for eco-sustainability. Because much of this seemed to be beyond the scope of his assignment, or was essentially covered in chapter 1, the editors were forced to prune it rather drastically for lack of space. It is to be hoped that, as a biologist, Professor Moser will recall that roses, too, must be pruned to make them bloom more abundantly. I have also added some parenthetical remarks in a few places in Professor Moser's text.

Introduction

Technologies cannot be assessed in isolation. Sustainable technologies must satisfy a number of requirements and constraints. These include (i) the limited capacity of the biosphere to absorb wastes and recover from injury, both globally and on a regional level, (ii) the limits of cultural and social acceptance, (iii) economic feasibility, and (iv) technical feasibility. In addition, it is obvious that technological "fixes" alone will not suffice to assure long-term sustainability, although technology plays an essential role. The main aim of this paper is to evaluate the potential of bioprocessing and to clarify its likely contribution to long-term sustainability.

The current situation: The status of biotechnologies

Four main fields of technical application (apart from food and beverages) are well known. These are health care, agriculture, environmental remediation, and industrial materials processing. These are discussed briefly in the following pages.

Health care (pharmacology and medicine)

The health-care field of biotechnology includes the production of vaccines, hormones (such as insulin), therapeutics, diagnostics, and antibiotics via conventional process routes, such as cell cultures, using natural organisms. Antibiotics are normally made in this way. For instance, penicillin, the first antibiotic, is produced by a fungus. Increasingly, however, "modern" pathways are being exploited, based on genetically engineered organisms (GEOs). These GEOs either lack certain genes or contain genes from other organisms.[1] As a result they have properties not found in the natural versions of those organisms.

Editor's note: Most of the early applications of genetic engineering technology have been in this field, owing to the high value of some pharmaceutical products.[2] For example, Eli Lilly began producing human insulin by recombinant DNA techniques in 1982. Interferon, human and animal growth hormones, and monoclonal antibodies are examples of early applications. Public attention is usually drawn to the advertised benefits of these innovations for society, especially the possibility of sharply cutting the costs of important categories of drugs. Most of these short-term benefits have been consistently overestimated, and the length of time needed to take a new drug or diagnostic technique through the tedious and complex approval process is consistently underestimated. Nevertheless, by the late 1980s several biotechnology firms – especially Amgen – had developed successful and profitable products and a number of others had been sold to international pharmaceutical giants.

Agriculture and food technology

Older agriculture shaped natural plants and animals to human uses by means of breeding techniques. The modern branch of agriculture uses chemicals derived from biological materials (such as hormones and plant growth regulators, single cell protein, vaccines), microbial cultures, and new plants and animals created deliberately by genetic engineering modifications of existing organisms by recombinant DNA methods. Potential and obviously desirable future applications of genetic engineering are to introduce nitrogen fixation capability and/or disease resistance into important crops, such as potatoes, corn, or rice.

Public debate reflects serious safety concerns here, too.

Environmental biotechnology

Environmental biotechnology is understood in a broad sense as the application of biotechnologies – mainly micro-organisms – to the solution of existing environmental problems, including the treatment of sewage, waste water, and even soil decontamination. Early applications include biogas systems. Genetically engineered organisms are also increasingly used in this field, resulting in the same public concerns about safety mentioned above.

Industrial biotechnology

Industrial biotechnology is an established field, including cheese-making, wine-making, the brewing of beer, and the production of baker's yeast, vinegar, alcohol, acetone, acetic acid, citric acid, etc. from carbohydrates and sugars, mainly by fermentation. GEOs are not yet being applied in this area, although it would seem to be an inevitable evolutionary development.

It is quite important for the evaluation of biotechnologies to consider the normal life cycle of technologies. The different stages of development are marked by the production of molecules of increasing complexity (e.g. bulk chemicals, single cell protein, drugs).

A rather visionary, more distant future stage can be denoted "eco-technology," or simply "eco-tech." The name is intended to convey the idea that biotechnology eventually begins to substitute for more conventional technologies in a wide range of applications, resulting in significant environmental benefits and a much closer approach to long-term sustainability.

Scientifically the advantages of bioprocessing over chemical processing can generally be characterized as follows:

- bio-catalysts are highly active, specific, and selective; their regeneration is easier than in the case of chemical catalysts; there are no environmental problems as with heavy metals;
- reaction conditions are mild (temperature, pressure, and also concentrations);
- internal energy is supplied by energy-enriched compounds, e.g. ATP, which are formed during metabolism;
- impure, diluted, and inactive raw materials can be used, owing to the high specificity and selectivity of bio-catalysts;
- bio-products are biodegradable in natural cycles.

The competitiveness of biotechnologies in comparison with chemical technologies is discussed later in this chapter. The most competitive opportunities for biotechnology, at present, lie in the domain of high-price/low-volume "specialty" products. However, increasing success in this domain, together with rising prices for petroleum and other fossil hydrocarbons, suggests that opportunities will gradually increase over coming decades in the domain of low-price/high-volume "commodity" products.

Two observations apply to biotechnologies in general. In the first place, to produce highly complex and specific products such as pharmaceuticals, or to degrade toxic substances in the environment, the biological path is already clearly superior to the chemical path in many cases. A similar competitive break-point can be expected in the near future in several other cases, where bioprocessing becomes yearly more competitive. To be more specific, the most successful current applications of bio-processes are as follows:

- the production of foods (e.g. cheese, yogurt, soya sauce) and beverages (wine, beer);
- the production of complex molecules on the industrial scale for use in health care for humans, animals, and plants (pharmaceuticals and therapeutics, antibiotics, proteins, steroids, etc.);
- the degradation/purification of wastes and toxic substances in the environment (sewage, industrial wastes, water treatment, etc.);
- sequential reactions in one-step processes (e.g. the production of steroids), highly selective stereospecific conversions, etc.

There are other domains where the advantages of "biologicals" compared with "chemicals" are likely to be established soon. These include the reclamation of soil, the recycling or sequestration of carbon dioxide, the production of biofuels from waste agricultural or forest biomass, the creation of new and more productive plants capable of surviving in different climates, resisting diseases, etc. The beneficial products of bioprocessing will surely increase in the next decade.

A second observation is that process economics for biotechnological products (thus far) suffer generally from the fact that they depend on growth cultures. The latter involve lower concentrations, higher water content, and, consequently, higher energy requirements for separation and purification than does chemical processing, in general. The need for more sophisticated equipment, and more highly educated technicians, also contributes to the current competitive disadvantage of biotechnologies as compared with chemical processing.

Thus, despite their potential benefits in terms of long-term sustainability, most bio-processes are not yet economically competitive. Biotechnology is not expected to become competitive on a wide range of fronts before the year 2030 (OECD 1989). Even this forecast will prove overoptimistic unless efforts toward commercialization are accelerated, especially by strengthening process engineering sciences (Moser 1994). Research programmes in bio-process engineering have been recently stepped up in Japan (1992), the United States (1992), and Europe (1993).

In the following section, the status of the various biotechnologies is considered in more detail.

Potential and promises

The near-term opportunities for bioprocessing can be summarized briefly as follows:
- the production of organic chemicals with the aid of bio-catalysts, e.g. enzyme technology (fine chemicals, starch and cellulose, biopolymers), fermentation products (ethanol, single cell protein, antibiotics, nitrogen fixation for fertilizers), and animal and plant cell cultures;
- the use of biomass for fuel and energy production;
- food production and processing;
- the production of industrial materials (e.g. vegetable oils, pulp, and paper) from biomass.

A few examples will help to put the situation in perspective.

Bio-catalysts (enzymes)

Enzymic conversions, as a consequence of the potential advantages mentioned, are in an excellent position to contribute to a cleaner environment. The use of enzymes offers industry an opportunity to replace processes using aggressive chemicals with mild bio-processes exhibiting minimal impact on the environment. The raw materials come from agriculture. Also the effluents are non-toxic, although they contain nitrogen, phosphorus, and organic matter. This leads to high amounts of wastes in the water. The major part of the spent dry matter is collected as a sludge and then spread on nearby farmland. The sludge consists of dead biomass, filter aid, nutrient surplus, and an insoluble residue.

In 1990, Novo Nordisk, a Danish pharmaceutical manufacturer, reused 500,000 m^3 of sludge containing 5 per cent dry solids including 800 metric tons of nitrogen and 285 metric tons of phosphorus. The sludge instead acts as an efficient slow-releasing N-P fertilizer: more than 90 per cent of N is bound in organic matter, which means that the evaporation of ammonia is minimal. Figure 3.1 depicts the situation of this enzyme production plant, which fits nicely into an ecological cycle with agriculture (Falch 1991; Novo Nordisk 1993). The full-scale process, now in operation, is shown in the diagram.

Biological control agents (bio-pesticides)

A bio-pesticide is a living organism or a product derived from micro-organisms or plant sources that kills the pest in order to sustain its

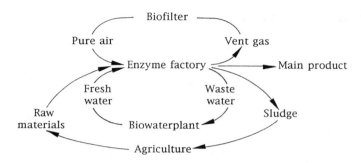

Fig. 3.1 **Closed-cycle technology in the Novo Nordisk enzyme production plant** (Source: Falk 1991)

own growth cycle. The characteristics of a bio-pesticide are pest specificity, environmental stability, safety, and low cost. Bio-control agents, despite being new entrants in the field, have already made substantial contributions in preserving the fertility of the soil, maintaining an ecological balance, and preventing resurgence of pests. This has been achieved with little harm to non-target animals and plants and with few side-effects. The potential of bio-toxins being active as insecticides, herbicides, and fungicides is basically known. However, widespread practical application is still in the wings, mainly owing to high costs.

A good example of application is in India, where the bio-pesticide market is around 100,000 tons per year, representing 3 per cent of the total market. Biologicals have a market share of 0.5 per cent of global chemical pesticides, as of 1995, while in the year 2000 a penetration rate of about 10 per cent is expected by some experts, out of a total global pesticide market of US$40–45 billion. At the moment the biotoxins produced from *Bacillus thuringiensis* (Bt) dominate, with nearly 70 per cent of the market.

Bio-pesticides can already substitute effectively for some chemical pesticides in agriculture (e.g. protection of cotton, sugar cane, oilseeds such as groundnut, rapeseed) as well as floriculture and horticulture. They have uses too in public health (e.g. control of disease vectors of malaria, filariasis, and encephalitis with *B. sphaericus* and *B. thuringiensis* formulations). Bio-pesticides can be broadly classified into the following categories, indicating a broad diversity in species as well as in specific actions:
– predators
– pathogens

- parasites/parasitoids
- pheromones
- kairomones
- neem oil

Predators
Commonly used predacious species are *Cryplolaemus nontrouzuri*, *Chrysopa*, *Scymnus*, *Coccivera*, and *Nephus* spp. against mealy bugs and *Cerilocorus nigritus* and *Pharoscymnus houri* against scale insects. *Ladybird beetles* are used to protect rice (against brown plant hopper), fruits such as citrus and grapes, and plantation crops such as coffee.

Pathogens (viral, fungal, bacterial)
Among the different entomopathogens, referred to as "biorational pesticides" as viral pathogens, the most important are the bacillo viruses. More than 10 types of such viruses have been isolated and extensively studied for their potential in pest management. Of these, nuclear polyhedrosis viruses (NPV) and granulosis virus (GV) are found to have good potential for pest control. The use of fungi to control pathogens that incite plant disease is another concept that has been in existence for some time. Insects infected with fungus exhibit general lethargy, slow growth, cessation of feeding, and changes in colour. The difference between fungi and other pathogens is that fungi do not have to be consumed by the insect to cause disease; instead they grow through the insect's skin. Many fungi are found to be pathogenic to a number of pests such as *Metarhizium anisopilae*, *Beauveria brongniartii*, *Anopheles stephensi*, and *Trichoderma*.

The most prominent bacteria in biological control are in the genus *Bacillus*, the group of Gram positive, rod-shaped bacterium. *Bacillus thuringiensis* (Bt) is the most widely known and researched aerobic spore-forming bacterium within this group for insecticidal properties and is differentiated from other spore-forming bacilli by the presence of a parasporal body that is formed within the sporangium during sporogenesis. The parasporal body is a high molecular mass protein crystal that is referred to as crystalline protein delta-endotoxin. The insecticidal activity of *B. thuringiensis* products is based on the delta-endotoxin. *Bacillus thuringiensis* is primarily a pathogen of lepidopterous pests. Being a natural protein, Bt endotoxin is highly biodegradable. It is also degradable by ultraviolet radiation. As a result, it is environmentally safe, because it cannot leave behind any residues to contaminate the soil, water, or food. Naturally occurring Bt are spore-forming bacteria. The spores are resistant to desiccation, high temperature, UV, and biodegradation.

Parasites/parasitoids
The families *Mermithidae, Steinernematidae, Romanomernis culicivoran, Goniozus nephantidis, Bracon brevicormis, Sturmiopsis inferens*, and *Trichogramma* are of special importance as examples of insect parasitic forms.

Pheromones
Insects rely on a sense of smell and communicate with each other by releasing specific chemicals (odours) to indicate their selection of food plants, sites to lay eggs, location of prey, defence and offence, mate attraction, and courtship. These specific chemicals that deliver intra-specific communications between individuals of single species are called *pheromones*. Between 600 and 1,000 pheromones have been isolated, identified, and synthesized, many for insects.

Kairomones
Kairomones are compounds emitted by an insect to convey a behavioural response to a member of a different species. They carry an advantage to the receiver (e.g. compounds used by parasites to locate a host). They are utilized in conjunction with *Trichogramma* to improve their efficiency in parasitization.

Neem oil
Extracts of *Neem* seed provide various crops with resistance to insect pests. Neem oil contains several chemicals of which the most potent one, "Azadirachtin," interacts with the reproductive and digestive processes of insects. Neem oil acts in a number of subtle ways, especially as a repellent and anti-feedant. It also has a growth regulatory effect by disturbing the insect's metabolism during various phases of development.

Another interesting field of research is *allelopathy*, where the metabolic substances produced by one plant inhibit the growth of another plant. This can be regarded as a potential alternative to the use of chemical herbicides and the evolution of herbicide-resistant crops. Plants also offer quite innovative chances for new applications in the area of removal of heavy metals from the environment, e.g.

"phytoremediation" (Salt et al. 1995), especially from soil, e.g. "phytoextraction" (Kumar et al. 1995), and from aqueous media, e.g. "rhizofiltration" (Dushenkov et al. 1995).

Bio-leaching of ores

Bio-leaching utilizes sulphur-loving bacteria that live in the ore itself. Examples include *Thiobacillus ferroxidans*, *Thiobacillus thiooxidans*, and *Leptospirillum ferroxidans*. When exposed to oxygen and carbon dioxide they obtain metabolic energy by reacting oxygen with sulphur, producing sulphuric acid as a metabolic waste. Compared with conventional heap leaching methods (using sulphuric acid recovered from ore roasting), bio-leaching can offer real economic advantages. Typically the economic feasibility differs for several plants on several site-specific factors such as concentrations, leaching rates, and residence times. Bio-leaching is commercially applied for the recovery of copper and uranium in the United States and for gold in South Africa and Brazil. The main obstacle is the investment in conventional plants (TME 1992).

The Biox® Genmin process for gold leaching involves the oxidation of a sulphitic concentrate slurry in a series of stirred tanks. Large volumes of compressed air are sparged into the tanks to fulfil the oxygen and carbon dioxide demand of the bacteria. A retention time of 3–5 days results in more than 90 per cent conversion of gold. The oxidized slurry then flows into a series of counter-current decantation thickeners to separate solids from acidic solutions. After neutralization to a pH of 11, cyanide is added and the gold is dissolved. Bio-oxidation currently offers real economic advantages over roasting and pressure oxidation for production plants with a capacity of less than 1,200 tons per day.

Denitrification of drinking water

In the denitrification of drinking water, denitrifying bacteria reduce nitrates and nitrites to harmless nitrogen gas and oxygen, which they use for metabolic purposes. A full-scale denitrifying plant is in operation in Austria, using a 2 m^3 fixed-bed bio-reactor system, operating with a natural population of microbes as denitrifiers. Because it is based on a naturally existing strain of bacteria, which accumulates during the start-up phase itself, sterile process operation is unnecessary. The process economics of denitrification are shown quantita-

Table 3.1 **Process costs for the denitrification of drinking water, comparing biological and chemical paths**

		Costs (US\$/m^3)		
	Investment	Running		Total
Biological + ethanol	0.15–0.27	0.10–0.15		0.26–0.47
Heterotrophic de-NO$_3$		Biological	Physical	
	p	0.024	0.011	
		0.048	0.023	
	m	0.022	0.020	
		0.034	0.030	
		0.057	0.046	
	c	0.067	0.067	
	w	0.003	0.124	
	a	0.001	0.002	
Physical–chemical electrodialysis	0.21–0.38	0.20–0.26		0.39–0.52

Source: Moser (1996).
a: analyses; c: chemicals; m: maintenance; p: personal; w: waste removal.

tively in Table 3.1, which compares biological and physico-chemical approaches (Moser 1996).

Biopolymers

Nowadays a large number of synthetic polymers are produced from petroleum derivatives because they are cheap, are available, can be prepared and processed easily, and are subject to few fluctuations of quality. Moreover, synthetic polymers offer a wider range of characteristics than natural polymers. However, genetic engineering offers at least the possibility of producing natural polymers with equivalent properties without the need for large-scale chemical processing.

There are two different ways to obtain polymeric materials from plants that are useful for engineering purposes:
1. making use of the original polymeric structure of the plant material by conserving most of it and chemically modifying only side chains;
2. degrading the plant material chemically, or having it degraded by animals or micro-organisms, and subsequently synthesizing new polymers by means of chemistry or biotechnology.

Quite a few classes of plant polymers can be used as engineering materials without degrading the polymer backbone. Cellulose is one.

The biosphere is abundant in cellulose, from timber, cotton, flax, and hemp. (Cellulose is the basis of rayon, cellophane, and celluloid.) Other natural polymers include natural rubber (a cis-polyisoprene), gutta-percha, lignin, polyphenols, and gums. Technologically useful polymers derived from animals also include proteins, such as wool, silk, leather, horn, gelatin, casein, chitin, and chitosan.

Some polymers with possible industrial application are produced by micro-organisms. Biopolymers (e.g. polysaccharides), with properties and applications similar to those of plant gums, are secreted by certain bacteria and can be obtained by means of biotechnology. In the 1980s processes were developed to produce polyhydroxy-alkanoates (PHAs) as thermoplastics on an industrial scale. PHAs are polyesters that are produced by a great variety of micro-organisms as a cellular storage material. The most widespread type of PHA is PHB (polyhydroxybutyrate). However, its properties are not quite suitable to serve as a thermoplastic. This is why methods to produce similar substances with improved processing and application properties are sought.

As a result of these efforts a copolymer of polyhydroxybutyrate and polyhydroxyvalerate (PHB/V) has been developed, with properties very much like polypropylene. This biopolymer, called "biopol," is produced by ICI in Great Britain by a fermentation process using glucose and propionic acid as organic substrates. The latter is currently derived from mineral oil but there are also ways to produce it from renewable raw materials by biotechnological methods. Biopol is biodegradable and therefore can be used for packaging products for quick disposal. In Germany a shampoo bottle made of biopol is on the market. This may be only the beginning (Moser 1994; Braunegg and Lefebvre 1993).

Use of genetic engineering

"Modern biotechnology" consists of new techniques, based on recombinant DNA technology, monoclonal antibodies, hybridoma techniques, cell fusion, vector-initiated gene techniques, and novel methods of cell and tissue cultures, resulting in genetically engineered organisms (GEOs).

The complexity, as well as the costs of development, increase in the following sequence (Swaminathan 1992): biological nitrogen fixation, plant tissue culture, embryo transfer, monoclonal antibody production, plant protoplasm fusion, rDNA for disease diagnosis, biocontrol agents, animal vaccine development, rhizobia improvement, plants, animals. Regardless of the high costs, there is no debate over the question of whether or not developing countries should begin genetic species engineering. Even the poorest should be thinking about a "survival kit" based in modern techniques; for example, a country with root crops as a staple food should initiate a tissue culture laboratory to facilitate the importation of tissue cultures of virus-free clones developed abroad. This would also allow rapid propagation if the plants proved adaptable to local conditions and acceptable to local producers and consumers. Table 3.2 gives some examples of genetic engineering activities and their actual and potential benefits.

It is generally agreed that the potential use of genetic techniques is very promising. Their application can further promote sustainability by, e.g., diversification of agricultural, forest, and fishery production systems, supplementation of genetic resources, and development of life forms appropriate to formerly impossible agricultural situations. A major consequence is considered to be the reduction of economic risk, but environmental risk is also likely to be reduced.

Current technologies can modify a single gene or chromosome. Major future breakthroughs will require more complex transfers. For example, at least six gene modifications would be involved in transferring nitrogen-fixing ability to cereals. Longer-term progress thus depends on further advances in basic science, notably in such areas as genome mapping. Bio-engineering applications are still extremely limited. The potentials have barely begun to be exploited. They are currently being held in check by the need for still more research to identify more useful genes plus more research to avoid harmful effects and bio-safety hazard.

To decide whether an activity is pro- or contra-nature, I have suggested a series of four eco-principles (Moser 1996):
1. non-invasiveness
2. embeddedness
3. sufficiency
4. efficiency
Table 3.3 applies principle (1) to various types of biotechnology.

Indigenous technologies: Food and health care

Ancient knowledge is a source of inspiration for sustainable technology development. Meso-American cultures had wide technological activities resulting from the combination of cultural, biological, and

Table 3.2 **GEO success stories**

Agronomic trait	Breakthrough	Crop	Potential benefit
Insect resistance	Immunity from boll-worm, caterpillars, corn borers, hornworms ...	Cotton	Reduced pesticide costs, reduced crop losses (*c.* US$1.5 billion), increased yields
Disease resistance	Protection against tobacco mosaic virus, rice tungro virus, cucumber mosaic virus ...	Tomato, rice, cucumber	Increased yield (25% for tomatoes)
Herbicide resistance	Tolerance for non-selective roundup herbicides	Sugar beet, maize, cotton, tobacco, potato	Less labour-intensive weeding needed
N-fixation	Stimulation of nodule-like structures in roots	Rice, wheat	Reduction in fertilizer costs
Drought resistance	Genes inserted from species growing in deserts, e.g. cacti	Wheat, corn, soybean et al.	~40% less water needed
Baking	Gene modification	Baker's yeast	
Cold-tolerating microbes	Deletion of gene for ice-nucleation protein	Potato, strawberry	~30% profit increase
Crop-ripening qualities	Antisense gene to block enzyme formation involved in softening/ripening	Tomato	Increased solid content and longer shelf-life
Disease-attacking microbes	Seedling roots soaked in a solution of modified bacteria	Stone fruits, nuts, roses	Losses reduced at minor cost (~US$1/litre)
Insecticidal microbes	Modified *Bacillus thuringiensis*	Various	Replacement of chemical insecticides, reduced costs

ecological diversities (Lopez-Mungia et al. 1994). A famous example in agriculture comes from the Incas, who were able to grow cereals at an altitude of 4,000 m with extraordinarily high productivity (10 tons/ha), although modern techniques (with chemical fertilizers) yield only 4 tons/ha. This 3,000-year-old "*waru-waru*" process is completely natural, having a renaissance in Bolivia under the name of "*socca*

Table 3.3 **Classification of bio-processes and biotechnologies by degree of invasiveness**

Non or low invasive (wisdom or common-sense based)
Use of those natural strains of micro-organisms, plants, and animals widely available in classical biotechs for food and feed and waste treatment
Use of simple selection and mutation (natural screening methods)
Use of GEOs where proved to fulfil all eco-requirements/eco-principles
Use of enzymes in fully biocompatible, aqueous systems

Medium invasive; based on classical natural and agro-sciences such as microbiology, biochemistry, cell biology, and engineering
Use of species cultivated in "modern biotech" laboratories (e.g. within the pharmaceutical industry and in plant and animal breeding) using modern mutation and selection methods (scientific screening)
Use of enzymes in non-biocompatible, non-aqueous media

Highly invasive; based on molecular biology and genetic engineering
Use of genetically modified organisms with modifications on the gene/genome level
Use of transgenic species; gene transfers on the level of "high biotech" (monoclonal antibodies, biocide-resistances) using, e.g., hybridoma techniques, cell fusion, vector-initiated gene technology

---

collos." The plants are grown on platforms 1 m in height, 4–10 m wide and 10–100 m long, made from soil dug from the canals. Water absorbs the sun's heat by day and radiates it back by night, protecting the crops against frost by creating a layer at +4°C. By capillary effects water ascends to the roots of the plants. Sediments from nitrogen-rich algae and plant and animal remains serve as fertilizer.

When Europeans arrived, the Incas had domesticated between 60 and 80 edible plants after centuries of interaction with ecosystems and species. In addition, more than 600 non-cultivated plants with adequate nutritional value, 300 species of fish, and 101 species of insects were used as food. Although much of this knowledge has evidently been lost, some of it may be recoverable. Surely the effort would be worth while. Meanwhile, the simple fact that such knowledge did exist at one time constitutes a powerful argument for preserving biodiversity.

Indigenous technologies are also very rich sources for human health care (bio-drugs). Some international firms have initiated joint ventures with tropical countries to identify active compounds from roots and plants (Girardet 1987). Table 3.4 lists some examples of products from indigenous processes.

Table 3.4 **Products stemming from indigenous technologies**

Basic techniques in agriculture
Waru-waru: sophisticated nature-integrated agriculture in the Andes
Chinapas: the "floating gardens" in the lakes, i.e. artificial isles
Others described in *"Codices Florentino"*

Medicinal plants
Echinacea purpurea ("red sun heat"): antiseptic, antibiotic, antiviral
Sepherdia rotundifolia ("buffaloberry"): ointment against eye infections
Artemisia tridenta ("big sagebrush"): against rheumatism and colds
Ayahuasca
Balche
Borrachero
Guatillo
Ololiuqui
Chicha
Teonancatl
Ayurvedic medicine (India)

Colourings
Cochinilla (*coccus cacti* L.), red pigment
Indigo from *"xiuhquilitl"* (*indigofera sufruticosa*), blue
    (recombinant E. coli based industry in Mexico)
Orange ink from *achiyotl* (*bixa oreyana*)
Red ink from *haematoxylum brasiletto*
Xantophyles from flowers of *cempazuchitl* (*tagetes erecta*)
Chilli (*annus capsicum*)

Bio-fertilizers

The growing need for fertilizers to enable a relatively fixed amount of arable land to support a growing human population is clear. Are chemical or biological fertilizers the best choice? A strong argument for replacing water-soluble chemical fertilizers such as urea, used in quantities up to 250 kg/ha, is that as much as about half of it goes directly into the groundwater and much of the remainder is lost to denitrifying bacteria. Bio-fertilizers such as *Rhizobium* can be applied in lesser amounts – as little as 0.5 kg/ha – potentially resulting in reduced costs.

For example, one can imagine an interrelated system combining a bio-fertilization plant (*Rhizobium*) with a sugarcane plantation and ethanol production where the main mass fluxes are consumed internally within the three operations. Further products could be added (food and feed, biological control agents such as *Bacillus thuringiensis*,

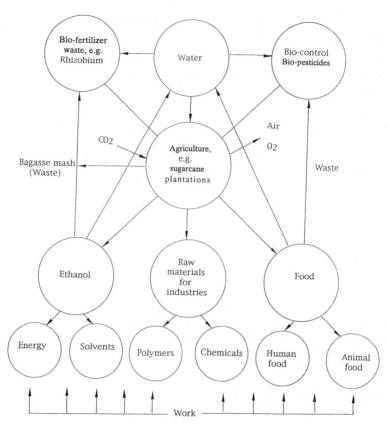

Fig. 3.2 **Example of a technology mix utilizing agriculture-integrated bioprocessing**

biopolymers for packaging materials, industrial raw materials, etc.), as shown schematically in figure 3.2 (Moser 1996).

It is known that in tropical countries there are a great number of plants that are able to live in symbiosis with nitrogen-fixing bacteria such as *Rhizobium* species (for leguminous plants) or associated symbiotics, e.g. *Azosperillum* for sugar cane. Genetic manipulation is possible, in the case of *Rhizobium* species, for further improvement. Some plants depend symbiotically on other microbes for nitrogen fixation. Recently it has been found that such microbes live not only in the roots but sometimes also on the surface of the plant (Doebereiner 1994). There are also non-symbiotic N-fixing bacteria (e.g. *azobacter, cyanobacteria*, blue and green algae). Research in this area is still at the earliest stages and the very fact that much of value remains to be learned constitutes a strong argument for preserving biodiversity.

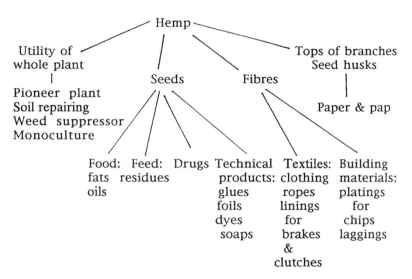

Fig. 3.3 **Hemp (*cannabis sativa*) as a typical renewable material for a diversity of applications**

Plant-matter-derived products

There is a renaissance of plant-derived bulk raw materials in the United States (Robbelen et al. 1991). In the past decade, technological advances have lowered the cost of producing high-quality products from plant matter, while environmental regulations have raised the cost of using petroleum-derived products. Another potential source of renewable materials is the large amount of waste organic material from agriculture and forestry, especially paper-pulping, municipal solid wastes, and food processing. The total is nearly 350 million metric tons/year in the United States alone.

The potential of using plants as industrial raw materials, instead of crude oil, has been neglected up to now owing to the low cost of petroleum. Consequently petrochemicals are the primary source of several categories of industrial materials. In effect, oil has replaced plant-derived matter not only for most textiles but also for significant uses of glass, metals, wood, and even paper. As one example of the potential for increasing the use of plant matter, the case of hemp is illustrated in figure 3.3. Practically all products can, in principle, be produced from plant materials. The basic technologies exist; only cost considerations, and sometimes quality differences, are preventing introduction to the market. The full potential of plant materials for replacing petrochemicals is shown schematically in figure 3.4.

PLANT MATERIALS   PRODUCTS

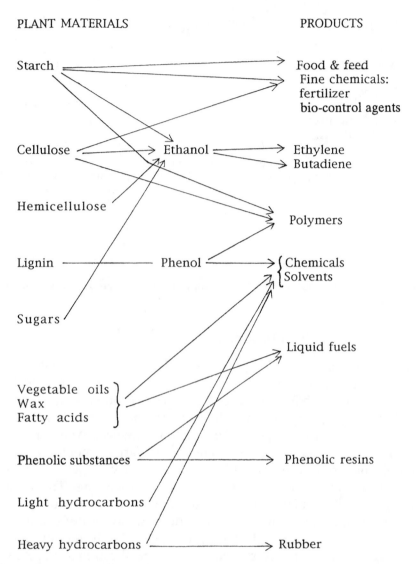

Fig. 3.4 **Production paths from renewable raw materials to industrial products**

Agro-based "industrial ecosystems"

An example of a possible interconnected but self-contained network of different activities to exploit plant-derived materials was shown in figure 3.2. There are other interesting possibilities for arranging a series of interconnected conversions, where each step uses the waste

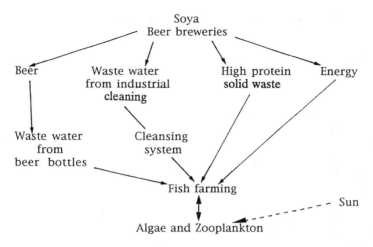

Fig. 3.5 **"Zero emissions research initiative" applied in the beer brewing industry (Source: Pauli 1994)**

stream from the step before, with the final result that very little bio-mass is wasted.[3] A second example (Pauli 1994) is the case of beer brewing, shown in figure 3.5, where the liquid waste stream is used as nutrient for fish farming for the production of proteins. An indirect advantage is that the production of 1 kg protein via fish needs only 30 per cent of the feed (in caloric terms) needed to obtain red meat from animals.

Another good example of an integrated bio-process is the use of "green juice" from grass and potatoes for the production of dried grass pellets and co-products such as lactic acid, amino acids, other fermentation products, biogas, and inorganic fertilizers (Kiel 1992). A further example of combining many kinds of specialized workshops or factories into a unified ecological complex is that of Aoxue Companie in Anyang/Henan province in China (Wang 1995). This began in 1988 as a simple cornstarch factory. This factory has been innovative in finding uses for wastes. Most of the original wastes are now utilized through "food-chain" adding successive processes to produce higher-valued by-products. The range now includes flour, corn syrup, inositol, corn oil, corn wine, protein forage, and protein powder. Other interesting cases from "eco-villages" have been compiled (Swaminathan 1994, table 7).

Table 3.5 presents a pattern of different activities characteristic of some "eco-villages" in India and China.

Table 3.5 **Main eco-technologies in China's "eco-villages"**

Biogas digester using wastes
High-efficiency production in agriculture
Edible mushroom production using crop and animal by-products
Earthworm raising
Fly pupae production
Chicken waste used as swine feed
Rice-field fishery
Multi-layer fish culture
Raising of natural enemies of pests
Biological control of erosion
Windbreak building
Firewood production
Agro-forestry techniques
Biological wastewater treatment
Intercropping
Solar heater

Market penetration by biotechnology

The processing of plant matter into final industrial products or consumer products is potentially much less environmentally burdensome than the processing of fossil fuels. The latter requires additional chemicals, resulting in a serious disposal problem. In particular, the pyrolysis process applied to plant materials generates no harmful wastes.

A decade age, virtually the only plant-matter-derived products on the market were adhesives and lubricating oils and a handful of intermediate chemicals. Today, plant-derived products compete in just about every major product category. They enter the market by displacing some petroleum-derived product in a portion of its market, and then gradually increase their market share. This is outlined in more detail in table 3.6. Fourteen product categories represent over 90 million of the 108 million metric ton (m.t.) commodity petrochemical market. In all cases, the prices of competitive bio-products have dropped since 1985; for example, in the case of inks this drop was over 30 per cent.

Admittedly, most plant-derived consumer products are not yet competitive with their petrochemical counterparts. But the price premium for plant-derived products has dramatically diminished. Even when their costs are higher, plant-based products are gaining market share as a result of a combination of "green" consumerism

Table 3.6 **Near-term potential in the United States for plant-matter-based industrial products**

Industrial product	Current production (million m.t. per year)	Derived from plants (%)		Cost (US$/kg)		Reduction in cost of plant-based products (%)		Projected increase in plant-based products by 1996 ('000 m.t.)
		1992	1996	Oil derived	Plant derived	Since 1985	By 1996	
Wall paints	7.8	3.5	9.0	0.50	1.20	14	10	429
Special paints	2.4	2.0	4.5	0.80	1.70	3	5	60
Pigments	15.0	6.0	9.0	2.00	5.80	20	15	465
Dyes	4.5	6.0	15.0	12.00	21.00	25	20	405
Inks	3.5	7.0	16.0	2.00	2.50	30	10	315
Detergents	12.6	11.0	18.0	1.10	1.70	–	10	882
Surfactants	3.5	35.0	50.0	0.50	0.50	20	5	525
Adhesives	5.0	40.0	48.0	1.60	1.40	15	2	400
Plastics	30.0	1.8	4.3	0.50	2.00	–	50	750
Plasticizers	0.8	15.0	32.0	1.50	2.50	20	20	136
Acetic acid	2.3	17.5	28.0	0.33	0.35	5	2	241
Furfural	0.3	17.0	21.0	0.75	0.78	10	2	12
Fatty acids	2.5	40.0	55.0	0.46	0.33	5	5	375
Carbon black	1.5	12.0	19.0	0.50	0.45	10	25	105

Data sources: *Chemical Marketing Reporter; Chemical & Engineering News; US Industrial Outlook*, US Department of Commerce.

and government regulation. A number of plant-based products have established their reliability and quality, not to mention environmental value. The cost of bio-products should continue to drop and their market share should continue to expand. As table 3.6 reveals, the amount of these eco-products was projected to increase by over 5 million tons by 1996. This would almost double the amount of plant matter used for industrial purposes from the 1990 level. Detergents and plastics account for one-third of the projected market expansion.

For example, inks based on soya oil first entered the US market in 1987. By 1991, 50 per cent of the 9,100 magazines and 75 per cent of daily newspapers were printed with soy-based ink. Aside from price, the key obstacle to the introduction of inks based on vegetable oils has been their slow drying time, which poses fewer problems in newspaper printing but more in magazine printing. This fact constitutes a significant technical challenge.

The interplay of public regulation, consumer sophistication, and private entrepreneurship has brought "biologicals" produced from renewable raw material into almost every major product category. Much larger markets can be achieved through concerted marketing and commercialization. Spurred by the surplus of agricultural crops, governments and some trade associations have targeted new market developments, focusing on those new markets as alternative crops that impact directly on the consumption of fossil fuels. Currently, the best return to biomass is available by displacing petroleum from high-value specialty chemical markets. These markets tend to be very small except for half a dozen chemicals. About 90 per cent of all petroleum products are presently used as fuels, the fuel market is the most interesting long-term prospect.

Active research continues to develop processes for the conversion of lignocellulose to ethanol. Although potential margins in this area appear to be greater than in starch-based ethanol conversion, they are realized only if markets can be found for carbon by-products such as lignin or furfural. Unfortunately, given the disparity between fuel requirements and chemical markets, these by-products would saturate existing chemical markets even at relatively modest levels of ethanol production.

More than 20 oilseed crops are grown in the United States, with soybean dominating. About 1 million tons of vegetable oil are used as feedstocks for industrial products such as plastics, surfactants, adhesives, and lubricants, with prices varying from 32 cents per kg for sunflower oil to almost US$10/kg for jojoba oil. Table 3.7 summarizes

Table 3.7 **Yields and prices of potential and conventional oil-crop raw materials used for fuel and industrial production in the United States**

Material	Crop yield (m.t./ha)	Oil yield (m.t./ha)	Oil price (US$/kg)	Important product categories
Bladderpod	10.0	3.9	–	Plastics, fatty acids, surfactants
Buffalo gourd	14.0	5.1	–	Epoxy fatty acids, resins, paints, adhesives
Castor	4.4	2.3	0.80	Dyes, paints, varnishes, cosmetics, polymer resins, bio-pesticides
Coconut	11.0	8.0	0.46	Polymer resins, cosmetics, soap, pharmaceuticals, plasticizers, lubricants
Corn	34.0	7.0	0.62	Ethanol, fermentations, resins
Crambe	7.5	3.0	1.55	Paints, industrial nylons, lubricants, plastic, foam suppressors, adhesives
Cuphae	10.0	4.0	–	Surfactants, lubricants, glycerine, biochemicals
Euphorbia	9.0	4.5	–	Surfactants, lubricants, paints, cosmetics
Honesty (money plant)	10.0	4.0	1.53	Plastics, foam suppressors, lubricants, cosmetics, industrial nylon
Jojoba	15.0	8.3	9.60	Cosmetics, pharmaceuticals, inks, plastics, adhesives, varnishes
Lesquerella	7.5	1.8	–	Paints, lubricants, hydraulic fluids, cosmetics
Linseed	5.2	2.1	0.50	Drying oils, paints, varnishes, inks, polymer resins, plasticizers
Meadowfoam (limnathes)	11.2	3.2	–	Cosmetics, liquid wax, lubricants, rubber, higher fatty acids (C20–C22)
Palm oil	–	12.5	0.34	Fermentation products, soap, wax, tin plating, fuel processing, polymers
Rapeseed	10.0	4.0	1.30	Plastics, foam suppressors, lubricants, cosmetics, adhesives
Safflower	7.0	2.8	0.80	Paints, varnishes, fatty acids, adhesives
Soybean	9.5	1.9	0.40	Inks, paint solvents, plasticizers, resins, pharmaceuticals, adhesives

Table 3.7 **(cont.)**

Material	Crop yield (m.t./ha)	Oil yield (m.t./ha)	Oil price (US$/kg)	Important product categories
Stokes aster	9.0	3.9	–	Plastic resins, plasticizers, paints
Sunflower	5.8	4.3	0.32	Plastic resins, plasticizers, fuel additives, surfactants, agro-chemicals
Vermonia	7.5	1.7	1.60	Plastics, alkyd paints, epoxy fatty acids

Data sources: USOTA (1992); Robbelen (1992).

the situation of oil-crop raw materials for fuels and industrial products manufactured in the United States (USOTA 1992; Robbelen et al. 1991).

Stricter environmental regulations may provide attractive alternatives for stimulating the biomass industry by targeting environmentally friendly products. The costs involved can sometimes be internalized in the producer's economics. But, more often, they entail external social costs, which allows government to make the cost–benefit analysis and provide incentive programmes.

In summary, chemicals from biomass, whether from new or from existing crops, face two major obstacles. The first is that high production entails competing for large-volume, low-margin markets. These markets tend to be volatile, as are the traditional feed/food commodities markets. The second obstacle is that high-margin products tend to have low-volume markets. Commodity chemicals have large markets and are usually low in costs, selling for US$1–3/kg. Specialty chemicals tend to have smaller markets (e.g. about US$56 billion in the United States) and command prices over US$4/kg.

Despite these obstacles, biomass-based commodities could eventually displace many petroleum-based products in the fuel and chemical markets, even without major price increases for petroleum. Obviously, the rate of market penetration would be increased if (or when) petroleum prices rise. The production of biomass-based commodities could potentially reduce dependency on non-renewable resources. Diversification into such areas also opens up new opportunities for the agro-forestry sector, at least where overproduction has been a problem in the past (as in Europe).

Barriers to penetration

To implement and accelerate these changes, a number of conditions must be met. Most of the points made in this section have already been made, but need emphasis. For one thing, it is vitally important to preserve biodiversity, not just for its own sake, but to preserve the genetic information embodied in living organisms. It is not just a question of finding whole organisms with valuable properties. It may be equally important to find organisms with just *one* valuable property that can be traced to a particular gene or group of genes. It is this possibility that raises hopes of giving food crops the ability to fix nitrogen, or to resist insects, or to tolerate saltier water or colder or hotter temperatures, or to metabolize and break down chlorinated aromatics, such as PCBs, and so on.

It is also important to focus more research on bioprocessing. The potential for substituting organic enzymes for inorganic catalysts is worthy of far more attention than it has ever received. The same is true of the use of micro-organisms for processing low-grade metal ores or purifying industrial wastes containing heavy metals.

Of course, it is important to develop and to use genetically engineered organisms (GEOs) in a sustainable way. This will require extensive and coordinated research in other sciences, including social and cultural factors. A series of open questions must be asked and answered concerning any application of GEOs.

There are scientific arguments for questioning the scientific validity of the basic premises of genetic engineering. A major assumption is that each specific feature of an organism is encoded in one or a few specific, stable genes so that transferring a gene results in the transfer of a discrete feature, and nothing else. This, however, represents an extreme form of genetic reductionism. It fails to take into account the complex interactions between genes and their cellular, extra-cellular, and external environments. Changing a gene's environment can produce a cascade of further unpredictable changes that could conceivably be harmful.

In the case of genetic transfer to an unrelated host it is literally impossible to predict the consequences: the stabilizing "buffering" control circuits for a gene are exposed to disruption and may be ineffective in new hosts. Owing to the high degree of complexity of any living organism, firm predictions of outcomes are nearly impossible because genomes are known to be "fluid." In other words, they are subject to a host of destabilizing processes such that the transferred gene may mutate, transpose, or recombine within the genome. It can even be transferred to a third organism or another species. In short, the evolutionary stability of organism and ecosystem may be disrupted and threatened. Like the genie in the bottle (in the tale of Aladdin's lamp), once a GEO is deliberately released, or inadvertently escapes from containment, it can never be recalled, even if adverse effects occur. GEOs may migrate, mutate, and multiply.

In addition, there are serious ethical issues concerning the patenting and ownership of life-forms, including implications for cultural values and for indigenous peoples and poor countries.

Editor's note: It is impractical to summarize these issues here, but it is clear that there are many legitimate concerns. Scientists and the business world tend to take the view that the general public should be excluded from the inner circles of decision-making, on grounds of inadequate technical knowledge. But this attitude is essentially undemocratic. It is also likely to backfire. It is worthwhile recalling that nuclear power technology has been discredited largely as a result of public distrust of what the so-called "experts" in government and industry were telling them. To overcome the public knowledge gap, some countries are organizing lay conferences (e.g. NEM 1996).

As an exemplary case, Norway's Gene Technology Act, section 10 (Norway 1993), includes four criteria for a GEO to be acceptable:
• safe to people
• safe to the environment, i.e. the entire ecosphere
• beneficial to the community
• contributing to sustainable development.
Of course, these criteria are quite general. There are endless arguments over how these criteria should be tested and measured. More specific criteria to qualify a micro-organism as "environmentally safe" have been put forward. For instance (Lelieveld et al. 1993):
• non-pathogenic for plants and animals
• unable to reproduce in the open environment (including by delayed reproduction of survival forms such as spores)
• unable to alter equilibria irreversibly between environmental microbial populations
• unable, in the open environment, to transfer genetic traits that would be noxious in other species.

Editor's note: The overriding concern will be safety. It is all too easy to envision GEOs escaping into the natural environment and causing irreversible changes in natural ecosystems. The damage that can be caused by species being introduced inadvertently into environments where they have no natural enemies are well known. A few reminders will help make the point. The rabbit, no problem in Europe, became a major pest when it was introduced into Australia. The sea lamprey, introduced into the Great Lakes via the Welland Canal, has caused great harm to the freshwater fishery there. Dutch elm disease, imported to North America from Europe, has virtually wiped out the most beautiful shade trees of the eastern part of the continent. Another disease of unknown origin has totally wiped out the American chestnut trees, which once dominated the eastern forests. The Japanese beetle also caused enormous damage to agriculture before it was brought under control by pesticides. If such damage can be caused by species that already exist, some sceptics will (and do) argue that the problem could be worse with deliberate genetic manipulation in the picture.

But even the foregoing criteria are ambiguous in a number of ways, because it is unclear how it is to be determined whether or not the criteria are satisfied. It is likely that, in practice, the process of testing and certification for GEOs will be no less rigorous (and possibly much more so) than the current process for drug testing in the United States. Moser takes the view that deliberate ecosystem modification (whether or not GEOs are involved) is wrong and should be prohibited on the grounds of being contra-natural (owing to "invasiveness"). In principle it is easy to agree, but in practice it seems unlikely that Moser's view will prevail.

Apart from safety and environmental security, there are a number of other questions to be asked and answered with respect to any proposed application. These include questions concerning costs, benefits, and secondary impacts (e.g. reduced need for extractable raw materials, reduced CO_2 emissions, remediation of polluted rivers, lakes, or soil, and the maintenance of biodiversity). But, again, it is impossible to go further into detail here.

Final remarks

To summarize, a number of conclusions can be set forth. In the first place, it is safe to say that biotechnologies can and doubtless will contribute significantly to long-run sustainability. They can contribute to solving existing problems such as food security, especially in the developing world (China, India). There is still significant potential for improving the yield and productivity of crops (e.g. rice) and animals, as well as improving nutritional value and taste, disease and pest resistance, storage life, and tolerance of heat, cold, saltiness, wetness, and aridity. A great and likely innovation of the coming decades will be the development of nitrogen-fixing staple crops, such as corn, wheat, and rice. Enormous strides can be expected in aquaculture, fishery management, and food processing, not to mention drinking water purification, composting of garbage, sewage treatment, biomass-based energy production, soil fertility, and decontamination. Developments such as "boneless" breeds (e.g. of trout), "seedless" fruits, and "antifreeze" genes (e.g. for salmon, tomatoes) will also make life interesting.

"Eco-technology" as a vision needs further elaboration and application. To achieve more general acceptance the vision must be sufficiently matured to be able to offer plausible alternatives and to describe transition pathways, from both economic and technological perspectives, such that the solving capacity is regarded as higher than the existing approach. This will require extensive research, development, and experience ("learning by doing"). Some examples are quantified in table 3.8 (Moser 1996).

Genuine practicality in making suggestions requires detailed knowledge of a particular region or country – its history, culture, biosphere, social structure, manpower situation, etc. There is no single set of recipes for a solution. Only general recommendations can be made, as depicted here.

Nevertheless, the direction seems inevitable. In the long run, principles of life must apply. The imperatives of the long-run survival of the human species surely imply that humans must learn to work within nature – as the so-called "indigenous" peoples had to do – rather than treating nature as an enemy to be overcome. This long-

Table 3.8 **Quantitative data on the reduction of the environmental impact (η_{eco}) in the case of some recently elaborated "eco-tech" processes, using the SPI index for the quantification of the production processes (not including the application of the products)**

Production process	η_{eco}
Drinking water denitrification: micro-organisms versus electrodialysis	2–5
Bio-pesticides: renewable versus fossil raw materials used	10–100
Biopolymers: polyhydroxy-butyric acid versus polyethylene	0.5–3.0
Bio-fertilizers: rhizobium strains as soil bacteria versus chemical synthetic fertilizer (urea)	$>5 \cdot 10^4$

run survival imperative necessitates the preservation of biodiversity, as well as human cultural and social diversity. In this context, technology becomes a powerful tool to assist us to achieve the sort of eco-restructuring that will be required to achieve long-run sustainability.

Notes

1. Technically, genetic engineering involves cutting and splicing molecules of the substance called deoxyribonucleic acid (DNA). The artificially modified forms are known as recombinant DNA or rDNA.
2. Indeed, as of 1994, well over 90 per cent of all worldwide venture-capital funding for biotechnology was targeted at this field of application.
3. See, for instance, the United Nations University's zero emissions research initiative (ZERI) (Pauli 1995).

References

Braunegg, G. and G. Lefebvre (1993) Modern developments in biodegradable polymers. *Kemiza u industriji* **42**(9): 313–322.

Doebereiner, J. (1994) Comments. In: M. S. Swaminathan (ed.), *Proceedings of Ecotechnology and Rural Development Conference, April 12–15 1993*, pp. 99–119. Madras, India: Macmillan India Press.

Dushenkov, V., P. Kumar, H. Motto, and I. Ruskin (1995) Rhizofiltration: The use of plants to remove heavy metals from aqueous streams. *Environmental Science and Technology* **29**: 1239–1245.

Falch, E. (1991) *Industrial Enzymes: Developments in Production and Application*. Budapest, Hungary: General Meeting, IUPAC, August.

Girardet, H. (1987) *Jungle Pharmacy*. Video film for TV for the Environment.

Kiel, P. (1992) Bioconversion of agricultural residues. In: K. Soyez and A. Moser (eds.), *Proceedings of Internal Workshop on Ecological Bioprocessing*, pp. 147–152. Potsdam, Germany: University of Potsdam.

Kumar, Nanda P., V. Dushenkov, H. Motto, and I. Ruskin (1995) Phytoextraction: The use of plants to remove heavy metals from soils. *Environmental Science and Technology* **29**: 1232–1238.

Lelieveld, H. et al. (1993) *EFB workgroup on biosafety*. Working Paper. Basel, Switzerland: EFB, 18 February.

Lopez-Mungia, A., C. Rolz, and A. Moser (1994) Integracion de technologias indigenas y biotechnologias modernas: Una Utopia? *Intersciencia* **19**: 177.

Moser, Anton (1994) Trends in biotechnology: From high-tech to eco-tech. *Acta Biotech.* **141**: 315–335.

——— (1996) Ecotechnology in industrial practice. *Ecological Engineering* **7**: 117–138.

NEM (1996) *Panel Report: Lay Conference on Genetically Modified Food*. Oslo, Norway: National Committee for Research and National Committee for Ethics.

Norway (1993) *Gene Technology Act*, Act No. 38. Oslo, Norway, 2 April.

Novo Nordisk (1993) *Environmental Report*. Denmark: Novo Nordisk.

107

OECD (1989) *Report on Biotechnology*. Paris: Organization for Economic Cooperation and Development.

Pauli, G. (1994) *The Breakthrough: What Society Urgently Needs*. Tokyo: United Nations University.

—— (1995) *Zero Emissions Research Initiative: Status Report*. Tokyo: United Nations University, June.

Robbelen G. et al. (eds.) (1991) *Oil Crops in the World*. New York: McGraw-Hill.

Salt, D. E., M. Blaylock, P. Kumar, V. Dushenkov, B. Ensley, I. Chet, and I. Ruskin (1995) Phytoremediation: A novel strategy for the removal of toxic metals from the environment using plants. *Biotechnology* **13**: 468–474.

Swaminathan, M. S. (1992) *Contribution of Biotechnology to Sustainable Development within the Framework of the United Nations System*. Special Report, IPCT 148. Vienna, Austria: UNIDO.

—— (1994) Comments. In: M. S. Swaminathan (ed.), *Proceedings of Ecotechnology and Rural Development Conference, April 12–15 1993*. Madras, India: Macmillan India Press.

Thomas, Lewis (1974) The technology of medicine. In: *Lives of a Cell: Notes of a Biology Watcher*. New York: Viking Press.

TME (1992) *Biotechnology as a Clean Technology*. Delft, Netherlands: TME, prepared for UNEP.

USOTA (United States Office of Technology Assessment) (1992) Agricultural commodities as industrial raw materials. *Chemical Marketing Reporter*, 9 March.

Wang, R. (1995) State-of-art of eco-engineering in China. Paper presented at International Ecological Engineering Conference, Beijing, China.

4

Materials futures: Pollution prevention, recycling, and improved functionality

Pradeep Rohatgi, Kalpana Rohatgi, and Robert U. Ayres

Editor's introduction

This chapter addresses a key problem in the context of eco-restructuring, namely the extent of technological possibilities for radically increasing materials productivity. It will be recalled that two premises of the book are (1) that economic growth must continue, at least for the foreseeable future, and (2) that the nature of that growth must change radically in order to satisfy the basic requirements of long-run sustainability. That change has two fundamental implications. First, the fact that non-renewable resource stocks are finite dictates that the rate of extraction of non-renewable materials cannot increase significantly over its present level, globally, and must eventually approach zero. Second, the fact that the habitability of the earth for humans depends on the health of the biosphere dictates that the rate of emissions of chemically active – hence potentially harmful – wastes into the environment must be decreased even more drastically, and even sooner.

There are two generic strategies for reducing waste emissions. The first is known as "end-of-pipe" treatment. It is the strategy that has been favoured overwhelmingly up to now. And it will remain essential. But it is ultimately limited in its effectiveness by the fact that wastes can never be completely inert as long as they differ chemically or physically from the composition of the environmental medium into which they are discarded. The other generic approach is to reduce the use of materials, especially non-renewable extractive materials. This is often taken to imply a reduced standard of living, even reversion to a sort of Gandhian lifestyle. It need not imply any such thing. What it does imply is that the economy must generate much more output (GDP) for each unit of physical materials and energy input. In other words, the productivity of materials and energy must be sharply increased and must continue to increase over time.

To increase materials and energy productivity there are several approaches. One that has been discussed frequently in the past is "dematerialization", i.e. to use less material *for a given function* than in the past. This approach depends partly on scientific progress in materials science, enabling materials to perform better. It also depends on more mundane changes to encourage less wasteful practices in the materials cycle itself – especially less dependence on dissipative uses of materials (such as solvents, cleaning agents, pigments, lubricants, etc.) and more efficient re-use, recovery, and remanufacturing of durable goods. This approach is sometimes called "clean technology," to distinguish it from waste treatment.

When the use of materials is considered from a lifecycle perspective, it is clear that efficient recovery, repair, renovation, remanufacturing, and recycling depend very strongly on how the material is utilized in the first place. Products that are dissipated in use (such as solvents or detergents) cannot be recovered for re-use. Products that are very difficult to disassemble cannot be repaired, renovated, or remanufactured. Clearly, these "end-of-life" issues must be taken into account at the beginning, i.e. at the stage of product design. Design for environment (DFE) is an emerging discipline that attempts to deal with this aspect of the problem. DFE requires that products be designed not only for performance and low manufacturing cost, but also for long life, efficient disassembly, and remanufacturability, and – where remanufacturing is not possible – for efficient recycling.

Clearly the problem of increasing materials productivity raises an enormous number of peripheral issues with respect to needed material performance characteristics. The present chapter deals primarily with the latter.

Background

As a point of departure, we begin with a truism: every substance extracted from the earth's crust, or harvested from a forest or fishery or from agriculture, is a potential waste. Not only is it a potential waste; in almost all cases it soon becomes an actual waste, with a delay of a few weeks to a few years at most. The only exceptions worth mentioning are long-lived construction materials. In other words, materials consumed by the industrial economic system do not physically disappear. They are merely transformed into less useful forms.[1]

Table 4.1 **World production of metal ores, 1993**

Ore	Gross weight of ore (million m.t.)	Metal content (%)	Net weight of metal (million m.t.)	Mine and mill waste[a] (million m.t.)
Aluminium	106	19	19.8	86
Chromium	10	30	3.0	7
Copper	>2,500	0.4	9.4	>2,490
Gold	≈466	0.0005	0.002	≈466
Iron	989	52	517.0	472
Lead	>45	6.5	2.9	>42
Manganese	22	33	7.2	15
Nickel	>130	0.7	0.9	>129
Platinum group[b]	≈50	0.0005	0.0002	≈50
Uranium (1978)[c]	1,900	0.002	0.04	1,900
Zinc	>219	3.2	6.9	>212

Data source: *Minerals Yearbook 1993*.

a. Extrapolated from US data on ore treated and sold vs marketable product for 1993, using same implied ore grade.

b. Based on ore grades mentioned in text for mines in South Africa only.

c. Based on Barney (1980). No current data available.

In some cases (as with fossil fuels) they are considerably transformed by combination with atmospheric oxygen. In other cases (such as solvents and packaging materials) they are discarded in more or less the same form as they are used. It follows from this simple relationship between inputs and outputs – a consequence of the laws of physics[2] – that economic growth in the past has been accompanied by growth in waste generation and pollution.

Apart from fossil fuels, however, enormous quantities of minerals and metal ores are extracted from the earth's crust. Table 4.1 shows world consumption of concentrated (or selected) metal ores and metals,[3] and the rate of extraction is increasing rapidly (fig. 4.1).

Annual production (i.e. extraction) of metals in the United States is more than 1.5 tonnes per capita (down from a maximum of close to 2 tonnes in the early 1970s). However the decline merely reflects the fact that the United States is increasingly dependent on imported ores or metals. Allowing for ores processed elsewhere, the real US *consumption* level is now more than 2.5 tonnes per capita. Consumption levels in Europe cannot be much less, though figures are harder to find.

Each tonne of refined metal involves the removal and processing of at least 4 tonnes of ore (in the case of aluminium) and up to several

111

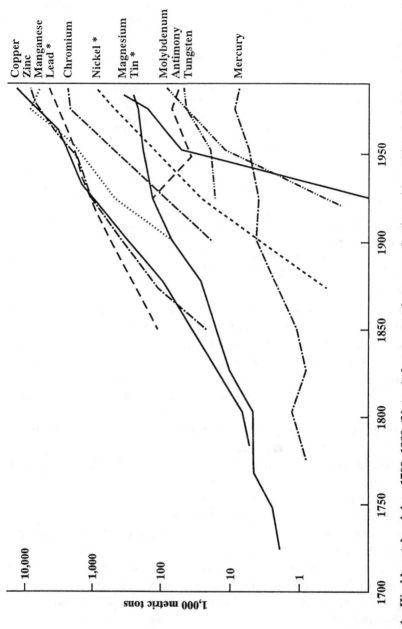

Fig. 4.1 World metals mining, 1700–1980 (Note: * denotes continuous production without historical data. Source: Josef Pacyna, "Atmospheric trace elements from natural and anthropogenic sources," in J. O. Nriagu and C. I. Davidson (eds.), *Toxic Metals in the Atmosphere*, New York: Wiley, 1986)

thousand tonnes of gangue and overburden, in the case of uranium, platinum group metals, or gold. These figures rise over time because the best grades of ore are used first. Thus, other factors remaining equal, energy consumption and costs of exploration, extraction, and beneficiation *per unit* would tend to rise over time. Only technological progress could compensate for this trend. The fact that resource prices have, on average, declined over many decades is regarded by resource economists as a strong indication of the power of technology – called forth by free markets – to keep resource scarcity at bay (see Barnett and Morse 1962; Smith 1979). It must be said that the neo-Malthusian worries about resource scarcity do not appear to be a near-term threat to economic growth, as has been suggested at times in the past.

Other threats are more immediate. The mining, beneficiation, and smelting of metal ores are inherently dirty. Even though modern technology permits the capture of most toxic waste pollutants from the process, these materials must still be disposed of somehow. A number of very toxic metals are by-products of copper, zinc, and lead, for instance. These include arsenic, bismuth, cadmium, cobalt, selenium, silver, tellurium, and thallium. Although many of these metals are recovered for use in other commercial products, the products in question – from pesticides, herbicides, fungicides, and wood preservatives to pigments and batteries – are almost entirely dissipated or discarded after use. (Toxic heavy metals are also dispersed into the environment via coal ash, which contains significant quantities of them.)

Non-metallic chemicals too are dissipated and lost either in use or after use. Such materials also constitute increasing pollution loads, with unknown environmental and health implications.

Until recently the only response to increasing pollution of the environment has been essentially localized "end-of-pipe" treatment. However, traditional approaches to pollution control seldom eliminate the wastes. They normally attempt to shift the wastes from a place where they can do harm to a place where they are less likely to do so. In some cases they are converted from a dangerously harmful form to a less potentially harmful form or location. Indeed, regulation has, in some cases, encouraged the recovery and treatment of wastes from one medium, only to find them reappearing in another. For instance, the burning of solid wastes may generate air pollution. Air pollutants, especially particulates and oxides of nitrogen and sulphur, can be (re)deposited on land via rainfall, only to be carried into rivers and streams via surface runoff.

The only possible way to reach a sustainable state is to find ways of using materials more efficiently in the first place, i.e. to begin to evolve closed (or nearly closed) materials cycles. In other words, we must learn how to get much more functional "bang for the buck" from materials – and not just the "high-tech" materials that get most of the attention. In this paper we adopt an engineering–technological perspective to increasing materials productivity, as described in the next section.

Strategies to increase materials productivity

In brief, there are three elements to the long-term materials productivity programme. The first is to reduce, and eventually eliminate, inherently dissipative uses of non-biodegradable materials, especially toxic ones (such as heavy metals). This involves process change and what has come to be known as "pollution prevention" via "clean technology." The second is to design products for easier disassembly and re-use, and for reduced environmental impact, known as "design for environment" (DFE). The third is to develop much more efficient technologies for recycling consumption waste materials, so as to eliminate the need to extract "virgin" materials that only make the problems worse in time.

It is not really necessary to describe in detail how this can be accomplished. It is sufficient to know that it is technically and economically feasible. (It remains, still, for policy makers to create the appropriate incentives to harness market forces. But this is a separate topic.) Of course, specific "scenarios" might be helpful in making such a conclusion more credible to doubters. However this would serve a communications purpose rather than an analytic one.

Returning to the specifics, we note four basic strategies for raising the productivity of material resources. These four generic strategies are:
1. **"De-materialization":** more efficient use of a given material for a given function. This can be achieved by increasing performance, reducing the need for materials by means of improved processing quality control, and/or better design. For instance, the need for built-in safety factors in many applications was established many years ago in terms of crude "rules of thumb." Computer-aided design (CAD), together with improved quality control, now permits significant reductions in materials thickness (and weight) for

many structural purposes – from engines to aircraft wings to build-ings – without compromising safety. In addition, there has been very rapid progress in recent years in micro-electronics and micro-machines. The minimum scale of electronic devices has decreased by at least a factor of 10^4 (to 0.5 microns) while the scale of machines has fallen by a factor of 100 (to 100 microns). The density of information storage capacity (i.e. computer memories) has increased by around two orders of magnitude per decade for the past four decades, and the rate of progress has not yet shown any tendency to decline.

2. **Substitution of a scarce or hazardous material by another material.** Again, either technology or policy can drive such a shift. For instance, cadmium has been largely eliminated from PVC stabil-izers and pigments. Lead pipes for water were replaced long ago by copper pipes. Lead arsenate has been eliminated as a pesticide for orchards; lead has also been phased out (to a large extent) as a pigment for exterior paints, and as an anti-knock additive for gasoline. It is also gradually being phased out of applications for soldering compounds and bearings. Similarly, mercury has been phased out of most uses as an anti-mould or anti-fungal agent (e.g. in paint) and in batteries – formerly its biggest use. It is also slowly being phased out of chlorine manufacturing.

3. **Repair, re-use, remanufacturing, and recycling.** For convenience we refer to this simply as the "recycling" strategy. Obviously all of these variants tend to reduce the need for virgin materials and (indirectly) all of the environmental damage and energy con-sumption associated with the extraction and processing of virgin materials, *including their toxic by-products*. Diesel engines are routinely remanufactured. The same could be done for automobile engines and other complex subassemblies, such as universal gears, transmissions, and compressors. One of the most attractive under-utilized candidates for remanufacturing is tyres. Aluminium cans, stainless steel automotive components, copper wire, and galvan-ized iron/steel are particularly good examples of candidates for more recycling. Arsenic and cadmium exemplify toxic by-products (of copper and zinc mining) that could be reduced thereby.

4. **"Waste mining":** utilization of waste streams from (currently) unreplaceable resources as alternative sources of other needed materials. This strategy simultaneously reduces (a) the environ-mental damage due to the primary waste stream, (b) the rate of exhaustion of the second resource, and (c) the environmental

damage due to mining the second resource. One attractive possibility is the use of so-called flue gas desulphurization (FGD) "scrubber" waste, which is virtually the same as natural gypsum, to manufacture plasterboard. Metallurgical slag is used for paving roads, but it can also be reprocessed into insulation competitive with fibreglass. Coal ash can be used in concrete products, or even as a source of aluminium and ferro-silicon. Phosphate rock processing waste can be a source of fluorine chemicals used in the aluminium industry (it already is in the United States). And so on. All of the above strategies can be further subdivided into two categories, namely *technology (and economics) driven* or *policy driven*. They are summarized, with examples, in the 4×2 matrix below. The choice of materials productivity strategy in each case will depend on economics and the available technology. We now review some areas of changing materials technology.

1A *De-materialization, technology driven* Example: micro-miniaturization in the electronics industry.	1B *De-materialization, policy driven* Example: imposition of Composite Average Fuel Economy (CAFE) standards for automobiles in the 1970s (USA) led to significant reductions in vehicle weight.
2A *Material substitution, technology driven* Examples: substitution of PVC for cast iron or copper water/sewer pipe in buildings; substitution of optical fibres (glass) for copper wire for point-to-point telecommunications.	2B *Material substitution, policy driven* Examples: ban on CFCs leading to replacement by HCFCs or HFCs in air-conditioners and refrigerators; ban on tetraethyl lead (TEL) leading to substitution by aromatics and alcohols (e.g. MTBE) as octane enhancers in gasoline.
3A *Recycling, technology driven* Examples: recycling of lead from starting-lighting-ignition (SLI) batteries used in motor vehicles; recovery of catalysts from catalytic convertors.	3B *Recycling, policy driven* Mandatory minimum levels of recycled pulp in paper products, e.g. in Germany; recycling of aluminium cans, Sweden; recovery of mercury from fluorescent lights, Sweden.
4A *Waste "mining," technology driven* FGD for oil and gas refineries with recovery of elemental sulphur; recovery of fluosilicic acid from phosphate rock processing wastes in the United States.	4B *Waste "mining," policy driven* Enforcement of FGD in non-ferrous metal smelters, with recovery of sulphuric acid; enforcement of FGD for electric power plants, with recovery of lime/limestone scrubber waste for use in wallboard production, Denmark.

Materials technology

Diversity is the most noteworthy characteristic of materials. It seems sensible, therefore, to begin this section with a taxonomy. The following is taken from the Table of Contents of a standard reference work (Lynch 1975):

Ferrous Alloys
Light Metals
Aluminum-Base Alloys
Nickel-Base Alloys
Other Metals
Glasses and Glass Ceramics
Alumina and other Refractories
Composites
Polymers
Electronic Materials
Nuclear Materials
Biomedical Materials
Graphitic Materials

The list can be further expanded. For instance, composites can be subdivided into metal matrix composites, ceramic matrix composites, and polymer matrix composites. Even a cursory summary of all these technologies in a short chapter is bound to be unbalanced and, in many ways, unsatisfactory. One can scarcely hope to do more than pick out a few salient topics.

A selection principle is urgently needed. It is therefore probably useful to start with the observation that the present economic importance of the material categories is virtually inverse to their present-day interest from a research perspective. Natural materials such as wood, paper, rubber, leather, cotton, wool, stone, and clay are still enormously important in the world economy, but they are declining in importance, if only because newer alternatives are increasingly available (Larson et al. 1986). The same is true of the "old" metals – copper (bronze, brass), lead, zinc (pewter), tin, silver, and gold.

From the research perspective, iron and steel, too, have largely had their day in the sun. The technology of iron smelting was essentially fully developed by the 1830s. The steel industry burst into prominence after 1860, after a long accumulation of incremental improvements in furnace design and metallurgy culminated in the great innovations of Bessemer, Kelley, Mushet, Siemens, Martin, and Thomas.

The metallurgy of steel and ferro-alloys progressed rapidly for the next half-century or so. However, although significant process improvements have continued since World War II, illustrated in figure 4.2, the potential of iron-based alloys technology has been largely (albeit not entirely) exhausted.[4] Newer technologies in this area include direct casting of strip (which cuts energy consumption) and wider use of high-strength low-alloy (HSLA) steels, which cuts the weight of structures such as auto and truck chassis.

Aluminium was a curiosity metal until the simultaneous invention in the 1880s (by Hall in the United States and Heroult in France) of a practical electrolytic reduction process. This process is still universal in the industry, though improved processes have been developed to the pilot stage. The problem for aluminium is that – aside for aircraft and structural components that can be produced by rolling, bending, or extrusion without machining (such as roof panels, window frames, and cans) – it is currently too expensive to substitute for steel for most uses. However, this limitation is now gradually being overcome in the auto sector, where aluminium is beginning to substitute for steel and even cast-iron (for engines). This substitution would likely accelerate in the event that light-weight battery-powered electric cars become more popular. The fact that aluminium is relatively easy to recycle (for example, cans) is a positive indicator for this development.

Since World War II, research emphasis in materials science has shifted to polymers, ultra-light composites, and special materials for limited applications such as semiconductors, supermagnets, superconductors, hard surfaces, and nickel- or cobalt-based "super-alloys." Most of these developments have been driven by military or aerospace requirements (for electronic equipment, airframes, and jet engines, for instance). In any case, copper, steel, and aluminium metallurgy – whether moribund or not – will not be considered further in this chapter. Nor will we discuss the properties or production processes of other old materials, including concrete, glass, wood, or paper.

To be sure, any of the "old" materials may enjoy a revival, in terms of research interest, because of either a new method of processing (e.g. plywood or fibreboard) or a new use (e.g. the superconducting properties of certain tin alloys). But, given the necessary brevity of this chapter and the enormous scope of its coverage, it seems justified to start by eliminating this group from further consideration.

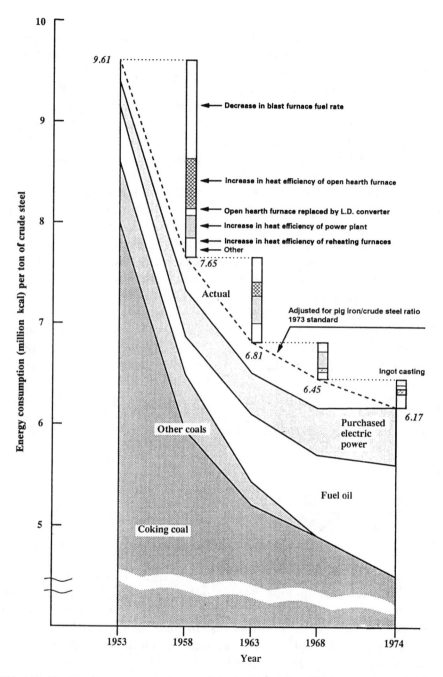

Fig. 4.2 **Process improvements in metallurgy, 1953–1974 (Source: NAS/NRC 1989)**

119

Material attributes

In general, material science is all about performance. It is tempting, at times, to try to measure technological progress for materials in terms of simple measures such as "tensile strength." Yet, even a moment's thought suggests that there are many other properties of importance. Each application calls for a different *combination* of properties. Generally speaking, it is the combination that matters. One of the attractive virtues of plastics – apart from light weight – is that customization of desired combinations has proven to be relatively easy (as compared, for instance, with metals or ceramics).

This point is especially well illustrated in the case of synthetic fibres. By and large, polymer-based materials have not (to date) competed significantly with metals. They do compete, in general, with wood, paper, natural rubber, and natural fibres. Recent developments in so-called "engineering" plastics have extended their range of competitiveness. Polymers that conduct electricity now appear to be very close to commercial realization.

The first "synthetic" fibres in the 1893–1895 era were cellulose-based (viscose rayon and cellulose acetate). The rayon industry boomed in the 1920s and 1930s. Later, completely man-made fibres were introduced, beginning with nylon (1935); see table 4.2. An effort to discern some meaningful trend was made by a "futures" consulting organization (Gordon and Munson 1982). A panel of experts identified four parameters as being "important" for synthetic fibres. The panel weighted the four attributes as follows:

Parameter	Panel weight
Tensile strength (g/denier)	0.2581
Elastic recovery (% recovery from % stretch)	0.2903
Modulus (g/denier)	0.2903
Moisture regain (%)	0.1613
	1.0000

A comparison of the major man-made fibres is given in table 4.2 and figure 4.3. It is obvious that the index constructed from the above parameters, weighted as indicated *a priori* by the panel, does not explain the success of newer fibres. In fact, an early form of rayon (cuprayon) introduced in 1894 is superior to all the more recent fibres but one in terms of the composite index. Clearly, a number of other (perhaps less quantifiable) factors such as "feel" are important. Moreover, the optimum "mix" of factors evidently varies significantly from

Table 4.2 **Man-made fibres data**

Fibre	Year of introduction	Tensile strength (g/denier)	Elastic recovery (% recovery from % stretch)	Modulus (g/denier)	Moisture regain (%)
Visrayon	1892	2.40	74	11.10	13.00
Acerayon	1894	1.50	65	5.50	6.50
Nylon	1935	5.70	100	24.00	3.80
Orlon	1949	5.00	84	24.00	0.90
Dacron	1951	5.00	95	25.00	1.38
Vicara	1953	1.25	99.5	3.50	10.00
Acrilan	1953	3.00	75	30.00	1.70
Dynel	1953	3.00	87	9.70	0.40
Arnel	1955	1.40	84	5.20	3.20
Zefran	1959	3.50	92	11.00	2.50
Darvan	1959	2.00	75	7.00	3.00
Kodel	1959	3.00	87	11.00	0.40
Vycron	1962	8.00	60	0.16	0.60
Arnel 60	1962	2.30	70	10.00	4.00
Zefkrome	1964	4.20	84	11.30	2.50
Encron	1968	5.00	70	5.30	4.00
Sef	1972	2.60	99	3.00	2.50
Triacetate	1980	1.30	70	5.20	3.20

Source: *Textile World*, Man-made Fiber Chart, various years.

one fibre use to another. The salient feature of recent developments in this field is probably diversity itself.

Much the same point can be made about other categories of materials. Although alloy steels have not been getting significantly stronger or harder, in recent decades the number of specialized steel alloys with different combinations of properties continues to grow. The same trend is even more pronounced for other metal alloys, refractories, and ceramics, and for polymers and composites. In many instances properties such as fracture toughness have significantly increased owing to improvements in processing.

Material performance trends

We have noted already that the areas of greatest research interest in materials science and engineering are not necessarily the areas of greatest current economic importance. Having said this, however, it is of interest to look at recent trends in three of the areas of current economic interest, namely high-temperature materials, light-

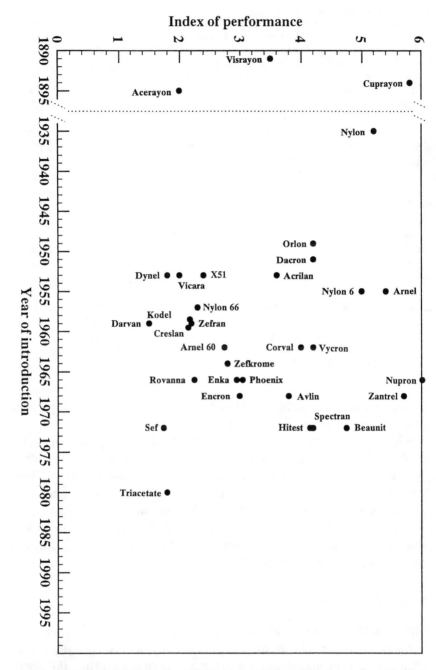

Fig. 4.3 **Man-made fibres performance index when values are non-dimensionalized by scaling between 0 and 1 (Source: Gordon and Munson 1982)**

122

weight materials, especially high-strength composites, and "electronic" materials. Potential areas of future application will be noted.

High-temperature materials

A requirement common to many material uses is a combination of toughness (i.e. ductility), strength at high temperatures, inflammability, corrosion and oxidation resistance, and minimum weight. Early uses for such materials were mainly for high-speed drilling and cutting tools (hence, "high-speed" steels). Jet engines and gas turbines currently exemplify this requirement. The essential point is that increased fuel economy and higher thrust-to-weight ratio are achieved by operating at higher temperature and pressures. A 150°F increase in inlet temperatures yields a 20 per cent increase in thrust (Clark and Flemings 1986). (For comparison, the thrust-to-weight ratio for large jet engines has somewhat more than doubled in the past 30 years; Steinberg 1986.) Airframes and re-entry vehicles (RVs) also require a combination of high strength and low weight at high temperatures. Increased fuel economy for aircraft is obviously very important in terms of increasing long-term resource productivity.

Two radically different cases can immediately be distinguished, depending on whether exposure to air is also essential or not. Thus carbon fibre, one of the strongest and lightest of all materials, cannot be used in engines, for instance, because of its combustibility. On the other hand, non-metallic refractories such as oxides, carbides, or nitrides are quite strong and not affected by the presence of oxygen. On the other hand, they tend to be brittle, i.e. they lack ductility. Thus, two major lines of development can be discerned. The first is metallurgical. The problem is to find metallic alloys with better combinations of strength and ductility for applications in oxidizing environments, especially for turbine engines.

Here again, a panel of experts identified three relevant parameters (taking non-flammability for granted) and weighted them (Gordon and Munson 1982):

Parameter	*Panel weight*
Rupture strength	0.333
Creep strength	0.333
Ductility	0.333
	1.000

Table 4.3 **High-temperature materials: Non-dimensionalized parameters and performance index**

Material	Year	Rupture strength	Creep strength	Ductility	Index
Nimonic	1941	0	0	0.812	0.271
S-816	1943	0.348	0.476	0.246	0.357
Nimonic 80A	1944	0.022	0.110	0.391	0.174
Nimonic 90	1945	0.040	0.110	0.971	0.374
L-605	1947	0.203	0.079	0.551	0.278
M 252	1949	0.384	0.215	0.087	0.229
Rene 41	1950	0.312	0.319	0.478	0.370
Udimet	1955	0.384	0.424	0.275	0.361
GMR 235	1955	0.565	0.476	0	0.347
Alloy 713c	1955	0.710	0.581	0.246	0.512
Udimet 700	1957	0.529	0.267	0.420	0.405
Nimonic 105	1958	0.268	0.168	0.493	0.310
Nimonic 115	1959	0.529	0.288	0.290	0.369
IN-100	1960	0.855	0.843	0.043	0.580
B-1900	1962	0.855	0.895	0.058	0.603
Alloy 713lC	1964	0.674	0.581	0.275	0.510
MM 509	1964	0.493	0.476	0.333	0.434
MM 246	1965	0.964	1.000	0.072	0.679
HA-188	1966	0.167	0.079	1.000	0.415
MM 200 (DS)	1966	1.000	1.000	0.072	0.691
Unitemp	1970	0.746	0.895	0.174	0.605

Source: Gordon and Munson (1982).
Note: Index weight factors 1/3 each.

Data for a number of high-temperature alloys introduced since World War II are shown in table 4.3. In this case (since the application is relatively unchanged), the single composite index, illustrated in figure 4.4, seems to have some explanatory power. However, even here there were two different applications, namely turbine blades and vanes.

For turbine blades, nickel-based alloys were preferred because of higher strength and stress resistance, whereas for vanes, cobalt-based alloys were preferred (because of reduced environmental degradation). The only three cobalt-based alloys in the study were S-816, MM 509, and HA-188. They show almost no upward trend in the composite index. There was a clear and rapid upward trend in the index of performance for nickel-based alloys, on the other hand, up to the mid-1960s. Since then, improvements have been achieved mainly

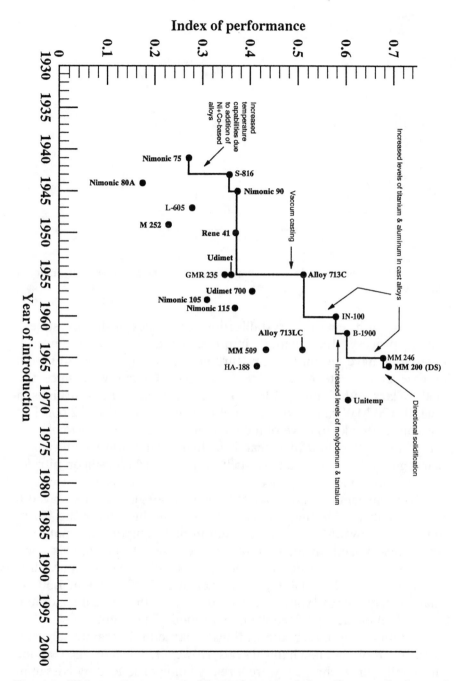

Fig. 4.4 **High-temperature materials performance index (Source: Gordon and Munson 1982)**

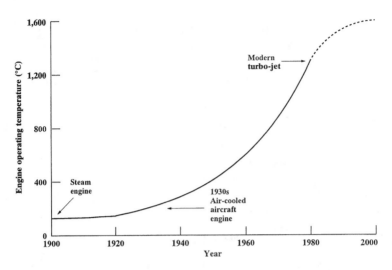

Fig. 4.5 **The steep climb in operating temperatures made possible by modern materials**

by the use of directional crystallization techniques in the investment casting process. Incremental improvements in high-temperature metallurgy have permitted gas turbine operating temperatures to increase at the rate of 10–12°F (about 6–7°C) per year since the 1960s (Clark and Flemings 1986). The development of gas turbines in the 120–150 MW range with turbine inlet temperatures of 2,600°F is envisioned, thanks to developments in advanced casting systems.

The alternative line of research in high-temperature materials is focusing on advanced ceramics, such as silicon carbide, silicon nitride, and lithium aluminium silicate. Concern over possible shortages of cobalt, chromium, and other so-called "strategic" metals played a major role in accelerating the research effort in this field in the 1970s. Figure 4.5 shows the continuing trend in high-temperature materials capabilities. Based on their known properties, ceramic–matrix composites seem to offer a potential of raising turbine inlet temperatures from about 1,850°F (1,000°C) to as much as 2,700°F or about 1,500°C (Clark and Flemings 1986). This would increase theoretical maximum turbine fuel efficiency, if realized, by around 27 per cent.

As of 1996, the major applications of structural ceramics are still for cutting tools and mechanical seals. However, a decade ago ceramic automobile turbo-chargers were already being produced by Nissan in Japan and ceramic glow plugs and precombustion chambers for diesel engines are being made by Isuzu (Robinson 1986). Ford and Garret

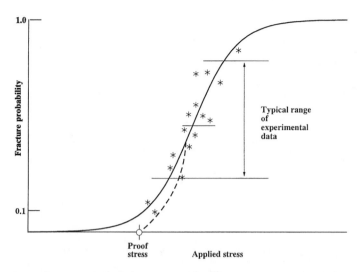

Fig. 4.6 **Typical strength variability curve for a ceramic (Source: NMABNRC 1975)**

Corporation were about to test a 100 hp gas turbine engine with a metal housing and ceramic parts in contact with the hot gases (Robinson 1986). However, little further progress has been reported since then, at least in terms of practical applications.

The problems of utilizing advanced ceramics such as silicon nitride for engines or other purposes where they compete with metals are not so much their well-known brittleness (i.e. lack of ductility) as their low fracture toughness and tendency to fail unpredictably. This, in turn, is because the distribution of microscopic defects – which concentrate and propagate stress – cannot be predicted *a priori*, owing to scatter in the experimental data, as shown in figure 4.6. A theoretical possibility is to "proof test," namely to test all ceramic parts up to a certain level of performance and throw away those that fail. This greatly decreases the odds of random failure among the survivors, as shown in figure 4.7. However, under present conditions, yields are likely to be less than 20 per cent, which is far too low. Until yields of 70 per cent or better can be achieved in practice, the economics of advanced ceramics will remain unfavourable.

Part of the problem of unpredictability may have its origin in the traditional techniques of compaction and hot pressing (sintering). The quality of the product is dependent on the size of distribution and uniformity of the starting material. New processing techniques such as "sol-gel" processing may offer hope. A "sol" is a colloidal

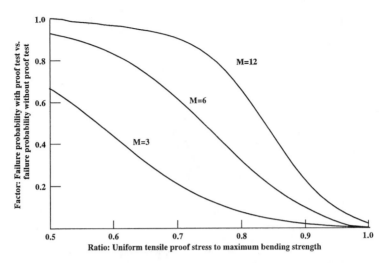

Fig. 4.7 **Effect of a uniform tensile proof test on failure probability of a bar in bending (Source: NMABNRC 1975)**

suspension of particles in sizes from 1 to 100 nanometers. As the "sol" loses liquid, it gradually becomes a "gel." Although the concept is old, this technique has been widely practised for only about three years, and its popularity is growing rapidly (Robinson 1986). New approaches in the field of ceramic–matrix composites are enhancing the fracture resistance of ceramics.

However, this growing interest in chemical-based techniques can be interpreted as evidence that the older physics-based techniques are reaching a dead end. At present, it appears safe to predict that advanced ceramics will rapidly grow in economic importance, but that they will not become serious competitors with metals (e.g. in auto, diesel, or jet engines) for at least another decade. This means that major technical improvements in engine performance – hence fuel economy – especially in large-scale applications cannot be expected for at least another 10 years, if not more. In the interim period, metal–matrix composites that contain ceramic particles or fibres will result in small incremental improvements in engine performance.

Strong light materials

De-materialization depends to some extent on the substitution of lighter materials for conventional ones, especially in structural applications. Strength-to-weight and (Young's) modulus-to-weight are obviously important characteristics in this context. For most practical purposes "strength" is a combination of two characteristics, namely resistance to stretching and resistance to bending (stiffness). The first is commonly measured in terms of the amount of pulling or tensile stress required to cause the sample to break (usually measured in psi, or pounds per square inch, of cross-section). The second is measured in terms of the tensile stress required in principle to stretch the sample to twice its original length, also measured in psi. This number is called "Young's modulus." For purposes of comparison, typical values of breaking strength and stiffness for standard engineering materials are as follows:

	Tensile strength $(\times 10^3)$ psi	Stiffness (modulus) $(\times 10^3)$ psi
Wood (spruce, along grain)	15	2,000
Bone	20	4,000
Glass (window or bottle)	5–25	10,000
Aluminium	10	10,500
Carbon steel (mild)	60	30,000

In principle, it seems obvious that these numbers must bear some relation to the attractive forces between atoms of the material. But if only inter-atomic forces were involved, materials should be 10 to 50 times stronger than they actually are. Very careful experiments in the 1940s and 1950s showed that flawless microscopic crystals or whiskers or very thin fibres of glass approached theoretical breaking strength much more closely than macro materials (Gordon 1973). Figure 4.8 shows that the strength-to-density ratios of today's engineering materials have increased by more than 50-fold, as compared with materials available at the beginning of the industrial revolution. This trend can be expected to continue for some time to come.

In the 1950s, theory (supported by newly available empirical data from X-ray microscopy and other new research tools) began to catch up, and the essential mechanisms of defect propagation in brittle materials and "crack-stopping" behaviour in ductile metals and natural composites (such as wood and bone) were finally understood (Gordon 1973). "Composites" are composed of two or more components, namely very strong small fibres (oriented or not) embedded in a much weaker matrix. A factor of 5 or so difference in strength between the two components is actually essential. This insight opened

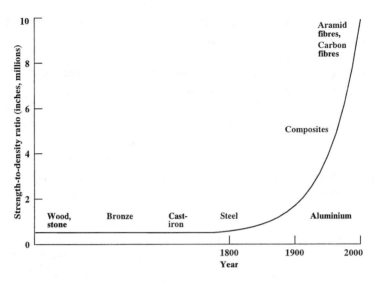

Fig. 4.8 **Progress in materials strength–density ratio, showing a 50-fold increase (Source: NAS/NRC 1989)**

the door to synthetic composites, of which the first commercially important one was fibreglass-reinforced plastic (FRP). FRP is still by far the most important composite commercially, but by the beginning of the 1970s a large family of new high-performance composites had been developed, largely by the aerospace industry.

The key to a practical composite material is the stronger and stiffer component, which can be a glass fibre, a mineral crystal such as sapphire (Al_2O_3), or boron (B), or graphite (C) fibre, a metallic crystal ("whisker"), or even a complex structure consisting of a silicon-carbide-coated boron fibre or a core of thin (e.g. tungsten) wire on which a coating of boron (B) or a boron-carbon compound (B_4C) has been vapour-deposited.

For almost all commercial applications, the matrix or binder is an epoxy or phenolic resin that can be easily moulded. However, if the composite material must also be heat resistant and non-inflammable, only mineral materials or metals can be used. In such cases, manufacturing techniques may be similar to those used in ceramic manufacturing (casting, powder compaction, followed by isostatic compression and sintering). As noted above, recent trends in advanced structural ceramic applications research suggest that physical techniques may be supplanted by chemical methods, such as the "sol-gel" method (Robinson 1986).

130

Another approach to the creation of metallic composites is to arrange a two-phase system of metallic crystals with the requisite difference in strength and stiffness. Such a system can be created by powder-forming techniques (metal–matrix composites) or by dissolving one metal in another and allowing it to crystallize as a separate phase within the melt under controlled conditions. The result is called a eutectic or "intermetallic" alloy. A number of combinations have been identified that have the requisite characteristics (e.g. Lynch 1975). In recent years a great deal of attention has been given to composites with intermetallic compounds as matrix materials reinforced by strong fibres. The most promising example at present is nickel aluminide (Ni_3Al), with small amounts of boron added to increase cohesion and small amounts of hafnium to increase yield strength (Claasen and Girifalco 1986). Other promising matrix materials include NiAl and TiAl.

The list of possible metal–matrix composites and eutectics may get much longer in time, but it is difficult to say whether significant improvements in absolute performance are likely. In any case, the primary objective of R&D over the next few years is to improve predictability, consistency, and formability, in order to decrease the cost per unit performance. Well over a decade after their initial introduction into the aerospace industry (for specialized uses in military aircraft and spacecraft), ultra-strong graphite-based composites finally appeared in a few selected commercial products such as tennis rackets, skis, and golf clubs in the late 1970s. They are gradually increasing market share as prices come down and designers learn how to utilize the new materials to best advantage. However, there are many other potential "civil" applications where strength, light weight, and corrosion resistance will make a difference. Bicycle frames, motorcycles, and small light aircraft would probably be the next obvious applications, followed by substantial use in commercial aircraft.

In principle, composites can replace aluminium for most of the structural parts of any aircraft, including the exterior "skin," and a significant part of the engine. Even small savings in weight in aircraft (or spacecraft) have a significant pay-off in terms of fuel economy or, equivalently, increased payload.

Undoubtedly, these materials will ultimately have a significant impact on the economics of air transportation. Commercialization has been slow, up to now, because of the long product "life cycle" in the aircraft industry, the specialized knowledge involved, and the fact

131

that most of it was initially proprietary to the aerospace industry. All of these factors result in rather high costs. However, most of the basic patents have already expired and the key "process" patents are currently expiring. This will open up the field to more intense competition. It can be expected that the ratio of "composites" to metals in newly designed subsonic aircraft will rise rapidly through the 1990s. For example, all the control surfaces on the Boeing 757 and 767 aircraft are made of graphite–epoxy composites, yielding a saving of 856 lb in weight and a 2 per cent saving in fuel (Clark and Flemings 1986).

Beyond aircraft applications, there will eventually also be important applications in automobiles. Until 1980 or so, only fibreglass (FRP) had found a significant automotive use (in the Chevrolet Corvette body). But an increasing number of bumpers and body panels and some complete metal automobile bodies are being replaced by unreinforced thermoplastic polymers, so the first major opportunity for lightweight composites may be to replace steel in the chassis and frame. The overall proportion of plastics in the weight of an average auto has increased quite sharply in recent years – it is now between 10 and 15 per cent – and this ratio can be expected to continue to grow in the future. Use of plastics in automobiles will accelerate if ways are developed to recycle the plastics more effectively than at present. (Currently, the plastics from junked cars are mainly dumped in landfills or incinerated, whereas the metals are largely recycled.)

Meanwhile, as noted above, ceramics may ultimately replace much of the metal in the conventional auto engine, and high-strength low-alloy steel will continue to replace mild steel in chassis and frame. The benefits of weight reduction in automobiles (and trucks) are not as great as in the case of aircraft but are nevertheless significant. Most of the increased fuel economy observed in automobiles since 1970 is attributable to lighter weight and better tyres – not to more efficient engines. However, it is clear that a great deal remains to be learned about large-scale manufacturing with composite materials before they can replace metals in mass-produced products.

Up until now, the auto industry has not invested much effort in this field. In view of the long lead-times in the industry, polymer–matrix composites (except FRP) cannot be expected to begin to replace steel in major automobile structural parts such as the chassis and frame until probably after 2010. However, ultralight metal–matrix composites such as aluminium–silicon carbide are beginning to replace old materials such as cast-iron in brake rotors, brake calipers, and engine blocks. The use of aluminium and magnesium will significantly increase in the next generation of motor vehicles, which will be half to two-thirds the weight of the current generation of cars. The weight reductions, together with engine performance improvements and continuing aerodynamic improvements (thanks to CAD) and continuing tyre performance improvements, will cut fuel consumption per vehicle-kilometre by at least a factor of two.

Another application would be for second-generation supersonic aircraft, now being developed by several countries. Such an aircraft would probably utilize up to 50 per cent polymer–matrix composites, plus 10 per cent meta–matrix composites, 15 per cent aluminium–lithium alloy, and 25 per cent other metals such as steel, aluminium, and titanium (Steinberg 1986).

Electronic materials

The category of electronic materials includes "ordinary" conductors, semiconductors, superconductors, photoconductors, photoelectrics, photovoltaics, photomagnetics, ferromagnetics, diamagnetics, paramagnetics, magnetostrictives, piezo-electrics, laser materials, and a host of others. Even a brief summary of the physical phenomena involved would be far too long for a chapter such as this.

Since the development of the transistor in 1947 – as a substitute for the electron tube or "vacuum tube" – research in the field of semiconductors has grown spectacularly. The rapid growth of basic knowledge about the materials has been driven by burgeoning demand for electronic devices, from telephone switchboards to radio, television, radar, sonar, and computers. The last application has proved the most important, especially after the successive development of integrated circuits (*c.* 1960) followed by the "microprocessor" (*c.* 1970), and then large-scale integration (LSI), very large-scale integration (VSLI), and now ultra large-scale integration (ULSI). Table 4.4 summarizes these dramatic changes.

One of the key technological driving forces, whose impact seems to have been consistently underestimated, is the close relationship between operating speed, power consumption, cost, and scale. The original motivation for the invention of the transistor was to cut down on the electric power consumption of the telephone switching systems. Miniaturization and large scale required the solution of many difficult technological problems such as controlling even smaller line widths (fig. 4.9). However, as these technical problems were solved, it proved to be a powerful cost-cutting strategy, because manufacturers'

Table 4.4 **The development of semiconductors**

Period of diffusion	Vacuum tube to 1945	Transistor 1955–	Integrated circuit		LSI 1975–	VLSI 1985–
			SSI 1965–	MSI		
Integration (elements per unit or per chip)	1 unit	1 unit	2–100	100–1,000	1,000–100,000	100,000–1,000,000
Functions per unit or per chip	1–2	1	100		10,000	100,000
Reliability per function	0.05	1	30		1,000	10,000
Price per function (per chip or per unit)	¥300	¥10	¥1		¥0.05	<¥0.05

Source: NIRA (1985).

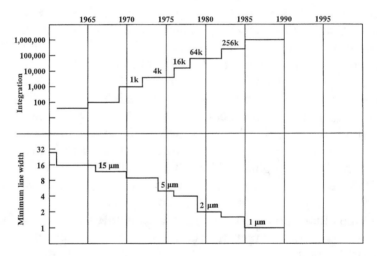

Fig. 4.9 **Changes in the scale of integration and minimum line width (Data source: Electronic Industries Association of Japan)**

sharply declining semiconductor circuitry costs, in turn, generated steady increases in demand, including wholly new applications (fig. 4.10).

The growth of demand for more "computer power" seems to be continuing unabated, as costs continue to fall. In fact, major new *categories* of computer and communications applications, such as voice

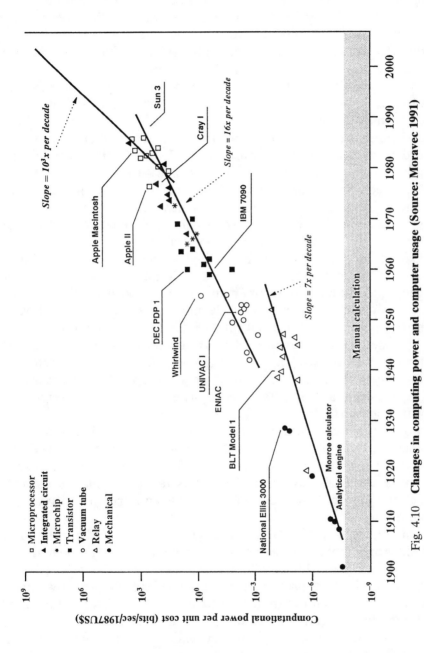

Fig. 4.10 **Changes in computing power and computer usage (Source: Moravec 1991)**

processing, vision processing, and "artificial intelligence," are just beginning to emerge (table 4.5). The silicon chip continues to dominate all challengers; its eventual replacement by other more exotic materials continues to be delayed into the indefinite future. However other (faster) semiconductor materials, such as gallium arsenide, may eventually have their day.

It is literally impossible to forecast with any confidence the "winners" and "losers" in this intense competition. A few conclusions can be drawn, however:

- Switching speeds and micro-miniaturization can still be increased by orders of magnitude, in principle, exploiting optical technologies now becoming ever more important (table 4.6).
- Manufacturing techniques are becoming more and more critical. The need for microscopic tolerances and ultra-low levels of impurity contamination require increasingly sophisticated (and expensive) and totally automated robotics facilities.
- Design complexity is becoming the limiting factor. Sophisticated CAD is already essential for "chip" design and every successive generation of more powerful memory or microprocessor chips[5] will certainly require correspondingly more powerful CAD software, probably including artificial intelligence (AI) to perform some of the functions performed by human designers at present. This, in turn, will emphasize the role of the very few research institutions capable of assembling a "critical mass" of front-rank AI researchers, applied mathematicians and logicians, and electronics and software specialists.

For the above reasons, the semiconductor, telecommunications, computer, and software industries are now inextricably linked and marching together. "New starts," small firms, and small countries are now essentially out of the game, as far as leading-edge microelectronics technology is concerned. (This is not true for software, of course.)

One of the major apparent opportunities for research in the field of electronic materials has been superconductors.[6] The advent of a practical commercial helium liquefier in the early 1950s resulted in an explosion of exploratory research in this field. Only a few superconductors were known up to that time, but by 1970 several hundred superconducting compounds and alloys had been identified. Moreover, by that time superconducting magnets were being sold commercially (by Westinghouse). Such magnets are now standard laboratory research tools, and will be used for any new large particle

Table 4.5 **Breakthroughs expected in electronics**

Field	Technological need	Current technology	New technology	Performance comparison
Communications	Large-volume transmission	Microwaves	Milliwaves	10 times
Information-processing	High-speed processing	Silicon LSI	GaAs	5–6 times
			Josephson-junction device	At least 10 times
	High-density memory	Horizontal magnetic recording	Perpendicular magnetic recording	At least 10 times
	Larger-scale integration devices	Planar integration	Three-dimensional circuit devices	–
Instrumentation and control	Improved sensitivity	–	Josephson-junction device	$(10^{-6}-10^{-7}\,\text{G})$
	Improved resolution	–	Ultrasonics (microscope)	$(1\ \mu m$ or less)

Source: Hitachi Research Institute (n.d.).

Table 4.6 **Breakthroughs expected in optics**

Field	Technological need	Current technology	New technology	Performance comparison
Communications	Large-volume transmission	Milliwaves (10^{11} Hz)	Laser light (10^{14} Hz)	1,000 times
	Long-distance transmission (relaying distance)	Electromagnetic waves (1 km)	Laser light (10–100 km)	10–100 times
	Transmission cost reduction (cable weight)	Coaxial cable (130 kg/m)	Optical fibre cable (70 g/m)	About 1/2000
Information-processing	High-speed processing	Josephson-junction device (6–7 picoseconds)	Laser light (10 picoseconds)	0.6 times
	Intra-CPU transmission (data volume/second)	Sequential processing	Parallel processing	Several dozen times
	Spatial image information-processing	Unidimensional development needed	Parallel processing of two-dimensional image possible	Advantageous for image information-processing
	High-density recording	Perpendicular magnetic recording (10M bits/cm^2)	Magneto-optic recording (20M bits/cm^2 minimum)	At least 2 times
Instrumentation and control	High reliability: Electromagnetic interference	Present	Absent	Light is advantageous
	Crosstalk	Present	Absent	
	Short circuits	Present	Absent	

Source: NIRA (1985).

accelerators or, probably, for future magnetic levitation ("mag-lev") rail systems.

On the other hand, the cost of liquid helium has not fallen significantly since 1960 and is not likely to. Many once active projects – such as the development of a superconducting computer (IBM) – have been dropped. As of 1975 the highest known critical temperature ($Al_{0.8}Ge_{0.2}Nb_3$) was only $20.7°K$, which was still below the boiling point of liquid hydrogen ($22.7°K$).

The first sign of a major breakthrough was the discovery in 1986 of a new class of barium-copper-lanthanum oxide superconductors, which achieved superconductivity at $35°K$. In January 1987 partial superconductivity in a similar compound was reported at $52°K$, under very high pressure. Only a few weeks later another metallic oxide compound was reported to be superconductive at $98°K$. More discoveries are to be expected. Dozens of laboratories around the world are now said to be searching for new compounds capable of superconductivity at even higher temperatures, and many physicists are now optimistic about the possibility of achieving superconductivity at room temperature (Sullivan 1987).

However the $77°K$ barrier, which has now been exceeded, was the truly significant one. Below that temperature only liquid helium is a feasible coolant (except in space), whereas above that point liquid nitrogen ($77°K$) can be used. Liquid nitrogen is available in industrial quantities as a by-product of the production of liquid oxygen used by the steel industry and for rocket propulsion. It costs only 10 per cent as much as liquid helium and is far less volatile. Thus, it is now realistic to think in terms of large-scale applications of superconductivity, e.g. power generation and transmission and magnetic levitation of high-speed trains. Neither of these applications is imminent. However, on a time scale of 50 years, both are rather good bets.

Photovoltaic (PV) materials are another category of potential importance as solar cells. Major candidates include silicon (crystalline or amorphous) and thin films. The latter may be made from gallium arsenide, copper indium diselenide, cadmium telluride, or other combinations not yet discovered. Silicon is by far the most widely used, at present, with achievable solar conversion efficiency of nearly 20 per cent for the crystalline form. Amorphous silicon has achievable conversion efficiency of at least 15 per cent, but it can be manufactured at much lower cost. Laboratory cells have already achieved over 30 per cent conversion efficiency, using concentrator cells, and 40 per cent or more is now regarded as likely by the end of the 1990s.

Some experts think that an 80 per cent conversion rate for sunlight to electricity is ultimately conceivable. This development is of the greatest possible importance. Each unit of electricity generated by photovoltaics instead of coal-burning eliminates emissions of sulphur and nitrogen oxides, volatile organics, coal ash carrying toxic trace metals, and carbon dioxide into the atmosphere.

Apart from progress in the fundamental science, there has been very rapid progress on the technological side. A number of new techniques for coating thin films of semiconductive materials onto a glass (or other) substrate have been developed, e.g. by Mobil-Tyco, Westinghouse, and Honeywell. Spectacular progress has also been made in reducing film thickness by a factor of 100, as compared with early cells (Zweibel 1987).

NASA, DOD, and Bell Laboratories supported much of the early R&D work in this field to obtain long-lived solar cells for application in satellites. The first solar cells, used mainly by NASA, cost US$1,000 per watt. An array of solar cells in 1975 cost about US$75 per watt of peak capacity (W_p) compared with US$5 per watt for a large nuclear power plant in 1975US$. The "energy crisis" of 1973–1974 precipitated an accelerated programme of R&D in this area, focused mainly on bringing down the cost of manufacturing. The US R&D programme was cut back sharply in the 1980s (from US$150 million in 1980 to US$43 million in 1987), but not before major progress had been made, as shown in figure 4.11 (Maycock 1982). The modest goals of US efforts to tap solar energy in recent years have been to achieve a competitive final price level of 6 cents per kWh by the year 2010, with module efficiencies of 15–20 per cent. Up until 1990 or so, the market for solar PV power had been restricted to remote locations and special-purpose applications (although the market was clearly growing). But the energy utility industry had not shown much interest. However it now appears likely that some big firms (notably Enron Corp.) have decided to invest in mass production of solar cells with the deliberate intention of bringing the price down more rapidly, perhaps even by 2000. More recent progress in this field is discussed in chapter 7 in this book.

Another important category that is worth discussing briefly is ferromagnetic materials (White 1985). In a way, this is surprising, because the phenomenon of ferromagnetism has been known for such a long time. However, as in the case of "strong materials," the relationship between magnetic fields on the micro (inter-atomic) scale and the macro scale was not adequately understood until the 1940s

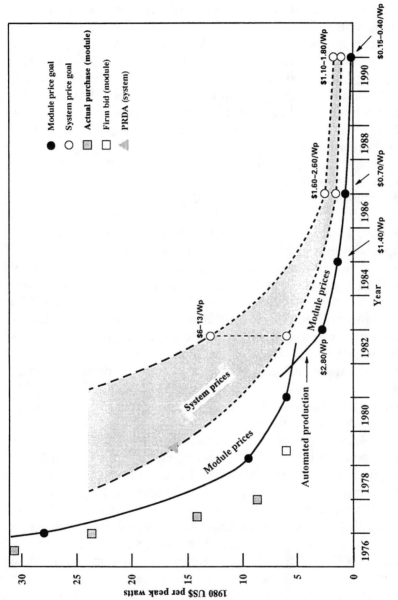

Fig. 4.11 Photovoltaic module and system price goals (Source: Maycock 1982)

141

when Neel, Kittel, and others developed the basic physical concepts that have dominated subsequent R&D in magnetism. The progress in basic physics of ferromagnetism was rapidly translated into increased practical interest, especially because of the growing importance of magnetic materials.

Ferrites – a new class of magnetic oxide materials, mainly Fe_2O_3 – were first used for data recording in the 1930s.[7] Ferrites also rapidly found applications in transformers, radar, communication equipment, and (by the late 1950s) computer memories. Discrete ferrite "core" memories have long been superseded by high-speed semiconductors; but ferrite-based magnetic tapes and disks remain the major form of read-in/read-out medium- to long-term data storage system. (It is not yet clear to what extent optical storage devices will ultimately replace magnetic devices, if ever.)

New non-iron-based ferromagnetic alloys for permanent magnets also began to be discovered in the 1930s, beginning with the Al-Ni-Co family. This was mainly research by trial and error. In the 1950s Phillips Laboratories produced permanently magnetized ferrites based on iron oxides combined with strontium or barium, aligned in powder form, then compacted and sintered. The rare-earth-cobalt ($SmCo_5$) based permanent magnets (REPMs) were discovered in 1967 and first commercialized by 1970. A second-generation series based on Sm_2Co_{17} was introduced around 1981, and an important boron-based compound $Fe_{14}Nd_2B$ appeared in 1983.

For permanent magnets there are two important parameters, namely *energy product* (the amount of stored magnetic energy[8]) and *coercivity* (the resistance to reversal or demagnetization by an external field, H_c). Progress since 1900 in these two areas is shown in figures 4.12 and 4.13, respectively. It is interesting to note that the theoretical maximum value of stored magnetic energy for iron would be 10^7 mega-gauss oersteds (MGOe) (if all the micro-domains could be completely aligned), and in the case of other alloys it may well be much higher. Thus, there is still room for significant progress in this area.

Applications of permanent magnets are widespread in many types of devices, but perhaps the most important single application is for special-purpose electric motors. Recent improvements in magnet performance can be expected to be reflected in improved electric motor performance. In fact, a whole new class of compact motor designs now appears practical (White 1985). This, in turn, will result in at least some significant new applications. For instance, compact high-power electric motors could replace hydraulic motors in robots,

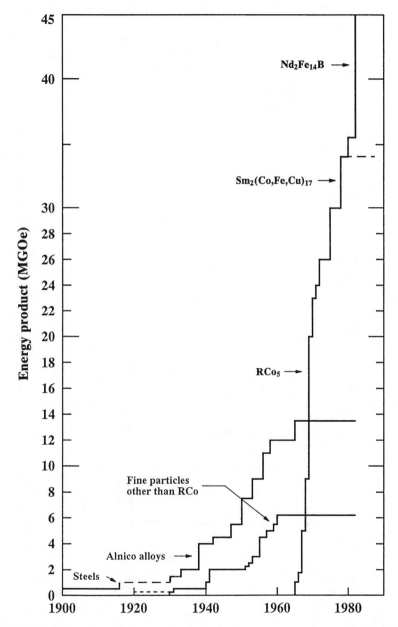

Fig. 4.12 **Change in energy product of various permanent magnet materials (Source: NAS/NRC 1989)**

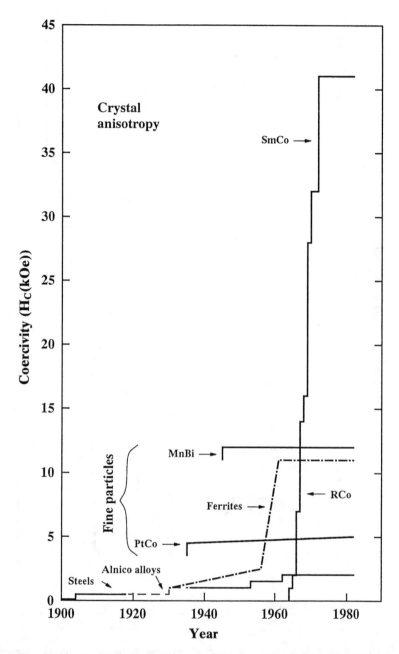

Fig. 4.13 **Change in coercivity of various permanent magnet materials (Source: NAS/NRC 1989)**

resulting in a substantial increase in speed of operation. However, the most attractive application for new types of powerful compact electric motors would be to propel electric vehicles. This is a major topic in itself, however, and we cannot discuss it at length here.

One final example of electronic materials worth mentioning is a class of organic liquids whose viscosity is strongly dependent on the imposed electric field. When a transverse field (voltage) is imposed, such a liquid becomes extremely viscous – almost glassy; yet when the field is removed it flows freely. This class of materials could conceivably become the basis for electrically controlled clutches, brakes, or robotic grippers, thus eliminating much of the mechanical complexity that now plagues such devices. However, much research remains to be done, primarily in the optimization of the molecular synthesis and the scale-up of manufacturing technology.

Conclusions

Materials are the underpinnings of technology – not only figuratively but literally. Some of the most important of all technological "breakthroughs" were associated with materials. The ability to make hard, impervious ceramic pots for the storage of liquids and seeds was one of the first requisites of urban civilization, around 8000 BC. The "Bronze" age and the "Iron" age were major technological milestones. The discoveries of paper and glass (not only for windows but, perhaps more important, for lenses) were only a little less significant in their time. Iron tools and weapons are an enormous improvement over bronze tools, but require much more advanced methods of smelting and working. Steel is as much an improvement over older forms of iron as iron was over bronze. The historian Elton Morrison called steel "almost the greatest invention," with some justice.

However, in some sense the "age of materials" is now past and the "age of information" is upon us. To be sure, most traditional uses of basic materials will continue for many decades, with gradual but cumulative reductions in the sheer mass of materials required for most purposes. Materials of all kinds are becoming more sophisticated and "information intensive," in the sense that they offer more service to the end-user.

But greatly overshadowing this rather broad trend is the enormously rapid increase in the uses of materials specifically for purposes of energy conversion (e.g. magnets, photovoltaics) and processing or storing information. The semiconductors and ferrites

Table 4.7 **Breakthroughs expected in materials**

Field	Technological need	Breakthrough technology	Materials
Communications	Large-volume transmission	Milliwaves, laser beams	Compound semiconductors (InP, GaAlAs, etc.)
	Long-distance transmission	Low-loss optical fibre	Non-silicic material
Information-processing	High-speed operations	Compound semiconductors ICs	Compound semiconductors (GaAs, InP, etc.)
		Josephson-junction device	Superconductive materials (alloys, compounds)
	High-density recording	Perpendicular magnetic recording	Perpendicular magnetized film
		Magneto-optic recording	Magneto-optic recording materials
		Molecular memory	High polymers, biological substances (protein)
Instrumentation and control	Improvement in sensing performance	Josephson-junction device	Superconductive materials (alloys, compounds, etc.)
		Biosensor	Biological (micro-organisms, enzymes, etc.)
	Improved resistance to environmental conditions	Devices more resistant to environmental conditions	Compound semiconductors (GaAs, InP, etc.)
Energy conversion	Solar energy, especially in remote areas	Photovoltaics	Silicon (crystalline or amorphous) Ga-As, Cd-Te, Cu-In, Se
	More efficient generators, transmission lines	Superconductivity	Cu-Ba-La-O. Other methane oxygen compounds
Transportation	Magnetic levitation	Ferromagnets	Sm-Co, Nd-Fe-B
		Superconductors	Cu-Ba-La-O. Other metallic oxygen compounds

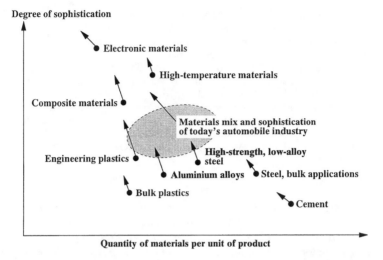

Fig. 4.14 **Relation between the quantity of materials in a product and its informa-tion content**

constitute the two obvious examples of the latter, but it can be argued that the dominant trend of the future is toward the development of materials that are "information intensive" in this narrower sense. A rough tabulation of the materials of greatest research interest today is given in table 4.7. The degree of sophistication and information con-tent of these materials is continually increasing (fig. 4.14). But they will also be more difficult to produce and to recycle. This will induce increasing interest in re-use and remanufacturing in coming decades.

Notes

1. Each tonne of fossil fuel burned results in the ultimate release of roughly 3 tonnes of CO_2 to the atmosphere, not to mention significant quantities of sulphur oxides (SOx) and oxides of nitrogen (NOx) – the main causes of environmental acidification. Atmospheric carbon dioxide concentration has increased by about 20 per cent since the nineteenth century.
2. Specifically, the first law of thermodynamics, i.e. the law of conservation of mass.
3. The quantities of ore removed from the earth are normally much larger, but physical sepa-ration techniques leave much of the excess material at the mine, where it is piled up into small mountains, but not put back into the ground. For instance, copper ores mined in the western United States contain less than 0.4 per cent copper, whereas concentrates delivered to refineries average 20 per cent copper. Thus, for every tonne of concentrate, at least 50 tonnes of crude ore were dug up and processed (by flotation ponds) at the mine. For 1 tonne of refined copper 250 tonnes of ore are processed. In some cases the quantities of ore pro-cessed are much larger. For example, roughly 140,000 tonnes of ore must be processed to yield 1 tonne of platinum group metals.
4. Applications of high-strength low-alloy (HSLA) steels are still continuing to increase how-

ever, especially in the auto industry. Major process innovations, notably the Basic Oxygen Process (BOF) and continuous casters, also appeared after World War II.

5. A 16 megabyte chip was announced in early 1987 by NTT (Nippon Telephone and Telegraph Co.). As of 1997 we are in the gigabyte range.

6. These are materials that lose all electrical resistivity at a temperature below some "critical" level so long as the magnetic field strength (including the field induced by the superconductive current itself) is below a critical level.

7. Data recording requires "soft" magnetic materials, i.e. materials that can easily be magnetized and demagnetized at high frequency without large "eddy current" losses. The latter requirement cannot be met by metals, but oxides fill the bill because of very high electrical resistivity.

8. Magnetic energy is measured in mega-gauss oersteds (MGOe).

References

Barnett, Harold and Chandler Morse (1962) *Scarcity and Growth: The Economics of Resource Scarcity*. Baltimore, MD: Johns Hopkins University Press.

Barney, Gerald (1980) *The Global 2000 Report to the President*. Technical Report, vol. 2. Washington D.C.: Council on Environmental Quality, US Department of State.

Claasen, R. S. and L. A. Girifalco (1986) Materials for energy utilization. *Scientific American* **255**(4): 85–92.

Clark, J. P. and M. C. Flemings (1986) Advanced materials and the economy. *Scientific American* **255**(4): 43–49.

Gordon, James E. (1973) *The New Science of Strong Materials*. Harmondsworth, UK: Penguin Books.

Gordon, T. J. and T. R. Munson (1982) *Research into Technology Output Measures*. Danbury, CN: The Futures Group.

Hitachi Research Institute (n.d.) *In Search of Future Technology in Electronics*.

Larson, Eric D., H. Marc Ross, and Robert H. Williams (1986) Beyond the era of materials. *Scientific American* **254**(6): 24–31.

Lynch, Charles T. (1975) *Handbook of Materials Science*. Cleveland, OH: CRC Press.

Maycock, P. D. (1982) Overview-Cost Goals in the LSA Project. Unpublished.

Moravec, Hans (1991) *Mind Children*. Cambridge, MA: Harvard University Press.

NAS/NRC (1989) *Materials Science and Engineering for the 1990s*. Washington D.C.: National Academy Press.

NIRA (National Institute for Research Advancement) (1985) *Comprehensive Study of Microelectronics*. Technical Report. Tokyo: National Institute for Research Advancement.

NMABNRC (National Materials Advisory Board) (1975) *Structural Ceramics*. Washington D.C.: National Research Council.

Robinson, Arthur L. (1986) A chemical route to advanced ceramics. *Science* **233**(4579), 4 July: 25–27.

Smith, V. Kerry (1979) *Scarcity and Growth Revisited*. Baltimore, MD: Johns Hopkins University Press.

Steinberg, M. A. (1986) Materials for aerospace. *Scientific American* **255**(4): 59–64.

Sullivan, Walter (1987) *New York Times*, 17 February.

White, R. M. (1985) Opportunities in magnetic materials. *Science* **229**(4708), 5 July: 11–16.

Zweibel, Kenneth (1987) Interview, *New York Times*, 13 February.

5

Global energy futures: The long-term perspective for eco-restructuring

Hans-Holger Rogner

Introduction

Since the mid-nineteenth century, world energy use has been growing, on average, by 2.1 per cent per year. This growth in energy use has fuelled an annual expansion of the world economy of 3.2 per cent. Most importantly, energy and economic growth have combined to raise world population from 1.2 to 5.3 billion, corresponding to an average growth rate of 1.1 per cent per year.

This account of past rates of growth is incomplete as long as it neglects the environmental degradation associated with industrial development, economic growth, and energy use, ranging from local air and water pollution, soil contamination, and reduced biodiversity, to stratospheric ozone depletion and the damage potentially caused by global climate change. Whereas initially the burdens placed by humans on the environment and their resulting consequences were primarily local, it is now apparent that the adverse impacts of human activity are rapidly approaching global dimensions. Foremost among these impacts is the potential for global climate change caused by a growing concentration of greenhouse gases (GHG) in the atmosphere. Climate change is likely to emerge as one of the greatest threats to the development of mankind during the twenty-first century. Scientific evidence linking unrestricted fossil fuel use to potential climatic change is increasingly gaining credibility (see IPCC 1990, 1992). The Second Assessment Report of the Intergovernmental Panel on Climate Change (IPCC) states that "the balance of evidence suggests a discernible human influence on global climate" (IPCC 1996a). However, fundamental disagreement in the scientific community exists as to the eventual impacts of global climatic change, especially at the regional level.

In large part the threat of climatic change is the result of greenhouse gas emissions from the energy system. The energy system is not the sole source of greenhouse gases, but it is the most important one, currently accounting for roughly half of all such emissions. More importantly, the global energy system is the fastest-growing emitter.

Stabilization of atmospheric GHG concentrations is a policy objective in several industrialized countries. GHG emission reduction targets are a key issue on the agenda of the United Nations Framework Convention on Climate Change (UNFCCC) where the so-called ANNEX I countries (OECD and Reforming Economies) have committed themselves to stabilization. Present energy research and environmental policy aim at the identification of energy technology options and strategies that mitigate greenhouse gas emissions. Technology responses analysed by numerous researchers range from efficiency improvements, fuel and technology switching, to GHG emission abatement or removal, and environmentally benign GHG disposal or sequestration. Presently, the discussion centres around issues such as the costs and benefits of different measures, least-cost and hedging strategies, etc. Yet these all focus on incremental and add-on technology fixes within the current energy sector, rather than on a systematic restructuring of the energy system.

What is missing in the current energy–environment debate is a zero-order understanding of the structure of a fully sustainable energy system. Long-term energy and environmental policy requires a reference or target energy system – a target beyond the issues of local air pollution and greenhouse gas emission levels. Once established, the long-term reference energy system then plays the role of a beacon for energy policy, for public investment in infrastructure changes beyond the capability of free market forces, for publicly funded research and development activities, as well as for private sector investments. This paper attempts to present a "reference" structure of a sustainable energy system that could serve not only as a long-

term target for energy and economic policy but also as a guideli
public and private investment.

In a world of continuous technical change, the "reference" energy
system is a moving target. Over a period of 50 years and more, technology forecasting based on current knowledge will certainly fail
to anticipate future inventions and rates of innovation. The target
energy system, therefore, should incorporate least-regret cost features, i.e. it is structured so that future innovation enhances the
system's performance rather than making previous infrastructure
investments obsolete. Despite the large uncertainties involved, it can
be shown that the overall system architecture and some fundamental
technological characteristics are quite robust even in a rapidly changing world of technology (Rogner and Britton 1991).

The environmental gains from restructuring the energy system will
be compounded if it takes place as an integral part of a fundamental
eco-restructuring of the entire economic production and consumption
process. Energy is not an end in itself; the prime purpose of energy is
to provide energy services such as heating, cooking, mobility, communication, consumption goods, and numerous industrial processes.
Eco-restructuring of the energy system, then, goes hand in hand with
changes in settlement patterns and transportation infrastructures,
workplace arrangements that include telecommuting, de-materializ-
ing of the production process, and recycling.

The fundamental features of a sustainable energy system can be
defined in terms of the following four compatibility constraints:
1. environmental compatibility,
2. economic compatibility,
3. social compatibility, and
4. geopolitical compatibility.

Regarding environmental compatibility, the fluxes to and from the
target energy system should be coherent with nature's energy and
material fluxes and should not perturb nature's equilibria. Only then
will it be possible to provide for economic growth without environmental costs undermining the gains. On the other hand, economic
reasoning demands that the costs of protecting the environment
should not exceed the benefits.

An effective and, in the long run, sustainable target energy system
should also consider the implications of the historically observed
linkage between per capita energy service requirements and demographics. In a world whose population has doubled in a single gen-

eration and which continues to grow at alarming rates, even drastic changes that one might be able to engineer in terms of specific energy efficiency improvements or environmental impacts over the next decades could well be swamped by the underlying demographic explosion.

Future energy systems and associated technologies need to be socio-politically acceptable in terms of convenience, level of risk, and economic affordability. Supply security and other potential geopolitical concerns including proliferation issues need also to be effectively resolved.

Once a target energy system is defined, the question of managing the transition must be addressed in terms of both energy system evolution and policy. Given the inherently long lifetime of existing energy infrastructures and lead-times from blueprint to operation of a dozen and more years for new production capacity, the energy system does not lend itself to quick adaptation or modification. The transition phase towards a sustainable energy system is likely to last well into the twenty-first century.

As regards policy measures, initiating the shift away from the potentially unacceptable burdens that the present system places on the environment will probably require more than the present measures ranging from energy price manipulations (green taxes), standards, regulated emission levels, and tradable permits to prescribed technology fixes. Present policy focuses primarily on short-term reductions in local air pollution, not on providing the market with guidelines and incentives for a transition toward an environmentally sustainable energy system. From the perspective of eco-restructuring, one of the most important policy steps would be to get the prices right by internalizing external costs. Still, the enormous changes in infrastructure associated with the transition towards a sustainable energy system are most likely beyond the domain of market forces. Therefore, effective energy policy must be based on a clear understanding of both the eventual shape and structure of the deep future energy system and the implications for the transition phase (Rogner and Britton 1992). This includes our understanding of the energy sources and principal technologies that will be key during this transition phase.

What is the energy system?

Energy analysts often use the term "energy system" when they are actually referring to the "energy sector." The energy sector is only

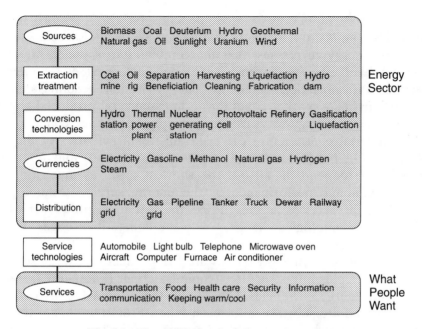

Fig. 5.1 **The architecture of the energy system**

the upstream part of the energy system. Figure 5.1 puts this difference into perspective by representing the architecture of the energy system as a series of vertically linked source-to-service pathways. The examples next to each system component are randomly chosen and do not represent any special correlation across the various columns.

The energy *sector* in figure 5.1 primarily focuses on the production and sale of energy currencies. Electric utilities generate and sell kWhs, while the oil sector explores for and produces oil, refines the oil into marketable products, and sells these in the market-place. The success of any particular agent within the energy sector is usually measured in terms of kWh or litres of gasoline sold. However, the reason people purchase kWhs of electricity or litres of gasoline is only indirectly related to these products. What people really want are energy services, i.e. information via electronic mail, the exchange of information through a telephone conversation, or the service of getting back safely from work to a comfortably temperature-conditioned home. It is important to note that the demand for energy services changes (in quantity and quality) as a function of demographics, income, technology, and location. But their fundamental nature does not change.

153

The supply of energy services depends on two or more inter-dependent inputs: one or more energy service technologies plus one or more energy currencies. It is the combination of the technology "automobile" and the currency "gasoline" that provides the energy service "transportation" – not the energy product gasoline alone.[1] The downstream market conditions – in essence oil products' ability to provide the energy services demanded by residential, commercial, and industrial consumers – drive the upstream activities of the oil industry. Oil product demand, end-use competition, and interfuel substitution depend, in all but the shortest term, as much on the techno-economic performance of the energy service technologies providing the services as they do on the actual oil product market prices. As technologies change, so do the competitive edges of the associated fuels.

More precisely, energy services are the product of energy service technologies plus infrastructures (capital), labour (know-how), mate-rials, and energy currencies. Clearly, all these input factors carry a price tag and are substitutes for each other. From the perspective of an energy service consumer, the important issue is the quality and cost of energy services. It matters very little what the energy currency is, and, even less, what the source of that currency was. It is fair to say that most energy services are blind to the upstream activities of the energy system.

But, for the development of civilization, it is the end-service tech-nologies, such as automobiles, aircraft, furnaces, electric motors, and computers, that are most important – or at least the most visible. It is these technologies (including associated infrastructures) and their mix that determine the quality and quantities of energy services peo-ple can buy.

The energy system is service driven, i.e. from the bottom up. Energy, however, flows top–down. It appears that the energy indus-try's priorities resemble the flow of energy – top–down – and approach zero once energy leaves the domain of the energy sector indicated in figure 5.1. Only recently have some energy sector industries begun to adopt a full source-to-service perspective, prompted in most cases by regulatory intervention. "Integrated resource planning" (IRP) and "demand-side management" (DSM) have been promoted to assist the industry in getting out of the energy sector "ghetto." In essence, IRP and DSM explicitly call for the inclusion of the end-use devices into the utilities' investment planning activity. Extending this to an example outside the utility domain, oil company subsidiaries might sell transportation services by leasing out highly efficient vehicles and charging for their use on a mileage basis only (the gasoline, car maintenance, etc., would be on the company).

With regard to the evolution of the architecture of the energy system depicted in figure 5.1, the following observations are in order:

1. the bottom–up, service-to-source architecture is time invariant;
2. the basic services of shelter (keeping warm), security, nutrition, communication, and health care are time invariant; and
3. the components of all chains from service technologies to sources are time "variant."

In the context of time variance or energy system evolution, there are several questions that must be addressed:

- Which components of which chains are most subject to change?
- What causes the change, i.e. is the change policy driven or innovation driven (market pull or technology push)?
- What is the rate of change (the dynamics of technology diffusion or evolution)?

Energy system inefficiencies

Most energy services have surprisingly low minimum energy input requirements. Figure 5.2 shows the average exergy[2] efficiency of electricity and total weighted average of selected energy services as a percentage of primary energy. The services considered are space heating, transportation, and lighting. There are many difficulties and definitional ambiguities involved in estimating the exergy efficiencies for comprehensive energy source-to-service chains or entire energy systems, and only few exergy efficiency estimates have been attempted to date. All estimates conclude that source-to-service exergy efficiencies are as low as a few percent. For example, Ayres (1988) calculates an overall source-to-service exergy efficiency of 2.5 per cent for the United States. Wall (1990) estimates a source-to-useful exergy[3] efficiency in Japan of 21 per cent, and Wall et al. (1994) calculate a source-to-useful exergy efficiency of less than 15 per cent in Italy. Schaeffer and Wirtshafter (1992) estimate a primary-to-useful energy efficiency of 32 per cent and an exergy efficiency of 23 per cent for Brazil. Other estimates include Rosen (1992) for Canada and Özdocan and Arikol (1995) for Turkey. Estimates of global and regional primary-to-service exergy efficiencies vary from 10 per cent to as low as a few percent (Gilli et al. 1990, 1995; Nakicenovic et al. 1993).

Figure 5.2 reveals that the present practice of energy service pro-

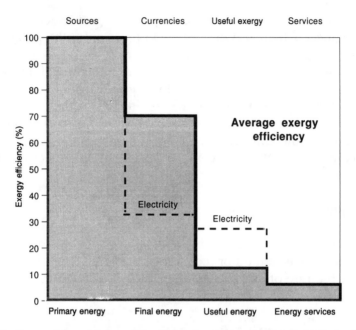

Fig. 5.2 **Source-to-service exergy efficiencies for a weighted basket of energy services (solid line) and exergy efficiency of electricity (dashed line) for the industrialized countries, 1990 (Source: adapted from Nakicenovic et al. 1993)**

vision in the industrialized countries is quite inefficient when compared with the ideal exergy efficiencies. The large inefficiency of the system indicates that most services could be provided with considerably lower energy inputs than those represented by current practice. With the exception of the electricity source-to-service chain, the present energy systems exhibit lowest efficiencies at the interface between the traditional energy sector and the domain of energy services (the service technology component of fig. 5.1). In the case of electricity,[4] the generating process provides the largest potential for efficiency improvement along the electricity source-to-service supply pathway. One should note, however, that electricity also has significant room for improvement at the useful-to-service interface.

Obviously, the opportunities for efficiency improvements suggested by figure 5.2, i.e. closing the gap to 100 per cent, are theoretical potentials that in real-life systems can never be fully exploited. Still, an overall exergy efficiency in the developed world of less than 10 per cent reflects a significant efficiency gap, a gap that represents opportunities for future innovation, policy incentives, and business devel-

156

opment. Energy and environmental policy should encourage public and private sector investment towards the narrowing of this gap wherever this is techno-economically feasible, because more efficient provision of energy services not only reduces the amount of primary energy required but, in general, also reduces material requirements and emission releases to the environment. Although efficiency is an important performance parameter influencing investment or purchase decisions, it is not the only one. Other, and often more important, issues include investments, operating costs, lifetime, peak power, ease of installation and operation, plus many other technical, economic, and convenience factors. For entire energy systems, further consideration must be given to regional resource endowments, conversion technologies, geography, information, time, prices, investment finance, operating costs, age of infrastructures, and know-how.

In essence, figure 5.2 contains one answer to the question of which system links are likely to change. It identifies energy service technologies as the critical component for overall energy system performance improvements. Not only is the energy system driven by service requirements, but the end-use technologies (e.g. the furnace linking final energy and useful energy) and infrastructures (e.g. building codes and insulation standards, which determine the share of useful space heating energy that becomes available for providing these energy services) constitute the system component with the largest potential for narrowing of the efficiency gap. As already mentioned, service technologies are intimately tied to settlement patterns, as well as to housing, transportation, and industrial production infrastructures. These infrastructures are as much responsible for the current inefficiency of the energy system as are the numerous energy conversion technologies associated with these infrastructures.

The deep future energy system

This section attempts to chart out the structure of a quasi zero-pollution energy system based on the single premise that local air-quality issues, in the short run, and greenhouse gas emissions, in the longer run, mandate the restructuring of the energy system to eliminate the use of fossil energy sourced carbon. If this premise stands the test of time, the configuration of the future energy system will be determined by the forces that render the current system obsolete. Most importantly, the future energy system will need to eliminate the unacceptable burdens that the present system places on the environment, and will ultimately be based on sustainable non-fossil sources and non-carbon currencies. However, the transition phase to the zero-carbon energy system will probably last a century or more. Hence the label "deep future."

Eco-restructuring

The term "industrial ecology" reflects the concept of a network of interacting industrial processes that utilize each other's material and energy wastes and by-products. Revised rules for the selection of technologies, products, and processes provide economic incentives that lead to superior efficiency and productivity in the supply of the goods and services demanded by our societies (Ausubel 1992). Rather than functioning as incremental improvements and add-ons, energy efficiency improvements and innovative energy technologies now complement the eco-restructuring process. The net result would be a significant decline in the energy intensity of economic production and consumption, the decarbonization of the energy system, and a drastic reduction in all energy-related GHG emissions. Eco-restructuring of the energy system means adopting industrial ecology features not only within the energy system (e.g. district energy) but also between the energy system and the commercial and industrial sectors.

An energy end-use system based primarily on non-fossil carbon currencies will differ greatly from the present system. Energy conversion efficiency improvements are a necessary but not sufficient prerequisite of the sustainable energy system. Equally important is the restructuring of those infrastructures intimately related to energy services. For example, building and settlement structures affect the quantities and types of service requirements as much as the technology performance of a furnace or vehicle. Although the restructuring of settlement and transportation infrastructures or industrial production processes falls outside the immediate domain of the energy system, these will certainly shape the evolving energy system. Eco-restructuring of anthropogenic production and consumption in general and the development of sustainable energy systems, therefore, are difficult to pursue independently from each other. Because of this interdependence, the momentum for the eco-restructuring of the energy system must start from the level of energy service technologies and related infrastructures.

158

Currencies and sources

In the introduction, sustainable energy systems were defined as systems in which the fluxes to and from the system are coherent with nature's fluxes and do not perturb nature's equilibria. "Coherent" implies that the energy system must mimic nature's energy flows. Coherent in this context means that the energy system utilizes technologies that exploit what nature would "waste" in any case (Häfele, et al. 1981) at rates consistent with the natural flows. Nature utilizes a symbiotic relationship between solar energy, hydrogen, oxygen, and carbon. The principal fuel of nature is hydrogen. Hydrogen fuels the sun. The "technology" photosynthesis utilizes the sun's radiated energy to split water into hydrogen and oxygen and, together with the carbon dioxide extracted from the atmosphere, to produce carbohydrates. Then, hydrogen weakly bonded to carbon fuels biological organisms including man (Hoffmann 1981). The human body is made up of some 100 trillion cells, each of which contains tens of thousands of nanobial organisms that use hydrogen to produce nucleic acids and protein (Braun 1990). Finally, hydrogen, oxygen, and carbon are emitted or rejected as a variety of differently composed molecules, with carbon, in particular, recycled as carbon dioxide and methane.

A sustainable energy system mimicking nature's approach to energy, therefore, should also be centred on this relationship between solar energy, hydrogen, oxygen, and carbon. Carbon in the deep future energy system would be recycled over time-spans consistent with the natural carbon cycle. In sustainably cultivated plantations, biomass would become the only carbon source in the system and would also serve the carbon sink. Biomass properly managed, e.g. the rate of timber harvesting and reforestation are in balance, is carbon neutral and would not contribute to an increase in atmospheric CO_2 concentrations. This would be coherent with nature's material fluxes.

Alternatively, solar energy technologies engineered by *homo technicus* to intercept sunlight could provide electric or thermal energy services. The energy of electromagnetic radiation from the sun reaching the earth's surface is in equilibrium with the energy radiated thermally back into space (in the form of infrared radiation). Because most energy services dissipate heat in the form of infrared radiation, this would be coherent with nature's energy fluxes.

The main characteristic of the deep future energy system outlined below is to be inherently non-polluting based on highly efficient energy service technologies and sustainable energy sources. This in effect limits the choice of currencies, giving hydrogen an edge over carbon-containing currencies. The conversion of hydrogen into energy services or electricity produces virtually no pollution; the by-product of electrochemical hydrogen conversion is water. In contrast, hydrogen combustion with air as the oxidant will also produce nitrogen oxide and nitric oxides. Although these pollutants can be effectively controlled by catalytic conversion technology, this represents an end-of-pipe clean-up approach. Likewise, carbon-containing currencies use ambient air as the oxidant and thus generate nitrogen compounds (in addition to carbon dioxide and carbon monoxide plus other emissions). Moreover, the most efficient use of currencies containing non-fossil carbon involves a reforming step to hydrogen at the point of use. In essence, hydrogen is a universal currency. It can be produced from all energy sources, which, although not all would be non polluting, is of importance for the transition phase, and can meet virtually all energy services. Because a significant share of services require electricity, which, in many instances, can be delivered more efficiently without a hydrogen involvement, hydrogen in the deep future energy system would be complemented by a well-established currency – electricity.

Figure 5.3 depicts the sustainable energy system in terms of figure 5.1. This system centres around the twin currencies electricity and hydrogen, both of which do not contain carbon and are compatible with all conceivable future energy service requirements.

Hydrogen and electricity complement each other as central components in the future energy system in the following ways (IPCC 1996b):

1. Hydrogen can be stored in any quantity; electricity cannot (at least from current technology perspectives; this may change drastically with the eventual advent of high-temperature superconductivity).
2. Hydrogen can be a chemical or material feedstock; electricity cannot.
3. Electricity can process, transmit, and store information; hydrogen cannot.
4. Hydrogen and electricity can be readily converted to one another.

These four compatibilities combine to provide excellent synergies between the two currencies. From these synergies it becomes obvious that hydrogen will be a strong candidate currency – in fact probably *the* candidate – that will substitute for oil-based liquid fuels in the

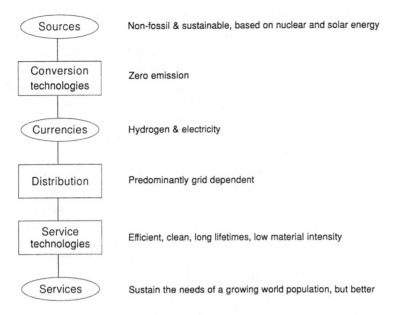

Fig. 5.3 **The deep future energy system**

longer term, while electricity will largely continue to do what it does today (Scott and Häfele 1989).

The outlook regarding the exact twenty-first-century energy sources from which the currencies hydrogen and electricity will be derived is less clear. Although the potential deep future options are known – nuclear power (fission and/or fusion), direct solar radiation (photovoltaics, central thermal solar conversion), and indirect solar energy (hydropower, wind, biomass, etc.), at present no single option is superior on all four compatibility constraints mentioned in the introduction.

The potential for nuclear energy to make a substantial contribution hinges upon the satisfaction of public concerns about operational safety, waste disposal, and proliferation. Without this satisfaction, nuclear power could wither away and play only a transitory role. Moreover, current nuclear fission practice is not necessarily sustainable unless breeding technology is employed. Fusion may become an option by the mid-twenty-first century, but to date has not been shown to be technically feasible – the conditions for a self-sustaining net power production controlled by man have not yet been achieved.

Solar and related renewable technologies are rapidly approaching economic viability in many niche applications, and their future potential is, in principle, enormous. However, uncertainty exists with respect to economic performance, in part related to their low specific-energy densities and intermittent availability, although the utilization of renewable energy sources offers substantial emission benefits compared with the use of fossil sources. One point is likely: eventually, the selection from this source option menu will become a socio-political choice at the regional rather than at the global level.

The lack of certainty or determinism regarding sources, however, is not a vice. Because the shape of future civilization depends on the currencies providing energy services – and not on energy sources *per se* – today's burning issues surrounding energy sources are put into a different time and priority scale. This may appear counter-intuitive given the current socio-political controversy surrounding the present and future use of nuclear power. But the absence of complementary hydrogen end-use technologies would be a much greater barrier to the sustainable energy system than keeping open the question (and the options) as to its eventual sources.

Certainly, if solar and/or nuclear energy are to replace fossil fuels, hydrogen must become their strategic partner. Unless solar and nuclear energy can be effectively stored and transported, they will not be able to displace fossil sources and currencies, especially in transportation. The key to this storage question is hydrogen. The hydrogen–solar/nuclear energy complementarity is illustrated in figure 5.4, the energy service "palette."

The palette is divided into two groups of energy services, one served by chemical fuels and the other served by electricity. Located at its periphery, the palette also contains two groups of energy source options: fossil sources and sustainable energy sources (labelled "new/ old hopes"). Fossil sources have unconstrained access to all services. This is not the case for the new/old hopes sources. Direct solar and most of the indirect solar options operate intermittently and are primarily locked into electricity generation. In addition, their availability profile is often discordant with the daily electricity load. Some may argue that "new/old hopes" sources can provide space heating services, or that biomass can be used as a feedstock for liquid fuel production. This is correct. But the relative importance of space heating is declining, and using biomass as the principal source for fuelling the global transportation service requirements of 10 billion people may be difficult to reconcile with sustainability, and may well

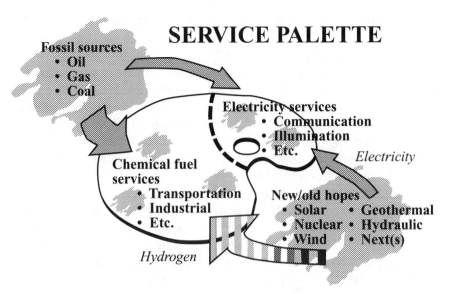

Fig. 5.4   **The energy service palette (Source: Scott 1992)**

be constrained by land availability. However, the utilization of solar and nuclear energies for hydrogen production via electrolysis, thermochemical water splitting, or biomass gasification and photolysis enables these non-fossil sources to supply all energy services, including transportation services.

Efficiency improvements

Improvements in the efficiency of energy service technologies are likely to be needed to counterbalance a potential drawback of the sustainable energy system. Harvesting renewable or nuclear energy sources for hydrogen production inherently shifts inefficiencies to the upstream operation of the energy system. Nuclear technologies utilize either steam or gas cycles for electricity generation and their efficiencies are subject to the limitations of heat engines. Renewable energy sources are dispersed and of low specific-energy density, in terms of joules per square metre, with large conversion capacities necessary to compensate for these low concentration or density levels. With the exception of biomass, the efficiency of renewable technologies is mostly an issue of installed capacity and investment costs and less a question of the actual source-to-currency conversion ratio. Still, efficiencies matter, especially when suitable siting locations, say for solar systems, become a constraint.

Producing carbon-free currencies is less efficient and currently generally more costly than producing carbon-containing ones.[5] However, the efficiency and cost disadvantages would improve substantially if energy service technologies designed to exploit the unique characteristics of hydrogen are used instead of adapting conversion equipment originally designed for hydrocarbon fuels. Electrochemical and catalytic energy conversion have the potential to become the technologies of choice for the production of many energy services, especially in transportation and distributed combined heat and power applications. The most promising electrochemical technology is the fuel cell. Fuel cells convert hydrogen directly into electricity without first burning it, which enables them to realize much higher conversion efficiencies than heat engines. Compared with internal combustion engines, fuel cells are expected to be twice as efficient, thus compensating for the lower hydrogen delivery efficiencies.

Technology change associated with the deep future energy system

Among the most important changes in energy technologies will be the decline of combustion technologies that close their fuel cycle of fossil carbon oxidation through the atmosphere. The remaining combustion processes will operate on either hydrogen, sustainable biomass, or biomass-derived hydrogen-rich fuels. Of course, by the mid-twenty-first century numerous additional environmental technologies will have enriched the menu of technology options. Carbon scrubbing and fossil-sourced hydrogen-rich fuel production may well eke out the fossil era. In any case, technological invention and innovation, in part stimulated by revised energy market prices that reflect their full social costs, will ensure a high degree of technology diversity.

From the perspective of sustainable energy systems and eco-restructuring, the coming of the hydrogen age seems inevitable. However, as the twentieth century draws to a close, the energy system is in the middle of the fossil era and its end is not apparently in sight. The question, therefore, is: When could the hydrogen age come? Are there any indications of the energy system positioning itself to accommodate hydrogen? The following section attempts to shed some light onto these questions.

Transition and the rate of change of the energy system

Elliot Montroll once observed: "Evolution is a sequence of replace-ments." The energy system is no exception. The historical develop-ment of global primary energy production and use has essentially been a sequence of technology replacements. Energy sources and infrastructures (embodied technologies) are intimately interrelated and the degree of use of any energy source is also a mirror of both upstream and downstream technology.

Energy infrastructures have inherently long lifetimes of several decades and more. To obtain a better understanding of the rate at which the energy system can evolve, it is necessary to take a long-term quantitative perspective spanning a century or more both back-ward and forward in time. Figure 5.5 shows the market shares of the world's most significant energy sources, starting in the middle of the nineteenth century. The rippled lines are the actual data; the straight lines are estimated curves based on a logistic substitution model that projects trends of primary energy source shares out to the year 2050.

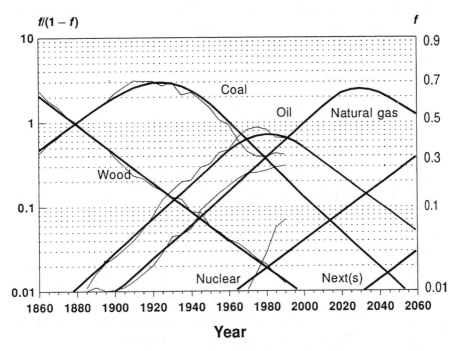

Fig. 5.5 **Global primary energy substitution (Note: f = market share. Source: adapted and updated from Marchetti and Nakicenovic 1979)**

165

On a market share basis, wood, once the dominant primary fuel, was replaced by coal. Then coal was replaced by oil. Today, natural gas is seriously cutting into oil's market leadership, and nuclear power is rising rapidly. These transitions have occurred despite the fact that resources of wood, coal, and oil were and are still plentiful. Today, well over a century after wood lost its pre-eminence, the world's annual biomass production exceeds the needs to fuel the world many-fold (Häfele et al. 1981). Likewise, coal was displaced by oil not because the world was running out of coal – the conventional view is that coal is by far the world's most abundant fossil resource.

Wood was abandoned because the first industrial revolution demanded a fuel with higher energy density and better transport and storage possibilities. Simultaneously, on the supply side, coal-mining and coal-use technology, notably the steam engine, developed to a point at which coal became a readily available energy source.

Similarly, oil displaced coal once a set of new and superior technologies both upstream and downstream were made available. Refined oil products proved superior to coal for powering trains, cars, and aircraft, generating electricity, heating homes and large buildings, etc. Except for aircraft, all these end-use applications can be, and initially were, served by coal. Refined oil products, however, are much better suited for these purposes (energy services), so that societies progressively abandoned coal for oil.

The historical inter-source substitutions were caused by innovation and technical change and not by global resource scarcity. Fossil energy resource availability is unlikely to be the driver for future shifts either; rather, the fact that fossil resources are plentiful and inexpensive (see fig. 5.6) is likely to be a delaying factor in the transition towards sustainable sources.

The cumulative carbon content of identified and inferred conventional oil, natural gas, and coal occurrences has been estimated to exceed 20,000 gigatonnes (Gt) of carbon (IIASA/WEC 1995). The application of a dynamic resource concept that accounts for long-run technical change in the exploration for, and extraction of, fossil sources shows a global fossil availability of some 3,000 Gt of carbon, which can be produced for less than US$30 (1995 prices) per barrel of oil equivalent (boe) (Rogner 1990, 1997; and Nakicenovic et al. 1993). To put this resource volume into perspective: the cumulative use of carbon by mankind to date amounts to some 230 Gt. If 200–300 Gt of carbon emissions give reason for severe concern about

US$(95)/boe

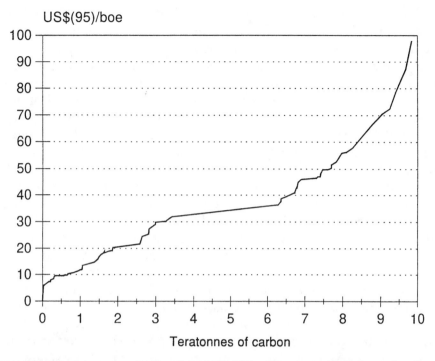

Teratonnes of carbon

Fig. 5.6 **The long-run cost of carbon availability (Note: costs include exploration, development, and extraction expenditures for coal, oil, and natural gas resources – conventional and unconventional, but excluding methane clathrates – and reflect future technology advances. Source: Rogner 1997)**

climate stability, it is obvious that most of the indicated 3,000 Gt of carbon will have to remain untapped in the ground.

Figure 5.5 projects natural gas as the next pre-eminent global energy source. Natural gas resources are plentiful and accessible by all the major economic centres worldwide. Natural gas is an established energy source with basically no public acceptance problem. Because natural gas is by far the cleanest fossil energy source, it is increasingly being touted as the fuel of least environmental resistance (Stern 1990). As regards the build-up of greenhouse gases in the atmosphere, natural gas represents the ideal hedging strategy. It automatically reduces CO_2 emissions (versus other fossil fuels) and thus buys time for sustainable energy sources and technologies to mature (Rogner 1988). The CO_2 benefits of natural gas, however, may not accrue if its enhanced use is accompanied by an increase in methane

(CH$_4$) emissions. Methane, the chief component of natural gas, is itself a greenhouse gas, with a greenhouse forcing potential per molecule up to two orders of magnitude larger than CO$_2$ depending on the time-horizon and the decay response of the underlying carbon model. IPCC reports a 56 times higher warming potential for methane over a 20-year time-horizon and 6.5 times over a period of 500 years (IPCC 1996a). Leakages from extraction, transmission, and distribution systems, as well as from end-use devices, therefore, need to be curbed substantially from present practice in order not to undermine the CO$_2$ gains.[6]

The dynamics of the energy source substitution model suggest that the fossil era will extend far into the twenty-first century – that a deep future hydrogen age will be preceded by a "methane age" (Lee et al. 1988). In fact, natural gas is the ideal bridge towards hydrogen for two reasons. First, a global market share of 50 per cent or more requires natural gas to expand into other than the traditional residential, commercial, and industrial markets. Electricity generation is certainly the market offering the largest opportunity for expansion in the short run. On a global scale, however, the electricity generation market is unlikely to be large enough to lift the gas market share to the level suggested by the substitution model. If gas is to achieve a 50+ per cent market share, natural gas would have to become a major source of transportation fuels. Today, natural gas already contributes to transportation fuel supply in three ways: as a feedstock in oil refining to improve the premium yield of the barrel; as a feedstock for upgrading heavy hydrocarbon sources such as oil sand bitumen; and directly as a vehicle fuel in the form of compressed natural gas (CNG). In absolute terms, however, the present market share in transportation is negligible.

The large-scale use of natural gas as a direct transportation fuel[7] will foster fundamental and far-reaching infrastructure changes that eventually would assist the hydrogen age. The path-breaking function of natural gas is the second reason the methane age is essential to a future hydrogen age. Both natural gas and hydrogen are gaseous currencies at ambient conditions. A natural gas market share of 50 per cent or more would advance gas-handling infrastructures and technologies. Innovative liquefaction technologies and cryogenic storage of liquefied natural gas (LNG) would become commonplace. Moreover, because the methane age may have a life cycle of 40–60 years, societies would have sufficient time to familiarize themselves with gaseous and cryogenic fuels. All these events would ease the large-scale introduction of hydrogen, especially with fuel cells being a key energy service technology. Finally, during the century-long transition phase towards a non-fossil energy system, natural gas is likely to become the predominant source for hydrogen production.

A 40–60-year methane window would also provide sufficient time for non-fossil technologies currently lacking economic feasibility to move down the technology learning curve and become commercially viable. For nuclear power, this time-horizon should suffice for the nuclear industry to develop and demonstrate new, possibly smaller-scale reactor designs incorporating "inherently safe" and "walk-away" features as well as efficient fuel cycles and waste disposal solutions. Also, fusion may become a viable option by the mid-twenty-first century. Other technology developments that enable the continued use of fossil sources even in a future of severely constrained greenhouse gas emissions may have advanced and their environmental implications become better understood. For example, although the technology to capture CO_2 after combustion is available, it is unclear whether the present storage and/or disposal options are environmentally acceptable or the capacities are large enough for long-term CO_2 disposal. Although the storage potential in oceans is estimated to be in excess of 1,200 Gt of carbon, not much is known about potential adverse environmental effects[8] or the actual ocean's CO_2 retention time. Offsetting CO_2 emissions through reforestation and forest management (carbon sequestration) is likely to be one of the least-cost mitigation options. The carbon captured from the atmosphere and fixed during the growth of forest, however, would have to be stored for a long time, and land availability may eventually limit the extent of carbon sequestration.[9]

De-materialization and decarbonization

De-materialization is a major cornerstone of the global economic eco-restructuring process. Within the energy system, decarbonization can be viewed as analogous to de-materialization. De-materialization implies a shift in emphasis from quantity to quality, from inefficiency to efficiency. Decarbonization of the energy system implies a shift in initiatives from energy supply to quality energy services.

Despite the exponential growth of energy-related carbon dioxide emissions since the early days of the industrial revolution, the energy system, in terms of carbon per unit of primary energy use, has been decarbonized at an average rate of 0.2 per cent per year (see fig. 5.7).

169

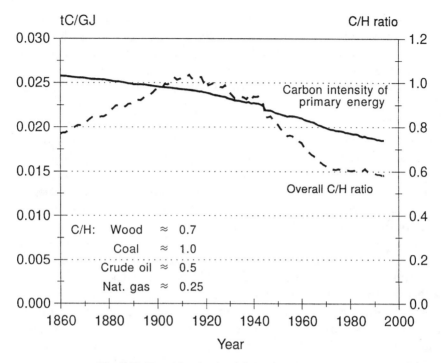

Fig. 5.7 **Decarbonization of the energy system**

The sequence of historical energy source substitutions shown in figure 5.5 can be viewed as an intermolecular substitution of hydrogen and carbon molecules. Figure 5.7 shows the historical variation of the average carbon-to-hydrogen ratio (C/H ratio) of the global primary energy mix. The C/H ratio declined steadily between 1920 and 1975, a trend that slowed down after the mid-1970s as a result of energy policy in many OECD countries. The oil price shocks of the 1970s and early 1980s were perceived as signs of oil and natural gas resource depletion. As a consequence, energy policy banned oil and natural gas from electricity generation and endorsed the use of coal as a secure and inexpensive under-boiler fuel in industry and electricity generation.

Decarbonization of the energy system is likely to continue as natural gas, chiefly methane (CH_4), nuclear, and renewable energy sources take on a growing share in global energy supplies. In a methane age, with global primary energy supply dominated by natural gas, the C/H ratio would approach 0.25. Yet, given an expected world population of 10 billion people by 2050 and a corresponding increase in energy service demand, a C/H ratio of 0.25 may well be insufficient for the long-term target of stabilizing atmospheric greenhouse gas concentrations. Any reduction in carbon intensity well beyond a value of 0.25 requires non-fossil energy sources – nuclear power (fission and/or fusion), direct solar radiation (photovoltaics, central thermal solar conversion), and indirect solar energy (hydropower, wind, biomass, etc.).

North–South disparity and sustainable energy systems

The globalization of environmental deterioration is the direct consequence of population growth and industrialization. In 1990, some 23 per cent of the world population living in industrialized countries were responsible for some 80 per cent of GHG emissions. Future demographic developments will likely push global population close to 10 billion people by the year 2050. Clearly, with 96 per cent of the incremental population growth taking place in the developing countries, the historical link between population, industrialization, and environmental degradation must be decoupled. Yet, present per capita income and per capita energy use in the developing world are about one-tenth of the respective values for the OECD. These disparities between the "haves" and "have-nots" are highlighted in figure 5.8. In the light of these disparities, we must ask how the deep future energy system fits the realities of the developing countries. No doubt, at face value the sheer capital intensiveness of the sustainable energy system, in addition to the capital resources needed for the industrialization process, will far exceed their economic capability.

In the past, environmental degradation has been a steady companion of industrialization and urbanization. At a certain level of prosperity and income, however, societies appear to express a preference for environmental amenities. This preference manifests itself as an internalization of external costs. Clean air acts, mandatory zero-emission vehicles, or legislated flue gas desulphurization of coal-fired power stations are representative historical examples of the emergence of environmental awareness in the developed world. To a certain extent the industrialized societies have begun to pay a small part of the interest on the mortgaged environment used to establish their wealth. Most of the interest, not to mention the principal, is still owed.

The industrialized world may well have harvested the benefits of the environment to the point of rapidly decreasing returns. It would

171

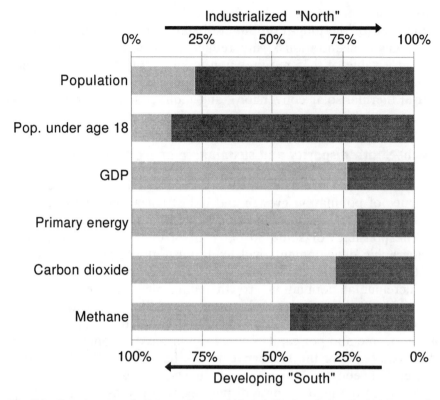

Fig. 5.8 **Development indicators for the industrialized and developing economies (Note: the CO₂ and CH₄ data include emissions related to the production and use of commercial energy only. Source: adapted from Grübler and Nakicenovic 1992)**

add insult to injury for the rich North to withdraw to a position where the developing countries are expected to forgo the benefits of industrialization so that the North can live an enjoyable life in a clean world that the South cannot afford. For sure the South will not consider the preservation of the North's wealth at the expense of their own development as equitable burden sharing.

Still, there is growing concern about a potential conflict between economic advance in the developing countries and the protection of the environment. Addressing this concern requires us to ask the fundamental question: What would be the environmental impact of no economic advance?

The industrialized and developing countries are faced with the following dilemma. Successful business-as-usual industrialization will take its toll on the environment. Compounded by the anticipated population growth, even small per capita income improvements may soon put the South on a par with the North, in terms of GHG emissions. However, lack of economic growth and development translate into increased poverty and population growth, which in turn lead to accelerated environmental deterioration through deforestation, soil erosion, and groundwater degradation. Moreover, agriculture-based economies may be more vulnerable to climatic hazards than industrialized economies where agriculture accounts for less than 3 per cent of gross domestic product (GDP) and the bulk of production is little affected by climate conditions.

Is a clean environment a matter of affordability? The answer is yes. Thus, economic development of the South is a necessary prerequisite for global environmental stability. Sustainable energy system development in the developing countries, therefore, is likely to depend on international action such as science and technology transfer. The costs of this transfer should, to the extent it is benefiting the protection of the atmosphere, be borne by the North. It can be said that the North's environment mortgage has matured and the principal including the accrued interest is now due for redemption.

Ideally, this repayment would be financed from the revenue generated by the monetary incentives, green taxes, or other mechanisms deemed suitable for correcting the present market imperfection of free use of the environment. Consequently, the concept of an internalization of external costs that is neutral in terms of tax revenue would have to be abandoned in favour of a capital transfer to the developing countries.

Economic potency demands that the North initiate the transition to the deep future energy system. From the perspective of system evolution, the initial step is under way already – the increasing role of natural gas in meeting global energy service requirements. The redemption of the North's environment mortgage will assist the South in the development of sustainable energy systems. In addition, the combating of global environment degradation may lead to the recognition that a dollar spent in the South may generate higher marginal environmental returns than one spent in the North.[10]

Concluding remarks

Planning for the future is a routine activity in the energy industry. Given present blueprint-to-operation lead-times for new-capacity additions of a decade and more, the inherent longevity of energy infrastructures, and the large up-front capital requirements, the temporal scope of the energy sector planning process is among the longest in private sector business planning.

At the level of government policy, planning has focused on national energy resource management, energy supply security, geopolitics, and issues of national and regional monopoly control. Because of the huge capital requirements of many energy projects, which often exceed private sector financial capabilities, governments have also been involved in energy project financing through subsidies, loans, or loan guarantees.

Yet, on the whole, it is fair to say that there has been a lot of planning but no plan. Clearly, there was never a private or public sector master plan to become reliant on fossil energy sources. This reliance is the result of an evolutionary optimization process within the energy system driven by the human needs for energy services. It has so happened that fossil-sourced carbon fuels have been best suited to meet past and present service demand. Moreover, fossil resources are plentiful and extraction costs are low. The summation of millions of individual choices has been a vote in favour of fossil energy.

Environmental imperatives are about to change the energy industry planning process fundamentally. Utility regulators increasingly enact system-oriented planning approaches. Public policies for the protection of the environment are spreading fast. Yet present public policy has been primarily of the command and control type, with a focus on improving specific local environmental conditions such as urban smog or acid deposition. To that extent, it has been adaptive.

Adaptive policy- and decision-making are inadequate tools for combating the potential threat of global climatic change. Given the long residence times of most GHGs in the atmosphere, and the fact that the energy system does not lend itself to quick fixes, policy must become anticipatory and deal with uncertainty.

Anticipatory policy needs a target, a plan, and contingencies. Regarding the policy response to the threat of climatic change, the target is a sustainable energy system, the plan is the accelerated transition to low-carbon energy sources, i.e. natural gas, and the contingencies centre around technology change and innovation.

The target – an energy system designed around the currencies hydrogen and electricity – is consistent with the target of sustainability and is open to innovation and technical change. In particular, such a target system does not require an early decision on the nature of its eventual no-carbon sources. What is important, however, is the build-up of an adequate and highly efficient energy service supply infrastructure suitable for the effective use of hydrogen-rich fuels and ultimately hydrogen.

It is key to recognize that the hydrogen network is likely to grow out of today's natural gas network, just as the ancestors of today's natural gas network originally moved town gas. In future, this includes not only the pipeline but also the cryofuel/LNG infrastructure. As much as gaseous hydrogen can use the natural gas transport and distribution grid, liquid hydrogen can piggyback on the LNG experience and infrastructure. Similar to the transition from town gas to natural gas, adjustments to the infrastructure will become necessary that account for the unique properties and safety requirements of hydrogen. The important point is, however, that this adjustment occurs at a mature point of the infrastructure's learning curve, leading to a transition that is technologically straightforward and socio-politically acceptable.

The plan – a larger reliance on natural gas – is therefore consistent with the target of sustainability. Indeed, the greater the dominance of natural gas in the evolving energy system – a Methane Age – the easier will be the eventual transition to hydrogen. The transition towards a Hydrogen Age is unlikely to be established much before the end of the twenty-first century and the actual time-frame will depend on many factors, particularly on the probability of occurrence of climate instability. More important is that natural gas paves the way towards hydrogen, potentially minimizing blunders and thus providing a least-regret cost strategy.

The contingency – that the "target" energy system cannot be cast in stone – is essential in a world of continuous technical change. Over a period of 50 years and more, technology forecasting based on current knowledge will certainly fail to anticipate the actual inventions and the rate of innovation. The target energy system and the plan, therefore, must incorporate least-regret cost strategies where future innovation enhances the system's performance rather than making previous infrastructure investment obsolete. The most important contingencies relate to the commercialization and market introduction of renewable technologies, the eventual resolution of the nuclear controversy, and the balance between eco-restructuring of the economic production consumption process, in general, and the energy system, in particular.

Even if the greenhouse effect becomes a non-issue, we end up with an energy system that is better in all respects: less polluting on all counts, more efficient, more resilient to surprise, and closer to sustainability. In summary, many of the prudent things to do about the greenhouse effect may well turn out prudent things to do anyway.

Notes

1. Obviously, the service "commuting to work" also requires a road infrastructure. Such infrastructures, however, although representing embodied technology, know-how, materials, and energy services, are only indirectly considered part of the energy system.
2. Exergy defines the maximum amount of work theoretically obtainable from a system as it interacts to equilibrium with the environment. While the energy of 11 litres of water at 80°C and 1 kWh of electricity is approximately the same, it should be obvious that 1 kWh of electricity enables the production of more useful work than the 11 litres of hot water. Exergy, therefore, is a quality measure for different types and forms of energy. Moreover, unlike energy, exergy is not conserved and the initial exergy potential is destroyed by the irreversibilities present in any conversion process. Contrary to energy efficiencies, the use of exergy efficiency relates actual efficiencies to the ideal maximum. Although this maximum can never be reached, exergy efficiencies provide a means to identify those areas with the largest improvement potentials or applications where there is a mismatch between the energy service and the energy supplied to provide that service.
3. Useful exergy is defined as the exergy supplied by the service conversion technology (e.g. the mechanical energy at the wheel of an automobile engine, the heat supply to a room by a radiator, or the luminosity of a light bulb), while the corresponding services could be measured in person-kilometres travelled, the desired temperature in a room, or adequate illumination for reading.
4. Generating efficiencies are based on the current OECD production mix, which is dominated by thermal power plants.
5. The overall efficiency from crude oil production to the supply of gasoline to an internal combustion engine of a vehicle is, on average, 80 per cent. The overall efficiency of hydrogen produced for the same vehicle, while depending on the primary energy source and subsequent conversion steps, is certainly lower. For example, one possible source-to-currency onboard pathway commences with nuclear-generated electricity, which is used to split water electrolytically into hydrogen and oxygen. The hydrogen then is liquefied (using nuclear electricity) and distributed to the filling station, stored, and dispensed to the cryogenic tank of the vehicle. Based on future technologies, the overall efficiency is expected to range between 20 and 25 per cent. If photovoltaic technology replaces nuclear electricity in this chain at an assumed conversion efficiency of 15 per cent, the overall efficiency of this pathway ranges between 6 and 9 per cent. If the solar radiation is considered free, then the pathway efficiency becomes some 50 per cent. Another pathway could utilize biomass for methanol production. Distribution and dispensing could use the present oil product infrastructures. Onboard the vehicle, the methanol would be re-formed on demand to generate hydrogen. The estimated efficiency is 45–55 per cent.
6. The technologies for effective leakage control exist but are often too capital intensive to be considered economical under present market conditions.
7. There are four routes for a substantial expansion of the role of natural gas in transportation. Two routes use natural gas directly as onboard fuels, i.e. CNG or LNG (liquefied natural gas). The other two routes, methanol and hydrogen, use natural gas indirectly. Although methanol has been promoted as a clean substitute for gasoline, it is unlikely that it will have a major impact on the transportation fuel market. Methanol appears attractive because,

unlike the other natural gas options, it is a liquid at ambient conditions and thus can use the existing gasoline distribution and storage infrastructure. Still, the production and use of methanol generates considerable CO_2 emissions. Used in internal combustion engines, the greenhouse gas emissions from methanol are comparable to those from oil products, whereas a significant reduction could be achieved after re-formation and use in fuel cells. Large-scale use of fossil-derived methanol is neither compatible with nor in support of objectives such as eco-restructuring, de-materialization, or carbon-free energy service production. Fossil-sourced methanol is, therefore, at best an incremental transition solution. However, the outlook for methanol would change markedly if it were biomass sourced.

8. Storage in depleted natural gas and oil fields is another option; the storage capacities, however, are considerably smaller than ocean disposal and are unlikely to offer permanent solutions to CO_2 emissions from the long-term use of fossil energy sources.

9. An alternative to growing forests for carbon fixation from fossil fuels, however, is to grow biomass sustainably as an energy substitute for fossil fuels.

10. The United Nations Framework Convention on Climate Change (UNFCCC) addresses the issue of technology and capital transfer from the North to the South under the label Activities Implemented Jointly (AIJ). At the First Conference of the Parties held in Berlin in the spring of 1995, it was decided that a pilot phase should be established for AIJ projects. However, no credits to ANNEX I will occur as a result of GHG emissions reduced or sequestered from activities implemented jointly (UNFCCC 1995).

References

Ausubel, J. H. (1992) Industrial ecology: Reflections on a colloquium. *Proc. Natl. Acad. Sci. USA* **89**, 879–884.

Ayres, R. U. (1988) *Energy Inefficiency in the US Economy: A New Case for Conservation*. Pittsburgh: Carnegie-Mellon University.

Braun, H. (1990) *The Phoenix Project: An Energy Transition to Renewable Resources*. Salt Lake City, UT: Publishers Press.

Gilli, P.-V., N. Nakicenovic, and R. Kurz (1995) First- and second-law efficiencies of the global and regional energy systems. WEC 16th Congress, 8–13 October 1995, Tokyo, Japan.

Gilli, P. V., N. Nakicenovic, A. Grübler, and F. L. Bodda (1990) *Technischer Fortschritt, Strukturwandel und Effizienz der Energieanwendung – Trends weltweit und in Österreich*. Band 6, Schriftenreihe der Forschungsinitiative des Verbundkonzerns, Vienna, Austria.

Grübler, A. and N. Nakicenovic (1992) *International Burden Sharing in Greenhouse Gas Reduction*. Environment Working Paper No. 55. Washington D.C.: World Bank Environment Department.

Häfele, W. et al. (1981) Renewable energy resources. In: *Energy in a Finite World – A Global Systems Analysis*, chapter 6. Cambridge, MA: Ballinger.

Hoffmann, P. (1981) *The Forever Fuel: The Story of Hydrogen*. Boulder, CO: Westview Press.

IIASA/WEC (International Institute for Applied Systems Analysis and World Energy Council) (1995) *Global Energy Perspectives to 2050 and Beyond*. London: WEC.

IPCC (Intergovernmental Panel on Climate Change) (1990) *Climate Change, The IPCC Scientific Assessment*, ed. J. T. Houghton, G. J. Jenkins, and J. J. Ephraums. Cambridge: Cambridge University Press.

—— (1992) *Climate Change 1992: The Supplementary Report to the IPCC Scientific Assessment*, ed. J. T. Houghton, B. A. Callander, and S. K. Varney. Cambridge: Cambridge University Press.

—— (1996a) *Climate Change 1995: The Science of Climate Change. Contribution of Working Group I to the Second Assessment Report of the Intergovernmental Panel on Climate Change*, ed. J. T. Houghton, L. G. Meira Filho, B. A. Callander, N. Harris, A. Kattenberg, and K. Maskell. Cambridge and New York: Cambridge University Press.

—— (1996b) *Climate Change 1995: Impacts, Adaptations and Mitigation of Climate Change: Scientific-Technical Analyses. Contribution of Working Group II to the Second Assessment Report of the Intergovernmental Panel on Climate Change*, ed. R. T. Watson, M. C. Zinyowera, and R. H. Moss. Cambridge and New York: Cambridge University Press.

Lee, T. H., H. R. Linden, D. A. Dreyfus, and T. Vasko (1988). *The Methane Age*. The GeoJournal Library. Dordrecht: Kluwer Academic Publishers.

Marchetti C. and N. Nakicenovic (1979) *The Dynamics of Energy Systems and the Logistic Substitution Model*. RR-79-13. Laxenburg, Austria: International Institute for Applied Systems Analysis (IIASA).

Nakicenovic, N., A. Grübler, A. Inaba, S. Messner, S. Nilson, Y. Nishimura, H.-H. Rogner, A. Schäfer, L. Schrattenholzer, M. Strubegger, J. Swisher, D. Victor, and D. Wilson (1993) Long-term strategies for mitigating global warming. *Energy* **18**(5), Special Issue.

Özdocan, S. and M. Arikol (1995) Energy and exergy analysis of selected Turkish industries. *Energy* **18**(1): 73–80.

Rogner, H.-H. (1988) Technology and the prospects for natural gas. *Energy Policy*, February: 9–26.

—— (1990) Analyse der Förderpotentiale und langfristigen Verfügbarkeit von Kohle, Erdgas und Erdöl. In: Enquete-Kommission Protection of the Atmosphere of the German Parliament, *Energie und Klima, Band 4: Fossile Energieträger*, pp. 7–86. Bonn: Economica Verlag.

—— (1997) An assessment of world hydro carbon resources. *Annu. Rev. Energy Environ.* **22**: 217–262.

Rogner, H.-H. and F. E. K. Britton (1991) Energy, growth and the environment: Towards a framework for an energy strategy. Think-piece submitted to the Directorate General for Energy (DG XVII), Commission of the European Communities, Brussels, December.

—— (1992) Energy, growth and the environment. In: E. U. von Weizsäcker and R. Bleischwitz (eds.), *Klima und Strukturwandel*, pp. 227–244. Bonn: Economica Verlag.

Rosen, M. A. (1992) Evaluation of energy utilization efficiency in Canada. *Energy* **17**: 339–350.

Schaeffer, R. and R. M. Wirtshafter (1992) An exergy analysis of the Brazilian economy: From energy products to final energy use. *Energy* **17**: 841–855.

Scott, D. S. (1992) *Hydrogen in the Evolving Energy System*. TR92-102. Institute for Integrated Energy Systems (IESVic), University of Victoria, B.C.

Scott, D. S. and W. Häfele (1989) The coming hydrogen age: Preventing world climatic disruption. Proceedings 14th Congress World Energy Conference, Montreal, September 1989. Feature Paper, Section 2.3.3, pp. 1–23.

Stern, J. P. (1990) *European Gas Markets: Challenge and Opportunity in the 1990s.* London: Royal Institute of International Affairs.

UNFCCC (United Nations Framework Convention on Climate Change) (1995) *Conclusions of Outstanding Issues and Adoption of Decisions. Conference of the Parties, Berlin, March 28–April 7, 1995.* FCCC/CP/1995/l.14.

Wall, G. (1990) Exergy conversion in the Japanese society. *Energy* **15**: 435–444.

Wall, G., E. Scuibba, and V. Naso (1994) Exergy use in the Italian society. *Energy* **19**: 1267–1274.

6

Fuel decarbonization for fuel cell applications and sequestration of the separated CO$_2$

Robert H. Williams

The challenge of stabilizing the atmosphere

Since the pre-industrial era, the concentration of CO$_2$ in the atmosphere has increased from 280 parts per million (ppm) to 350 ppm, mainly as a result of the burning of fossil fuels. The consequences of the ongoing build-up are troubling though uncertain (IPCC 1990; Manabe and Stouffer 1993, 1994). Stabilizing the atmosphere at less than a doubling of the atmospheric concentration of CO$_2$ would require radical change in global energy technology. According to the Intergovernmental Panel on Climate Change (IPCC), stabilizing the atmospheric concentration of CO$_2$ at 450 ppm would require that cumulative emissions over the period 1990–2100 be no more than 630–650 GtC, corresponding to an average emission rate of 5.7–5.9 GtC/year (IPCC 1996). For comparison the mean estimate of actual emissions in 1990 is 7.4 GtC (of which 6.0 GtC was due to fossil fuel burning). Moreover, IS92a, the reference scenario for global energy generated by the IPCC, involves emissions increasing to 20 GtC/year by 2100, with cumulative emissions amounting to 1,500 GtC over 1990–2100 (IPCC 1994).

Recent advances relating to the prospects for renewable electric

180

power-generating technologies – especially wind, photovoltaic, solar thermal–electric, and biomass power technologies – have led various groups to be optimistic about the prospects for curbing emissions from the electric power sector over a period of many decades (Johansson et al. 1993; WEC 1994; Anderson and Ahmed 1995).

Although this new outlook for renewable electric technologies is auspicious, successful development of a wide range of renewable electric technologies by itself would not make it possible to stabilize the atmosphere at near current levels, because most CO_2 emissions are from non-electric sources. In 1990, the electricity sector accounted for 36 per cent of global primary commercial energy use but only 29 per cent of global CO_2 emissions from fossil fuels; in the IS92a scenario, it is projected that the electricity sector in 2100 will account for 44 per cent of primary energy use but just 25 per cent of total CO_2 emissions from fossil fuel use (despite a 6.3-fold increase in electricity demand over the period 1990–2100, compared with a more modest 4.2-fold increase in total primary energy use in this period), because of projected growing contributions to power generation from renewable and nuclear power sources (IPCC 1992).[1]

The major greenhouse challenge will be to avoid enormous increases in CO_2 emissions arising from the production of synthetic fuels from coal.[2] In the IS92a scenario, synthetic fluids account for 75 per cent of all liquid and gaseous fuels used in 2100, and the amount of coal used for synthetic liquid and gaseous fuels production then is 4.2 times the total amount of coal use in 1990.

Synthetic fuels can be produced from non-fossil fuel sources. The prospect that low-cost photovoltaic (PV) power systems could become available (circa 2010–2020) with amorphous silicon and/or other thin-film PV technologies led in the late 1980s to a detailed technical/economic analysis painting a picture of a world energy economy in which PV technology would be widely used not only to provide electricity that is used directly but also to provide hydrogen derived electrolytically from this electricity, for transport and various stationary markets (Ogden and Williams 1989). Although the outlook for low-cost PV technology based on thin-film devices is as good today as it was at the time of the Ogden and Williams study (Carlson and Wagner 1993; Zweibel and Barnett 1993), it is now known that the production of hydrogen from biomass via thermochemical gasification would be a much less costly route for producing hydrogen from a renewable energy source than hydrogen derived electroly-tically from any source[3] other than off-peak power[4] – even if cost goals for thin-film PV technology are fully realized; moreover, the prospects are good that this biomass-derived hydrogen would be no more costly than hydrogen derived from coal via thermochemical gasification in many instances (Williams et al. 1995a,b).

The growing of biomass for use with modern energy conversion technologies, either in large plantations or on many small energy farms (Larson et al. 1994), has been identified as an attractive climate-friendly energy strategy that simultaneously could provide an energy base for rural industrialization and employment generation in the developing world and make it possible to phase out agricultural subsidies in the industrialized world (Williams 1994a). Although it is inherently easier to grow biomass for energy in environmentally acceptable ways than is the case for food production (Larson et al. 1995), various groups are sceptical that biomass can be produced for energy at large scales in environmentally acceptable ways (WEC 1994; Flavin and Lenssen 1994).

This paper explores a strategy for decarbonizing fuels (both fossil and biomass) that would make it possible to achieve deep reductions in CO_2 emissions, prospectively at a relatively low incremental cost for energy services, while reducing the amount of land resources needed for making energy from biomass and avoiding the large cost penalties associated with a possible premature commitment to solar electrolytic hydrogen in the quest for an energy future compatible with sustainable development goals.

Flue gas decarbonization vs. fuel gas decarbonization

A technically feasible but costly option for achieving deep reductions in greenhouse gas emissions is to extract the CO_2 from flue gases of large fossil fuel combustors (e.g. at fossil fuel power plants) and to isolate the CO_2 so recovered from the atmosphere (Blok et al. 1989). This "flue gas decarbonization" strategy is costly largely because of the expenses associated with separation of the CO_2 from flue gases (in which the concentration of CO_2 is only 8–15 per cent); once the CO_2 is separated out, the incremental cost of isolating the re-covered CO_2 from the atmosphere can often be relatively modest (van Engelenburg and Blok 1993; Hendriks 1994).

A much more promising approach involves fuel decarbonization:

the production of hydrogen or a hydrogen-rich fuel from a carbon-rich fuel, in the process of which a stream of essentially pure CO_2 is separated as a by-product at low incremental cost – a process that might more appropriately be labelled "fuel gas decarbonization" (see Appendix A). Pioneering work on fuel gas decarbonization has been carried out at the University of Utrecht (Blok et al. 1989; Hendriks 1994) and at Shell in the Hague (van der Burgt et al. 1992) in conjunction with the production of electricity from coal via integrated gasification/combined cycle power plants. Although the cost penalty for fuel decarbonization and sequestration of the separated CO_2 with this approach is far less than that for various flue gas decarbonization schemes, the electricity produced this way would nevertheless be about 30 per cent more costly than with a conventional coal integrated gasifier/combined cycle power plant (Hendriks 1994), simply because there are no direct economic benefits (only environmental benefits) arising from fuel gas decarbonization.

Because the production of hydrogen is inherently costly, it is desirable to use it in conversion equipment where it is worth more than conventional fluid fuels – especially because there is little prospect that the prices of conventional hydrocarbon fuels will rise high enough in the foreseeable future to the point where hydrogen will be able to compete on a $-per-GJ-equivalent basis. The true value of hydrogen should be determined not by a comparison of fuel costs but by a comparison of the costs of providing an energy service such as the cost per vehicle km of travel.

The use of hydrogen in low-temperature fuel cells for transport and distributed combined heat and power applications could provide the needed high value. Fuel cells offer high thermodynamic efficiency and zero or near-zero local pollutant emissions without the need for pollution control equipment. Moreover, for combined heat and power applications, the absence of scale economies for production units, the lack of need for operating personnel, low maintenance requirements, and low noise levels make it possible to site low-temperature fuel cells near users where the produced energy is more valuable than at centralized facilities.

Until recently it has not been practical to take advantage of these attributes. The only commercial fuel cell is the phosphoric acid fuel cell. Its power density is too low for it to be considered for automotive applications, and its prospective costs in mass production are not especially low. However, recent advances relating to the proton-exchange-membrane (PEM) fuel cell indicate a hopeful future for this technology for both distributed combined heat and power (Little 1995; Dunnison and Wilson 1994) and transport (Williams 1993, 1994b; Mark et al. 1994) applications.[5] When mass produced for transport applications, its costs could be low, approaching the costs of internal combustion engines.[6]

Low-temperature PEM fuel cells can very efficiently utilize hydrogen or methanol that is re-formed with steam to produce a gaseous H_2/CO_2 mixture onsite or, in transport applications, onboard the vehicle.[7] Such fuels have good prospects for becoming major energy carriers in the "post-combustion" era, when electrochemically based fuel cells will have become well established in the energy economy. The least costly ways of producing these energy carriers are from chemical fuel feedstocks – initially natural gas and later coal and biomass (Williams et al. 1995a,b).

Whereas the alchemists failed in their attempts to transmute base metals into gold, the technology for making hydrogen from carbon is well established. Specifically, a carbon-rich fuel feedstock can be processed to produce hydrogen or methanol (a hydrogen carrier) by first converting the feedstock into "syngas" (a mixture of CO and H_2) via steam re-forming (in the case of natural gas) or via thermochemical gasification (in the case of coal or biomass) and then shifting the energy contained in the CO to H_2 by reacting the CO with steam – a process requiring very little net energy input (see Appendix A). In the final stages of the manufacturing process, CO_2 is separated from the fuel product (e.g. using pressure swing adsorption [PSA] in the case of hydrogen production or Selexol in the case of methanol production) in a virtually pure stream that is available as a by-product at low incremental cost (see table 6.1).[8]

If there were no greenhouse problem, this stream of pure CO_2 would be vented to the atmosphere. In a greenhouse-constrained world, consideration might be given to isolating this CO_2 from the atmosphere because of the large potential and relatively low costs involved. If this stream of separated CO_2 could be stored in isolation from the atmosphere, CO_2 emissions would be sharply reduced.

Lifecycle CO_2 emissions – without and with CO_2 sequestration

Without sequestration of the separated CO_2 there would be no significant reduction in lifecycle CO_2 emissions per GJ of fuel provided, in shifting from reformulated gasoline to methanol or hydrogen derived from natural gas; moreover, lifecycle emissions would roughly double in shifting from reformulated gasoline to methanol or hydrogen derived from coal (see table 6.1). The only options based on the thermochemical conversion of fuels that offer significant greenhouse benefits without sequestration of the separated CO_2 are methanol and hydrogen derived from biomass that is grown on a sustainable basis; in these instances lifecycle emissions are just 5 and 10 per cent of those for reformulated gasoline (see table 6.1).

With sequestering, the balances are sharply changed. Lifecycle emissions for methanol produced from coal would be no more than for gasoline or for methanol produced from natural gas, while lifecycle emissions for hydrogen produced from either natural gas or coal with sequestering would be only about half of the emissions from gasoline (see table 6.1).[9]

In the case of biomass grown on a sustainable basis, net lifecycle emissions with sequestering would be strongly negative (because the carbon in the plant matter was originally extracted from the atmosphere in photosynthesis) and, absolutely, more than twice as large for hydrogen production[10] as for methanol production (see table 6.1). This characteristic of systems that involve the production of hydrogen-rich fuels from biomass with sequestering of the separated CO_2 makes it possible to achieve deep net reductions in global greenhouse gas emissions even if some countries are unable to achieve deep reductions or choose to ignore the greenhouse problem (see, for example, Appendix B).

If the end-use technology is taken into account, the emissions reduction potential with sequestration can be even more dramatic. Consider lifecycle emissions, measured in gr C per km of vehicular travel, for fuels used in fuel cell vehicles (FCVs) compared with emissions for gasoline internal combustion engine vehicles (ICEVs). Operated on gasoline, methanol, and compressed hydrogen, FCVs are expected to be, respectively, 1.8, 2.4, and 2.8 times as energy efficient as comparable gasoline ICEVs (see table 6.2). As a result, lifecycle emissions per km of travel for FCVs operated on methanol derived from coal with CO_2 sequestering are only two-fifths as large as for gasoline ICEVs. For FCVs operated on hydrogen derived from natural gas or coal with CO_2 sequestering, emissions per km are less than one-fifth of those for gasoline ICEVs and one-third of those for gasoline FCVs (see table 6.2).

Table 6.1 **CO₂ emissions characteristics of alternative transport fuel options (kg C/GJ of transport fuel produced)**

Fuel option	Lifecycle CO$_2$ generation rate[a]	Photosynthetic offset[b]	Potential CO$_2$ sequestration rate[c]	Net lifecycle emissions with photosynthetic offset and/or CO$_2$ sequestration
Reformulated gasoline	22.6	–	–	22.6
MeOH from natural gas	23.0	–	–[d]	23.0
H$_2$ from natural gas w/o CO$_2$ sequestering	21.8	–	–10.7	21.8
H$_2$ from natural gas w/CO$_2$ sequestering	21.8	–	–10.7	11.1
MeOH from coal w/o CO$_2$ sequestering	40.8	–	–18.6	40.8
MeOH from coal w/CO$_2$ sequestering	40.8	–	–18.6	22.3
H$_2$ from coal w/o CO$_2$ sequestering	41.2	–	–29.8	41.2
H$_2$ from coal w/CO$_2$ sequestering	41.2	–	–29.8	11.4
MeOH from biomass w/o CO$_2$ sequestering	42.8	–40.5	–11.1	2.3
MeOH from biomass w/CO$_2$ sequestering	42.8	–40.5	–11.1	–8.8
H$_2$ from biomass w/o CO$_2$ sequestering	38.9	–33.5	–23.8	5.4
H$_2$ from biomass w/CO$_2$ sequestering	38.9	–33.5	–23.8	–18.4

a. Williams et al. (1995a,b) provide estimates of emissions of CO₂ that occur throughout the entire cycle of fuel production, fuel transport, additional processing (if any), and final use for the primary energy source/energy carrier combinations shown here, in gr C per km, for internal combustion engine vehicle and fuel cell vehicle applications. Lifecycle emissions per km of travel are converted here to emissions per GJ of energy carrier consumed by taking into account the fuel economy of the vehicle (see note b to table 6.2).

b. This is the CO₂ extracted from the atmosphere in growing biomass. It is not quite as large as the lifecycle emissions associated with the production of H₂ or MeOH from biomass, because of the various fossil fuel inputs involved in biomass production – e.g. for cultivation, harvesting, and hauling equipment, and for fertilizers and herbicides.

c. This is the C in the pure CO₂ stream produced at the fuel production facility as a "free" by-product of the production of H₂ or MeOH (from Katofsky 1993).

d. There is no CO₂ recovery at plants producing methanol from natural gas, because fuel processing does not involve the water–gas shift reaction (see Appendix A); the H/C ratio needed for methanol is the same as that for methane, the principal constituent of natural gas.

Table 6.2 **Net lifecycle CO_2 emissions with photosynthetic offsets and/or CO_2 sequestration for alternative transport fuel options**

Fuel option	Emissions per unit of transport fuel provided[a] (kg C/GJ)	Emissions per unit of transport service provided[b] (gr C/km of car driving)	
		ICEV	FCV
Reformulated gasoline	22.6	71.6	38.7
MeOH from natural gas	23.0	64.9	30.7
H_2 from natural gas w/o CO_2 sequestering	21.8	59.9	25.0
H_2 from natural gas w/CO_2 sequestering	11.1	30.5	12.7
MeOH from coal w/o CO_2 sequestering	40.8	115.1	54.5
MeOH from coal w/CO_2 sequestering	22.3	62.9	29.8
H_2 from coal w/o CO_2 sequestering	41.2	113.0	47.2
H_2 from coal w/CO_2 sequestering	11.4	31.3	13.1
MeOH from biomass w/o CO_2 sequestering	2.3	6.6	3.1
MeOH from biomass w/CO_2 sequestering	−8.8	−25.3	−11.9
H_2 from biomass w/o CO_2 sequestering	5.4	14.7	6.1
H_2 from biomass w/CO_2 sequestering	−18.4	−50.1	−20.7

a. From table 6.1 (right-most column).

b. Net lifecycle emissions E_{km} (in gr C per km of driving) are obtained from net lifecycle emissions E_{GJ} (kg C per GJ) of the energy carrier via

$$E_{km} = (1000 \text{ gr/kg})*(0.0348 \text{ GJ/litre})*E_{GJ}/FE,$$

where *FE* is the fuel economy of the vehicle, in km/litre of gasoline equivalent. (Gasoline has a higher heating value (HHV) of 0.0348 GJ/litre.) Emissions E_{km} are given both for internal combustion engine vehicles (ICEVs) and for fuel cell vehicles (FCVs). For ICEVs, the gasoline-equivalent fuel economies are assumed to be: for gasoline, 11.0 km/litre (25.8 mpg); for MeOH, 12.4 km/litre (29.1 mpg); and for H_2, 12.7 km/litre (29.9 mpg). For FCVs, the gasoline-equivalent fuel economies are assumed to be: for gasoline, 20.4 km/litre (47.7 mpg), based on the use of onboard partial oxidation; for MeOH, 26.1 km/litre (61.5 mpg), based on the use of an onboard steam re-former; and for compressed H_2 gas, 30.4 km/litre (71.6 mpg). See Williams et al. (1995a,b).

Options for sequestering CO_2

The most-discussed option for CO_2 disposal has been piping CO_2 to depths greater than 3 km in deep ocean basins. So doing would eliminate the rapid transient build-up of CO_2 in the atmosphere and delay equilibration with the atmosphere by several hundred years; resulting interactions with calcite-rich sediments would probably reduce the long-term (> 2000-year) atmospheric concentration by a significant amount (~50 per cent) (Wilson 1992). But many questions remain about the dynamics of the processes involved, and many environmental issues have been raised – including concerns about the effects on ocean life of pH change from CO_2 injection, and the impacts on benthic organisms and ecosystems as hydrate particles are deposited on the ocean floor. Much more research is needed on such issues before deep ocean disposal can be pursued with confidence that the environmental risks are acceptable (Turkenburg 1992).

Among other options, disposal in depleted natural gas and oil fields stands out as being especially secure, as long as the original reservoir pressures are not exceeded (van der Burgt et al. 1992; Summerfeld et al. 1993), and potentially low in cost (Blok et al. 1989; van der Burgt et al. 1992; Koide et al. 1992; Hendriks 1994). The global sequestering capacity associated with past production, proved reserves, plus estimated undiscovered resources is estimated to be 410 GtC for natural gas fields and 105 GtC for oil fields (Hendriks 1994). For comparison, global CO_2 emissions from fossil fuel burning totalled 6.0 GtC in 1990.

The capacity of natural gas fields to sequester carbon at the original reservoir pressure is generally greater than the carbon content of the original natural gas and depends on the depth of the reservoir, the geothermal gradient, and the pressure gradient. Hendriks (1994) has shown that, for typical gradients, the ratio of carbon in CO_2 to that in the original natural gas is 3.0, 1.8, and 1.4 for depths of 1, 2, and 3 km, respectively, and that worldwide, on average, about twice as much carbon can be stored (as CO_2) in depleted reservoirs as was in the original natural gas.

If a hydrogen production facility could be sited near a depleted natural gas field the costs of long-distance pipeline transport of CO_2 could be avoided. Moreover, the cost of injection into the reservoir could be offset to some extent by recovery of additional natural gas. When primary production of natural gas at a reservoir ceases, it is not because the contained natural gas has been exhausted but rather because the reservoir pressure falls below a certain level (typically of the order of 30 bar) at which it is no longer economic to continue pumping out natural gas. But with CO_2 injection, the reservoir is repressurized, so that enhanced natural gas recovery is possible. Because of the order of 80 per cent of the natural gas in place is recovered in primary production, the amount of additional natural gas that can be produced is not large – but the enhanced production could pay for part of the incremental costs of CO_2 storage.

Based on data characteristic of large natural gas reservoirs in the Netherlands, Blok et al. (1997) have assessed the prospects for enhanced natural gas recovery with CO_2 injection, the implications for the net costs of CO_2 sequestration, and the impacts on the costs of producing hydrogen or methanol from natural gas. For the reservoir conditions they studied, extra natural gas production would contribute between 3.5 per cent and 8.5 per cent of the natural gas feedstock requirements for a hydrogen production plant over the first 15 years of its assumed 25-year operating life, depending on whether there were large or small permeability differences, respectively, between adjacent layers of the natural gas reservoir. The material balances for their analysis of the case where there are small permeability differences are shown in figure 6.1. In this example, the reservoir is capable of sustaining a CO_2 injection rate of 15,000 tonnes per day. Injection begins after 20 years of primary natural gas production, by which time the reservoir pressure has fallen to 30 bar, from the original pressure of 350 bar. During the next 15 years there is enhanced natural gas recovery that makes it possible to provide about 8.5 per cent of the natural gas requirements for the hydrogen production facility, as a result of reservoir repressurization via CO_2 injection. (This

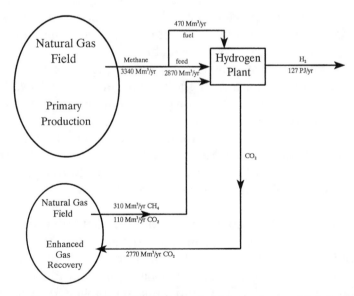

Fig. 6.1 **Wellhead production of hydrogen from natural gas with injection of the separated CO_2 into a depleted natural gas field and enhanced natural gas recovery as a result of reservoir repressurization (Source: based on data developed in Blok et al. 1997)**

corresponds to the case with "high credit for enhanced natural gas recovery" in table 6.4.) The reservoir pressure reaches about 130 bar after 15 years of CO_2 injection. The recovered gas is about three-quarters natural gas, the rest being CO_2. It is assumed that the small level of overall contamination ($<$ 5 per cent of the total gaseous input to the hydrogen production plant is CO_2) is readily managed in the hydrogen production process. The hydrogen production plant is sized to match the depleted reservoir capacity for accepting CO_2. For details, see Blok et al. (1997).

There would be considerable capacity in depleted natural gas fields for sequestering CO_2 recovered from decarbonizing fuels other than natural gas. For example, when hydrogen is produced from natural gas, the CO_2 recovery rate – 10.7 kg C/GJ of produced hydrogen (see table 6.1) or 9.0 kg C/GJ of the natural gas from which it is derived (assuming all energy inputs are provided by natural gas) – is equivalent to just two-thirds of the carbon in the original natural gas (13.5 kg C/GJ). Since, on average, the CO_2 sequestering capacity is equivalent to about twice the carbon contained in the original natural gas, the production of hydrogen from natural gas would thus leave about two-thirds of the sequestering capacity available for CO_2 derived from other sources. In addition, the sequestering capacity associated with past natural gas production and future production that will not be associated with the manufacture of hydrogen and the sequestering of the separated CO_2 would be available.

The limitation on strategies for CO_2 sequestration in depleted natural gas and oil fields is their limited geographical availability. This should not be a significant constraint on hydrogen manufactured from fuel conversion facilities sited near the natural gas fields, because the produced hydrogen could be distributed long distances via pipeline at acceptable costs (see table 6.7 below and Appendix C), serving markets just as natural gas pipelines do today. However, it would be desirable to have sequestering options that are more widely available as well.

The most widely distributed reservoirs for potential sequestering of CO_2 are saline aquifers located deep below the earth's surface underlying most of the area of sedimentary basins throughout the world. The areal extent of these basins is equivalent to nearly half of the land area of the inhabited continents (see table 6.3). Aquifers are porous underground beds, consisting mainly of sand, that are permeable to the flow of fluids. The pore spaces are usually filled with water and, occasionally, with petroleum or natural gas as well. In order

Table 6.3 **Areas of sedimentary basins in relation to total land areas**

Region	Total land area (10^6 km^2)	Sedimentary basin[a] Area (10^6 km^2)	% of total land area
Asia	27.60	11.34	41
Former USSR	22.40	9.71	43
Europe	4.93	2.76	56
South America	17.80	9.07	51
North America	24.20	9.21	38
Africa	30.30	15.23	50
Australia and Oceania	8.51	7.47	88
World	135.74	64.79	48

a. Source: Koide et al. (1992).

to be able to store the CO_2 at high supercritical fluid densities, only aquifers deeper than 750 metres are considered as potential storage reservoirs for CO_2. Aquifers containing fresh water are normally found at much shallower depths. If CO_2 were stored at a depth of 750 metres or deeper, it would generally take 2,000 years or more to reach a freshwater reservoir, and even then it will probably reach the freshwater reservoir in low concentrations; the main effect of the CO_2 that would enter the freshwater reservoir would be to increase the hardness of the water, because carbonates will dissolve (Hendriks 1994).

Hendriks (1994) has estimated the CO_2 storage capacity of such aquifers under the assumption that the injected CO_2 displaces water. He has made alternative estimates that depend on the extent to which structural traps are needed for secure storage (see table 6.4). Without a structural trap, the injected CO_2 might eventually migrate from the injection site to other subterranean sites where storage is not desirable or even to where it can escape to the atmosphere. If structural traps are not needed, the estimated worldwide sequestering capacity of aquifers is about 15,000 GtC; if structural traps are necessary, the sequestering capacity is 60 GtC (Hendriks 1994). A recent multinational, multi-institutional study (Holloway 1996) carried out for the European Commission concluded that structural traps might not be necessary to achieve a reasonably high degree of confidence in the security of aquifer storage, if the CO_2 is injected far enough from the aquifer boundary that it is predicted not to reach the boundary.

Table 6.4 **Order-of-magnitude estimates of the CO_2 storage capacity of aquifers (GtC)**

Region	Sequestering capacity	
	Structural trap required	No structural trap required
Western Europe	3	700
Eastern Europe	8	2,000
North America	11	2,700
Latin America	11	2,700
Africa	11	2,700
Middle East	3	700
Oceania and Asia	14	3,400
World	60	15,000

Source: Hendriks (1994).

It estimated that the underground CO_2 storage potential for the European Union plus Norway is more than 200 GtC – equivalent to 250 years of total CO_2 emissions for all of OECD Europe; most of this storage capacity is in aquifers under the North Sea. The study pointed out, however, that, to ensure adequate storage security in large aquifers, large amounts of data would be needed regarding reservoir integrity.

Framing the cost analysis for CO_2 sequestration

The costs[11] of alternative options for hydrogen production and use/ CO_2 disposal are estimated here for hydrogen produced from natural gas, coal, and biomass, with a focus on automotive applications of the produced hydrogen.[12] Storage of CO_2 in both depleted natural gas fields and saline aquifers is considered. Various hydrogen production/ CO_2 disposal scenarios are investigated. Costs are estimated for hydrogen production, for delivering hydrogen to users, and for using hydrogen. The estimated costs for CO_2 sequestration include the costs for drying and compressing the CO_2 to the pressures required for CO_2 transport and injection,[13] the costs of pipelines for transporting the CO_2 to the sequestering sites,[14] and the costs for wells and surface facilities at the storage sites.[15]

Hydrogen production cost estimates under alternative assumptions about sequestration are presented in table 6.5 for natural gas, table 6.6 for coal, and table 6.7 for biomass feedstocks, as functions of feedstock prices. In all cases it is assumed that the CO_2 separated (at 1.3 bar) at the hydrogen production facility must be dried and compressed to 110 bar for delivery to a CO_2 pipeline or natural gas disposal well. In table 6.8 hydrogen costs to consumers for transport applications are presented for base case scenarios for each feedstock as a function of the feedstock price, without and with sequestration, assuming typical sequestration costs in the latter instance.

For hydrogen production from natural gas with sequestration, it is assumed that the hydrogen plant is sited at a depleted natural gas field, in which the recovered CO_2 is sequestered, thereby avoiding long-distance CO_2 transport costs. Credit is taken for the modest increase in natural gas production that results from repressurization of the natural gas reservoir. It is assumed that: (i) as in the analysis of Blok et al. (1997), the increased natural gas production would contribute between 3.5 and 8.5 per cent of the natural gas feedstock requirements for the hydrogen production plant; (ii) increased production takes place after 20 years of primary production; (iii) after 15 years of CO_2 injection there is no more increased production; and (iv) the benefits of increased production accrue to producers of hydrogen from natural gas for the situation where conversion plants are located near the disposal site.

Because natural gas field disposal sites are geographically limited, it is assumed for the base case scenarios that in order to reach typical final consumers the produced hydrogen is transported 1,000 km further than is required for hydrogen that might be produced from coal or biomass at sites other than at depleted natural gas fields. To take advantage of the scale economies of pipeline transport of hydrogen, it is assumed for the base case scenarios that the outputs of five large production plants (each having a production capacity of 19.1 PJ of hydrogen per year – see table 6.5) are combined for hydrogen transport in a single 1,000 km pipeline. The cost of hydrogen to consumers is estimated by assuming that, after the initial 1,000 km hydrogen transport journey, the produced hydrogen is further transported 100 km in intermediate-sized pipelines, followed by transport 10 km in small-diameter pipelines to refuelling stations for automobiles, where the final costs tabulated in table 6.9 are incurred.

Costs for hydrogen from natural gas with sequestration are compared with costs for two alternative configurations for making hydrogen from natural gas without sequestration: one in which hydrogen is produced near the natural gas field and piped to distant markets; and

Table 6.5 Cost of producing hydrogen from natural gas near depleted natural gas fields (US\$/GJ of H_2)

Cost component	With venting of the recovered CO_2[a]	With sequestration of the recovered CO_2			
		High credit for enhanced NG recovery		Low credit for enhanced NG recovery	
		Low-cost sequestration	High-cost sequestration	Low-cost sequestration	High-cost sequestration
Base H_2 plant costs[b]					
Fixed capital	1.26	1.26	1.26	1.26	1.26
Working capital	0.10	0.10	0.10	0.10	0.10
Labour, maintenance	0.61	0.61	0.61	0.61	0.61
Purchased energy	0.41	0.41	0.41	0.41	0.41
Feedstock	$1.115*P_{ng}$	$1.115*P_{ng}$	$1.115*P_{ng}$	$1.115*P_{ng}$	$1.115*P_{ng}$
Credit for enhanced NG recovery[c]	—	$-0.079*P_{ng}$	$-0.079*P_{ng}$	$-0.033*P_{ng}$	$-0.033*P_{ng}$
CO_2 compression/drying[d]					
Capital	—	0.06	0.06	0.06	0.06
O&M	—	0.02	0.02	0.02	0.02
Electricity	—	0.22	0.22	0.22	0.22
Subtotal	—	0.30	0.30	0.30	0.30
CO_2 storage[e]	—	0.03	0.14	0.03	0.14
Total	$2.38 + 1.115*P_{ng}$	$2.71 + 1.036*P_{ng}$	$2.82 + 1.036*P_{ng}$	$2.71 + 1.082*P_{ng}$	$2.82 + 1.082*P_{ng}$

a. Lifecycle emissions are 21.8 kg C/GJ of H_2 with venting of the separated CO_2, and 11.1 kg C/GJ if the separated CO_2 is sequestered (see table 6.1).

b. For a plant producing 19.1 PJ/year of H_2 at 75 bar via steam re-forming. The overnight construction cost is US\$188.3 million; land + working capital are US\$18.2 million; external electricity requirements are 8.2 kWh/GJ of H_2 (Williams et al. 1995a,b). Assuming a 3-year construction period, a 25-year plant life, and an annual insurance charge of 0.5 per cent, the annual fixed capital charge rate is 0.1277, while the annual capital charge rate for land + working capital is 0.10. It is assumed that the purchased electricity price is US\$0.05/kWh. Here P_{ng} is the price of natural gas (NG) feedstock, in US\$/GJ.

c. Following Blok et al. (1997), it is assumed that the extra NG available from repressurizing the reservoir via CO_2 injection is 3.5–8.5 per cent of total NG requirements averaged over a 15-year period after primary NG production ceases; the value of enhanced production levelized over the 25-year life of the plant is 2.9–7.1 per cent of NG feedstock needs.

d. CO_2 is produced at the H_2 plant in a 750,000 tonnes/year stream at 1.3 bar and 40°C, with 1.5 per cent moisture (Katofsky 1993). It is assumed that the CO_2 must be dried to less than 10 ppm and compressed to 110 bar (Farla et al. 1992). The capital cost $CC = US\$10.35*10^6US\$$), from $CC = 0.351*(CAP)^{0.51117}$ (Farla et al. 1992), where CAP is the capacity (in 10^3 tonnes of CO_2/year). Assuming a 1-year construction period, a 25-year plant life, and an insurance charge of 0.5 per cent per year, the annual capital charge rate is 0.1172. It is assumed that annual O&M costs are 3.5 per cent of the capital cost. In this capacity range, electricity requirements, EL (in kWh/tC), are given by $EL = 1097.5*(CAP)^{-0.1509}$ (Farla et al. 1992), or 404 kWh/tC.

e. For injection into depleted NG fields at a depth of 2 km, Hendriks (1994) has calculated that storage costs range from US\$2.6 for an injection rate of 20 Nm^3/s to US\$13.3/tC for an injection rate of 2 Nm^3/s.

Table 6.6 **Cost of producing hydrogen from coal (US$/GJ of H₂)**

Cost component	With venting of the recovered CO_2 [a]	Coal transported to depleted NG field for H₂ production and sequestration of recovered CO_2 in depleted NG field [a]		Sequestration of recovered CO_2 in an aquifer 250 km from the H₂ production plant [a]	
		Low-cost sequestration	High-cost sequestration	Low-cost sequestration	High-cost sequestration
Base H₂ plant costs [b]					
Fixed capital	3.27	3.27	3.27	3.27	3.27
Working capital	0.21	0.21	0.21	0.21	0.21
Labour, maintenance	1.36	1.36	1.36	1.36	1.36
Purchased energy	1.51	1.51	1.51	1.51	1.51
Feedstock	$1.292*P_c$	$1.292*P_c$	$1.292*P_c$	$1.292*P_c$	$1.292*P_c$
CO₂ drying [c]	–	0.02	0.02	0.02	0.02
Coal transport [d] or CO₂ pipeline [e]	–	0.55	0.55	0.60	0.60
CO₂ storage [f]	–	0.08	0.40	0.28	1.02
Total	$6.35 + 1.292*P_c$	$7.00 + 1.292*P_c$	$7.32 + 1.292*P_c$	$7.25 + 1.292*P_c$	$7.99 + 1.292*P_c$

a. Lifecycle emissions are 41.2 kg C/GJ of H₂ with venting of the separated CO_2, and 11.4 kg C/GJ if the separated CO_2 is sequestered (see table 6.1).

b. For a plant producing 37.8 PJ/year of H₂ at 75 bar using a Shell oxygen-blown gasifier, for which the overnight construction cost is US$924.4 million; land + working capital are US$78.2 million; external electricity requirements are 27.8 kWh/GJ of H₂ (Williams et al. 1995a,b). Assuming a 4-year construction period, a 25-year plant life, and an annual insurance charge of 0.5 per cent, the annual fixed capital charge rate is 0.1337, while the annual capital charge rate for land + working capital is 0.10. It is assumed that the purchased electricity price is US$0.05/kWh. Here P_c is the price of the coal feedstock, in US$/GJ.

c. From Farla et al. (1992) the cost of drying the CO₂ to <10 ppm is US$0.073/tC for steam (at 8 MJ/tonne of CO_2) plus US$0.416/tC for capital (for a capital cost $CC = 1.48*(CAP)^{0.7} =$ US$3.99 million when $CAP = CO_2$ recovery rate = $4.125*10^6$ tonnes/year of CO_2; assuming a 25-year plant life and an annual insurance charge of 0.5 per cent per year, the annual capital charge rate is 0.1172) plus an annual O&M cost of 2.1 per cent of the capital cost per year, or US$0.074/tC. Thus the total cost of drying is US$0.563/tC, or US$0.017/GJ of produced H₂.

d. The cost of transporting coal from where it is produced to a depleted NG field site for a hydrogen production facility is taken to be US$0.35/GJ, the difference between the import price of Australian coal (with a higher heating value of 27.2 GJ/tonne) imported into Europe and its export price from Australia in 1993 (IEA 1995). This translates into a cost penalty of US$0.55/GJ of produced hydrogen.

e. Skovholt (1993) has calculated the pipeline cost, PC, in US$/tC (including costs of compression of CO_2 from atmospheric pressure to 110 bar) for 250 km of pipeline transmission of CO_2, for pipelines of capacities of 3–100 million tonnes of CO_2/year. A regression yields $PC = 43.85*(CAP)^{-0.54786}$, where CAP is the capacity in million tonnes of CO_2/year. For a plant with $CAP = 4.125$ million tonnes of CO_2 per year, $PC = US$20.18/tC$ or US$0.60/GJ of H_2.

f. For injection into saline aquifers (depleted NG fields) at a depth of 2 km, Hendriks (1994) has calculated the storage cost to range from US$9.2/tC (US$2.6/tC) for an injection rate of 20 Nm³/s to US$34.3/tC (US$13.3/tC) for an injection rate of 2 Nm³/s.

197

Table 6.7 **Cost of producing hydrogen from biomass (US$/GJ of H₂)**

Cost component	With venting of the recovered CO_2[a]	With biomass transported to a depleted NG field for H₂ production and sequestration of the recovered CO_2 in the depleted NG field[a]		With sequestration of the recovered CO_2 in an aquifer 250 km from the H₂ production plant[a]	
		Low-cost sequestration	High-cost sequestration	Low-cost sequestration	High-cost sequestration
Base H₂ plant costs[b]					
Fixed capital	2.68	2.68	2.68	2.68	2.68
Working capital	0.19	0.19	0.19	0.19	0.19
Labour, maintenance	1.39	1.39	1.39	1.39	1.39
Purchased energy	1.09	1.09	1.09	1.09	1.09
Feedstock	$1.366*P_b$	$1.366*P_b$	$1.366*P_b$	$1.366*P_b$	$1.366*P_b$
CO₂ drying[c]	–	0.02	0.02	0.02	0.02
Biomass transport[d] or CO₂ pipeline[e]	–	1.48	1.48	1.30	1.30
CO₂ storage[f]	–	0.06	0.32	0.22	0.82
Total	$5.35 + 1.366*P_b$	$6.91 + 1.366*P_b$	$7.17 + 1.366*P_b$	$6.89 + 1.366*P_b$	$7.49 + 1.366*P_b$

a. Lifecycle emissions are 5.4 kg C/GJ of H₂ with venting of the separated CO_2, and −18.4 kg C/GJ if the separated CO_2 is sequestered (see table 6.1).

b. For a plant producing 7.73 PJ/year of H₂ at 75 bar using a Battelle Columbus Laboratory indirectly heated biomass gasifier, for which the overnight construction cost is US$170.3 million; land + working capital are US$14.7 million; external electricity requirements are 21.7 kWh/GJ of H₂ (Williams et al. 1995a,b). Assuming a 2-year construction period, a 25-year plant life, and an annual insurance charge of 0.5 per cent, the annual fixed capital charge rate is 0.1215, while the annual capital charge rate for land + working capital is 0.10. It is assumed that the purchased electricity price is US$0.05/kWh. Here P_b is the price of the biomass feedstock, in US$/GJ.

c. From Farla et al. (1992) the cost of drying the CO_2 to <10 ppm is US$0.073/tC for steam (at 8 MJ/tonne of CO_2) plus US$0.714/tC for capital (for a capital cost $CC = 1.48*(CAP)^{0.7} = US\$1.12$ million when $CAP = CO_2$ recovery rate $= 0.674*10^6$ tonnes/year of CO_2; assuming a 25-year plant life and an annual insurance charge of 0.5 per cent per year, the annual capital charge rate is 0.1172) plus an annual O&M cost of 2.1 per cent of the capital cost per year, or US$0.128/tC. Thus the total cost of drying is US$0.915/tC, or US$0.022/GJ of produced H₂.

d. Assuming that wet biomass has a higher heating value of 10 GJ/tonne and that the cost per tonne of transporting biomass or coal from where it is produced to a hydrogen production facility at a depleted NG field site is the same, the transport cost per GJ for biomass would be 2.7 times the cost for Australian coal, or US$0.94/GJ if the benchmark for coal is as assumed in note d, table 6.6. This translates into a cost penalty of US$1.48/GJ of produced hydrogen.

e. Following the approach outlined in note e, table 6.6, the pipeline cost in US$/tC for 250 km of pipeline transmission of CO_2 is $PC =$ $43.85*(CAP)^{-0.54786} =$ US$54.44/tC of produced hydrogen, for $CAP = 0.674$ million tonnes of CO_2/year.

f. For injection into saline aquifers (depleted NG fields) at a depth of 2 km, Hendriks (1994) has calculated the storage cost to range from US$9.2/tC (US$2.6/tC) for an injection rate of 20 Nm^3/s to US$34.3/tC (US$13.3/tC) for an injection rate of 2 Nm^3/s.

Table 6.8 **Delivered costs of hydrogen produced from alternative feedstocks[a] (US$/GJ of H₂)**

Cost component	H₂ from natural gas			H₂ from coal[d]		H₂ from biomass[e]	
	H₂ plant at the NG field[b]	H₂ plant at the city gate[c]	H₂ plant at the NG field[b]				
CO₂ sequestration?	No	No	Yes	No	Yes	No	Yes
Production	$2.38 + 1.115 \cdot P_{ng}$	$2.67 + 1.115 \cdot P_{ng}$	$2.77 + 1.059 \cdot P_{ng}$	$6.35 + 1.292 \cdot P_c$	$7.60 + 1.292 \cdot P_c$	$5.35 + 1.366 \cdot P_b$	$7.19 + 1.366 \cdot P_b$
H₂ pipeline T&D[f]							
1,000 km pipeline	0.50	–	0.50	–	–	–	–
100 km pipeline	0.10	–	0.10	0.05	0.05	0.24	0.24
10 km pipeline	1.69	1.69	1.69	1.69	1.69	1.69	1.69
Subtotal	2.29	1.69	2.29	1.74	1.74	1.93	1.93
Refuelling[g]	5.07	5.07	5.07	5.07	5.07	5.07	5.07
Total	$9.74 + 1.115 \cdot P_{ng}$	$9.43 + 1.115 \cdot P_{ng}$	$10.13 + 1.059 \cdot P_{ng}$	$13.16 + 1.292 \cdot P_c$	$14.41 + 1.292 \cdot P_c$	$12.35 + 1.366 \cdot P_b$	$14.19 + 1.366 \cdot P_b$
Total with a US$52/tC CT[h]	$10.87 + 1.115 \cdot P_{ng}$	$10.54 + 1.115 \cdot P_{ng}$	$10.71 + 1.059 \cdot P_{ng}$	$15.30 + 1.292 \cdot P_c$	$15.00 + 1.292 \cdot P_c$	$12.63 + 1.366 \cdot P_b$	$13.23 + 1.366 \cdot P_b$
Lifecycle CO₂ emissions (kg C/GJ of H₂)	+21.8	+21.4	+11.1	+41.2	+11.4	+5.4	−18.4

a. Assuming average values for sequestration costs in tables 6.5, 6.6, and 6.7. Here P_{ng} is the wellhead NG price (in US$/GJ); P_c and P_b are, respectively, the prices of coal and biomass delivered to the conversion facility.

b. For the pipeline transmission and distribution (T&D) system associated with producing H₂ from NG near the NG field, it is assumed that the output for a cluster of five plants (a production rate of 95.45 PJ/year or 850.3 million scf/day) is transported 1,000 km in a 81.3 cm (32 inch) pipeline, for which the inlet and outlet pressures are 75 bar (1,087.5 psia) and 48 bar (697 psia), respectively. At the end of this pipeline, the output is divided into 5 equal parts, each of which is transported another 100 km in 30.5 cm (12 inch) pipelines, for which the outlet pressure is 20.3 bar (294 psia). At the ends of these pipelines the H₂ is transported 10 km further to refuelling stations in 4.2 cm (1.7 inch), 1 million scf/day (0.113 PJ/year) lines for which the outlet pressure is 14 bar (200 psia).

c. In this instance NG is piped from the NG field via 1,000 km and 100 km pipelines (similar to those described in note b) to a H_2 conversion plant at the city gate. The cost of compressing the NG and transmitting it to the city gate adds US$0.64/GJ to the cost of H_2 production. Because the plant is so close to the market, the H_2 recovered from the PSA unit need not be compressed to high pressure at the production plant. Here it is assumed that H_2 is instead sold at the 20.3 bar pressure at which it is recovered from the PSA unit, saving US$0.35/GJ in compression costs. This compression saving is much larger than the cost of compressing NG at the gas field to 75 bar. The lifecycle CO_2 emissions are reduced slightly as a result of this compressor work savings.

d. It is assumed that the output for a single plant producing H_2 from coal (a production rate of 37.76 PJ/year or 336.5 million scf/day) is transported 100 km in a 32.3 cm (12.7 inch) pipeline, for which the inlet and outlet pressures are 75 bar and 20.3 bar, respectively. At the end of this pipeline, the H_2 is transported 10 km further to refuelling stations in 4.2 cm (1.7 inch), 1 million scf/day lines for which the outlet pressure is 14 bar.

e. It is assumed that the output for a single plant producing H_2 from biomass (a production rate of 7.73 PJ/year or 68.9 million scf/day) is transported 100 km in a 17.7 cm (7 inch) pipeline, for which the inlet and outlet pressures are 75 bar and 20.3 bar, respectively. At the end of this pipeline the H_2 is transported 10 km further to refuelling stations in 4.2 cm (1.7 inch), 1 million scf/day lines for which the outlet pressure is 14 bar.

f. Hydrogen T&D costs presented here are illustrative rather than definitive. (The pipeline/compressor systems are not optimized.) Flow rate and cost calculations are based largely on Christodoulou (1984). However, it is assumed that pipeline unit costs are never lower than about US$180/m, the actual installed cost for a 2,700 m pipeline rated for 1,000 psia with $D = 3$ inches (Ogden et al. 1995); thus, for small-diameter pipelines, it is assumed that the cost per metre of pipe is independent of the pipe diameter. It is assumed that pipelines last 50 years, so that the annual capital charge rate (including an insurance rate of 0.5 per cent per year) is 0.1059.

g. See table 6.9.

h. This is the carbon tax (CT) required to make the cost of H_2 produced from NG with sequestration in the depleted NG field equal to the cost of H_2 produced from NG at the city gate without sequestration. At this tax level, the cost of H_2 produced from coal with sequestration is also less than the cost of H_2 produced form coal without sequestration.

another in which natural gas is piped to a hydrogen production facility near these distant markets (see table 6.8). Siting the facility for producing hydrogen from natural gas near hydrogen markets for one of the cases without sequestration is included because pipeline transport is less costly for natural gas than for hydrogen.

Two scenarios are considered for coal and two for biomass. In one scenario for each feedstock, the base case, it is assumed that the recovered CO_2 is transported by pipeline 250 km to a site where sequestration is feasible in a saline aquifer. Because saline aquifers are so widely available, it is assumed that the pipelines required to bring the produced hydrogen to market are much shorter than for the case where hydrogen is produced from natural gas with sequestration. Specifically, it is assumed that the produced hydrogen is transported 100 km in an intermediate-sized pipeline, followed by transport 10 km in small-diameter pipelines to refuelling stations for automobiles, where the final costs tabulated in table 6.9 are incurred. In the other scenario the coal or biomass is transported to a hydrogen production facility located near a depleted natural gas field, where the separated CO_2 is sequestered. However, it is assumed in this instance that: (i) natural gas field disposal of CO_2 occurs after disposal has already taken place there for hydrogen produced from natural gas, and (ii) unlike the natural gas case, no additional enhanced natural gas production can be credited against the cost of hydrogen produced from coal or biomass.

The costs of hydrogen to consumers from natural gas, coal, and biomass feedstocks, as functions of feedstock costs, are presented in table 6.8, without and with sequestration, and without and with a carbon tax of US\$52/tC – a tax large enough to make the cost of hydrogen from natural gas with sequestration at the gas field equal to that for hydrogen produced from natural gas at a site 1,100 km from the natural gas field, near large remote hydrogen markets, when the wellhead natural gas price is US\$3/GJ, and for average sequestration cost and average credit for enhanced natural gas recovery (see table 6.5). The charge against the fuel cost to the consumer from this carbon tax is levied at the net lifecycle CO_2 emission rate for a given fuel, as indicated in table 6.1. Hydrogen costs to consumers, along with gasoline costs for comparison, are also shown in figures 6.2 and 6.3 for specific feedstock prices – both without sequestration and for low and high estimates of sequestration costs. (All fuel taxes are excluded in these figures.) In figure 6.2, these costs are presented per unit of delivered energy (US\$ per GJ); in figure 6.3, they are pre-

Table 6.9 **Estimated cost of hydrogen refuelling**[a]

Cost component	US$/GJ of delivered H_2
Capital for H_2 storage at the refuelling station[b]	2.00
Capital for compressor[c]	0.61
O&M for compressor[d]	0.02
Electricity for compressor[e]	1.08
Hydrogen dispenser and controls[f]	0.36
Labour[g]	1.00
Total	5.07

a. For a large refuelling station providing 10^6 scf/day (0.132 million GJ/year) of gaseous hydrogen, based on a design by Ogden et al. (1995). It is assumed that fuel cell cars have a 250 mile (400 km) range and that the average fuel economy of these cars is 71.6 mpg (30.4 km/litre) of gasoline equivalent, so that refuelling requirements are 0.46 GJ/car, and 787 cars are refuelled per day. Further it is assumed that H_2 is stored onboard cars at 552 bar (8,000 psia), and that the compressor discharge pressure at the refuelling station is 558 bar (8,400 psia).
b. Storage cylinders for the refuelling station having a maximum operating pressure of 8,400 psia, a capacity of 6,005 scf each, and an installed cost per vessel of US$10,500. The refuelling station needs 150 cylinders, so that the total capital cost is US$1.575 million. The cylinders are expected to last 10 years. The annual capital charge rate (including an insurance rate of 0.5 per cent per year) is thus 0.1677.
c. The compressor capacity required for the refuelling station (for inlet and outlet hydrogen pressures of 200 psia and 8,400 psia, respectively) is 270 kW$_e$, its installed cost is estimated to be US$1,919/kW$_e$, and its lifetime is expected to be 100,000 hours (11.4 years), so that the annual capital charge rate (including an insurance rate of 0.5 per cent per year) is 0.1559.
d. Ogden et al. (1995) estimate the annual cost for the compressor to be US$3,000.
e. Electricity requirements are 6.49 kWh/1,000 scf (17.93 kWh/GJ) of H_2. It is assumed that the electricity price is US$0.06/kWh.
f. The capital costs of the hydrogen dispenser, priority panel, and sequencer are estimated to be US$285,500. This equipment is expected to last 10 years. The annual capital charge rate (including an insurance rate of 0.5 per cent per year) is thus 0.1677.
g. The annual labour cost is US$131,400 per year, assuming a labour plus benefits rate of US$15/hour.

sented per unit of transport energy services provided (cents per km of driving), assuming the hydrogen is used for automobiles. The estimated total lifecycle costs of owning and operating fuel cell cars fuelled by hydrogen derived from alternative sources are shown in figure 6.4.

The feedstock prices assumed for the construction of figures 6.2, 6.3, and 6.4 are indicative for the period near 2010 when hydrogen might begin to come into the market in some areas: US$3.0/GJ for natural gas, US$1.35/GJ for coal, and US$2.0/GJ for biomass. The gasoline cost shown in these figures is for reformulated gasoline derived from US$23/barrel (US$3.75/GJ) crude oil (the world oil price projected for 2010 by the US Department of Energy – EIA 1995). The assumed natural gas price is the average natural gas wellhead price projected for the year 2010 for the United States by the US Department of Energy (EIA 1995), while the coal price is the average price projected for US electric utilities in that year (EIA 1995). The biomass price is what could be widely realizable for plantation biomass in developing countries in this time-frame, based on commercial plantation technology from Brazil;[16] for the industrialized countries, plantation biomass prices based on present technology would be higher. However, if R&D goals for plantation biomass can be realized, biomass prices as low as US$1.5/GJ appear to be feasible for the time-period near 2020 for large-scale plantation biomass production in the United States.[17] It is not likely that biomass would begin to be used for hydrogen production before 2020.

Major findings of the sequestration cost analysis

The results of the sequestration cost analysis are best understood in the context of the relative costs for energy services for transport using alternative fuel/vehicle combinations, without the sequestration of separated CO_2.

Consider first a comparison of costs without sequestration on a $/GJ of fuel basis (see fig. 6.2). The first observation one can make about these costs is that gasoline would be far less costly than hydrogen derived from any source. Second, the least costly option for providing hydrogen is from natural gas, for which the cost per GJ to the consumer is likely to be nearly 60 per cent higher than the gasoline price. Third, the cost of hydrogen is about the same for both coal and biomass, despite the assumption that the biomass price is about 50 per cent higher than the coal price – a reflection of the facts that costly sulphur removal is not needed for biomass and that biomass is more reactive than coal and thus easier to gasify (Williams et al. 1995a,b). Fourth, the cost of hydrogen from biomass or coal is about 10 per cent higher than for hydrogen from natural gas. Fifth, all the electrolytic hydrogen options are far more costly than hydrogen derived thermochemically from natural gas, coal, or biomass; for the least costly electrolytic option, which represents what might plausibly be realizable for advanced thin-film photovoltaic technologies,[18] the cost of hydrogen to the consumer is 60 per cent higher than the indicated cost of hydrogen from biomass.

A more meaningful comparison than the cost of fuel *per GJ* is the cost of fuel *per km of driving the vehicle* that the fuel might be used in. The consumer prices and lifecycle CO_2 emissions for hydrogen shown in figure 6.2 are converted in figure 6.3 to fuel costs and life-cycle CO_2 emissions per km of driving a fuel cell vehicle (FCV), along with a comparison of gasoline costs and lifecycle CO_2 emissions per km of driving, for both internal combustion engine vehicle (ICEV) and FCV applications. The reference gasoline ICEV is a year-2000 version of the Ford Taurus automobile with a fuel economy of 11.0 km/litre (25.8 mpg). The hydrogen FCV has performance characteristics that are comparable to those for this ICEV and a gasoline-equivalent fuel economy of 30.4 km/litre (71.6 mpg) (Williams 1995). The cost of hydrogen derived from natural gas and biomass without sequestration of the separated CO_2 would be 1.49 and 1.73 cents/km, respectively, compared with 2.65 cents/km for gasoline. Initially fuel cell cars would probably be operated on gasoline converted to a hydrogen-rich gaseous fuel mixture via a process that begins with partial oxidation. The estimated fuel economy of such a fuel cell car having the same performance as the internal combustion engine alternative would be 18.0 km/litre (42.3 mpg). The fuel cost per km for this vehicle would be 1.62 cents/km (see fig. 6.3).[19]

Consider next the penalties for sequestration associated with hydrogen derived from natural gas for the situations depicted in figure 6.2. These penalties are low – increasing the cost of hydrogen to the consumer by only 0.8 to 2.6 per cent. The low value of the penalty is a result of: (i) being able to sequester the separated CO_2 near where it is produced (thus avoiding the costs of long-distance CO_2 pipeline transport), (ii) the relatively low penalty for storage in depleted natural gas fields compared with aquifers,[20] and (iii) receiving a modest credit for extra natural gas produced as a result of repressurization of the natural gas reservoir – a credit almost large enough to cover the incremental cost of sequestration.

The penalties for sequestration shown in figure 6.2 for natural gas feedstocks are for the case where hydrogen is produced at the natural gas field both without and with sequestration. In this case the carbon tax needed to make equal the costs of hydrogen with and without sequestration, and thereby induce hydrogen producers to sequester the separated CO_2, is US$9–32/tC, depending on the cost of sequestration and the magnitude of the credit for enhanced natural gas recovery (see table 6.5). Such a carbon tax would increase the hydrogen cost by US$0.2–0.7/GJ, some 1.6 to 5.5 per cent of the cost of

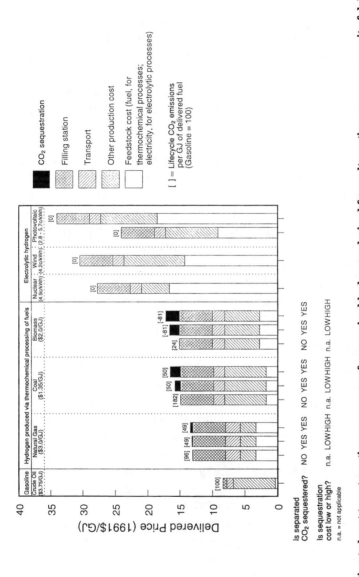

Fig. 6.2 **The estimated cost to automotive consumers of pressurized hydrogen derived from alternative sources, per unit of delivered energy (Note: the cost of hydrogen derived from natural gas without sequestration is for a plant sited at a depleted natural gas field. The sequestration costs shown for coal and biomass are for sequestration in saline aquifers located 250 km from the hydrogen production facilities. The costs for hydrogen derived electrolytically from nuclear and wind (photovoltaic) sources are for the indicated AC (DC) electricity prices, assuming an 85 per cent efficiency for electrolysis and a 96 per cent efficiency for rectification. The cost of transporting electrolytic hydrogen from production facilities to refuelling stations is assumed to be the same as for hydrogen derived from coal. In all cases, production costs include the costs for pressurization to 75 bar at the production plant. For the intermittent renewable electric sources, costs for hydrogen storage are also included in production costs)**

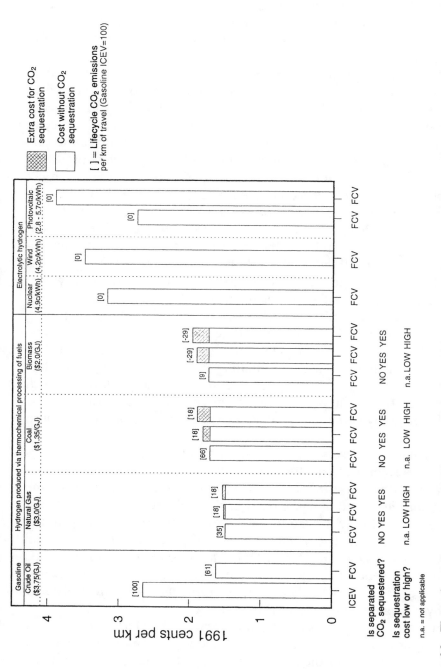

Fig. 6.3 **The estimated cost to automotive consumers of pressurized hydrogen derived from alternative sources, per km of driving fuel cell cars. Costs for gasoline used in internal combustion engine cars and fuel cell cars are shown for comparison**

207

hydrogen to consumers without sequestration. The magnitude of the carbon tax in this instance is independent of the length of the hydrogen transmission line and thus would apply equally to situations where large potential hydrogen markets are located near the natural gas field.

If instead hydrogen production without sequestration were to take place 1,100 km from the natural gas field near major remote hydrogen markets (see table 6.8), the hydrogen cost penalty to the consumer for sequestration would increase to the range 3.2–5.1 per cent, for a natural gas wellhead price of US$3/GJ. In this instance the carbon tax required to make equal the costs of hydrogen produced without and with sequestration is US$39–63/tC; with this carbon tax in place the cost of hydrogen to the consumer would be 7–11 per cent higher than without sequestration and with no carbon tax.[21] Though the impact of this tax on the cost of hydrogen to the consumer is still modest, it is considerably higher than for the scenario where hydrogen production without sequestration takes place near the natural gas field. Since the latter scenario is most realistic for situations where there are large potential hydrogen markets near the natural gas field, the sequestration option is likely to be pursued first in such regions – e.g. in the Netherlands and Texas. If nearby hydrogen markets can be served, there is no need to seek the economies of large-scale hydrogen transmission capacity by building very large hydrogen production plants. This makes it possible to begin sequestration much earlier in the evolution of a hydrogen economy than would be the case if the only potential hydrogen markets were remote from natural gas fields.

For the base case sequestering scenario for coal, in which CO_2 is sequestered in aquifers, the cost penalty is higher – giving rise to a 6–11 per cent increase in the cost of hydrogen to the consumer for the situations indicated in figure 6.2. For the high sequestration cost estimate, the cost of hydrogen to the consumer per km of driving would still be 29 per cent less than the cost of gasoline with an internal combustion engine. In this instance, a carbon tax of US$29–54/tC would be needed to make equal the costs of hydrogen without and with sequestration, a tax that would increase the cost to the consumer of hydrogen derived from coal by 8–15 per cent.

For the base case sequestering scenario for biomass, the cost penalty is somewhat higher but still modest – giving rise to a 10–14 per cent increase in the cost of hydrogen to the consumer for the situations indicated in figure 6.2. But even if the high sequestration cost estimate proves to be valid, the cost of hydrogen to the consumer per km of driving would still be 26 per cent less than the cost of gasoline with an internal combustion engine.

The percentage cost penalties associated with sequestering the separated CO_2 would be smaller still if calculated as a contribution to the total cost of owning and operating a car, to which the cost of fuel makes a relatively modest contribution (see fig 6.4).[22] Consider, for example, the total lifecycle cost of owning and operating a fuel cell car operated on hydrogen derived from coal without sequestering the separated CO_2. The estimated cost is 20.1 cents/km (slightly less than for a gasoline internal combustion engine car of comparable performance) for the assumptions indicated in figure 6.2, of which the price of hydrogen fuel accounts for only 1.71 cents/km. With a carbon tax sufficient to induce producers of hydrogen from coal to sequester, the lifecycle cost of the car would increase only 0.14–0.25 cents/km, or 0.7–1.3 per cent.

These calculations suggest that deep reductions in CO_2 emissions can be achieved in the transport sector at low incremental cost by shifting to hydrogen or a hydrogen carrier derived from chemical fuel feedstocks. Such cost calculations could of course be refined as more knowledge is gained about the various technologies involved. But this basic finding is robust. It is not sensitive to the outlook for the relative prices of the three feedstocks considered. If natural gas prices remain low for the indefinite future, and if high estimates of remaining ultimately recoverable natural gas resources prove to be valid, hydrogen would be predominantly natural gas based in many parts of the world for decades to come, and sequestration could be pursued on large scales at very low incremental cost. If, instead, natural gas prices rise rapidly beyond the year 2010,[23] then biomass- and coal-based hydrogen production strategies would eventually supplement hydrogen supplies provided by natural gas.

Biomass without sequestration would tend to be favoured over coal with sequestration wherever adequate land resources are available for biomass production,[24] because hydrogen production costs would be as low or lower under most conditions (for all the cases considered here – compare tables 6.6 and 6.7), and because lifecycle emissions would be only half as large (see table 6.1). However, in regions where coal is cheap and the availability of land for biomass production is limited, coal-based hydrogen strategies would be favoured.

Biomass-based production strategies with sequestration would be favoured where land-use constraints limit the extent of hydrogen

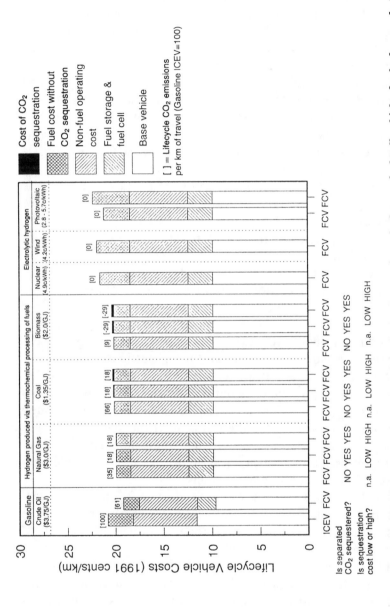

Fig. 6.4 **The estimated lifecycle cost to consumers of owning and operating a hydrogen fuel cell vehicle, for hydrogen derived from alternative sources, per km of driving. Estimated lifecycle costs for gasoline-powered internal combustion engine and fuel cell cars are shown for comparison (Note: operating lifetimes of 241,000 km and 193,000 km are assumed for fuel cell vehicles and internal combustion engine vehicles, respectively. Sources: vehicle performance and cost characteristics based on Ogden et al. 1994; fuel costs from fig. 6.3)**

production from biomass,[25] or when it is desired to offset emissions from other sectors or parts of the world.

The largest uncertainties underlying this analysis are: (i) the extent to which society will adopt low-temperature fuel cells and their fuels for transportation and distributed combined heat and power applications, (ii) the prospects for converting existing natural gas transmission lines to hydrogen service and building new pipelines dedicated to hydrogen, and (iii) the extent and security of saline aquifers as storage reservoirs for separated CO_2.

Major research, development, and demonstration commitments are needed on the hardware for low-temperature fuel cell technology and for the production, storage, and transport of hydrogen and hydrogen carriers. Although there is rapidly growing R&D activity on low-temperature fuel cells for transportation applications, the overall level of the R&D effort in this area is still minuscule. Moreover, there is very little ongoing R&D on the production of hydrogen from coal or biomass.

The issues relating to converting existing natural gas transmission and distribution lines to hydrogen service are discussed in Appendix C. Being able to make this conversion would be especially important for the already industrialized world, where a large natural gas pipeline infrastructure is already in place. It appears to be feasible to convert low-pressure distribution lines without great difficulty, but hydrogen embrittlement looms as a serious issue for high-pressure transmission lines. Technical fixes might be possible. For example, would mixing trace quantities of another gas with the hydrogen be a suitable strategy for coping with the embrittlement problem (see Appendix C)? More research is needed to find out.

More research is also needed on the various issues raised regarding sequestration in depleted oil and gas fields and saline aquifers – especially the latter.

Appendix A: The importance of the water–gas shift reaction in fuel decarbonization

It is feasible to convert a carbon-rich fuel to a hydrogen-rich fuel at relatively high overall efficiency by taking advantage of the thermodynamics of the so-called water–gas shift reaction.

Suppose it is desired to make hydrogen (H_2) out of carbon (C). The first step is to gasify C by partial oxidation to produce carbon monoxide (CO):

$$C + 1/2\, O_2 \rightarrow CO, \; \triangle H_R = -110.5\,MJ/mol.$$

Note that, with complete oxidation,

$$C + O_2 \rightarrow CO_2, \triangle H_R = -393.5 \, MJ/mol,$$

which shows that the CO produced in partial oxidation retains 71.9 per cent of the higher heating value (HHV) of the original C:

$$HHV_{CO} = 283.0 \, MJ/mol,$$

$$HHV_C = 393.5 \, MJ/mol.$$

The HHV of H_2 is approximately the same as the HHV of CO:

$$HHV_{H_2} = 285.8 \, MJ/mol.$$

The next step is to use the water–gas shift reaction:

$$CO + H_2O_{(g)} \rightarrow CO_2 + H_2, \triangle H_R = -41.2 \, MJ/mol,$$

a slightly exothermic reaction that makes it possible to "shift" the energy contained in the CO to H_2. The needed steam (gaseous water, $H_2O_{(g)}$) can be raised by evaporating liquid water ($H_2O_{(l)}$), a phase change that requires just slightly more heat than is generated in the water–gas shift reaction:

$$H_2O_{(l)} \rightarrow H_2O_{(g)}, \triangle H_{PC} = +44.0 \, MJ/mol.$$

Note that the extra heat required ($44.0 - 41.2 = 2.8 \, MJ/mol$) can be met using just 2.5 per cent of the heat released via the initial partial oxidation of C.

The final step in the production of H_2 from C involves separating out the H_2 from the gaseous H_2/CO_2 mixture – for example, using commercial pressure swing adsorption (PSA) technology, which can recover 90 per cent or more of the produced H_2 at up to 99.999 per cent purity. (PSA exploits the ability of porous materials to adsorb specific molecules selectively at high pressure and desorb them at low pressure; the cyclic pressure *swing* is what gives the process its name.) A by-product of the process is a stream of pure CO_2 that is potentially available for sequestration in some secure reservoir.

This discussion shows that it is possible in theory to generate 1 mole of H_2 from 1 mole of C at an overall efficiency $n = 100^*(285.8/393.5) = 72.6$ per cent. In the real world, H_2 fuel would be made from natural gas, coal, or biomass. H_2 can be produced from natural gas at an overall real-world efficiency of 84 per cent via a process that begins by reacting natural gas with steam (Williams et al. 1995a,b). This efficiency is higher than for making H_2 from C because natural gas (mainly methane, CH_4) already contains a great deal of H_2. The real-world efficiencies for making H_2 from coal (whose chemical composition can be represented as $\sim CH_{0.8}O_{0.08}$) via oxygen-blown gasification and from biomass (whose chemical composition can be represented as $\sim CH_{1.5}O_{0.7}$) via steam oxidation are each about 64 per cent (Williams et al. 1995a,b).

Appendix B: Biomass CO_2 emission offset potential in a world where some coal-rich regions cannot or will not reduce emissions

Consider a world situation in 2100 where the hydrogen fuel cell vehicle is a well-established technology and where natural gas resources are in limited supply, so that the primary options for producing hydrogen at low cost are from coal and biomass. Suppose further that some regions with a capacity to produce biomass on large scales agree to seek to help bring about deep reductions in global CO_2 emissions, but that other regions must depend on coal and either have no ready access to secure sequestering sites or are unwilling to incur the cost penalties for storage, however modest. In these circumstances it may still be feasible to achieve low global emissions levels because of the large "emissions offset potential" offered by biomass-derived hydrogen (see tables 6.1 and 6.2).

To illustrate the possibilities, suppose that: (i) the world population in 2100 is 10.5 billion; (ii) there are then 0.4 cars per capita in the world (the average for the industrialized market countries in 1985) – some 4.2 billion cars altogether (10 times the present number); (iii) the average car is driven 13,400 km/year (the average for industrialized market countries in 1985); (iv) these cars are all equipped with hydrogen fuel cells; (v) the average automotive fuel economy is 42.5 km/litre (100 mpg) of gasoline equivalent.

With so many cars, would it be possible to have zero net CO_2 emissions worldwide from the automotive sector, if some cars were run on hydrogen derived from coal without sequestration of the separated CO_2 (so that net lifecycle emissions would be +41.2 kg C/GJ of hydrogen – see table 6.1) and if the rest were run on hydrogen derived from biomass with sequestration of the separated CO_2 in saline aquifers and/or depleted natural fields (so that the net lifecycle emissions would be −18.4 kg C/GJ of hydrogen – see table 6.1)?

Under the above conditions, there would be zero net emissions from the automotive sector if a fraction "a" of all cars is operated on coal-derived hydrogen, where "a" is determined from the following equation based on the net lifecycle emission rates for the two hydrogen-producing systems: $41.2^*a - (1-a)^*18.4 = 0$, or $a = 0.31$. Thus net global emissions from cars would be zero if 31 per cent of the hydrogen were derived from coal and 69 per cent from biomass. The amount of hydrogen consumed worldwide for cars would be 46 EJ per year. Assuming an efficiency of 64 per cent for making hydrogen from coal or biomass (see Appendix A), some 22 EJ and 51 EJ per year of coal and biomass, respectively, would be needed for fuelling automobiles in 2100. For comparison, total global coal consumption in 1985 was 90 EJ per year; and 50 EJ per year is approximately the average rate at which non-commercial biomass is consumed in the world today (Hall et al. 1993). Assume that in 2100 all this biomass would be grown on plantations. It is reasonable to expect an average yield of, say, 20 dry tonnes per hectare per year at that time (Williams 1995). With an energy content of 20 GJ/dry tonne, some 128 million hectares of plantation area would be needed worldwide. There will very likely be far more land available for biomass energy plantations than this (Larson et al. 1995). The required sequestering rate of 0.75 GtC per year is modest in relation to the estimated capacities of aquifers and depleted natural gas and oil fields.

213

Appendix C: Pipeline transport of hydrogen

Transport costs for new pipelines

The cost of hydrogen pipeline transport is higher than for natural gas. Pottier et al. (1988) estimate that the cost of the pipe would typically be 50 per cent higher than for natural gas transmission lines, largely because embrittlement-resistant steels would be specified. Also, the optimized pipe diameter would be perhaps 20 per cent larger for hydrogen to achieve the same energy flow rate (Leeth 1979). The cost of installation would also be higher, because special care would be needed with welds. And much larger compressors would be needed to achieve the same energy flow rates, because the volumetric energy density of hydrogen is just 35 per cent of that for natural gas.

But hydrogen pipeline transport costs would not be prohibitive, for two reasons. First, the diversity of supply options implies that hydrogen would often be available from sources that are relatively close to where the hydrogen is needed (Ogden and Nitsch 1993). Second, even where long-distance pipelines are needed, the costs involved are relatively modest compared with the total cost of hydrogen to the consumer, and the total cost per unit of service provided would typically still be less than for conventional transport fuels. For example, the transport of hydrogen 1,110 km to consumers for use in fuel cell vehicles from a production facility located at a natural gas field contributes less than one-fifth of the total cost of hydrogen to the consumer (see fig. 6.2 and table 6.8).

Transport costs for pipelines converted to hydrogen from natural gas

In many parts of the industrialized world extensive pipeline networks designed for use with natural gas are already in place. Could these pipelines be converted to hydrogen? Even neglecting considerations of embrittlement, these pipelines are not optimized for use with hydrogen, whose energy density and viscosity are very different from the values for natural gas. Nevertheless, from a fluid dynamics perspective, the mismatch would not be severe. For a given pipe diameter and operating pressure, the energy flow rate for hydrogen would be about 85 per cent of that for natural gas with partially turbulent flow and 90 per cent of that for natural gas with fully turbulent flow (Christodoulou 1984). Seals, joints, and metering equipment would probably have to be replaced with conversion. Moreover, almost three times as much compressor power would be needed to obtain the same energy flow rate as for natural gas; and reciprocating rather than centrifugal compressors would be needed. Nevertheless, there could be large savings associated with the sunk costs of the pipelines themselves, if conversion were feasible.

Hydrogen embrittlement

A major concern about converting natural gas pipelines to hydrogen service is "hydrogen environment embrittlement," which refers to the degradation of mechanical properties that takes place when a metal is exposed to a hydrogen environment.

The available evidence indicates that this is not an issue for existing local natural gas distribution systems, which could therefore be converted to hydrogen with only minor modifications (Ogden et al. 1995). However, because of the higher pressures (up to 70 bar or 1,000 psia) and materials used, hydrogen environment embrittlement could be a serious problem for existing long-distance natural gas transmission lines that would transport pure hydrogen. The primary mechanisms are fatigue crack growth under cyclic loading and slow crack growth under stable loads near welds and other "heat-affected" zones in pipes.

Various countermeasures have been suggested, including adding gases to inhibit embrittlement, preloading with an inert gas, coating pipelines, and selective replacement of steels susceptible to embrittlement. The most promising approach seems to be gas additives. Available research indicates strong inhibition of fatigue crack growth with oxygen, at concentrations ranging from 100 ppm to 1 per cent (Ogden et al. 1995). A high priority for hydrogen research should be given to gas additives and other countermeasures for inhibiting embrittlement in existing natural gas transmission lines that might be converted to hydrogen.

Acknowledgements

Financial support for this research was provided by the Geraldine R. Dodge Foundation, the Energy Foundation, the W. Alton Jones Foundation, and the Merck Fund.

Notes

1. The use of coal for power generation in the IS92a scenario accounts for 19 per cent of total CO_2 emissions from fossil fuels in 2100, the same percentage as in 1990.
2. If there were no coal and if those concerned about climate change had only conventional oil and gas resources to worry about, it might be feasible to stabilize the atmospheric concentration of CO_2 near the present level. According to the US Geological Survey (Masters et al. 1994), remaining ultimately recoverable conventional oil and gas resources (proved reserves plus estimated recoverable undiscovered resources) amount (as of 1992) to 11,300 exajoules (EJ) of oil and 12,500 EJ of natural gas. Assuming CO_2 emission coefficients of 19.5 million tonnes of carbon per EJ (MtC/EJ) for oil and 13.5 MtC/EJ for natural gas, cumulative emissions associated with burning all conventional oil and gas resources amount to 390 GtC, which is within the range of cumulative emissions consistent with stabilizing the atmosphere at the present concentration of CO_2 (IPCC 1996).
3. Hydrogen produced electrolytically is more costly than hydrogen derived from fuels largely because electricity is far more expensive than fuel per unit of contained energy. Averaged over all users in the United States in 1993 the electricity price was three times the price of all petroleum products, five times the price of natural gas, and 14 times the price of coal (EIA 1995). Hydrogen derived from electricity will be even more expensive than the electricity "feed" used in its manufacture, both because of inefficiencies in electrolytic conversion and because of the capital needed for electrolytic equipment.

   Although hydrogen derived from carbon-rich fuels via thermochemical processes will be more expensive than these feedstocks per unit of contained energy, it will not be nearly so expensive as electrolytic hydrogen, because the basic processes involved in "turning carbon into hydrogen" (see Appendix A) are relatively simple and not nearly so capital intensive as the process of making electricity.

4. When hydrogen is derived electrolytically from off-peak power sources that have low running costs, it can be economically attractive, because the capital charges can be avoided. However, the total quantities of hydrogen potentially available via this route are tiny in relation to the demand for fluid fuel. Nevertheless, hydrogen derived electrolytically from off-peak hydroelectric power will play important roles in providing hydrogen for various demonstration projects and other niche applications in helping launch a hydrogen economy.

5. In late 1995, Ballard introduced a 60 passenger, 275 hp, hydrogen PEM fuel cell "commercial prototype" bus having a 400 km (250 mile) range. It has sold three hydrogen fuel cell buses each to the Chicago Transit Authority and to BC Transit in Vancouver, British Columbia; the first bus was delivered to Chicago in September 1996. In 1998 Ballard expects to be producing commercially 75 passenger, 275 hp, hydrogen fuel cell buses having a 560 km (350 mile) range. In collaboration with Ballard and using Ballard fuel cells, Daimler-Benz has introduced three experimental fuel cell vehicles: a proof-of-concept hydrogen PEM fuel cell van (NECAR I) in April 1994, a prototype hydrogen-powered fuel cell passenger van (NECAR II) in April 1996, and a small prototype methanol-fuelled fuel cell passenger car (NCAR III) with an onboard fuel processor in September 1997. In joint ventures with Ballard, Daimler-Benz hopes to produce 100,000 engines per year for fuel cell vehicles by 2005. Also Toyota has introduced two experimental fuel cell vehicles: a prototype hydrogen fuel cell passenger car using metal hydride storage in October 1996, and a prototype methanol fuel cell passenger car with onboard fuel processing in September 1997.

6. In one study carried out for the US Department of Energy by the Allison Gas Turbine Division of General Motors (AGTD 1994), it is estimated that, in mass production, the cost for a 60 kW_e continuous output ($\sim$90 kW_e peak output) automotive electrochemical engine system based on use of the PEM fuel cell operated on methanol would be US\$3,899 – consisting of US\$1,752 for the fuel cell stack, plus US\$1,077 for the fuel processor, US\$195 for the heat rejection and water management system, and US\$875 for system auxiliaries – so that the total unit installed cost would be US\$65/kW_e continuous (US\$46/kW_e peak).

    In another study carried out for the US Department of Energy by Directed Technologies, Inc. (James et al. 1994), the cost of mass-produced automotive hydrogen/air PEM fuel cells (for production at a rate of 10^6 units per year in the year 2004) is estimated to be US\$31/kW_e, and the cost of an 85 kW_e hydrogen/air PEM fuel-cell-based automotive power system (including the cost of the fuel cell, the heat management system, the power conditioning, an ultracapacitor for peak power, an electric motor, and storage tanks for compressed hydrogen) is estimated to be US\$4,400–5,100, compared with US\$3,000–4,000 for the cost of the internal combustion engine equipment that would be displaced.

7. At the site or, in transport applications, onboard the vehicle, methanol is "re-formed" to produce a gaseous mixture of hydrogen and carbon dioxide via reactions that are summarized as:

$$CH_3OH + H_2O_{(g)} \rightarrow CO_2 + 3\,H_2.$$

    This gaseous fuel mixture can be utilized directly by proton-exchange-membrane fuel cells, which (unlike the alkaline fuel cells used in the space programme) are not poisoned by CO_2.

8. Hydrogen and methanol can be produced from natural gas with commercially available technology. These energy carriers can also be produced from coal using commercially ready oxygen-blown coal gasifiers plus commercially available technologies for the needed further processing. In the case of biomass, the fuel-processing technologies downstream of the gasifier are also commercially available. Although suitable gasifiers tailored to biomass are not commercially available, such gasifiers could be commercially available by 2000 with a relatively modest R&D effort (Williams et al. 1995a,b).

9. When hydrogen is produced from natural gas, the carbon content of the natural gas feedstock amounts to 15.2 kg C per GJ of produced hydrogen, and the CO_2 stream separated at

the PSA unit has a carbon content of 10.7 kg C per GJ of produced hydrogen. When hydrogen is produced from coal, the carbon content of the coal feedstock amounts to 31.8 kg C per GJ of produced hydrogen, and the CO_2 stream separated at the PSA unit has a carbon content of 29.8 kg C per GJ of produced hydrogen.

10. When hydrogen is produced from biomass, the carbon content of the biomass feedstock amounts to 34.4 kg C per GJ of produced hydrogen, and the CO_2 stream separated at the PSA unit has a carbon content of 23.8 kg C per GJ of produced hydrogen.

11. In this paper, all costs are presented in 1991US$ and lifecycle costs are evaluated using a 10 per cent real (inflation-corrected) discount rate. Corporate income, property, and sales taxes are neglected. Also, the energy content of fuels is given in terms of the higher heating value.

12. The present analysis is limited to hydrogen because the sequestration potential is much larger than for methanol production (see table 6.1). However, the general finding that sequestration costs are low holds for methanol as well. In fact, the costs for CO_2 compression would be less with methanol production. In this case, the CO_2 is generally released at higher pressures using Selexol CO_2 separation technology (e.g. 13 bar for methanol produced from biomass using the Battelle Columbus Laboratory biomass gasifier and 21.8 bar for methanol produced from coal using the Shell gasifier – Katofsky 1993) than is the case for the PSA technology used in hydrogen production (1.3 bar). If the CO_2 must be compressed to 110 bar, the required compression ratio is just 8.5 for biomass- and 5.0 for coal-derived methanol, compared with 85 for hydrogen produced from natural gas, coal, or biomass.

13. The costs for drying and compressing CO_2 to the pressures needed for pipeline transport and reservoir injection are based on Farla et al. (1992) at Utrecht University – see note d, table 6.5.

14. The costs of CO_2 transport by pipeline are based on analyses carried out at the Statoil R&D Centre in Trondheim, Norway (Skovholt 1993) – see note e, tables 6.6 and 6.7.

15. The costs for disposal in both depleted natural gas fields and saline aquifers are based on the work of Hendriks (1994) at Utrecht University – see note e, table 6.5, and note f, tables 6.6 and 6.7.

16. Drawing on commercial plantation experience in Brazil (Carpentieri et al. 1993), biomass supply curves (potential production vs. long-run marginal production cost) have been generated on a country-by-country basis for Africa, Latin America, and Asia, for the year 2025, taking into account land requirements for food production at that time (Larson et al. 1995). Marginal costs were related to prospective yields, and prospective yields were estimated via a correlation with rainfall. It was found that 70 EJ/year (35 EJ/year) of biomass could be produced on 10 per cent (5 per cent) of "available" land in those countries where biomass can be produced at or below this cost. Available land is defined here as non-forest, non-wilderness land that is not needed for producing food crops. To put these energy quantities into perspective, consumption of coal, oil, and natural gas in 1990 was 35.8 EJ, 40.5 EJ, and 12.2 EJ, respectively, for developing countries.

17. In a major assessment carried out by a team with participants from the Oak Ridge National Laboratory and the US Department of Agriculture, it is estimated that if R&D goals for plantation biomass in United States can be realized, 5 EJ/year of plantation biomass could be produced in 2020 on 17 million hectares at a long-run marginal cost of US$1.5/GJ (Graham et al. 1995). For comparison, about 3 EJ/year of biomass would be required to support a fleet of 120 million cars (the total number in the United States in 1992) powered by hydrogen fuel cells, assuming the gasoline-equivalent fuel economy of these fuel cell cars is 34 km/litre (80 mpg).

18. The least costly electrolytic option is for a photovoltaic (PV) module efficiency of 18 per cent, a PV installed system cost of US$1,030/kW, and a plant siting in an area of high insolation (270 W/m^2). These PV performance and cost parameters are optimistic but plausible for advanced thin-film PV technologies (Ogden and Nitsch 1993).

217

19. With a cost of service comparison, even costs for electrolytic hydrogen used in fuel cell vehicles are not much different from the 2.65 cents/km cost of gasoline for an internal combustion engine vehicle – ranging from 2.75 to 3.90 cents/km for the electrolytic options shown in figure 6.3.
20. Storage costs estimated by Hendriks (1994) range from US$3/tC to US$13/tC for depleted natural gas fields, compared with US$9/tC to US$34/tC for saline aquifers.
21. For comparison, a carbon tax in the range US$39–63/tC would increase the retail price of gasoline shown in figure 6.2 by 11–17 per cent.
22. It is assumed that hydrogen is stored onboard vehicles in carbon-fibre-wrapped aluminium tanks at high pressure (550 bar). Because of the bulkiness of gaseous hydrogen storage, the hydrogen FCV is designed for a range between refuellings of 400 km, compared with 640 km for a gasoline ICEV. The weight of the hydrogen FCV is estimated to be 1.3 tonnes, compared with 1.4 tonnes for the ICEV. Initial costs are estimated to be US$17,800 for an ICEV and US$25,100 for a hydrogen FCV (in mass production). The initial cost for a gasoline FCV is assumed to be US$21,700, the same as the estimated cost for a methanol FCV (Ogden et al. 1994). Retail fuel taxes are included under "other non-fuel operating costs" at the average US rate for gasoline used in ICEVs; to ensure that road tax revenues are the same for all options, it is assumed that retail taxes are 0.75 cents/km for all options (equivalent to 8.2 cents/litre or 31 cents/gallon for gasoline used in ICEVs).
23. The US Department of Energy has projected that the wellhead price of natural gas in the United States will increase at an annual average rate of 3.1 per cent per year, 1993–2010 (EIA 1995).
24. Considerable hydrogen production from biomass is likely to be possible before land scarcity becomes a major limiting factor for the growing of biomass. See, for example, the calculation presented in Appendix B, and discussions of land-use availability for industrialized countries in Williams (1994a) and for developing countries in Larson et al. (1995).
25. With sequestration of the separated CO_2, the amount of biomass grown on a given land area could make a much larger contribution in reducing global emissions than without sequestration.

References

AGTD (Allison Gas Turbine Division), General Motors Corporation (1994) *Research and Development of Proton-Exchange Membrane (PEM) Fuel Cell System for Transportation Applications: Initial Conceptual Design Report.* Prepared for the US Department of Energy, Office of Transportation Technologies, Report DOE/CH/10435-01, Contract No. DE-AC02-90CH10435, February.

Anderson, D. and K. Ahmed (1995) *The Case for Solar Energy Investments.* World Bank Technical Paper No. 279, Energy Series. Washington D.C.: World Bank.

Blok, K., C. Hendriks, and W. Turkenburg (1989) The role of carbon dioxide removal in the reduction of the greenhouse effect. IEA/OECD Expert Seminar on Energy Technologies for Reducing Emissions of Greenhouse Gases, Paris, 12–14 April.

Blok, K., R. H. Williams, R. E. Katofsky, and C. A. Hendriks (1997) Hydrogen production from natural gas, sequestration of recovered CO_2 in depleted gas wells and enhanced natural gas recovery. *Energy* **22**(2–3): 161–168.

Burgt, M. van der, J. Cantle, and V. Boutkan (1992) Carbon dioxide disposal from coal-based IGCCs in depleted gas fields. In: K. Blok, W. Turkenburg, C. Hendriks, and M. Steinberg (eds.), *Proceedings of the First International Conference on Carbon Dioxide Removal*, pp. 603–610. *Energy Conversion and Management* **33** (5–8), Oxford: Pergamon Press.

Carlson, D. and S. Wagner (1993) Amorphous silicon photovoltaic systems. In T. B. Johansson, H. Kelly, A. K. N. Reddy, and R. H. Williams (eds.), *Renewable Energy: Sources for Fuels and Electricity*, pp. 403–435. Washington D.C.: Island Press.

Carpentieri, A., E. Larson, and J. Woods (1993) Future biomass-based electricity supply in Northeast Brazil. *Biomass and Bioenergy* **4**(3): 149–173.

Christodoulou, D. (1984) Technology and economics of the transmission of gaseous fuels via pipelines. M.Sc. in Engineering thesis, Department of Mechanical and Aerospace Engineering, School of Engineering and Applied Sciences, Princeton University, April.

Dunnison, D. (Ballard Power Systems) and J. Wilson (The Dow Chemical Company) (1994) PEM fuel cells: A commercial reality. In: *A Collection of Technical Papers: Part 3, 29th Intersociety Energy Conversion Engineering Conference*, pp. 1260–1263. Monterey, CA, 7–11 August.

EIA (Energy Information Administration) (1995) *Annual Energy Outlook 1995, with Projections to 2010*. DOE/EIA-0383(95). Washington D.C.: US Department of Energy.

Engelenburg, B. van and K. Blok (1993) Disposal of carbon dioxide in permeable underground layers: A feasible option? *Climatic Change* **23**: 55–68.

Farla, J., C. Hendriks, and K. Blok (1992) Carbon dioxide recovery from industrial processes. Report prepared for the Integrated Research Programme on Carbon Dioxide Removal and Storage, Department of Science, Technology, and Society, Utrecht University, Utrecht, the Netherlands, December.

Flavin, C. and N. Lenssen 1994. *Power Surge: Guide to the Coming Energy Revolution*. New York: Norton.

Graham, R., E. Lichtenberg, V. Roningen, H. Shapouri, and M. Walsh (1995) The economics of biomass production in the United States. In: *Proceedings of the Second Biomass Conference of the Americas, Portland, OR, 21–24 August*, pp. 1314–1323. NREL/CP-200-8098, DE 95009230. Golden, CO: National Renewable Energy Laboratory.

Hall, D., F. Rosille-Calle, R. Williams, and J. Woods (1993) Biomass for energy: Supply prospects. In: T. B. Johansson, H. Kelly, A. K. N. Reddy, and R. H. Williams (eds.), *Renewable Energy: Sources for Fuels and Electricity*, pp. 593–651. Washington D.C.: Island Press.

Hendriks, C. (1994) Carbon dioxide removal from coal-fired power plants. Ph.D. thesis, Department of Science, Technology, and Society, Utrecht University, Utrecht, the Netherlands.

Holloway, S. (1996) An overview of the Joule II Project. *Energy Conversion and Management* **37**(1–2): 1149–1154.

IEA (International Energy Agency) (1995) *Energy Prices and Taxes: Second Quarter 1994*. Paris: OECD.

IPCC (Intergovernmental Panel on Climate Change) (1990) *Climate Change: The IPCC Scientific Assessment*, ed. J. T. Houghton, G. J. Jenkins, and J. J. Ephraums. Cambridge: Cambridge University Press.

——— 1992. *Climate Change 1992: The Supplementary Report to the IPCC Scientific*

219

Assessment, ed. J. T. Houghton, B. A. Callander, and S. K. Varney. Cambridge: Cambridge University Press.

―――― (1994) *Radiative Forcing of Climate Change: The 1994 Special Report of the Scientific Assessment Working Group of the IPCC*, ed. J. T. Houghton, L. G. Meiro Filho, J. Bruce, Hoesung Lee, B. A. Callander, E. Haites, N. Harris, and K. Maskell. Cambridge: Cambridge University Press.

―――― (1996) *Climate Change 1995: The Science of Climate Change*, ed. J. T. Houghton, L. G. Meiro Filho, B. A. Callander, N. Harris, A. Kattenberg, and K. Maskell. Cambridge: Cambridge University Press.

James, B., G. Baum, and I. Kuhn (1994) Technology development goals for automotive fuel cell power systems: Final Report to Argonne National Laboratory. US Department of Energy, ANL-94/44, August.

Johansson, T., H. Kelly, A. Reddy, and R. Williams (1993) Renewable fuels and electricity for a growing world economy: Defining and achieving the potential. In: T. B. Johansson, H. Kelly, A. K. N. Reddy, and R. H. Williams (eds.), *Renewable Energy: Sources for Fuels and Electricity*, pp. 1–71. Washington D.C.: Island Press.

Katofsky, R. (1993) *The Production of Fluid Fuels from Biomass*. PU/CEES Report No. 273. Princeton, NJ: Center for Energy and Environmental Studies, Princeton University.

Koide, H. et al. (1992) Subterranean containment and long-term storage of carbon dioxide in unused aquifers and in depleted natural gas reservoirs. In: K. Blok, W. Turkenburg, C. Hendriks, and M. Steinberg (eds.), *Proceedings of the First International Conference on Carbon Dioxide Removal*, pp. 619–626. *Energy Conversion and Management* **33**(5–8), Oxford: Pergamon Press.

Larson, E., L. Rodriguez, and T. Rexende de Azevedo (1994) Farm forestry in Brazil. Paper prepared for BioResources '94, Bangalore, India, October.

Larson, E., C. Marrison, and R. Williams (1995) CO_2 mitigation potential of biomass energy plantations in developing regions. Center for Energy and Environmental Studies, Princeton University, draft MS.

Leeth, G. (1979) In: K. E. Cox and K. D. Williamson (eds.), *Hydrogen: Its Technology and Implications; Volume II: Transmission and Storage*. Cleveland, OH: CRC Press.

Little, A. D. (1995) Fuel cells for building cogeneration applications – Cost/performance requirements, and markets. Final Report prepared for the Building Equipment Division, Office of Building Technology, US Department of Energy, NTIS, Springfield, VA.

Manabe, S. and R. Stouffer (1993) Century-scale effects of increased CO_2 on the ocean–atmosphere system. *Nature* **362**(6434): 215–217.

―――― (1994) Multi-century response of a coupled ocean–atmosphere model to an increase of atmospheric carbon dioxide. *Journal of Climate* **7**(1): 5–23.

Mark, J., J. Ohi, and D. Hudson (1994) Fuel savings and emissions reductions from light duty fuel cell vehicles. In: *A Collection of Technical Papers: Part 3, 29th Intersociety Energy Conversion Engineering Conference*, pp. 1425–1429. Monterey, CA, 7–11 August.

Masters, C., E. Attanasi, D. Root (1994) World petroleum assessment and analysis. In: *Proceedings of the 14th World Petroleum Congress, Stavanger, Norway*. New York: Wiley.

Ogden, J. and J. Nitsch (1993) Solar hydrogen. In: T. B. Johansson, H. Kelly, A. K. N. Reddy, and R. H. Williams (eds.), *Renewable Energy: Sources for Fuels and Electricity*, pp. 925–1009. Washington D.C.: Island Press.

Ogden, J. and R. Williams (1989) *Solar Hydrogen: Moving Beyond Fossil Fuels.* Washington, D.C.: World Resources Institute.

Ogden, J., E. Larson, and M. DeLuchi (1994) *A Technical and Economic Assessment of Renewable Transportation Fuels and Technologies.* Report to the Office of Technology Assessment, US Congress, Washington D.C., May.

Ogden, J., E. Dennis, M. Steinbugler, and J. Strohbehn (1995) *Hydrogen Energy Systems Studies.* Final Report from the Center for Energy and Environmental Studies, Princeton University, to the National Renewable Energy Laboratory on US DOE Contract No. XR-11265-2, 18 January.

Pottier, J., E. Blondin, and A. Garat (1988) Large-scale transmission and storage of hydrogen. In: T. N. Veziroglu and A. N. Protosenko (eds.), *Hydrogen Energy Progress VII, Proceedings of the World Hydrogen Energy Conference.* Moscow, 25–29 September.

Skovholt, O. (1993) CO_2 transportation systems. *Energy Conversion and Management* **34**(9–11): 1095–1103.

Summerfield, I. R. and S. H. Goldhorpe (British Coal Corporation, Coal Research Establishment) and N. Williams and A. Sheikh (Bechtel Ltd.) (1993) Costs of CO_2 disposal options. IEA Carbon Dioxide Disposal Symposium, Christchurch College, Oxford, England, 29–31 March.

Turkenburg, W. (1992) CO_2 removal: Some conclusions. In: K. Blok, W. Turkenburg, C. Hendriks, and M. Steinberg (eds.), *Proceedings of the First International Conference on Carbon Dioxide Removal*, pp. 819–823. *Energy Conversion and Management* **33**(5–8), Oxford: Pergamon Press.

WEC (World Energy Council) (1994) *New Renewable Energy Resources: A Guide to the Future.* London: Kogan Page.

Williams, R. (1993) Fuel cells, their fuels, and the US automobile. Proceedings of the First Annual World Car 2001 Conference, University of California at Riverside, Riverside, CA, 20–24 June.

——— (1994a) Roles for biomass energy in sustainable development. In: R. H. Socolow et al. (eds.), *Industrial Ecology and Global Change.* Cambridge: Cambridge University Press.

——— (1994b) Fuel cell vehicles: The clean machine. *Technology Review*, April: 21–30.

——— (1995) Variants of a low CO_2-emitting energy supply system (LESS) for the world. Prepared for Working Group IIa (Energy Supply Mitigation Options) of the Intergovernmental Panel on Climate Change, in support of Chapter 19 (Energy Supply Mitigation Options) of the IPCC's Second Assessment Report, Report No. PNL-10851, Pacific Northwest Laboratories, Richland, Washington, 99352, USA.

Williams, R., E. Larson, R. Katofsky, and J. Chen (1995a) Methanol and hydrogen from biomass for transportation. *Energy for Sustainable Development* **1**(5): 18–34.

——— (1995b) Methanol and hydrogen from biomass for transportation, with comparisons to methanol and hydrogen from natural gas and coal. PU/CEES Report No. 292, Center for Energy and Environmental Studies, Princeton University, Princeton, NJ, July.

Wilson, T. (1992) The deep ocean disposal of carbon dioxide. In: K. Blok, W. Turkenburg, C. Hendriks, and M. Steinberg (eds.), *Proceedings of the First International Conference on Carbon Dioxide Removal*, pp. 627–633. *Energy Conversion and Management* **33**(5–8), Oxford: Pergamon Press.

Zweibel, K. and A. Barnett (1993) Polycrystalline thin-film photovoltaics. In: T. B. Johansson, H. Kelly, A. K. N. Reddy, and R. H. Williams (eds.), *Renewable Energy: Sources for Fuels and Electricity*, pp. 437–481. Washington D.C.: Island Press.

7

Photovoltaics

Paolo Frankl

Introduction

Photovoltaic (PV) cells are semiconductor devices that convert sunlight directly into electricity. Apart from using the inexhaustible, zero-cost, solar primary energy source, PV systems show several advantages, even when compared with other renewable energy technologies. These include low environmental impact, simplicity, modularity, long lifetimes, and low maintenance requirements.

Despite these advantages and despite a rapidly evolving technology, PV systems have not found large-scale use up to now. Almost all PV penetration scenarios developed in the past have proven to be overoptimistic. Certainly, the major barrier to widespread adoption of PV systems is their continuing high cost. These costs have fallen significantly, but not as rapidly as was hoped.

Given these facts, the question might be raised to what extent PV can actually play a significant role in a future sustainable energy scenario. People participating in the debate on this question are roughly divided in two opinion groups. Some people think that PV is one of the most promising energy conversion technologies for the twenty-first century. Their optimism is based mainly on three factors: the inexhaustible primary energy resource, the wide range of applications, and, above all, the enormous potential for technological improvement. PV technology is still young. As technology improves and market demand grows, PV electricity prices should fall sharply, making PV fully competitive with other conventional and renewable energy sources. Other people think that PV technology will have only a minor role in the future world energy system. These people claim that PV acceptance is impeded not only by high costs but also by other major drawbacks, namely low efficiency, the large surface areas required, and intermittent power supply source.

The aim of the present paper is to discuss these two positions in some detail and to address two fundamental questions:

- Is PV compatible with the long-term targets of a sustainable energy system?
- What roles can PV play in the eco-restructuring transition?

In order to answer these questions, the paper will first analyse the technological potential of PV (the technology "state-of-the-art" and its rate of change). Second, it will go into the details of the main barrier to the widespread use of PV, its present high cost. Then, it will identify a possible PV market diffusion strategy. Finally, it will suggest possible scenarios for PV penetration in the twenty-first-century energy system.

The paper argues that PV is fully compatible with the *long-term* targets of a sustainable energy system (in environmental, economic, social, and geopolitical terms, as defined by Rogner in chap. 5 of this volume). PV is compatible with a decarbonized energy system based on the delivery of energy *services,* with electricity and hydrogen as energy vectors. Because it is extremely flexible in terms of technological options, range of applications, synergisms with other energy technologies, and the actors involved, PV is consistent with all sustainable energy patterns open to innovation and technological change. Therefore, PV will play a major role within the twenty-first-century energy system.

The technological potential of PV

The basics of PV systems

The fundamental element of any PV system is the PV *cell.* A PV cell is a particular semiconductor device that is able to convert sunlight directly into electricity (direct current). PV cells are inherently low-voltage, high-current-density devices. Several series-connected cells

How PV cells work

The possibility of producing electrical energy directly from sunlight is based on some properties of semiconductor materials, and particularly on the inter-action occurring in certain solid materials between photons (light packets or "quanta") and the electrons of the solid-state atomic matrix.

Semiconductors are characterized by the existence of a so-called "energy band gap." This is the finite difference between the energy level of electrons in a stable position in the crystal structure – the *valence band* – and the next allowed electron energy band level, known as the *conduction band*, in which an electron can move freely through the material. The magnitude of the gap is different for each semiconductor material.

In an equilibrium situation at room temperature with no external applied fields, the semiconductor valence band is completely filled by the valence (external orbital) electrons, whereas the conduction band is completely free of electrons. When the semiconductor is exposed to sunlight, photons with an energy content higher than the band gap can excite electrons from their stable energy level (the valence band) to higher energy levels (the conduction band), leaving a so-called *hole* in the valence band. In this state, if an external electric field is applied, the material is able to carry electricity.

However, in order to *produce* electricity, a further step is needed. In the absence of an electric field, the excited electrons in the conduction band will recombine with the holes. That is, they will "relax" into the vacant, lower-energy levels in the valence band, and no current will be observed. In effect, the electrons excited by the photons need to be oriented by an electric field to produce useful current. The basic concept of a PV device is to produce this electric field *internally* in the solid. This is achieved by combining semi-conductor materials with different characteristics to form a *junction*. Two configurations, namely homojunctions and heterojunctions, are possible. In homojunctions, two differently doped layers of the same semiconductor are combined, whereas heterojunctions are made by two (or more) semicon-ductors with different energy gaps.

In the junction zone a *built-in* electric field is established, which is able spa-tially to separate the photo-excited electrons from the holes and start them drifting in opposite directions. If the cell material quality is good enough, the carriers will reach the external electric contacts of the cell and a voltage between the latter will be observed (photovoltaic effect). If an external load is applied, direct current will pass through the electric circuit. The PV cell is then gen-erating useful electrical power.

PV cells are inherently low-voltage, high-current-density devices. A typical commercial crystalline silicon cell (10 cm × 10 cm area) can produce a current of up to 3 amperes at a voltage of only 0.5 volts. Several series-connected cells are therefore needed to form a module, the basic commercial component of PV systems. A commercial silicon module ($0.4 \ m^2$ area) produces between $40 \ W_p$ and $50 \ W_p$ at 17V voltage. Several modules are then connected to form a string. The in series and/or in parallel connection of different strings makes it possible to obtain practically any desired operating voltage for the final PV system (from low voltage for household applications to 20kV for large power plants).

are needed to form a *module*, the basic commercial component of PV systems. Several modules are then connected to form a string. The in series and/or in parallel connection of different strings makes it possible to obtain practically any desired operating voltage for the final PV system.

Depending on the type of electrical connection, there are two main categories of PV systems: the autonomous (stand-alone) and the grid-connected systems.

In the stand-alone systems, the PV field is connected to a means of energy storage (usually electrical batteries). The energy produced can thus also be used when the sun does not shine.

In the grid-connected systems, usually no accumulation systems are employed and the electricity is fed directly into the grid. Power conditioning systems are needed to operate the system at maximum power and to avoid stability problems in the electricity network. Finally, an inverter is needed to convert the direct current produced by the PV modules into useful alternating current. However, it should be noted that many appliances (e.g. all electronic devices and several high-efficiency lamps) could run on direct current. Several companies are exploring the possibility of introducing a dual supply for their products.

The final part of a PV system is its supporting structure. There are two categories of system: those mounted on purpose-built structures (i.e. power plants in open fields and PV systems on flat roofs), and building-integrated systems, which use part of the building structure for support.

In current terminology there are two basically different parts to a PV system: the PV *module*; and all other structures and means by which the electricity produced by the module can be delivered to the grid or to the final users. This so-called "Balance-of-System" includes all supporting structures, power conditioning systems, wiring, and eventual energy storage systems.

PV technologies

There are many different possible technologies for manufacturing PV cells and modules. A classification can be made with regard to system types, manufacturing processes, and semiconductor materials. One main distinction can be made between *crystalline semiconductor cells* and *thin-film* devices.

Thanks to the related experience of the electronics industry, *crystalline silicon cells* dominate the PV market at present. In 1993 they had 84 per cent of market share (Vigotti 1994a). Crystalline silicon cells use scraps from the electronics industry as a feedstock. Today, this mature technology is the only one that can simultaneously offer high stability, long lifetimes, high module efficiencies (15.3 per cent for high-purity monocrystalline Si modules and 11.1 per cent for polycrystalline Si modules of slightly lower purity), and advanced production status (see also table 7.1).

However, this particular technology will have to give way to other PV technologies in the near–mid future, for at least two reasons. First, demand by the PV industry will soon exceed the amount of scrap material offered by the electronics industry. Second, and more important, the present technology derives directly from the electronics industry and is *not optimized* for PV cell production. The present manufacturing processes of crystalline silicon cells are very inefficient in terms of the consumption of both primary energy and raw materials. This is also reflected in the present high cost of PV systems.

In the near future, so-called "solar-grade" crystalline silicon cells will most likely be used. Solar-grade silicon is much less pure than electronics-grade silicon, but pure enough for PV cells. Solar-grade silicon manufacturing processes rely on completely different purification processes of metallurgical silicon. These processes are much simpler than the ones currently used for silicon cells derived from electronics scraps. They are also expected to be much more efficient as far as primary energy consumption and raw materials use are concerned. Up to 1995, there had been no large-scale production of solar-grade silicon. However, solar-grade silicon production has top priority on the agenda of several PV industries, particularly in Europe and in Japan.

In the mid–long term, the large-scale use of *thin-film* PV devices is expected. Thin films are based on yet another completely different approach and manufacturing process from those employed for crystalline PV cells. Whereas crystalline silicon requires a thickness of about 200 microns to absorb 90 per cent of incident light, thin films need only a few microns of active material to collect the same amount of radiation. Consequently, far less semiconductor material is needed. This greatly decreases costs and reduces primary material resource use and primary energy consumption during manufacturing. Secondly,

Table 7.1 Conversion efficiency of various PV technologies at the different stages of their development (%)

Cell type	Largest standard commercial module[a]	Best prototype module	Area (cm²)	Best laboratory cell	Area (cm²)	Theoretical limit	Production status
CRYSTALLINE SEMICONDUCTOR							
Silicon							
Monocrystalline Si	15.3	20.8	743	24.0	4.00	30–33	Large-scale
		19.5	3,080	21.6	47.00		
Polycrystalline Si (p-Si)	11.1	17.0		17.2	100.00	22	Large-scale
EFG-band p-Si				14.7	50.00		Small-scale
Dendritic Web				17.0	4.00		Pilot prod.
GaAs							
Monocrystalline on GaAs				29.0	0.05		Small-scale
Monocrystalline on other substrate				17.6	1.00		Pilot
THIN FILMS							
Amorphous silicon (a-Si)	6.8	10.2	933	12.7	1.00	27–28	Large-scale
				12.0	100.00		
p-Si on ceramic (100 microns thick)		11.2	225	14.9	1.00	20	
Polycrystalline silicon				15.7	1.00		
Polycrystalline GaAs				8.8	8.00		
CdTe	7.25	10.0	3,528	15.8	1.00	28	Pilot
		7.7					
CIS		11.1	3,880	15.9	1.00	23.5	Pilot
		9.7		13.9	7.00		
Mechanically stacked a-Si and CIS				15.6	4.00		
GaAs[b]		22.0		29.3	0.50	42	
GaAs on GaSb[b]				34.0			
				37.0	0.05		

Sources: Green and Emery (1994), Kelly (1993), IAEA (1992), *Proceedings of the 1st PV World Conference* (1995).

a. Typical commercial PV module areas range from 0.5 to 0.75 m².

b. Concentrator systems: in these systems *direct* radiation is concentrated on a small cell by means of a Fresnel lens.

thin-film production techniques are particularly well suited for large-scale production. Thin-film deposition is done by directly spraying or sputtering the active material onto a glass or metal substrate. This continuous process is far more efficient than the batch processes of crystalline cell production. Moreover, it allows a manufacturer to produce cells as large as complete crystalline modules. This increases the effective active area and eliminates the problems and costs of connecting a number of cells together to form a module. Moreover, by stacking several thin-film layers, multijunction cells can be produced. In such a cell, each layer absorbs a different part of the light spectrum. In principle, the theoretical efficiency limit of multijunction cells is much higher than that of conventional cells. Finally, several thin-film modules are semi-transparent. Therefore, they can be used in buildings as PV "windows" or PV glazing surfaces.

In table 7.1, the conversion efficiencies[1] of the various PV technologies at the different stages of their development are summarized. The important thing to note is that efficiencies much higher than those of commercial modules have been achieved in the laboratory. Thus there is still considerable potential for further improvement between the theoretical and commercial limits. Uncertainties regarding production costs, the investments needed, and the rapidity of technological improvement make it impossible to select a single best or most likely PV system for the future.

However, it is much more important to realize that all PV technologies are in rapid evolution. Figure 7.1 shows the past efficiency evolution over time for different types of cells. Moreover, the fact that *several* technology development paths seem capable of providing comparable PV cell efficiencies and costs in the future means that there is likely to be competition between different design approaches. In turn, this is likely to accelerate improvements in PV technology and the industrialization process and to reduce manufacturing costs.

PV applications

PV systems are highly modular and therefore offer a wide range of applications. As already mentioned, the series and/or parallel connection of different modules and/or strings allow one to obtain practically any desired operating voltage for the final PV system. Figure 7.2 summarizes the applications of PV systems as a function of installed peak power. As shown, the range of possible applications

229

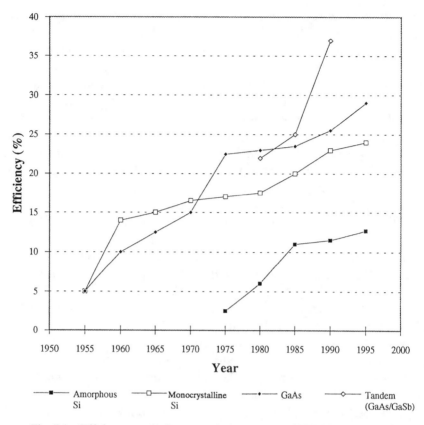

Fig. 7.1 **Efficiency evolution over time per type of PV laboratory cell**

extends from very small devices such as solar calculators or watches to the grid-connected multi-megawatt power plants.

Today, PV systems for communications and solar home systems have the largest market share (21 per cent and 15 per cent respectively) (EPIA 1995). Up to 2010, the two largest markets expected are (a) solar home systems in developing countries, and (b) grid-connected, mainly building-mounted systems in industrialized countries (see also the section on "A PV market diffusion strategy").

PV is very well suited to provide electricity to rural and remote areas in developing countries. Whereas taking the electricity grid to the people living in those areas would imply enormous investments and might take decades, small PV stand-alone solar home systems with a small battery storage are cost effective and can meet some basic needs such as lighting and TV. This would tremendously increase the

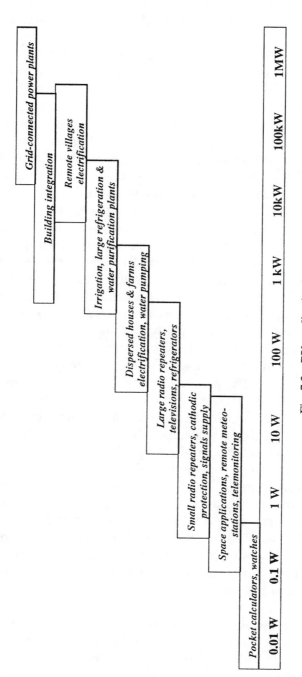

Fig. 7.2 **PV applications**

quality of life of the local population. It would also encourage people to stay in their communities rather than migrate to a megalopolis in the hopes of increasing their standard of living. Although the cost of a solar home system today (around US$500) is relatively expensive for rural conditions, it could be subsidized by low-interest financing programmes. This is currently being done by the World Bank in some Asian countries.

The application of building-integrated PV systems is particularly interesting, because it shows several advantages compared with "conventional" PV power plants. First, the occupation of surfaces already used for other purposes substantially reduces the main environmental obstacle to the adoption and diffusion of PV, namely land requirements. As a consequence, it greatly increases the potential applicability of PV in areas of high population density. Second, integration into already existing or planned supporting structures and the substitution of building envelope materials reduce total system costs. Because total energy consumption during the manufacturing and installation of the systems is reduced, the energy payback time[2] of the PV system is also reduced and its (indirect and low) environmental impacts are further lowered. Finally, this application actually *expands* the technological potential of PV systems, because in buildings they can play more roles than solely producing electricity. For instance, building-integrated PV panels can save energy when used as sun-shading systems. Moreover, in buildings, there is the possibility of recovering a significant fraction of the thermal energy dissipated by the PV panels. This thermal energy can be used directly for room heating in winter and for pre-heating of water in all seasons. Potentially very interesting is the coupling of PV building-integrated systems with other solar-passive, bioclimatic architecture and energy-saving measures. This has significant environmental implications. Recent Life Cycle Analysis studies show that already building-integrated PV systems can "avoid" over twice the CO_2 emissions compared with conventional PV power plants (Frankl 1994).[3] These environmental benefits will increase with future PV technologies as conversion efficiencies increase and energy consumption during manufacturing decreases.

This application is poised to take off right now (1995), because practically all PV manufacturers worldwide are getting involved in developing new products to be integrated with buildings. Some non-PV cell producers are specializing in this sector as well, by purchasing cells and selling specific products for the buildings market. Products range from PV roof-tiles, to facades, construction materials, and colour modules. Applications range from office, residential, and industrial buildings up to carpark roofs and highway sound barriers.

This phenomenon could have enormous implications, because it raises the number of interested and involved actors by orders of magnitude, on both the supply and the demand side. The result will be to promote competition and investment in the PV sector. PV will be a subject of interest not only for the limited number of PV industries and electricity utilities around the world, but potentially for millions of architects and engineers, as well as for their clients.

PV costs

The major obstacle to the widespread use of PV is currently the high capital and installation costs of the system. Owing to the absence of moving parts and to the simplicity and reliability of PV systems, operating and maintenance costs can be very low if the lifetime is long enough. "Fuel" costs are obviously zero.

At present, installation costs are more or less equally shared between module costs and "Balance-of-System" (BOS) costs. PV module costs have fallen sharply during the past two decades as the global market grew to 61 MW peak power worldwide shipments in 1994. The average selling price of complete PV modules[4] fell from around US$50 per peak watt production in 1976 to less than US$5.5 in 1994 (Strategies Unlimited 1995) (see fig. 7.3).[5] In terms of current US$/$W_p$ prices, this corresponds to a general trend of price decline (about 10 per cent per year) over the past decade. In 1988–1990, however, supply shortages of crystalline silicon wafer scraps led to briefly higher prices of PV modules (actually a slower price decline, in real terms). After 1991, the previous rate of price decline resumed, owing to additional capacity coming on-line and a new surplus of electronics-grade silicon feedstock. The present (1995) PV market situation is characterized by over-capacity combined with increased price competition in the power module market (Vigotti 1994a). In the near term, price declines can be expected to continue.

But what can be said about long-term forecasts? Will PV module prices continue their historical downward path? At what rate of decline? Will there be a saturation point?

According to optimists, there is enormous potential for further PV cost reduction through technological innovation and economies of scale. This situation is depicted in the "PV learning curve" shown in

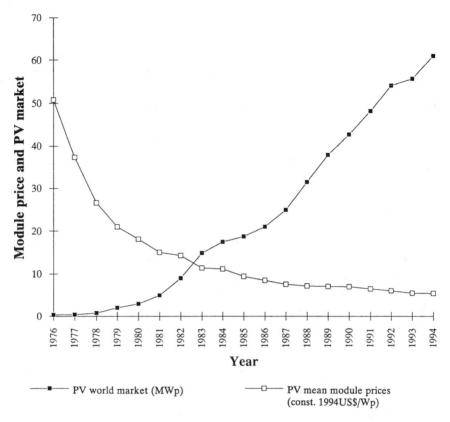

Fig. 7.3 **PV mean module prices and PV market**

figure 7.4. Based on the historical average price pattern, possible PV specific module prices down to US$1/$W_p$ for a world PV market of 1–10 GW_p are forecast. Pessimists, on the other hand, point out that this learning curve does not reflect the time variable. So, although the cost decline will almost certainly happen eventually, in fact it could be delayed for a considerable time.

However, there are at least three good reasons to be optimistic about specific cost reductions (US$/$W_p$) of PV systems. The first reason is that, until now, crystalline silicon modules using electronics-grade silicon scraps as a feedstock have dominated the world PV market. As already mentioned, their manufacturing processes derive from the electronics industry and are not optimized for PV cell production. The annual production capacity is fairly low (max. 5 MW_p/year for a single plant). Electronics-grade silicon scraps are becoming

234

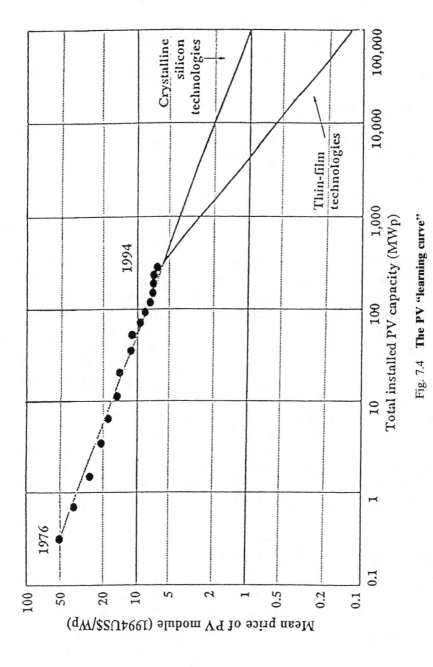

Fig. 7.4 The PV "learning curve"

235

scarce and expensive. Significant cost reductions will be achieved as soon as dedicated production facilities for solar-grade silicon are justified by demand. As a matter of fact, Siemens Solar recently announced a target price of US$2/$W_p$ for Czochralsky-based silicon crystal modules to be achieved through wafer geometry, process changes, and materials handling measures within a typical production capacity of 25–100 MW_p per year (Strategies Unlimited 1994). On the same occasion, Solarex Corp. presented its module production cost goal of US$1.20/$W_p$ within the framework of the US Department of Energy PVMat programme, to be reached by improved cutting, automated module assembly, and a threefold increase in production capacity.

Even sharper module cost reductions can be expected in the case of thin-film PV cells, irrespective of the basic semiconductor employed (amorphous silicon, CdTe, CIS, or others). First, this is due to the use of a much smaller amount of semiconductor material and to much lower energy consumption rates. Secondly, thin-film manufacturing techniques (direct deposition) allow the direct manufacturing of 1,000 cm^2 integrated solar modules (i.e. a-Si) and are particularly well suited for mass production.

The cost goals for thin-film modules are summarized in table 7.2 (Kelly 1993). In accordance with other authors (Coiante and Barra 1992), these considerations have been incorporated in figure 7.4 by assuming that another learning curve, with a faster-declining slope, will apply in the case of thin films. Such a two-slope learning curve is nothing new in the history of technology. Several products, and particularly semiconductor devices, have actually followed this type of historical pattern (Ayres and Martinas 1992). The present market situation, on the verge of a change in the slope of the learning curve, just reflects a maturing PV industry, emerging from the laboratory and entering the real energy market.

Table 7.2 **Cost goals for thin-film PV modules**

Semiconductor material	Module efficiency (%)	Annual production capacity (MW_p/year)	Expected module cost (US$/$W_p$)
Amorphous silicon	15	25	1.11–1.21
CdTe and CIS	10	10	1.19–1.86
All	15	150	0.50–0.78

Source: adapted from Kelly (1993).

236

In fact, in late 1994, a US natural gas company (Enron Corporation) entered into a joint venture with an oil company (Amoco Corporation) to form Amoco/Enron Solar and acquire 50 per cent ownership of Solarex (Strategies Unlimited 1994). Under the venture, it will participate in the US Department of Energy (DOE) Solar Enterprise Zone project, building up a 100 MW_p amorphous silicon solar power plant to be completed by 2003. Beginning in 1997, the PV electricity produced will be sold at the remarkable price of US$0.055/kWh, which is fully competitive with conventional electric power sources. Of course, this is the result of the DOE subsidy. However, most important, and for the first time in history, the development of a sustained long-term market will allow the venture to make large-scale production investments. This would induce a quantum step down the PV learning curve towards substantial cost reduction. The venture will eventually enable Solarex to be the largest world PV module manufacturer, with 10 MW_p annual output capacity expected in 1997, to be doubled again by the year 2000.

A final reason for optimism is that *several* types of laboratory test cells show much higher efficiencies than those of present commercial modules (see table 7.1 above), which still remain far below the theoretical limits. These very encouraging results will probably be transferred to the market within the next few years. For example, the 24 per cent efficient buried contact technology silicon cell is expected to go into mass production before 2000.[6] The first commercial modules, using low-cost, low-purity polycrystalline feedstock material, will have 15 per cent efficiency, with the potential for later improvements up to 22 per cent. Thus, observing that a wide range of technological patterns are in contention for the PV market, it can be concluded that some or several of them will achieve commercialization at competitive prices in a reasonable time-span.

More efficient modules need less area to produce the same amount of energy. As a consequence, efficiency gains will lead to a reduction in both specific (US$/$W_p$) module costs and "Balance-of-System" (BOS) costs, which also account for a high percentage of current costs.

There are reasons for substantial optimism that PV could soon enter a "virtuous circle" leading to competitiveness as far as the "Balance-of-System" too is concerned. For instance, "learning by doing" in large demonstration projects led to cost reductions of 50 per cent between 1984 and 1994 (see table 7.3). The world's largest operating PV power plant in Serre, Italy, showed BOS costs in the

Table 7.3 **BOS cost reduction in large demonstration projects**

PV power plant	Year of construction	Total power installed (kW$_p$)	"Balance-of-system" costs (US$/W$_p$)
Carrisa Plant (USA)	1984	760	6.56
Kerman Project (USA)	1992	500	3.02
Serre (Italy)	1994	3,300	3.20[a]
Possible replicas		1,000–5,000	2.00

Sources: adapted from Cunow (1994), Iliceto et al. (1994).
a. Original data in ECU; a 1994 exchange rate of 1 ECU = US$1.2 was assumed.

Table 7.4 **Total system costs for different PV technologies and applications**

Year	Module type	System type	Module price (US$/W$_p$)	BOS cost (US$/W$_p$)	Total system cost (US$/W$_p$)
1994	Crystallized silicon	Large power plant	4.25[a]	3.20	7.45
2000	Thin film	Building-integrated	2.50	1.00	3.50
2010	Thin film	Building-integrated	0.80	0.70	1.50

Sources: estimated on the basis of Kelly (1993), Iliceto et al. (1994), TERES (1994).
a. Large modules in quantity are usually sold at a price 20–25 per cent lower than the average selling price of all modules.

order of US$3.2/W$_p$.[7] An assessment of further possible improvements in industrial replications suggests further reduction potential in the range of 40 per cent, leading to an eventual cost of US$2/W$_p$ (Iliceto et al. 1994).

Potentially far more effective BOS cost reductions are likely to be achieved by the high diversification process of PV market products related to PV integration in buildings. At present, BOS costs of building-integrated PV demonstration systems are generally higher than those of power plants. However, as soon as more standardized market products and installation procedures are introduced, BOS costs will drop. Substantial improvements in both performance and cost reduction are also expected through the adoption of solid-state electrical inverters. The best building-integrated system costs could be as low as half the costs of some conventional centralized PV power plant systems as early as the year 2000 (TERES 1994). This would lead to significant total system cost reductions, as summarized in table 7.4.

238

Moreover, the installation costs of PV in buildings have to be considered within the framework of total building construction or retrofit costs. As regards conventional PV power plants, there are savings both because already existing (or at least planned) supporting structures are used and because PV panels are used instead of planned cladding components. In fact, it was recently estimated that PV panels on highway sound barriers in Switzerland could be cost effective in the immediate future (Strategies Unlimited 1994).[8]

Finally, PV integration in buildings also allows useful thermal energy recovery. In addition, the PV daily power supply curve coincides with the typical electricity demand curve, where that is driven by buildings-related energy final uses, such as air-conditioning.[9] Both of these "services" (co-generation and an electricity supply where and when it is needed) actually increase the value of the energy provided by PV systems in buildings.

In fact, the integration of PV in buildings could be enormously effective in providing the momentum needed for the PV industry to move along the learning curve.

A PV market diffusion strategy

In many energy "future" studies it has been assumed that PV will be competitive with other energy sources only if or when the long-term module price goal of US$1/$W_p$ is reached. At that price, 15 per cent efficient PV modules in a sunny area could provide electricity for around US$0.10/kWh (Kelly 1993).[10] However, if US$1/$W_p$ is the "break-through" point for base-load electricity production, there are other market segments in which PV could become competitive at an earlier developmental stage, because the actual cost of conventional electricity for these applications is substantially higher than average electricity prices.

Following this approach, the International Energy Agency (IEA) has developed a PV market diffusion strategy. This approach envisages PV entering and diffusing through a series of six expanding markets, namely remote customer applications, remote communities and islands, grid-connected building-integrated systems, local utility grid support, peak power supply, and (lastly) bulk power supply.

Two competitiveness parameters are defined, namely the "entry price" and the "deployment price." The "entry price" is the lowest price at which PV is likely to find "niche" opportunities to enter the market. As soon as PV reaches the "deployment price," it is fully

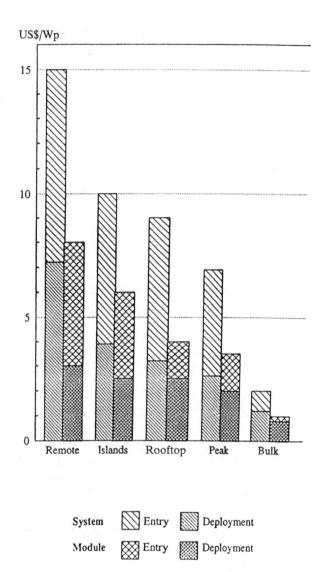

Fig. 7.5 **Entry and deployment pricing of PV power applications (Source: Vigotti 1994a)**

competitive in the market and large-scale diffusion will begin to occur. For completeness of information, both system and module prices are indicated in figure 7.5.

The resulting market diffusion strategy for six different PV system applications is summarized in figure 7.6.

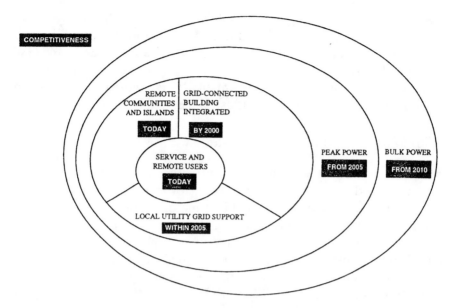

Fig. 7.6 **Diffusion strategy of PV system applications (Source: Vigotti 1994a)**

Remote applications

PV systems have already proved to be cost effective for a wide range of small applications to power remote communications, safety, and control devices (in the range of 10W to 10 kW).

Remote communities and islands

PV systems are also cost effective, or at least very close to competitiveness, when supplying power for local grids in remote villages and small islands (10 kW to 1 MW power range). Both applications have been successfully demonstrated in industrialized countries and have an enormous application potential in developing countries because of missing or incomplete electricity supply and distribution infrastructures in those regions. PV is one of the most appropriate technologies to meet the increasing demand for rural electrification. In fact, there has been a very high recent growth in remote solar home systems in India. Indonesia is already a proven market for these stand-alone systems. The potential for this kind of application is also very high in China, Central Asia, southern Africa, and the Maghreb region. Hybrid diesel–PV systems for supplying villages

241

have recently been successfully applied in Brazil and have proved to be cost effective. The overall potential of a decentralized PV systems market in developing countries has been estimated to be up to 140 GW (Vigotti 1994a). This huge market potential could certainly have a positive impact on the development of PV technology, and also on grid-connected applications in industrialized countries.

Grid-connected, building-integrated systems

In the short term, PV could be competitive in building-integrated grid-connected systems. In certain cases (for instance, in sunny places and when expensive building cladding materials are replaced by PV modules), such systems have entered the market already. This is the fastest-growing market sector for PV in Europe. The IEA estimates that further substantial system cost reductions down to US$4/$W_p$ will be necessary for PV building-integrated systems to be fully competitive and become widespread. However, the IEA model does concentrate only on electricity production. It does not take into account the possibility of recovering useful heat from PV panels, or the possibility of PV–energy-saving coupling measures (e.g. using PV panels as sun-shading systems, PV integration into bioclimatic architecture design, or using PV as a means of promoting demand-side management). As a consequence, PV competitiveness as a wider "energy-service supply technology" in the building sector could actually be greater than it appears at first glance.

This has significant general implications. In the first place, the share in energy final use of the building sector is quite high. In Europe, it accounts for almost 40 per cent of total energy consumption. Second, direct solar energy conversion technologies (both active and passive) are the only renewable energy technologies that can be used in urban areas. This very simple consideration is relevant for both industrialized and developing countries. For the latter, electrification as a means of increasing the quality of life in rural areas remains a top-priority issue, but urban pollution in developing countries' megalopolises raises strong environmental concerns as well. Moreover, integration of PV into buildings greatly increases the potential applicability of PV in areas of high population density and substantially reduces the main environmental obstacle to the diffusion of PV, namely land requirements. The theoretical potential of PV on rooftops is impressive indeed. Although there has been no systematic detailed assessment of the potential as yet, a rough estimate of 2,800 km^2 and 8,400 km^2 of "available" rooftops has been reported for European and OECD countries, respectively (van Brummelen and Alsema 1994). Assuming a (future) module efficiency of 20 per cent, this would correspond to an installed capacity of 560 GW$_p$ and 1,680 GW$_p$, respectively. Consequent annual electricity production would be, at an overall 15 per cent system efficiency, around 475 TWh and 1,950 TWh, corresponding to around 27 per cent and 29 per cent of Europe's and OECD countries' 1990 electricity production, respectively (CEC 1993).

A very detailed study on rooftop PV potential in Puglia, a southern Italian region, has shown that PV on roofs could cover 27 per cent of the current total electricity demand of the region, corresponding to 94 per cent of demand in the residential sector (Vigotti 1994b).

Local utility grid support and peak power supply

At a system cost of US\$3/W$_p$, PV would be a cost-effective option for electricity utilities for both local utility distribution grid support and peak power supply. At this cost, the more than 80 electricity utilities that have formed the Utility Photovoltaic Group (UPVG) estimate a short-term 7,500 MW$_p$ PV potential in this market sector in the United States (Moore 1994). The IEA estimates that PV will be competitive in this sector by 2005.

Bulk power supply

Once the most promising market sectors have been at least partially exploited, scale economies would further reduce module and system costs down to the target US\$1/W$_p$ threshold, making PV fully competitive in the bulk power sector as well. This is not likely to occur before 2010, but is very likely to come about soon after that.

The IEA diffusion strategy is only one of the possible paths – albeit a plausible one – along which PV could become a significant option in the energy market. The previously mentioned strategy of Enron Corporation for cheap baseload electricity production is an example of another possible parallel path. However, the IEA model clearly emphasizes the diversification of the actual energy system. Carefully taking into account the local realities of actual energy system infrastructures, it certainly opens more opportunities for PV diffusion.

Possible PV adoption and diffusion scenarios

It is very difficult to forecast exactly the extent to which PV will contribute to the mid-twenty-first-century energy system. Apart from the rates of innovation and cost reduction of PV technology itself, it will depend on many other factors, including:

– innovation in and prices of *all* competing (renewable and non-renewable) energy technologies;
– the definition and implementation of environmental protection policies;
– national and international energy policies;
– the internalization of environmental costs in market prices;
– an increase in the lifecycle efficiency of energy chains;
– the availability of investment capital for renewable energies in industrialized countries and developing countries;
– institutional and infrastructure reforms.

Depending on the evolution of some or several of these parameters,[11] very different future scenarios could result. However, several statements can be made with a high degree of confidence.

On the demand-side
• World primary energy demand will increase strongly in coming decades, driven mainly by population growth and economic growth. The price elasticity of demand is close to unity, which means that energy demand will grow roughly in inverse proportion to the fall in energy prices (in relative terms).
• Developing countries' share of primary energy demand (and eventually of emissions) is actually expected to increase by more than 50 per cent by 2020 (Khatib 1993; IEA 1993).
• Electricity intensity will increase in both industrialized countries and developing countries. In the latter, it is expected to rise at twice the rate of economic growth. According to the "accelerated policies" scenario of the International Panel on Climate Change (IPCC), the present developed countries will be responsible for over 60 per cent of world electricity demand in 2050. Figure 7.7 shows the predicted increase in electricity demand from 2000 to 2050 for different groups of countries.
• It has been estimated that in 1990 over 2 billion people – 37 per cent of the world population and 48 per cent of developing countries' population – still had limited or no access to electricity.

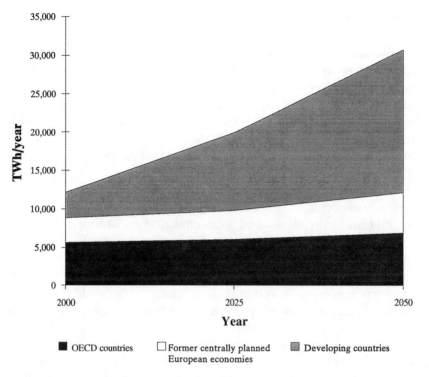

Fig. 7.7 **World electricity demand according to IPCC's "accelerated policies" scenario**

Giving this population access to basic electricity-driven services remains a top-priority issue.

On the supply side
Current progress is slow because PV has to compete with several alternative (and currently cheaper) energy technologies. However, PV provides a set of unique features, including the following:
• Owing to its high modularity, PV has extreme flexibility for powering a wide range of electricity-driven services, from very small applications to large power plants.
• PV is very well suited to providing electricity to rural and remote areas in developing countries. PV solar home systems could meet some basic needs of the people living in those areas, significantly increasing their standard of living. These PV applications can be installed rapidly and are more cost effective than taking the electricity grid into those regions. Most developing countries have

245

excellent potential for the direct use of solar energy, the majority having higher insolation than world average values and large areas (e.g. deserts) suitable for solar panels.

• Direct solar conversion technologies are in practice the only renewable energy technologies that can be used in urban areas. The coupling of PV building-integrated systems with other solar-active or solar-passive and/or energy-saving measures substantially increases the technological and economic potential of PV in these areas. This is true for both industrialized countries and developing countries.

• As described earlier, PV technology is rapidly evolving. Substantial improvements in both technological performance and cost reduction are expected.

• The theoretical potential of solar energy is enormous. PV has very few physical utilization limits. With reasonable PV efficiencies available in the very short term, surfaces available for PV would be more than enough to meet the whole electricity demand in both industrialized and developing countries.[12] The main missing element is a means of storing electrical energy. This will be needed to balance supply and demand patterns, both day/night and summer/winter. In the very short term, the storage problem could be overcome by appropriately using other energy sources such as hydroelectric dams. In the long term, hydrogen would seem to be the most likely storage medium and carrier for PV energy. Thus, there are no major long-term resource or technological constraints to PV diffusion. The main factors that will limit the speed of PV expansion in the energy market are economic ones.

Given these premises, some plausible scenarios up to 2050 are presented in the next part of the paper.[13] Other assumptions have also been incorporated in these scenarios:

– only electricity production has been considered;
– no cost-effective storage means is available (prior to 2050);
– PV electricity introduced directly to the grid never exceeds 10 per cent of total annual electricity demand;
– from 2010 on, the PV electricity production cost is assumed to be comparable with those of other renewable (and non-renewable) electricity sources.

2000

At the turn of the century, PV diffusion is likely to be strongly limited by economic constraints, because it will still have to compete with much cheaper energy technologies. Crystalline silicon technology is still likely to dominate the market, although the implementation of the world's two biggest planned PV power plants (150 MW$_p$ in China and 100 MW$_p$ in the United States) will certainly give a great impetus to amorphous silicon technology. Other thin-film technologies will still be in the very early stages of commercial production.

PV module production will still largely be restricted to industrialized countries. Only system assembly and maintenance steps will be locally performed in developing countries, almost totally for rural electrification purposes (with the exception of China's 100 MW central power plant project). In Europe, applications will shift from demonstration plants and remote systems to decentralized, grid-connected systems. This will occur as building-integrated systems prove to be fully feasible and more attractive than other systems. This is also likely to happen in the United States. Moreover, the big PV power stations planned for the United States will demonstrate the value of PV for supplementary power production during peak hours of daytime demand.

Overall installed PV capacity will be very limited by 2000. A 15 per cent yearly mean market growth would imply a worldwide installed capacity of 1 GW$_p$. This should be considered as the lower-limit, "business-as-usual" (bau) case. It should be noted, however, that, if proposed R&D policies were fully implemented and all environmental and social costs were fully taken into account, a capacity level of 5 GW$_p$ would be possible in Europe alone (TERES 1994). Extrapolating this value for the entire world[14] would imply a potential total worldwide installed PV capacity of 50 GW$_p$. Although this is unlikely to happen, it gives an idea of the magnitude of the gap between present "business-as-usual" patterns and an alternative future pattern in which all environmental burdens are accounted for.

2010

By 2010, thin-film technologies could be strong competitors to crystalline silicon technology, thus sharply reducing PV module costs and making PV much closer to competitiveness with other energy technologies over the full range of applications. This outcome strongly depends on the success of demonstration projects and on the implementation of accelerated R&D policies during the first decade of the new century. Uncertainty about this explains the gap by a factor of over 60 between the most conservative and the most optimistic fore-

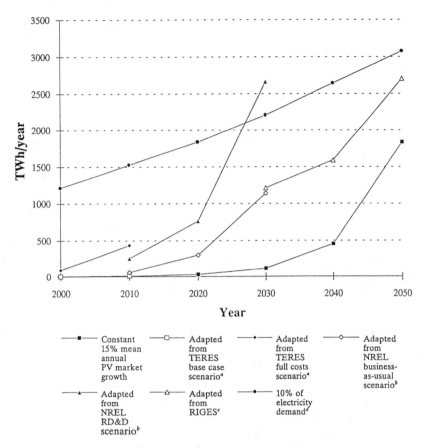

Fig. 7.8 **PV worldwide electricity production scenarios (Notes: A daily mean insolation of 4.6 kWh/m^2/day was considered in all calculations, where necessary. *a*. TERES 1994, assuming regional solar energy demand shares as indicated by the WEC 1994; *b*. NREL 1990, assuming regional solar energy demand shares as indicated by the WEC 1994; *c*. Johansson et al. 1993, assuming a PV share in all intermittent renewables of 18 per cent in 2030 and 28 per cent in 2050; *d*. as indicated in the IPCC "accelerated policies" scenario)**

cast values for 2010 (from 4 GW$_p$ to 265 GW$_p$ installed worldwide – see also fig. 7.8).

As electricity demand strongly increases in the developing world, solar energy demand will also dramatically rise in those regions. According to the World Energy Council scenario (WEC 1994), in 2010 Asian countries alone will account for one-third of world solar demand. At that time local mass production of entire PV systems (including modules) is likely to begin in China, India, and other

South-East Asian countries. In these countries and in some regions of Latin America, PV applications will likely include building-integrated systems in highly polluted megalopolises and large power plants for big remote applications and for local grid support. In Africa the main demand will still come from rural electrification systems.

In Europe, the full implementation of R&D and environmental accounting programmes will possibly lead to the installation of a 25 GW_p capacity (practically all decentralized, grid-connected systems), providing 3.4 per cent of annual electricity demand at that time (TERES 1994). In 2010, PV is not likely to have expanded strongly in the former centrally planned East European economies (including the CIS) because their priority is likely to be given to energy-saving and other infrastructural measures.

Finally, according to the NREL study, PV capacity of 9–40 GW_p could be installed in the United States, depending on whether R&D programmes are implemented (NREL 1990). According to World Energy Council projections, this would correspond to about 25 per cent of the total world PV demand.

2030

In 2030, all the various PV technologies will eventually have reached a high level of maturity and be economically competitive with other energy sources.

Given their extremely high electricity demand (more than all OECD countries together), Asian countries will not only be the largest PV "consumers" (accounting for around 40 per cent) but could eventually be among the world's biggest PV producers. In those countries, PV could meet 5 per cent of total electricity demand (Johansson et al. 1993). Larger proportions could be supplied only with some large-scale storage systems (hydropower stations or hydrogen production).

Overall, developing countries are expected to account for 50–60 per cent of worldwide PV demand in 2030. The major uncertainty for 2030 regards former centrally planned East European economies. On the one hand, high electricity intensity, the need to substitute for obsolete coal and nuclear power plants, and the high technical skill of local engineers and scientists would suggest rapid and extensive PV diffusion in those countries. On the other hand, because of non-optimal insolation, other competing (renewable and non-renewable) technologies might be preferred. According to these two different scenarios, former centrally planned East European economies could account for 8–21 per cent of worldwide PV demand.

2050

In 2050, the regional distribution of PV demand is likely to be similar to that in 2030: 60 per cent of demand will come from the developing countries. Asian countries alone will be responsible for up to or even more than 40 per cent of total world demand, while PV penetration in Africa and Latin America is expected to be lower because of abundant biomass resources. Europe will account for only 5 per cent of demand because of non-optimal insolation and land constraints. Japan will account for 3 per cent. The rest, with some degree of uncertainty owing to factors mentioned earlier, will mainly be shared between the United States and former centrally planned East European economies.

In table 7.5, PV electricity production figures for different countries are reported from the "Renewables-Intensive Global Energy

Table 7.5 **PV electricity production in different world regions in 2050**

Countries[a]	Yearly PV electricity production (TWh/y)	Share of electricity demand[b] (%)
Western Europe	121	5
United States	332	10
Canada	62	12
Japan	68	9
Australia	16	10
Total OECD countries	599	9
Former centrally planned European economies	539	10
Total industrialized countries	1,139	9
Latin America	92	3
Africa	59	3
Middle East	168	10
China & planned economies	623	10
South/East Asia	621	10
Total developing countries	1,562	8
Total world	2,701	9

Source: adapted from Johansson et al. (1993) assuming a PV share of 28 per cent in total intermittent renewables.
a. Classification of OECD, industrialized, and developing countries as of 1995.
b. As indicated in the IPCC "accelerated policies" scenario.

Scenario" (RIGES – Johansson et al. 1993), assuming a 28 per cent PV share in total intermittent renewables (all solar for electricity production and wind).

Interestingly, *all* scenarios for 2050 (see fig. 7.8) forecast a world total installed PV capacity of between 1,000 GW_p and 2,000 GW_p. The electricity produced would then be of the same order of magnitude of 10 per cent of world electricity demand (3,075 TWh/year according to the IPCC "accelerated policies" scenario – see fig. 7.7).

Although this is a significant figure for PV diffusion in 2050, it should be not taken as an upper limit to PV expansion in the future, mainly because by that time the direct input of electricity from an intermittent source into the grid will no longer be a major technological issue. As pointed out by Johansson et al. (1993), the contribution of total intermittent renewables (all solar and wind) to total electricity demand will be locally very high (up to 37 per cent) in 2050. This will be possible owing to two factors. First, wind and solar are independent, not correlated, intermittent sources. By 2050 advanced electricity network optimization methods will be available that will allow the maximum contribution to be achieved from these intermittent sources together. Second, additional great flexibility will be guaranteed by advanced natural gas and coal combined-cycle turbine power plants for peak generation, which are able to adjust output quickly and which will be the best complement to intermittent renewable energy technologies.

Thus, although a 28 per cent share for PV in total intermittent renewables is significant, larger percentages are in principle possible. In fact, whereas wind and solar thermal stations (for electricity production) are most suitable for mid-power generation in isolated areas (>100 kW_p), PV systems are the only renewable technology likely to be used for electricity generation in urban areas. Given the potential for roof-integrated systems in OECD countries (van Brummelen and Alsema 1994), a relevant fraction of the total PV systems could come from roof-integrated systems. Moreover, the coupling of PV building-integrated systems with other solar-active or solar-passive and/or energy-saving measures, and the fact that power is supplied where and when needed, substantially increases the attractiveness of PV systems compared with solar thermal and wind systems. This holds for both industrialized and developing countries. These two factors (*not* taken into account in the previous scenario) could lead to even higher shares of PV in total intermittent renewables, thus leading to higher PV penetration, as indicated in figure 7.8.

Finally, by the middle of the twenty-first century, electrolytic hydrogen production from intermittent sources is very likely to be a well-established and mature technology. This would definitely solve the storage problem of solar-produced electricity. This is not likely to happen before 2030 because of the lack of the huge hydrogen storage and transportation infrastructures needed, and because hydrogen would eventually be mainly produced by much cheaper steam re-forming of natural gas and biomass.

In 2050 however, large-scale hydrogen diffusion infrastructures will begin to appear, and advanced and efficient hydrogen storage methods will be available.[15] Of course, other advanced electricity storage means, from advanced electrical batteries to superconductivity, could also be available at that time. With such storage systems, there would be no more technological limits to PV expansion.

Concluding remarks: PV and eco-restructuring

Today, major economic constraints limit the diffusion of PV in the world energy system. However, it is argued that this renewable energy technology will play a major role in the eco-restructuring transition leading towards a sustainable energy system for the twenty-first century.

First, PV is fully *compatible with the long-term targets* of such a sustainable system. It is *environmentally benign*, because it uses the sun as a fully clean source. It is fully compatible with a decarbonized system using electricity and hydrogen as energy vectors. A major part of PV systems will be installed on surfaces already occupied by buildings (the theoretical potential of PV on rooftops alone could satisfy up to one-third of world electricity demand), thus significantly limiting the main environmental impact of PV, namely the occupation of land. Other indirect environmental burdens (i.e. generated during module manufacturing) are already low and will decrease with future PV technologies. PV will be *economically compatible* in the long term, because module and installation costs will decrease, as a result of technological innovation and economies of scale. It is a *socially compatible* energy technology, because it has a wide range of applications and involves a wide set of actors and users. Owing to some unique features, such as modularity, flexibility of use, silent and clean use, it has hardly any problems of public acceptance (even fewer than for other renewables, e.g. wind). Moreover, PV is *geopolitically compatible*. The sun is a "shared" primary energy resource throughout the world. Most developing countries have excellent potential for the direct use of solar energy. The majority of them have higher insolation than world average values and large areas (e.g. deserts) suitable for solar panels. Today, PV modules are produced almost entirely in industrialized countries, but in the future developing countries (particularly Asian countries) will be both major users and producers of PV.

Second, PV is very *open to innovation and technical change*. The key feature of PV is its extraordinary *flexibility* in terms of technological options for different PV devices, and in terms of the wide range of applications. In contrast with other energy technologies, PV involves not only utilities but also many other interested actors, from energy distribution companies, to architects, up to final users. PV is strongly oriented towards the delivery of *energy services*, particularly as far as applications in buildings are concerned. In fact, building-integrated PV systems can also act as energy-saving systems (e.g. as sun-shading devices) and as small co-generation systems. Furthermore, PV in buildings has great synergy with other solar-active and solar-passive energy technologies, with energy-saving measures, and also with demand-side management.

Finally, PV is fully *compatible with hydrogen energy technologies*. The solar–hydrogen energy technology cycle is the most likely target for a sustainable energy system for the mid-twenty-first century. The cycle includes the direct use of solar energy, the electrolytical production of hydrogen, the use of hydrogen as a chemical energy storage means and as an energy vector, and the eventual re-electrification of hydrogen by means of fuel cells. It is a fully clean cycle that uses electricity and hydrogen as energy vectors and that is capable of providing *all energy services* needed. The use of hydrogen as a means of energy storage is the final solution to the intermittent nature of the solar primary energy source, and virtually eliminates the ultimate technological limit of PV.

By 2050, PV is likely to supply about 10 per cent of world electricity demand. Most importantly, however, PV is open to a lot of other benign energy technology options. *PV is consistent with all sustainable energy patterns* and has no real long-term limits on its exploitation potential. It will therefore play a major role in the eco-restructuring transition and in the world energy system of the second half of the twenty-first century.

Notes

1. The PV cell conversion efficiency is normally defined as a ratio:

   (electric power produced by the cell)/(light power arriving on cell surface under standard conditions)

   The standard conditions are: air-mass $(AM) = 1$ (no clouds); temperature $(T) = 25°C$; incident light power density $= 1\,kW/m^2$.
2. The energy payback time is the time required for the energy system to "repay" the energy needed for its construction.
3. As far as quantitative results are concerned, it was assumed that PV substituted for electricity produced by the European mix of supply sources, and the thermal energy recovered substituted for heat produced by natural gas.
4. Including consumer indoor applications and large tax-subsidized grid-connected government demonstration projects.
5. Prices in constant 1994 US$.
6. This was announced at the 1st PV World Conference, Hawaii, December 1994.
7. For 1 ECU = US$1.2.
8. The potential for this application sector has been estimated at 300 MW_p for Switzerland alone. This potential market is five times the present total world PV market.
9. Summer electricity consumption due to air-conditioning systems has increased heavily in recent years in both industrialized countries and developing countries. To mention just a few European cases: Greece's newly installed air-conditioning capacity increased nine-fold between 1987 and 1990 while in Italy, Spain, and Portugal the use of air-conditioning has been growing at a rate of 20 per cent per year (Ambiente Italia 1995).
10. Assuming 1,800 kWh/m^2 annual average insolation and a 6 per cent real discount rate. In the longer term, some thin-film or concentrator technologies can be expected to supply electricity at 3.5–7.0 cents/kWh (Kelly 1993). PV electricity costs of course depend on several factors, some of them being technology specific (module and system efficiencies, lifetimes, and installation costs), others being site specific (insolation) or economic, such as capital cost discount rates.
11. Many of these issues also require an international cooperation effort (never before seen) to define international standards and rules tackling global environmental issues.
12. It is worth remembering that, within OECD countries, the average per capita available surface on *roofs* alone has been estimated to be 10 m^2 (van Brummelen and Alsema 1994). Were such an area available for every person worldwide, even with present PV technology available on the market today, this would correspond to an installed capacity of around 5,500 GW_p and yearly electricity production of about 9,300 TWh/y. This value exceeds present total world electricity demand.
13. Several other scenarios were taken into account and adapted to extrapolate worldwide PV diffusion – WEC (1994), TERES (1994), NREL (1990), Johansson et al. (1993). The mean installed PV capacity was always calculated from annual electricity by considering a daily mean insolation of 4.6 $kWh/m^2/day$.
14. By assuming regional solar energy demand shares as indicated in the WEC (1994) scenario.
15. Hydrogen storage is currently the major technological issue in hydrogen energy technology.

Bibliography

Ambiente Italia (1995) Passive building cooling: Technology and strategies to reduce energy and power demand. EU-funded research project, private communication, January.

Ayres, R. U. and K. Martinas (1992) Experience and the life cycle: Some analytic implications. *Technovation* **12**(7): 465–486.

Brummelen, M. van and E. A. Alsema (1994) Estimation of the PV-potential in OECD countries. Proceedings of the 12th European Photovoltaic Solar Energy Conference, Amsterdam, the Netherlands, 11–15 April.

CEC (Commission of the European Communities) (1993) *Energy in Europe – Annual Energy Review*, Special Issue. Brussels: Commission of the European Communities, April.

Coiante, D. and L. Barra (1992) Can PV become an effective energy option? *Solar Energy Materials & Solar Cells* **27**(1).

Cunow, E. (1994) Large PV power plants – Past experience and future direction. SIEMENS report. In: G. N. Belcastro and F. Paletta (eds.), *Proceedings of the Workshop on Modular PV Plants for Multimegawatt Power Generation held in Paestum, Italy, 7–9 July 1994*. Rome: IEA, October.

EPIA (European Photovoltaic Industry Association) (1995) *Photovoltaics in 2010*. Report to the Commission of the European Communities, Directorate General for Energy (DG XVII), within the ALTENER programme, Brussels.

Frankl, P. (1994) Ciclo di vita del fotovoltaico e ciclo di vita degli edifici [Life cycle of photovoltaics and life cycle of buildings]. Proceedings of the ISES Conference "Energie Rinnovabili: Architettura e Territorio" [Renewable energies: Architecture and territory], Rome, Italy, 5–7 October.

Green, M. A. (1993) Crystalline- and polycrystalline-silicon solar cells. In: T. B. Johansson, H. Kelly, A. K. N. Reddy, and R. H. Williams (eds.), *Renewable Energy: Sources for Fuels and Electricity*, chap. 7. Washington D.C.: Island Press.

Green, M. A. and K. Emery (1994) Solar cell efficiency tables (version 4). *Progress in Photovoltaics* **2**(3): 231–234.

IAEA (International Atomic Energy Agency) (1992) *Renewable Energy Sources for Electricity Generation in Selected Developed Countries*. IAEA-Tecdoc-646, Vienna, Austria, May.

IEA (International Energy Agency) (1993) *World Energy Outlook to the Year 2010*. Paris: IEA/OECD.

Iliceto, A., A. Previ, V. Arcidiacono, and S. Corsi (1994) Progress report on ENEL's 3.3 MWp PV plant. In: G. N. Belcastro and F. Paletta (eds.), *Proceedings of the Workshop on Modular PV Plants for Multimegawatt Power Generation held in Paestum, Italy, 7–9 July 1994*. Rome: IEA, October.

Johansson, T. B., H. Kelly, A. K. N. Reddy, and R. H. Williams (1993) A renewables-intensive global energy scenario. In: T. B. Johansson, H. Kelly, A. K. N. Reddy, R. H. Williams (eds.), *Renewable Energy: Sources for Fuels and Electricity*. Washington D.C.: Island Press.

Kelly, H. (1993) Introduction to photovoltaic technology. In: T. B. Johansson, H. Kelly, A. K. N. Reddy, and R. H. Williams (eds.), *Renewable Energy: Sources for Fuels and Electricity*, chap. 6. Washington D.C.: Island Press.

Khatib, H. (1993) Solar energy in developing countries. Proceedings of the World Solar Summit, UNESCO Headquarters, Paris, France, 5–9 July.

Masini, A. (1995) Analisi del ciclo di vita di sistemi fotovoltaici in silicio cristallino [Life-cycle analysis of crystalline silicon PV systems]. Internal report, Dipartimento di Meccanica e Aeronautica, Università di Roma "La Sapienza," Rome, Italy, May.

Moore, T. (1994) Emerging markets for photovoltaics. *EPRI Journal*, October/ November.

NREL (National Renewable Energy Laboratory) (1990) *The Potential of Renewable Energy*. An Interlaboratory White Paper prepared for the Office of Policy, Planning and Analysis, US Department of Energy. Golden, CO: NREL, March.

Proceedings of the 1st PV World Conference, Waikoloa, Hawaii, 5–9 December 1994 (1995) IEEE Cat. No. 94 CH 3365–4.

Roskill (1991) *The Economics of Silicon and Ferrosilicon 1991*, 7th edn. London: Roskill Information Services.

Strategies Unlimited (1994) *Solar Flare*, no. 94-6, Mountain View, CA, December.

——— (1995) *Solar Flare*, no. 95-2, Mountain View, CA, April.

TERES (The European Renewable Energy Study) (1994) *The European Renewable Energy Study – Prospects for Renewable Energy in the European Community and Eastern Europe up to 2010*. Report within the framework of the ALTENER Programme. Brussels: Commission of the European Communities.

US Bureau of the Census (1993) *Statistical Abstract of the United States 1993*. The National Data Book, US Department of Commerce, Economics and Statistics Administration, Washington D.C.

Vigotti, R. (1994a) International PV programmes: Status, prospects and strategy for PV power system application. Proceedings of the 12th European Photovoltaic Solar Energy Conference, Amsterdam, the Netherlands, 11–15 April.

——— (1994b) Il fotovoltaico nell' edilizia: esperienze e prospettive [Photovoltaics in the building sector]. Proceedings of the ISES conference "Edilizia pubblica e privata: fonti rinnovabili, nuove tecnologie e materiali innovativi [Public and private building sector: Renewables, new technologies and innovative materials], Lecce, Italy, July.

WEC (World Energy Council) (1994) *New Renewable Resources: A Guide to the Future*. London: Kogan Page.

Zweibel, K. and A. M. Barnett (1993) Polycrystalline thin-film photovoltaics. In: T. B. Johansson, H. Kelly, A. K. N. Reddy, R. H. Williams (eds.), *Renewable Energy: Sources for Fuels and Electricity*, chap. 10. Washington D.C.: Island Press.

Part II
Restructuring sectors and the sectoral balance of the economy

8

Global eco-restructuring and technological change in the twenty-first century

Faye Duchin

Globalization

Visions about social and material conditions in the distant future are naturally surrounded by a great deal of uncertainty. One reason is that future outcomes depend on public and private decisions among alternatives that could have rather different long-term consequences. This paper describes some of the major, emerging directions of change that are likely to be important in the global economy of the twenty-first century. It attempts to situate within this context the kinds of choices that we face, including those surrounding technological changes that can be stimulated by eco-restructuring, and emphasizes the special role of environmental considerations in conditioning our decisions. The paper also illustrates the contribution of economic analysis in evaluating trade-offs among alternative choices on the regional and global levels.

Over the past few decades the globalization of the world's societies has become a physical reality and one that has relatively quickly become apparent to the general public. The two principal reasons for globalization are attributable to technological advances. Through modern telecommunications, people in all but the most remote locations are exposed instantaneously to the world's crisis situations and familiarized with the day-to-day realities in far-away places; and modern transportation has made it possible to travel, and to trade and shift investments, among distant locations more quickly and more extensively than ever before.

The other major stimulus to global thinking was the ability to view the whole planet from space and to measure and anticipate the possible effects of human activities not only on the water, the soil, and the minerals buried in it but especially on the quintessential global commons, the atmosphere. The desire to "save the planet" reflects a concern that is not just environmental but specifically global.

Eco-restructuring (also called Industrial Metabolism or Industrial Ecology) is an attempt to promote social well-being by designing and implementing technologies in a way that disrupts the biogeochemical systems of the planet as little as possible. Eco-restructuring is undoubtedly influencing the design considerations and the content of engineering for the twenty-first century, but it is not yet evident what forms this influence will take and how extensive the changes will be.

Economics provides a powerful conceptual framework for describing the world system in terms of the interdependence of human activities and decisions. An economic modelling framework can be used to analyse and evaluate alternative, more or less detailed stories – or scenarios – about the future, based, in part, on alternative initiatives that originate in eco-restructuring. A framework capable of playing this role needs to go beyond the concepts of equilibrium and marginal changes that still dominate economists' thinking and practices today. The framework needs to be guided by a broad conception of economic theory that describes the material structure, as well as the social structure, of the global economy. Scenarios need to be capable of reflecting substantive policy options related to major potential structural changes, and the challenges related to them. The overall structure has to be sufficiently integrated to capture the interdependencies that characterize this complex and dynamically changing system. I have written in other places about such a conceptual economic framework (see Duchin 1992, 1994, and forthcoming; Duchin and Lange 1994).

I shall first explore the growth of the world population and world economy in the twenty-first century, and then describe some of the major elements of environmental transformation. Projections about the likely future use of primary materials demonstrate the use of an economic model for the systematic assessment of the implications of various assumptions. I take up the production, use, and disposal of a specific material, plastics; and identify the major decisions that will have to be made regarding plastics, in order to demonstrate the kinds of challenges facing eco-restructuring.

Population growth and economic growth

The basic political and economic objective of the modern liberal state is to achieve increased prosperity through economic growth, which in turn is pursued through improvements in efficiency, new technology, and free trade. This outlook has prevailed in the two centuries since the industrial revolution, a period that has experienced accelerated growth of both population and material well-being. With the fall of communism, economic liberalization is virtually unopposed as a global political and economic philosophy. However, as population growth levels off, at least in the affluent societies, it is timely to consider the prospect for a levelling off of economic growth as well and new global agreements and institutions that govern the operation of more or less self-regulating markets.

Economists distinguish three categories of factor inputs needed for the production of goods and services: capital, labour, and land, where "land" is interpreted as shorthand for all categories of inputs from the natural world. For an economy operating with a given set of technologies, growth in the delivery of goods and services to final users requires more factor inputs. Clearly, population growth can generate economic growth with the simple replication of existing methods and a larger labour force, as well as more land and other inputs. Of course, on a per capita basis, consumption might not increase.

Malthus's concern about running out of land and food was at least temporarily put to rest by the enormous increases in yields resulting from new technology. "Artificial manure" proved remarkably successful in assuring "big and ever increasing harvests lasting eternally" (Liebig 1862, quoted in Krohn and Schäfer 1976, p. 31). Such confidence in unlimited increases in prosperity already sound dated, however. There is surely the possibility of continued advances and even dramatic breakthroughs in our ingenuity for wresting a living from nature. But there is also precedent for the collapse of entire ecosystems.

In the analysis of actual activities, economists in the twentieth century have focused their investigation of growth almost exclusively on changing inputs of capital and labour both in theoretical discussion and in the "production functions" chosen for most empirical analysis. This emphasis is largely explained by the fact that the extraction of primary materials in agriculture and mining utilizes a very small portion of the labour force in the rich, industrialized economies that have been taken as the model for development, and air and water were considered free of charge. However, demographic and environmental pressures are already shifting the attention of economists to the third factor of production, natural resources. Its operational definition will require attention to the distinctions among the individual energy raw materials that are neither renewable nor recyclable; the numerous mineral resources that are potentially recyclable; and water and soils of different qualities. The different categories of pollution and environmental degradation that are delivered back to the natural world also need to be accounted for as factors of production; they can be viewed as "negative inputs." Although capital and labour obviously cannot be ignored, the primary materials that increasingly occupy economists are also the inputs at the centre of attention in eco-restructuring.

A major reason for the developing countries taking on a new importance in the world economy is that they will continue to be the locus for virtually all population growth over the twenty-first century and therefore offer the easiest targets for the expansion of both production and consumption. The affluent societies can increase per capita consumption further through employing higher-quality factor inputs; the most practical avenue to exploit this option is through the upgrading of the skills and satisfaction of the labour force. New technologies can promote growth by enhancing the "productivity" of factor inputs; but they invariably involve not only a decrease in factor quantities per unit of output but also a change in the quality or at least the mix of inputs. Some consequences include the generation of novel wastes – such as chlorine-containing compounds. However, the opportunities for actually implementing new technologies are limited when they are applied to the upgrading of capacity that is already in place (in the industrialized countries) rather than the construction of entirely new facilities to expand capacity (in the developing countries). Individuals or firms in the rich countries may be able to generate more profit, if they are free to do so, by supplying the requirements of other countries with faster-growing populations rather than by investing in incremental improvements in production for domestic markets.

The size of the population may level off in the developing countries too in the course of the twenty-first century. With less political pressure continually to "create jobs" for increasing numbers of labour force entrants, concerns about depleting resources or degrading the physical environment could lead to a shift in emphasis from growth to improvements in the quality of life. For the medium term, however, the asymmetry in population dynamics between the rich and poor countries will strongly influence the nature of their interactions.

Environmental pressures for global change

Darwin's identification of competition as the mechanism for natural selection was influenced by the ideas of Malthus. The mutual reinforcement of the dominant role assigned to competition as the mechanism for change in both the biological and economic worldviews assured its fundamental role in Western thinking over the past century. It is significant that at the present time this view is being substantially moderated in our understanding of both the natural and the social spheres, as these reinforcing changes in perspective will be more influential than either one could be alone. Increasing numbers of contemporary biologists are subscribing to Margulis's view that accommodation through symbiosis is a major mechanism for evolutionary change: life "did not take over the world by combat but by networking" (Margulis and Sagan 1986, pp. 15 and 18). The parallels are striking with the emergence of the global economy.

The global economy is emerging at a time of great transformation as the ideological confrontation of East and West is replaced by economic conflict and negotiation (largely over trade and aid) between North and South.[1] The countries in transition to a market economy are aiming to join the ranks of the developed economies over the next several decades as Europe – Central and Eastern, as well as Western – proceeds toward increasing unification along various dimensions. Regional economic blocs, based initially on trade and investment agreements, are also developing in America, in Asia, and among the Pacific Rim countries. The international competition associated with *laissez-faire* capitalism is if anything more fierce than ever. At the same time, it is undeniably operating within a context of long-term regional integration and emerging global institutional arrangements and constraints.

Environmental concerns about the "global commons" will strongly reinforce other pressures toward global dialogue and negotiation. Only a small number of environmental disputes has so far been brought to court within the international trade community, but it is already clear that these conflicts raise questions far more complex than what conventional trade law can readily resolve. In anticipation of the avalanche of cases to come, the Secretariat of GATT (the General Agreement on Tariffs and Trade) was led to call for discussions about multilateral consensus on environmental objectives in the hopes of bypassing bilateral, case-by-case haggling in instances where new environmental concerns conflict with the older objective of removing barriers to trade to promote growth independently of any other considerations. The tuna and dolphin dispute between the United States and Mexico or the Danish bottle law and the reaction to it in Europe are two early examples (see Lee, 1993, for a brief description of 22 such cases). In surprisingly blunt language, the GATT Secretariat stated that it is "no longer possible for a country to create an appropriate environmental policy entirely on its own" (quoted in OTA 1992, p. 24).

Environmental concerns (coupled with the attempt to protect domestic producers) are leading countries to erect barriers to trade based on the production process and not just on the characteristics of the traded product. (This is true in the tuna and dolphin case or in potential restrictions on imports of electronics components manufactured using CFCs that are being analysed in connection with the Montreal Protocol.) These pressures to provide a product *produced using a particular technology* are a potent force for the further globalization of technology. There is already a tendency to adopt modern technologies in new manufacturing sectors in developing countries, especially in foreign-owned factories. But the pressures for international use of common techniques are likely to spread beyond manufacturing into areas that have until now been largely shielded from globalization by cultural differences. For example, trade-related requirements about the use of recycled materials affect people's lifestyles because recycling involves common procedures to be followed by individuals in their capacities as citizens and consumers; likewise, legislation governing water pollution is bound to be similar in different societies because it will need to promote compliance with common process specifications.

Other pressures toward uniform social practices can also be observed. One example is a universal concept of human rights; another is the state's assumption of responsibility for social welfare, which today absorbs roughly similar proportions of national income in the rich economies and in the formerly socialist economies but is virtually non-existent in most developing countries.

Scenario analysis and the use of materials

In this section I report the results of the analysis of a specific scenario about the future, focusing on the use of primary materials. In the modelling framework used for this analysis, the material structure of an economy is described in terms of its natural endowment of soil, water, primary materials, etc., the accumulation of built capital including roads, buildings, and machines, the pool of workers of different qualifications, and the characteristic ways in which these factors of production are used. Despite significant variation in the structures of different economies, one can distinguish a few basic patterns. Four groupings of regions will be discussed below: the rich, industrialized economies; the economies of Eastern Europe and the former Soviet Union; the newly industrializing countries; and the rest of the developing countries. The groups tend to differ with respect to their natural riches, the types of capital employed, the education, health, and productivity of the workforce, the amount of capital at the disposition of the average worker, and the per capita utilization of fuels and materials. Consequently, they also differ with respect to the technologies used in all sectors of the economy. With globalization, however, most economies tend to move in the direction of the industrialized economies in terms of their choices of technologies and the associated factor inputs.

In a recent study about global air pollution, Lange and I examined the consequences for the world economy (described in terms of 16 regions) over the period 1980–2020 of alternative assumptions about future choices of technology in the different regions (Duchin and Lange 1994). The scenario we analysed was intended to examine the outlook expressed in the Brundtland Report (WCED 1987), the publication that popularized the notion of sustainable development. It incorporates United Nations projections about population growth, optimistic assumptions about economic growth in both developed and developing countries, and assumptions about the adoption of clean and efficient technologies in the material-intensive and energy-intensive sectors in all regions over the next three decades. The scenario is optimistic in suggesting that sharply improved material standards of living in the developing economies, further increases in per capita consumption in the rich economies, and the volume of population increases that is anticipated for the twenty-first century can be compatible with reduced pressures on the environment provided that sensible technologies are adopted, such as extensive conservation of energy, recycling of metals, glass, and paper at rates approaching those achieved in only a few countries today, and the rapid incorporation of the cleanest and most efficient technologies currently available or near commercialization. Our objective was to investigate the plausibility of this scenario by documenting explicit assumptions about the adoption of new technologies in the different regions and creating a modelling framework to analyse them. The assumptions are developed in the course of 10 case-studies and include extensive recycling, highly fuel-efficient vehicles, energy conservation in homes and businesses, etc. The outcomes were compared with those of a business-as-usual scenario that assumed no technological changes.[2]

From an economic point of view the scenario is cost saving, especially in the rich countries, although it is far more capital intensive than the current mix of production techniques in developing countries. Despite substantial savings in energy and materials that are attributable to the new technologies, however, the pollutants that are tracked in the model all continue to grow, rather than fall, over the period studied. For the four groupings of regions, table 8.1 shows the levels of consumption of the 14 categories of primary materials in 1980 and 2020, the regional distribution of consumption, and consumption per million people. The rates of growth of consumption and of per capita consumption of these primary materials are reported in table 8.2.

Even under a scenario that is rather optimistic about conserving mineral resources, net consumption of all 14 food, fuel, and non-fuel resources increases over the 40-year period (see table 8.2). On a per capita basis, however, net consumption of eight of the resources actually falls because of technological changes – by as much as 36 per cent in the case of iron. This comparison strongly suggests that, over the next few decades, the impact of population growth on resource utilization will more than offset the economies that can be achieved by these technologies.

Population in the developing countries increases from 72 per cent of the total in 1980 to 81 per cent by 2020, and an even larger share can confidently be expected before world population stops growing. By 2020, per capita consumption of most materials is still highest in today's rich economies, followed by the formerly socialist economies, the newly industrializing countries of Asia and Latin America, and then the other developing economies (see table 8.1). However, there are some notable exceptions.

Not a single primary material among those in the tables is used by the two developing regions in proportion to their combined share of population in 1980 or even in 2020. However, the disparity among regions is much lower for food than for fuel and non-fuel minerals. None the less, the dominance of plant-based foods over animal products in the developing countries is clear even at this gross level of spatial discrimination. In the world as a whole, harvesting of edible raw materials grows faster than that of minerals between 1980 and 2020 even though it also starts from a lower gap between rich and poor countries. This growth reflects the steep rates of increased food consumption, especially of animal products, anticipated for the developing countries of Asia. A much closer look at the changing composition of the diet of different categories of households in all countries is clearly merited and amenable to this kind of approach, but it has not yet been carried out. A quantitative, structural analysis of household consumption, and of social welfare more generally, is far less developed than the multisectoral analysis of production. (See Duchin, forthcoming, for a detailed conceptual and applied framework for the multisectoral approach to household activities.)

Per capita use of fossil fuels declines by 2020 in the rich economies owing to a variety of measures including more fuel-efficient cars. Worldwide demand for natural gas actually doubles, with very steep increases in the developing economies. According to these projections, Eastern Europe and the former Soviet Union remain very energy-intensive economies because of their industrial mix and a rather low starting point for energy productivity. Despite massive increases in the use of energy in the developing economies, their per capita use of fossil fuels is still very low in 2020 by global standards. (Their use of nuclear fuels is quantified in Duchin and Lange 1994.)

Of the non-fuel minerals, only the use of bauxite increases worldwide on a per capita basis. Despite increased rates of recycling, total bauxite use more than doubles as aluminium increasingly substitutes for other materials in construction, in automobiles, and in other fabricated products. In the rich economies, demand for lead and iron actually falls and demand for nickel and copper is nearly flat. But the use of all of these metals, and of other materials not shown such as plastics and paper, will increase steeply in the developing economies even on a per capita basis.

The foregoing are the consequences of doing things "smarter" but without dramatic departures from today's technical practices. In terms of the use of all primary materials, such a scenario will clearly

Table 8.1 Consumption of primary materials in the world economy in 1980 and projections for 2020

1980

	Region[a]				
	RDE	NIE	ODE	ESU	World
Consumption[b]					
Fish	29.5	12.4	20.2	10.3	72.4
Livestock	116.9	41.6	61.3	42.5	262.3
Oil crops	45.6	25.4	68.1	30.9	170.0
Grains	392.5	160.5	644.8	248.3	1,446.1
Root crops	91.0	69.4	237.0	132.9	530.3
Copper	5.8	0.7	0.6	1.4	8.5
Bauxite	11.7	1.3	1.7	1.9	16.6
Nickel	486.2	30.0	33.5	176.4	726.1
Zinc	3.4	0.5	0.5	1.1	5.5
Lead	2.0	0.2	0.3	0.8	3.3
Iron	261.0	42.5	83.1	149.0	535.6
Petroleum	2,300.8	323.0	398.3	619.4	3,641.5
Gas	1,116.6	90.8	96.7	556.1	1,860.2
Coal	1,179.8	38.1	588.5	907.7	2,714.1
Population (millions)	845	505	2,711	377	4,438
Regional distribution of consumption (%)					
Fish	41	17	28	14	100
Livestock	45	16	23	16	100
Oil crops	27	15	40	18	100
Grains	27	11	45	17	100
Root crops	17	13	45	25	100
Copper	68	8	7	16	100
Bauxite	70	8	10	11	100

2020

	Region[a]				
	RDE	NIE	ODE	ESU	World
Fish	38.6	22.2	37.8	13.6	112.2
Livestock	202.8	131.1	270.1	69.8	673.8
Oil crops	92.8	81.8	256.4	58.7	489.7
Grains	780.3	583.5	2,163.1	460.8	3,987.7
Root crops	155.0	188.0	671.0	196.4	1,210.4
Copper	6.1	2.0	2.5	2.0	12.6
Bauxite	21.3	5.7	7.2	3.9	38.1
Nickel	493.4	77.4	118.8	198.6	888.2
Zinc	4.7	1.3	2.3	1.4	9.7
Lead	1.5	0.5	1.5	1.1	4.6
Iron	240.2	81.9	190.5	107.7	620.3
Petroleum	2,610.1	1,088.6	1,853.7	919.6	6,472.0
Gas	1,191.4	466.0	882.3	1,159.8	3,699.5
Coal	1,025.6	190.5	1,914.0	980.6	4,110.7
Population (millions)	1,048	914	5,631	470	8,063
Fish	34	20	34	12	100
Livestock	30	19	40	10	100
Oil crops	19	17	52	12	100
Grains	20	15	54	12	100
Root crops	13	16	55	16	100
Copper	48	16	20	16	100
Bauxite	56	15	19	10	100

Nickel	67	4	5	24	100	Nickel	56	9	13	22	100
Zinc	62	9	9	20	100	Zinc	48	13	24	14	100
Lead	61	6	9	24	100	Lead	33	11	33	24	100
Iron	49	8	16	28	100	Iron	39	13	31	17	100
Petroleum	63	9	11	17	100	Petroleum	40	17	29	14	100
Gas	60	5	5	30	100	Gas	32	13	24	31	100
Coal	43	1	22	33	100	Coal	25	5	47	24	100
Population	19	11	61	8	100	Population	13	11	70	6	100

Consumption per million people[b]

Fish	0.035	0.025	0.007	0.027	0.016	Fish	0.037	0.024	0.007	0.029	0.014
Livestock	0.138	0.082	0.023	0.113	0.059	Livestock	0.194	0.143	0.048	0.149	0.084
Oil crops	0.054	0.050	0.025	0.082	0.038	Oil crops	0.089	0.089	0.046	0.125	0.061
Grains	0.464	0.318	0.238	0.659	0.326	Grains	0.745	0.638	0.384	0.980	0.495
Root crops	0.108	0.137	0.087	0.353	0.119	Root crops	0.148	0.206	0.119	0.418	0.150
Copper	0.007	0.001	0.000	0.004	0.002	Copper	0.006	0.002	0.000	0.004	0.002
Bauxite	0.014	0.003	0.001	0.005	0.004	Bauxite	0.020	0.006	0.001	0.008	0.005
Nickel	0.575	0.059	0.012	0.468	0.164	Nickel	0.471	0.085	0.021	0.423	0.110
Zinc	0.004	0.001	0.000	0.003	0.001	Zinc	0.004	0.001	0.000	0.003	0.001
Lead	0.002	0.000	0.000	0.002	0.001	Lead	0.001	0.001	0.000	0.002	0.001
Iron	0.309	0.084	0.031	0.395	0.121	Iron	0.229	0.090	0.034	0.229	0.077
Petroleum	2.723	0.640	0.147	1.643	0.821	Petroleum	2.491	1.191	0.329	1.957	0.803
Gas	1.321	0.180	0.036	1.475	0.419	Gas	1.137	0.510	0.157	2.468	0.459
Coal	1.396	0.075	0.217	2.408	0.612	Coal	0.979	0.208	0.340	2.086	0.510

Source: My calculations. For description of assumptions, see text and Duchin and Lange (1994).

a. The regions are rich, developed economies (RDE), newly industrializing (NIE), other developing economies (ODE), and Eastern Europe and the former Soviet Union (ESU).

b. Crops and minerals are measured in millions of tons, except for nickel which is in thousands of tons. Fuels are in millions of tons of coal equivalent.

Table 8.2 **Growth in consumption of primary materials in the world economy, 1980–2020**

	Growth in consumption (2020/1980)					Growth in per capita consumption (2020/1980)				
	RDE	NIE	ODE	ESU	World	RDE	NIE	ODE	ESU	World[a]
Fish	1.31	1.79	1.87	1.32	1.55	1.06	0.99	0.90	1.06	0.85
Livestock	1.73	3.15	4.41	1.64	2.57	1.40	1.74	2.12	1.32	1.41
Oil crops	2.04	3.22	3.77	1.90	2.88	1.64	1.78	1.81	1.52	1.59
Grains	1.99	3.64	3.35	1.86	2.76	1.60	2.01	1.62	1.49	1.52
Root crops	1.70	2.71	2.83	1.48	2.28	1.37	1.50	1.36	1.19	1.26
Copper	1.05	2.86	4.17	1.43	1.48	0.85	1.58	2.01	1.15	0.82
Bauxite	1.82	4.38	4.24	2.05	2.30	1.47	2.42	2.04	1.65	1.26
Nickel	1.01	2.58	3.55	1.13	1.22	0.82	1.43	1.71	0.90	0.67
Zinc	1.38	2.60	4.60	1.27	1.76	1.11	1.44	2.21	1.02	0.97
Lead	0.75	2.50	5.00	1.38	1.39	0.60	1.38	2.41	1.10	0.77
Iron	0.92	1.93	2.29	0.72	1.16	0.74	1.06	1.10	0.58	0.64
Petroleum	1.13	3.37	4.65	1.48	1.78	0.91	1.86	2.24	1.19	0.98
Gas	1.07	5.13	9.12	2.09	1.99	0.86	2.84	4.39	1.67	1.09
Coal	0.87	5.00	3.25	1.08	1.51	0.70	2.76	1.57	0.87	0.83
Population	1.24	1.81	2.08	1.25	1.82					

Note: See table 8.1 for region names.

a. The growth in per capita consumption for the world as a whole is in several cases lower than growth for all component regions. Although the result may appear counter-intuitive, it is readily confirmed using the figures in table 8.1 and reflects the rapid growth of population in the regions with the lowest per capita consumption.

put more, not less, pressure on the environment over the next several decades because the combined effects of population increase and improving the material standard of living in the developing countries will more than offset the savings in primary materials associated with the substitutions among materials, recycling, and other technological changes. The results of this analysis provide the motivation for a more radical agenda for eco-restructuring.

The challenge for eco-restructuring

Much of the primary material that passes through the economic system, from automobiles to packaging or sewage pipes, ends up sooner or later as solid waste. There are several emerging rules of thumb for solid waste management: use less material in the first place (i.e. source reduction), re-use products or at least recycle materials to the extent that is practical, and dispose of remaining wastes in a manner that is environmentally benign. It is often necessary to reconceive product design and manufacturing to facilitate recycling, for example by preferring a single material to composites. It is clear that practices in several countries, which have already begun to move in these directions, will spread in the twenty-first century. But these prescriptions are far more complicated than they appear because there are many different ways of proceeding, all of which have different consequences that affect not only a single sector but many parts of an economy. For reasons that have already been discussed in this paper, we can expect a relatively rapid globalization of those solutions that appear to be successful. Then, for better or worse, there will tend to be a "lock-in" (Arthur 1988) on a global scale to these solutions, which will make it hard to replace them by superior ones for many decades to come.

One of the obstacles to the effective recycling of any material is the difficulty of assuring a uniform waste stream of predictable volume. The investment in recycling facilities cannot be justified from a business or from a social point of view unless a steady, reliable source of inputs can be assured. This problem is faced for many materials but none more so than plastics, and they provide an instructive case-study of the challenges for eco-restructuring.

All parties today agree about the need to reduce polymer solid waste in landfills by some combination of source reduction, degradability of the material, and recycling. The problems arise in achieving an appropriate and stable mix because the steps taken to satisfy one objective tend to thwart the other objectives.

One mechanism for source reduction is the substitution of other materials for plastics. However, the most celebrated comparisons, such as McDonald's former polystyrene foam "clamshell" package vs. the replacement of bleached paper/polyethylene wrappers, or disposable vs. cloth diapers, are inconclusive as to their environmental effects – in part because they have not yet been analysed within a sufficiently complete and integrated economy-wide framework. Source reduction can be achieved by lowering consumption; but, after the initial economies, this option is likely to require significant changes in lifestyle that consumers may be reluctant to make. Refilling plastic containers is another option that requires behavioural changes.

Achieving degradability is similarly complicated. Petrochemical-based polymers are not intrinsically degradable (Stein 1992, p. 836), and truly degradable ones are still in early stages of commercialization (Luzier 1992, p. 839). Of course, very little of the potential for

271

degradation is actually realized in waste disposal sites designed and managed as landfills rather than composting facilities. Furthermore, the shift in feedstock from hydrocarbons to biomass would have massive implications for the global economy.

A significant problem in the recycling of plastics is the expense of collection and the cost and difficulty of separation even among apparently homogeneous objects and polymers, not to mention objects of mixed composition and composite materials (Stein 1992, pp. 836–837). The relative importance of different polymers, and the material composition of many objects, would need to change substantially if large-scale recycling of polymers were to be implemented. Further technical development would be necessary for the separation of mixed plastics (Hegberg et al. 1992, p. 73). Of course, in the unlikely event of a massive substitution away from plastics in many uses, coupled with a reliance on biodegradable plastics, there would be inadequate raw material to justify investing in recycling.

One current prospect is for the development of completely biodegradable polymers from biomass. Polymers derived from starches of annual crops such as corn and potatoes are already in use in several applications such as golf tees and pharmaceutical capsules. A significant programme is also under way to commercialize polymers based on the jute crop of Bangladesh and India; it is hoped that this market will be able to replace the traditional uses of jute, which are lost as polypropylene displaces jute sacks for packaging grain, sugar, fertilizer, and cement (personal communication with Irv Koons, United Nations Development Programme).

Plastics are still displacing other primary materials and paper even in the rich economies, and their use is growing rapidly in developing countries. To the extent that polymers are fabricated from biomass, the demand for the hydrocarbon feedstock is reduced. It could also reduce the solid waste that needs to be disposed of and precipitate the shift from landfills to composting facilities. But it puts pressure back on the land used to grow renewable crops.

The alternative roles that plastics might play in the global economy over the next 50 years may be a particularly fruitful case to study from both a technological and a social and economic point of view. What actually happens, by conscious decision or otherwise, may be only one small contributing factor to the global "big picture," but the range of alternatives that were sketched in the previous few paragraphs demonstrates that although engineering innovation is necessary it is hardly sufficient.

Concluding remarks

Despite the difficulty of anticipating the technological practices of the future, it is clear that eco-restructuring will need to respond to social priorities for "internalizing the costs" of real and perceived environmental damage. It seems likely that engineering design will continue to economize on mineral fuels and non-renewable materials and probably rely increasingly on biotechnology industries for fuels and materials of biological origin. The latter are attractive because they are renewable and degradable and sequester atmospheric carbon in their growing phase. As this transition ripples through the economy, it will enhance the importance of new farming systems, new crops, and technologies for processing biological materials, relative to mining activities and the processing of petrochemicals and metals. However, the substitution of renewable for non-renewable resources, in combination with population increases, will intensify competition with food production for land and water. Trying to balance these interests will be a major challenge in the twenty-first century and one that merits the development and analysis of alternative scenarios.

The scope for computer-based automation continues to increase in existing and new applications, including process control or the integration and coordination on a large scale of formerly separate activities of all types. People in their personal capacities will gain unprecedented access to public and private information and to on-line networking capabilities.

Eco-restructuring will involve not only technological but also organizational changes. The handling of plastics provides one example; another has to do with transportation. There are prospects for phenomenal growth rates in the production and use of private automobiles in developing countries. Even moderate growth in per capita automobile use, coupled with substantial improvements in fuel efficiency, will still make the automobile a major source of increased global air pollution (especially that originating in China) by 2020. At the present time it may be hard to envisage a shift away from the use of private automobiles toward a combination of public transport and lowered mobility in the rich countries, and a similar shift in the aspirations of the developing countries. Given the powerful attraction of the private automobile, the burden is on eco-restructuring to demonstrate appealing "lifestyles" built around spatial organization and leisure activities that can be accommodated with many fewer cars per capita. This challenge is as important, and as daunting, as any faced by eco-restructuring.

The consequences of increasing globalization, population growth, and environmental stress that we will face in the twenty-first century could well result in a substantial deterioration in the quality of life for much of the world's population. Even the scenario of the Brundtland Report (WCED 1987), which is optimistic from an economic and social point of view, will increase rather than reverse environmental degradation. Eco-restructuring, based largely on technological innovations, holds promise for solving some of these problems. However, even aside from the formidable political challenges of achieving enough common purpose to implement such solutions on a large scale, the challenges for eco-restructuring should not be underestimated.

Notes

1. According to conventional usage, the North includes the rich, industrialized countries, the South is the developing countries, the West is the market economies, and the East is the formerly socialist economies.
2. A reviewer suggested that the scenario results be compared with those of the IS92 scenario of the IPCC. But the latter scenario does not have enough detail to provide a basis for comparisons.

References

Arthur, Brian (1988) Competing technologies: An overview. In: G. Dosi, C. Freeman, R. Nelson, and G. Silverberg (eds.), *Technology and Economic Theory*. London: Pinter Publishers.

Duchin, Faye (1992) Industrial input–output analysis: Implications for industrial ecology. *Proceedings of the National Academy of Sciences* **89**, February: 851–855.

——— (1994) Input–output analysis and industrial ecology. In: Braden R. Allenby and Deanna J. Richards (eds.), *The Greening of Industrial Ecosystems*. Washington D.C.: National Academy Press.

——— (forthcoming) Household lifestyles: The Social Dimension of Structural Economics. Manuscript submitted to the United Nations University, Tokyo, August.

Duchin, Faye and Glenn-Marie Lange (1994) *The Future of the Environment: Ecological Economics and Technological Change*. New York: Oxford University Press.

Hegberg, B. A., G. R. Brenniman, and William H. Hallenbeck (1992) *Mixed Plastics Recycling Technology*. Park Ridge, NJ: Noyes Data Corporation.

Krohn, Wolfgang and Wolf Schäfer (1976) The origins and structure of agricultural chemistry. In: Gerald Lemaine, Roy Macleod, Michael Mulkay, and Peter Weingart (eds.), *Perspectives on the Emergence of Scientific Disciplines*. The Hague: Mouton Publishers.

Lee, James R. (1993) Between process and product: Making the link between trade and the environment. Unpublished manuscript, School of International Service, the American University.

Luzier, W. D. (1992) Materials derived from biomass/biodegradable materials. *Proceedings of the National Academy of Sciences* **89**: 839–842.

Margulis, Lynn and Dorian Sagan (1986) *Microcosmos: Four Billion Years of Microbial Evolution*. New York: Summit Books.

OTA (Office of Technology Assessment, US Congress) (1992) *Trade and Environment: Conflicts and Opportunities*. OTA-BP-ITE-94. Washington D.C.: Government Printing Office, May.

Stein, R. (1992) Polymer recycling: Opportunities and limitations. *Proceedings of the National Academy of Sciences* **89**: 835–838.

WCED (World Commission on Environment and Development) (1987) *Our Common Future* [the Brundtland Report]. Oxford: Oxford University Press.

9

Agro-eco-restructuring: Potential for sustainability

Heinrich Wohlmeyer

Nature to be commanded first has to be obeyed. (Francis Bacon, 1561–1626, the founder of English empiricism)

Nature's demise spells the death of agriculture. (Edouard Saouma, former General Director of the FAO, opening address to the Conference on Agriculture and the Environment, 15–19 April 1991)

Editor's note

Agriculture is fundamental to human survival. As Wohlmeyer says, it feeds us. Organized agriculture (including managed forestry) now accounts for in the order of half of the total biomass of the earth. By the middle of the twenty-first century, to accommodate a doubled human population at (it is hoped) a higher standard of living, agriculture will necessarily be more intensive and probably more "industrial" than it is now. At least that is the conventional view. Some background data may be useful to put this set of problems in perspective. Wohlmeyer's contribution, which follows, addresses the possibility of an alternative approach to agriculture.

Agriculture and food production

Food production per capita in the developing countries increased 20 per cent during the 1980s. Yet, 800 million people in the world are undernourished and 500 million are chronically malnourished. Grain harvested per capita for the world as a whole rose 40 per cent from 1950 to 1984 (the peak year). However since then it has been falling at 1 per cent per year, with the biggest decline in the poorest countries. World grain planted area has been dropping since the early 1980s. Grain area planted per capita fell from about

0.24 hectares (ha) in 1959 to barely half that (0.13 ha) in 1992. This reflects loss of arable land to erosion and desertification.

Meanwhile, grain fed to livestock has doubled since 1950, aggregate meat production has more than tripled, and meat production per capita has increased by over 50 per cent (though not since 1988). The rising production of meat can be regarded at first blush as good news. However, it is not. It means that more and more basic plant calories are being diverted away from feeding people to feeding animals. In effect, the demands of the more prosperous segments of the world's population are aggravating the situation faced by the poorest.

Evidently, global food production is still rising but more slowly than in the past. Productivity gains per unit of cultivated land are continuing but becoming more and more difficult to achieve. High rice productivity per hectare in Japan is not a viable model for the rest of Asia – it is not only labour intensive, but also very energy and chemical intensive.

China is the focus of major controversy about the future of agriculture. In 1979 the leadership of China was taken over by Deng Xiaoping, a reformer. Under Deng, collective farming was gradually abolished. Though the land itself remained in the hands of the state, privatization of agriculture began to gain momentum during the early 1980s. Peasants were freed from central planning to plant, harvest, and sell as they chose. Food production jumped after 1980. By 1984 China had a record harvest; per capita production of rice in China was up to 90 per cent of Japan's level and the country was self-sufficient. In 1985 China exported grain. Diets continued to improve. In 1990 another record harvest was achieved, 10 per cent above the 1984 level. The year 1993 saw still another record harvest, despite continuing conversion of agricultural land to other uses. Production in 1995 was 465 million metric tons, according to Prime Minister Li Peng's latest report to the National People's Congress. The target for 2000 is 500 million metric tons. Simply extrapolating the recent trend, many economists have concluded that China will have no problem feeding itself for the foreseeable future.

In China, urban population in 1950 was 61 million; currently it is around 330 million; by 2050 it is expected to be around 1 billion, according to the United Nations' population projections. The situation in India is, of course, comparable if not worse. This urbanization will, among other things, remove very significant amounts of land from cultivation. In China, for instance, cities, towns, and infrastructure took 324,000 km^2 of land in 1994, as compared with 1,364,000 km^2 that were cultivated.[1] In 1988/89 alone, 174,000 ha (1,740 km^2) were lost to cultivation and converted to urban or industrial use. Assuming this modest rate of conversion continues unabated, only about 100,000 km^2 more land would be lost to cultivation in China by 2050. But if population increases as projected and the density of cities does not increase, urban area would have to increase by a factor of 3, i.e. to about 1 million km^2, largely at the expense of nearby land, most of which is cultivated at present. So the potential loss of cultivated land could be as much as 650,000 km² or close to half of the current total.

A closely related local/regional problem associated with urbanization and economic development is groundwater shortages. The cause of the water shortages now plaguing much of northern China is debatable, but the most likely cause is too many wells and too-intensive pumping of groundwater for industrial and municipal purposes. Wet rice cultivation and fish farming have both been abandoned in this region of China. The Heaven River no longer exists, and canals that formerly brought water to Beijing are now dry. In late 1993, the water resources minister of China (Niu Maosheng) said that 82 million rural Chinese were suffering water shortages, along with 300 Chinese cities, in 100 of which the shortages were "extreme" (Tyler 1993).

Projecting current trends, China will increase its per capita consumption of food, especially meat, while losing half its arable land to urbanization and industrialization by 2030. Unless agricultural productivity increases faster than it has in the past, China will necessarily become a large importer of food. For the above reasons, among others, Lester Brown of the World-watch Institute has again raised the alarm about China's future ability to feed itself.[2] This would force China into the world's food market as a major importer. This shift will quickly exhaust reserve capacity and create the conditions for shortages and rapid and sharp price increases. But, whereas the gasoline shortage merely caused lines at filling stations, food shortages can cause mass starvation.

Vaclav Smil takes issue, mainly, with one point in Brown's thesis, namely his assumption that China has little scope for further increases in agricultural productivity (Smil 1996). Smil argues (1) that China has at least 25 per cent and possibly 45 per cent more cultivated land than official statistics admit (owing to underestimation of cultivated area to avoid taxes), whence (2) yield is actually much lower than official statistics assume, leaving more room for future improvement than Brown allows for. Smil also argues that there is enormous waste in the Chinese irrigation and fertilizer production systems, and also in the food distribution system, all of which offer significant further room for increased food supply to consumers in the future. Nevertheless, Smil concedes, rather reluctantly:

It would be a mistake to dismiss Brown's predictions as just another scare. Concerns about China's long term food production capacity are valid and many knowledgeable people, both Chinese and non-Chinese, are far from optimistic in their long-term assessment of it. (Smil 1996, p. 33)

The most optimistic (and mainstream) view is presented by Dennis Avery of the Hudson Institute. Avery notes that increased food production per capita in the third world has been based on a virtually constant cultivated land area. It was mainly due to the so-called "green revolution," which

introduced new strains of rice that responded very well to increased fertilizer use. Avery expects further technological progress to continue this trend.
He states that the world can feed "another billion people, right now, without
stressing any fragile acres or putting on heavy doses of farm chemicals"
(Avery 1995, p. 388). He does not, however, suggest that there is room for
another 5 billion people, which is what the UN population projections have
suggested that we must expect.

The environmental impacts of industrial agriculture

The major mass flows and emissions associated with agriculture are nitrogen
losses (as ammonia and nitrous oxide) via various processes, methane
emissions from livestock, and soil erosion. Nitrogen losses must be made up
by organic recycling, nitrogen fixation by legumes, or the application of synthetic nitrogen fertilizers. Erosion is the major cause of phosphorus loss,
which must also be made up by the application of phosphate fertilizers.

A detailed nitrogen and phosphorus balance for five regions, including
world croplands, and all agro-systems for both the United States and China,
has been prepared (Smil 1993). According to this study, biofixation accounts
for only 17 per cent of global crop nitrogen inputs (25 per cent in the United
States, 11 per cent in China), with synthetic fertilizer supplying 43 per cent
of the nitrogen for world croplands (31 per cent in the United States, 52 per
cent in China). Smil also estimates the contribution from atmospheric deposition: 8.5 per cent of global N-inputs, 6.2 per cent of US N-inputs, and 3.7
per cent of Chinese N-inputs).[3] The remainder is from organic recycling.

Future growth in food production in Asia and Africa will evidently be
more dependent on synthetic ammonia production than on either organic
recycling or legumes. Worldwide, about 87 per cent of synthetic ammonia
production is used for fertilizer [*Info. Chimie* 346, 1993]. The World Bank's
World Nitrogen Survey projected a 37 per cent increase in consumption in
Asia between 1992 and 2000 (Constant and Sheldrick 1992).

Long-term projections of population growth and food production in
the developing world suggest huge increases in fertilizer use. To put the
problem in perspective, Food and Agriculture Organization (FAO) data for
1989 suggest that, in the wealthiest countries (Western Europe and North
America), grain yield is about 4.4 tonnes/ha with an input of 270 kg/ha of
fertilizer (cited in Huq 1994, fig. 8). For Eastern Europe and the former
USSR, yields averaged 3.5 tonnes/ha with fertilizer inputs of 145 kg/ha. East
Asia had yields of 3.3 t/ha with inputs of 135 kg/ha. Latin America had
yields of 2.3 t/ha for fertilizer inputs of 90 kg/ha. South Asia got 2.25 t/ha
with inputs of 77 kg/ha. Finally, sub-Saharan Africa enjoyed yields of 1.3 t/ha
with only 26 kg/ha of fertilizer inputs.[4]

When these data are extrapolated, it is clear that fertilizer use increases
non-linearly with yield. There are strong indications that nitrogen fertilizer

use in America and Europe may already be at saturation level. More fertilizer would not increase yields significantly, if at all. But, to raise grain yields in East Asia by 25 per cent – to current West European or US levels – fertilizer use in that region would have to double. For South Asia to double its grain yields, nitrogen fertilizer use would have to increase by something like 350 per cent. In the case of sub-Saharan Africa, low grain yields might conceivably increase three-fold, but fertilizer consumption would probably have to rise 10-fold. In summary, if the world population doubles by 2050, as UN projections imply, most of the increase will be in the developing countries. To allow for urbanization and for increased food consumption per capita, fertilizer inputs in the developing world will almost certainly have to quadruple or more. This implies very significant increases in global nitrogen mobilization.

Nitrogen losses for the world (*c.* 1990) were about 95 million metric tons (MMT). Losses exceeded synthetic nitrogen fertilizer inputs – around 75 MMT (N) – by 20 MMT. Smil assumes the balance is made up by "mineralization" of 30 MMT (from fossil biomass) and atmospheric deposition of 15 MMT (Smil 1993). This seems unlikely. For instance, it is hard to see why the world average from atmospheric deposition should be higher than the US average, considering that both ammonia emissions (from animals) and NOx emissions from combustion sources are much higher in the United States than in the rest of the world. It seems more likely that Smil overestimated this source of nitrogen as a global input. Many experts believe the global system is out of balance and that the soils of the developing world, especially Asia and Africa, are being "mined" of nitrogen content – which must ultimately be replaced. This implies a growing worldwide nitrogen deficit. It also implies an enormous future demand for fertilizer.

Of the 95 MMT worldwide N-loss estimated by Smil, the United States accounts for 14 MMT. Western Europe probably accounts for somewhat less, perhaps 10 MMT (in proportion to agricultural output). Evidently most of the global N-emissions (roughly 70 MMT) are occurring outside the OECD countries. Subtracting the probable OECD contributions, the rest-of-world (ROW) breakdown of losses seems to be roughly as follows:

Denitrification	15 MMT (21.5%)
Leaching into soil	10 MMT (14.5%)
Erosion losses	40 MMT (57%)
Volatilization of NH_3	5 MMT (7%)

The denitrification process (due to bacterial action) generates mainly di-nitrogen gas (N_2), but a small proportion (5–7 per cent) of the nitrogen is released as nitrous oxide (N_2O), which is a greenhouse gas. The fraction released as N_2O is not accurately known, and is certainly a function of local soil conditions and humidity. However, the best available estimate of the ratio is 16:1, which implies a global N_2O production of about 1.25 MMT, of which about three-quarters now comes from the ROW countries.[5]

This pattern of N-losses can probably be expected to continue for the foreseeable future, except that the totals can be expected to increase roughly in parallel with consumption of synthetic nitrogen fertilizer. In other words, nitrogen mobilization and N_2O emissions may be expected to quadruple by 2050. Nitrous oxide currently accounts for something like 7–8 per cent of greenhouse gas emissions. This fraction can be expected to increase.

The other major air pollutant emissions associated with agriculture are ammonia and methane. Ammonia is associated with livestock urine and manure, especially on large-scale feedlots. Most of the ammonia released is volatilized and eventually returned to the land as nitrates and sulphates, which are essentially fertilizers. Little if any harm is done, except that some of the nitrogen is lost to non-agricultural land or oceans. Contamination of groundwater is a more serious problem, however, because ammonia itself and many organic nitrogen compounds are toxic. Grazing animals, especially ungulates, also produce methane in their stomachs – the work of anaerobic bacteria that help with the digestion of grasses. Methane is also generated in large quantities from wet rice cultivation; it is caused by anaerobic decay bacteria in the mud. The OECD countries account for the great majority of cattle and sheep in the world, but wet rice cultivation is primarily an Asian phenomenon. Overall, methane from agriculture (wet rice cultivation) accounts for about 8 per cent of global "greenhouse potential" (WRI 1990, table 2.4).

Pesticide use in the developing world is also rising faster than agricultural production, as measured in monetary terms (WRI 1994, fig. 6.11). The reasons for this are similar to the reasons for expecting fertilizer use to increase faster than food production. Many pesticides banned or tightly restricted in the OECD countries are being used, and in some cases manufactured, in developing countries. Chlordane and DDT are two cases in point. Pesticide use in the OECD countries has levelled off or even declined in recent years. By contrast, pesticide use in many countries of the Asia–Pacific region has been growing at 10 per cent per annum or more, notwithstanding some progress toward integrated pest management (IPM). In India, treated cropland increased from 6 million hectares in 1960 to 80 million in 1985; pesticide production in that country increased 13-fold between 1970 and 1980 and now meets 90 per cent of domestic demand (not to mention exports). India, Indonesia, and Russia are major producers of DDT, for instance, though use of that chemical was supposedly ended in the early 1970s (Ayres et al. 1995).

Agriculture is a major consumer of carbon dioxide and producer of oxygen. For instance, annual above-ground production of harvested crops in the United States is between 500 and 600 MMT, plus a slightly smaller amount of above-ground residues, making a total of 1,100–1,400 MMT but not including grass consumed directly by animals (another 200 MMT). About half of this mass is water; the rest is a combination of carbohydrates, proteins, and fats, and a small percentage of mineral substance (ash). Year-to-year variation depends on rainfall and climate factors. Much of the unharvested crop residue in the United States is left on the land and recycled. In Asia and Africa as much as two-thirds of it is collected and burned – rather inefficiently – for cooking (Smil 1993).

For every 100 units of dry biomass – taken as sugar (ribose) – produced by photosynthesis, 146.7 units of CO_2 are extracted from the atmosphere and 106.7 units of oxygen are returned thence. However, it must be recognized that biomass fed to animals for metabolic purposes reverses the photosynthesis process, consuming oxygen and generating carbon dioxide again. In principle, agriculture and forestry need not affect the global carbon cycle in equilibrium. However, in present practice, they do.

Despite increasing efforts to develop alternative modes of cultivation – especially "no till" agriculture (now strongly promoted in the United States) – world dry-land agriculture, as currently practised, involves extensive ploughing of the soil, mainly for weed control. Ploughing exposes humus (partially decayed organic material) to rapid oxidation. On a net basis, global agriculture is losing humus faster than it is being replaced. No-till methods have a considerable potential to reduce this loss, but they require extensive re-education of farmers.

Erosion, flooding, and topsoil loss are major environmental problems in all countries. Erosion losses in the United States have been carefully monitored (and have been gradually decreasing in recent years). However, despite this, annual topsoil losses in the United States currently average 1.5 billion metric tons or a bit less. In Asia, Africa, and Latin America the erosion problem is not under control. Topsoil losses each year in the non-OECD (ROW) countries, taken as a group, are at least 20–25 times the US level. The fact that erosion accounts for a very large fraction of non-OECD losses of N is significant. It is also the only significant mechanism for loss of phosphorus. Evidently, erosion control would be a very potent tool for reducing demand for synthetic fertilizers. By extension, it would also reduce the very serious pollution problems that are caused by phosphate rock mining, beneficiation, and fertilizer production.

The other source of disequilibrium is deforestation. Deforestation (at present) occurs mainly in the tropics, either for logging or to open new land for cultivation or cattle-grazing. Forests are major storehouses of fixed carbon. Cutting (or burning) forests releases this carbon to the atmosphere as carbon dioxide.

The rate of deforestation is variously estimated, and the larger estimates are somewhat disputed. However, the World Resources Institute (WRI) estimated several years ago that deforestation alone contributed 14 per cent to global climate warming potential. Of this, 10 per cent was attributed to carbon dioxide release and 4 per cent to methane release (WRI 1990, table 2.4). (*For purposes of comparison, this implies that global deforestation contributes as much CO_2 as all the fossil fuels burned by the United States and the former USSR, combined.*)[6] The problem of deforestation is essentially limited to the tropical developing (non-OECD) countries of South-East Asia, Africa, and Latin America. In fact, Europe and the United States exhibit net reforestation, which partially counteracts the loss of tropical forests in terms of the global carbon cycle.

The broad situation

In nearly all scenarios of global development food supply is the major critical factor. At the same time mainstream agriculture is now increasingly considered to be not sustainable. There is overwhelming evidence that "efficient" (industrial) agriculture is not only mining the natural resource base but also influencing other parts of the environment in ways that are detrimental to the well-being of humankind. In addition, the availability of external inputs such as phosphates, fossil hydrocarbons (the current source of synthetic nitrates), and potash is limited.

The characteristic signs of unsustainability include soil erosion, deterioration of soil structure, exhaustion of soil nutrients, salinization of irrigated areas, overuse of water resources, desertification, deforestation, reduction of biodiversity, pest and disease build-up, and pollution from agricultural chemicals in groundwater. Toxic chemicals are finding their way into our food supply. Synthetic nitrogen fertilizer also contributes (via denitrification bacteria) to nitrous oxide emissions and climate warming. On the other hand, it is argued that this intensive pattern of production is necessary to feed the growing world population and, especially, the rapidly growing megacities.

Is humanity in a tragic trap? Is the inevitable fate of humankind – like the development pattern of a rapidly growing culture of microorganisms on a Petri dish – to consume our life support system, to end in autolysis?[7]

This chapter attempts to describe the dilemma in more detail. It also depicts a possible escape route without concealing the fact that far-reaching changes will be necessary. In order to be realistic, it is necessary to identify major social, economic, and ecological constraints that narrow the necessary pathway.

Identifying the limiting factors

One limiting factor is traditional basic cultivation patterns and mind-sets. In different social and ecological conditions very different cultivation methods and philosophies have evolved. The most marked difference is that between intensive gardening-like agriculture in densely populated areas of Asia and "industrial" agriculture in those areas of the world that were brought under cultivation by European emigrants or colonizers within the past 500 years.

In the old cultures, land was scarce and population was dense. Thus, a high yield per surface unit was the overriding need. In the Americas, on the other hand, land was abundant, the population was low, and labour was in short supply. Thus mechanization and large-scale agriculture were appropriate and successful. At present the latter model dominates world agriculture. Its domination is fortified by mainstream economic theory and international trade interests and rules, as well as by cheap transport and telecommunications. But will it be the proper long-term strategy for feeding the dramatically growing world population in a sustainable way? Would not the "outdated" agricultural models from China, (peasant) Europe, India, and Japan be a more appropriate starting point? Could these older models be modernized and adapted to the needs of the future?

Another limiting factor is underestimation of the real importance of agriculture in the industrialized economies.[8] Owing to its minor contribution to the GNP of industrialized economies (typically 2–5 per cent), agriculture is largely neglected in mainstream economic analysis. But agriculture plays a key role in every scenario as the *essential* life-support system.[9] This is due to five major features:

1. Because agriculture is the industry nearest to nature, ecological deficits become apparent much earlier here than in any other branch of the economy.
2. Agriculture satisfies the most basic needs of humankind: it feeds us.
3. The consequences of disregarding sustainable patterns have been more serious in agriculture than in any other sector of the economy; "modern" industrialized agriculture has turned out to be unsustainable within two generations.
4. The long-term prospects for the world food situation are so critical that, if civilized humankind is to survive, corrective action is urgent.
5. Agriculture is the indispensable source of organic material streams in a sustainable future world economy.

A further limiting factor is that modern economics and management theory have encouraged a short-term and reductionist view of agriculture. Successful industrial strategies, characterized by "lean production," rapidly changing technologies, short depreciation periods, and minimization of external influences in process design, are now being transferred to agriculture.[10] The evaluation of agricultural production strategies (systems) by impersonal "market forces" leads to a short-term calculus. But the physical and biological nature of the system itself implies that the appropriate time-frame for measuring sustainable and economically viable agricultural supply systems is much longer: at least 20 years (for example, to observe three periods of a seven-fold crop rotation requires 21 years) and perhaps as much as 100 years (Harrington 1992). Agriculture is an inherently interacting system that should make use of all natural synergisms.

To evaluate agricultural strategy on a short-term basis is to create inappropriate expectations. Thus agriculture is globally being driven towards the industrial model. But this systems coercion is in blunt contradiction to eco-systemic needs, which require biodiversity (CE 1995), site orientation, and a massive reduction of material flows.

There is a high degree of consensus that sustainable land use in developing countries should rely on small-scale mixed agriculture in order to husband environments with a low ecological buffering capacity as well as to feed and employ the population. But the opposite is demanded for industrialized countries (Schmidheiny 1992). The negative reaction of leaders in developing countries is not surprising. They consider this advice to be self-interested and neo-colonialist; they regard it as an attempt to preserve the oligarchic economic structure of the world economy. Hence they unwisely imitate the inappropriate patterns of the industrial world, even when they are not directly imposed by "Western-style" agro-business.

A logical consequence is that soil erosion and the leaching of agro-chemicals into groundwater are out of control in non-OECD countries. In fact, more than three-quarters of world soil destruction takes place in the third world. The massive problem of soil erosion demands a drastic change in production systems towards more stewardship and husbandry of soils and landscapes. The present pattern of production is leading to a decrease in the productive agricultural area by up to 16 million ha per year (ISOE 1995). Therefore, without change, a higher production volume for an increasing population would (will) have to be achieved on a decreasing area.

Another limiting factor is water. The exploitation of water resources, which brought nearly a 2 per cent increase in productivity in the first three post–World War II decades, cannot be augmented, at least not without major investments and dislocations (as in the Three Gorges project in China). Pollution of water resources by wasteful agricultural practices (especially excessive use of synthetic nitrogen fertilizers and pesticides) will have to be reduced in many cases in order to save drinking water reserves. Inputs of agro-chemicals must also to be limited in order to guarantee the integrity of food chains.

To compound the difficulties, most mainstream cultivation systems have been brought to a rather high level of productivity. This means that the law of diminishing returns has to be taken into account in planning the future. In the context of the standard model, this implies that higher industrial inputs will be necessary to increase productivity further, thus shortening the time-horizon within which non-renewable external resources (oil, natural gas, phosphates, potash) will still be available. These are the major raw materials for agro-chemicals (fertilizers, pesticides, and herbicides). These fossil resources are finite and will last at most for some 100 years, if consumption is not slowed down. But the opposite (i.e. acceleration) is the probable outcome of present policies.[11]

Yet another limiting factor is that the food potential of the oceans (and aquaculture) will not be a sufficient alternative at least as far as fish is concerned. There is strong evidence that the world's traditional fishery resources are also already overexploited (see, for example, Weber 1995).

Is a collapse of the agricultural system inevitable? The logic of the curve of population growth suggests that either humans are already overtaxing the carrying capacity of the environment, or they soon will. This implies a real danger that we will eventually consume our own "seed corn," i.e. our life-support system. Without a basic change in population growth rates, consumption patterns ("lifestyle"), and supply technology, present developments resemble a forest fire in a strong wind. The system's breakdown can be expected.

As far as agriculture is concerned, the limiting factors enumerated above can be summarized in a nutshell: intensified conventional mainstream high-input/high-output agriculture is not sustainable in the long run. This is because short-term advantages are offset by long-term disadvantages in the form of increasing destruction and loss of soil and water resources. In addition, the pattern of ever-increasing inputs of fossil energy and raw materials cannot continue indefinitely, for reasons of eventual scarcity as well as environmental reasons.

The food needs of an exponentially increasing world population could not be met, in the long run, even if we assume the most optimistic possible increases in area productivity. Besides slowing down population growth, increasing the efficiency of nutrition will be an indispensable supplementary measure (especially the reduction in luxury meat consumption).[12]

If the present trends of soil degradation and population growth are projected without change,[13] there would be very few regions in the world in 2025 able to satisfy the nutritional needs of their own population, even relying on a diet of grain, tubers, and legumes (i.e. cutting meat consumption to a minimum) (ISOE 1995). Therefore the often-heard argument that there is only one way to avoid serious social upheavals in the future, namely to feed the growing world population by employing intensified industrial patterns of production, cannot be a realistic solution.

This judgement is supported by the annual "State of the World Reports" by the Worldwatch Institute, which point to an approaching crisis. In recent times several events and studies have underlined the view that agriculture will be *the* crucial sector in world economic development. In 1991 the Conference on Agriculture and the Environment, organized by the Food and Agriculture Organization of the United Nations (FAO) and the Government of the Netherlands, analysed the world situation and worked out an Agenda for Action to meet food needs without mining the natural resource base and thus consuming the life-support systems of future generations and probably even of our own. The loss of 5–7 million hectares[14] of arable land per year through soil degradation was reported, with an annual global loss of topsoil running at 24 billion tons. (For an even bigger estimate, see ·Editor's Note above.) There was a general consensus that the situation demands urgent action. It was generally agreed that it is not only the *symptoms* of unsustainability in agriculture (land degradation, desertification and deforestation, water pollution, loss of soil productivity and natural processes, diminishing wildlife habitats and genetic diversity, air and climate effects, etc.) that have to be changed. The change must extend to the underlying dynamics of our societies.

Some other studies support this position (Hohmeyer and Gärtner 1992; FAO 1993; Pimentel et al. 1994; ISOE 1995). The reduction in vital agricultural reserve capacity implied by "business-as-usual" scenarios is likely to lead to increased starvation in developing countries and to mass migration. It may also lead to social, economic, political, and – last but not least – military conflicts. In worst-case scenarios, such catastrophes could destroy the social achievements that most countries value so highly and assume to be guaranteed.

Some economists dismiss these warning studies with epithets such as "neo-Malthusian," the implication being that Malthus was long ago disproved or discredited. There are even strategic papers, such as the "Study on the perspectives for the rural areas in the European Community" of the Netherlands Scientific Council for Government Policy (1992), that see such large long-term surpluses of agricultural goods that only about 50 per cent of the productive land of the European Union will be needed in the future.

Those who attack Malthusianism *per se* can be met by pointing out that there is a decisive difference between the present situation and that in the eighteenth and the nineteenth centuries. Even in the nineteenth century there were still large new areas available for colonization and cultivation, especially in the Americas. Moreover, older cultivated areas and species had not reached ecological limitations associated with monoculture, chemical use, and toxification of soil and groundwater.

As to the food surplus scenarios, it has to be pointed out that all these scenarios are based on the assumption that industrialized countries will continue to run their economies unsustainably. Societies that cover basic demands for organic raw materials and energy by plundering non-renewable fossil resources within a few generations have no need to reserve land for an enduring harvest of solar energy. By limiting agricultural production to the food sector and by boosting food production via cheap fossil-based inputs (chemicals and energy), they can and do produce artificial, but temporary, surpluses. These are not sustainable, however.

Because the introduction of general conditions of sustainability cannot be circumvented in the long run, agricultural politics is confronted with a (politically) painful dilemma. The choice is between short-term maximization – even to the point of generating unwanted surpluses – and long-term sufficiency. This dilemma cannot be resolved by relying on market forces alone, because the latter are unavoidably short term and private in nature and do not reflect the larger public interest.

Anticipatory strategies leading the market to a long-term optimum are therefore necessary. The reasons are evident: population growth cannot be stopped quickly; water resources have already become scarce, especially in developing countries (FAO 1993); the use of chemical fertilizers and pesticides in agriculture has to be controlled and curtailed in order to protect the groundwater, especially in developed countries (OECD 1993). The accepted principles of precaution and plausibility in risk management underline this position.

In this context a few remarks on international trade policy as it concerns agriculture are appropriate. The results of the Uruguay Round of the General Agreement in Tariffs and Trade (GATT) reflect the short-term market calculus (GATT 1994). Calls by environmentalists for measures allowing protection of future-oriented long-term sustainable agricultural systems *within* a system of fair trade are denounced by trade negotiators as "green protectionism." Trade negotiators argue that agriculture must accept the same rules as the industrial sector. Yet industrial undertakings normally do not need a site-oriented design. Their adaptation time to changing circumstances is shorter, and the same holds for the depreciation period. Further, the co-production of public goods (such as harmonious landscapes, biodiversity, and potable water) is, for practical purposes, non-existent in industry. The time-frame of the trade calculus is even shorter than the industrial one.

In addition, long-term food security concerns seem inconsistent with providing favourable trade treatment to regions that gain a short-term comparative advantage by operating unsubstainably. Examples include risking soil erosion through irrigation with "fossil" groundwater and clearing rain forests and steep hillsides to provide cattle pasture for less than a decade before the thin layer of topsoil is lost. Myopic decisions in international economic development planning are the rule, rather than the exception. Proven and sustainable cultivation systems are routinely sacrificed for unsustainable short-term advantages, not only in the Amazon or Central America and in disadvantaged areas such as the European Alpes-Maritimes and Ligurian Alps, terrace agriculture in Yemen, or mountain agriculture in India and Pakistan, but also in the advantaged areas of the northern hemisphere.[15]

The so-called "green box" measures (the "Blair House Agreement" of 1992) are an attempt to mitigate some symptoms.[16] This has broadly the character of a "social end-of-the-pipe treatment strategy," because the listed measures are strictly palliative. They leave the underlying dynamics unchanged. Therefore the environmental impacts of agriculture are not changed at the roots. (For more details see Editor's Note above.)

Does this mean that agriculturalists, as a minority that cannot significantly influence the economic mainstream, must be advocates of intensification of the presently dominating patterns of agricultural production in order to keep humanity alive and fed in the short run, in spite of the warnings of ecologists, environmentalists, and rural developers? The key to a strategy of hope is the answer to the following crucial question: Are there other systems of sustainable agriculture at our disposal that can achieve the high area productivity of mainstream (high-input/high-output) agriculture but that have the potential to feed the growing mega-cities of the future?

The technological feasibility of sustainable agriculture

It should not be necessary to emphasize yet again to the readers of this book that an essential characteristic of sustainable future economic systems must be to minimize the energy and material inputs per service (production) unit, in all sectors. In the realm of food production, organic agriculture is the most appropriate concept. By careful husbanding of soils and landscapes, by relying on site-oriented biodiversity in order to be able to use a maximum of natural synergisms, and by intensive nutrient recycling it minimizes external inputs. Thus, it achieves a maximum net harvest of solar energy in forms usable to humans. In this way it preserves and even improves the soil and achieves the highest possible yields in a way that can be practised for a virtually unlimited time-horizon. In the remainder of this paper, small-scale mixed agriculture in developing countries will not be addressed specifically. Its merits are widely accepted and documented (e.g. Hiemstra et al. 1992; Radtke 1995). I refer to the experience of institutions such as the Bakara Agricultural College in Molo, Kenya. This started as a conventional training school, but it has evolved into an exemplar of site-oriented small-scale mixed agriculture including agro-forestry in order to achieve a maximum of sustainable yield and a diverse diet, unburdened by the residues of agro-chemicals detrimental to human health.

The emphasis hereafter is on the potential of organic agriculture in the present bread-basket countries of the North (i.e. in the industrialized countries). In the following paragraphs, the principal concepts, historical examples, and actual comparisons are presented as evidence that there is a realistic and socially beneficial way out of the "Malthusian food trap" if we are prepared to surmount and challenge the rules of the present game.

The gardening concept

There is evidence that a gardening-like cultivation system with a high input of labour ($\sim$0.3 persons per ha), a high turnover of nutrients, and a balanced pattern of mixed cropping is capable of outproducing low-labour (mechanized) agricultural production systems by at least three-fold. In times of worldwide structural unemployment it would be a wise strategy to rely on this concept in order to meet future food shortages. But the intelligent intermediate step would be to preserve the skills needed to manage highly productive mixed agricultural systems that later can be more easily intensified towards a gardening-like pattern of cultivation. In this light, small-scale mixed agriculture can be seen as the starting block for stepping up agricultural productivity in the future in a sustainable way.

Germany in World War II

I observed an example of (enforced) low-input/maximum-output agriculture in my youth. I was adopted by a farmer family after my father was killed by the Nazis. According to all traditional expectations, Germany – being cut off from all external supplies of food, fertilizers, and agro-chemicals – should have come to starvation point within at least one or two years. But, in spite of massive military destruction, organic agriculture guaranteed the necessary minimum supplies until the end of the war. In fact, invading Allied forces found and captured strategic food reserves in storehouses. Over and above its own population, the German agricultural system had to feed an additional customer in the east because the Red Army could not rely on its own supplies. The dramatic (but temporary) food shortage of 1945 occurred because spring planting was impeded by warfare and seeds were destroyed or consumed for food throughout much of the countryside.

The example of German war agriculture also answers one standard argument against small-scale mixed agriculture, the argument that long-distance supply to towns and cities is not manageable. Even with primitive means (such as horse-drawn wagons and trucks powered by gas from wood pyrolysis), with processing and packaging mainly in small units by hand, an efficient system of collection, storage, and distribution was organized. This task would surely be achieved much more easily by employing advanced technology (microelectronics, informatics, and telecommunications) for networking and designing satisfactory supply systems. Crisis scenarios that were simulated in the 1980s for the Netherlands, Germany, and Finland confirm this past experience (Bakker 1985; Henze 1980; Kettunen 1986).

The potential of organic agriculture in temperate climates

Some preliminary remarks have to be made with respect to the validity of existing comparisons between conventional and organic agriculture.[17] First there is a general tendency to underestimate the productivity of organic agriculture for four reasons:

1. Organic agriculture stems from a revolutionary "bottom–up" movement. It still has relatively little scientific support, because R&D funding by government and industry is directed to support mainstream activities.
2. In order to achieve full productivity by building up the humus content of soils and optimizing the farmer's skills (including the choice of appropriate crop rotations and intermediate crops), a "learning" period of about 10 years is typically necessary.[18]
3. Organic farmers have always asked for support because of the initial yield-lag during the transformation phase.
4. In many cases shortage of affordable labour is a limiting factor, because the question of labour intensity cannot be addressed within the present system of agricultural support and mainstream economic philosophy. This bottleneck could be overcome by a future ecological tax reform that taxed the consumption of non-renewable materials and primary energy carriers on the one side and reduced the direct and indirect taxation of labour on the other.

Thus assessment of the productivity potential of organic agriculture has also to take into account these short-term temporary disadvantages. Comparisons between conventional and organic agriculture, assuming similar endowments of labour and machinery, suggest a much higher energy efficiency for organic agriculture. The improvement ranges from 48 per cent to 64 per cent. But there is a corresponding short-term drop in yield of up to 30 per cent (Haas and Köpke 1994; Berardi 1977). One study observed a 10 per cent reduction in natural produce yields when comparing 14 pairs of conventional and organic farms in the eastern central states of the United

States (Lockeretz et al. 1976). A 1980 study by the US Department of Agriculture (USDA 1980) in the US Midwest found not only a much higher energy efficiency for organic agriculture but also similar or better average yields per surface area unit. In the case of wheat there was no significant difference between the two. In the case of soybeans, organic methods produced 14 per cent higher average yields.

In Europe a number of similar studies have been made (Granstedt 1990; Rist et al. 1989). They have estimated a 20–30 per cent reduction in yields, based on the average performance of organic farms. Bechmann et al. (1992) propose compensating for the yield reduction by changing the European diet (reducing the present physiologically detrimental overconsumption of meat). Meyer (1989), building on a study by Rist, has calculated for the Canton of Zug (in Switzerland) that only 1,430–1,600 m^2 (0.14–0.16 ha) of organically farmed land would suffice to feed one adult person. This differs favourably from the 0.5 ha demanded by Pimentel et al. (1994) in order to provide a diverse nutritious diet of plant and animal products. To take an extreme case, a diet based largely on potatoes could feed an adult person from only 110 m^2 assuming maximum productivity and from 300–400 m^2 assuming average productivity (Walker 1979).

Based on these facts it is possible to make the following rough judgements. The earth is now providing about 4.6 billion ha of land usable for agricultural purposes. About one-third is arable land and two-thirds permanent grassland (ISOE 1995). Divided by a world population of 5.77 billion in 1996, the current world *per capita* endowment amounts to 0.25 ha of arable land and 0.50 ha of grassland. Thus there is still sufficient (but not ample) room for adjustment towards a global eco-restructuring of the agricultural supply systems without the threat of increased starvation. On the contrary, given appropriate incentives, humanity could save its resource base for future generations and still achieve food security.

In assessing future potentials, the performance of the best farmers should serve as a measuring rod, bacause they are the spearhead of future development. Personal observation of Austrian organic farms, especially the well-documented model farm of Hermann Pennwieser, shows that within a period of 10 years the humus content of soils increased by one-third (1.5–2 per cent per annum), and that soil life, soil structure, and water storage capacity also increased significantly (Sinabel 1991). One surprising effect is also that the incidence of plant diseases actually decreased, which indicates a strengthening of the plant's immune systems. The average yields of these organic farms are at the same high level as in comparable Austrian conventional farms.

Besides estimating the potential of sustainable organic agriculture, it is also important to assess the resource conservation potential of organic agriculture if it were adopted globally. The energy efficiency of organic agriculture has already been noted. In addition to the examples cited above, a US study by Lampkin (1990) concluded that conventional high-input/high-output agriculture consumes 2.3 times more energy compared with organic farms.

The contribution of organic farming *vis-à-vis* soil erosion is vitally important. There is clear evidence that soil erosion can be drastically reduced. Reganold et al. (1987) observed a yearly erosion of 8.3 t/ha on organic fields and 32.4 t/ha on conventional ones. Erosion is reduced by three major characteristics of organic agriculture:

- crop rotation, the concept of evergreen agriculture (continuous coverage of the soil by plants), mixed cropping, and underseeding reduce the susceptibility of soil to erosion (Lindenthal et al. 1996);[19]
- augmentation of the humus results in a better soil structure, a higher stability of aggregates, greater penetration by roots, and better water storage capacity (Gehlen 1987; Reganold et al. 1987; Maidl et al. 1988; Beyer et al. 1989; Unger 1989; Diez 1991; Mäder 1993);
- careful (soft) soil cultivation also cuts the risk of erosion.

Higher plant nutrient efficiency

It is usually argued that there are no alternatives to the present high inputs of nitrogen, phosphorus, and potassium (NPK). If all farmers of the world were to follow the high-input model, the minable deposits of phosphorus would be exhausted in about 80 years (Scheller 1991, 1993). The same holds for potassium and for fossil organic resources, which are the base of nitrogen fertilizers (Barney 1980). In addition, the high energy input for the supply of mineral fertilizers has to be taken into account. Nutrient-efficient cultivation techniques are, therefore, a *conditio sine qua non* for long-term sustainable food supply.

Organic agriculture tries to achieve maximum nutrient recycling by integrating plant and animal production and by using all by-products and wastes. Following this concept, nearly balanced nutrient cycles can be achieved (FAT 1994). As far as phosphorus and potassium are concerned, use of the nutrient reserves in the soils and of their geogenous potential, combined with the recycling of organic residuals, can be considered to be a proper intermediate strategy. In the very long term, agriculture must achieve a near closure of nutrient material cycles.

Nitrogen efficiency deserves a separate comment. Conventional agriculture now imports nutrients in nearly unlimited quantities, which have resulted in a nitrogen surplus (N-surplus) in areas where this has been going on for many years. In contrast, organic agriculture limits itself to nutrient recycling and to legumes as sources of nitrogen. In addition, organic farms normally observe the restriction of not more than two large animal units per hectare. Because organic farms are forced to economize on nitrogen inputs, the N-surplus on organic farms is much lower. For the agricultural areas of Germany, for the years 1991 and 1992, Isermann et al. (1994) have calculated a surplus of 145 kg N/ha. In contrast, organic agriculture caused smaller N-surpluses of 37–76 kg/ha (Haas and Köpke 1994). This is clearly reflected in the nitrate content of groundwater. Research in Bavaria found that on average the nitrate content was 79 ppm/litre under areas of conventional agriculture with livestock raising and 42 ppm/litre without livestock (Brandhuber and Hege 1992). Under organically farmed areas the nitrate content of groundwater was, on average, 27 ppm/litre, thus being within safe limits.

Agriculture has always tried to optimize the living conditions of plants and animals and to protect them. Organic agriculture has the same aim. Enlightened organic agriculture therefore does not refuse external aids completely (as some fundamentalists do), but it cuts them to a minimum and tries to rely mainly on the employment of natural synergisms and intensive care. Under these auspices, further increases in the effectiveness and productivity of organic agriculture can be expected. This judgement is underpinned by the fact that political support and public funding of research work in this field are also increasing (USNRC 1989; Lindenthal et al. 1996).

Based on the above evidence, it can be said that pragmatic organic agriculture is a realistic pathway to feed the growing world population and to secure the natural resource base needed for a long-term sustainable future. But it has to be complemented by other measures, especially efficiency of food distribution. Most important of all, there must be effective measures to stabilize world population in order to secure a high quality of life for all citizens of the globe in the long term.

The possible course towards sustainable change

All basic strategies need a rather long time-horizon in order to implement the necessary changes. As pointed out by Leo Jansen (1993), a realistic approach has to start simultaneously on three basic fronts:
- good housekeeping in the short term, i.e. increasing efficiency within the present patterns of supply and consumption;
- designing new more efficient and environmentally benign processes that are compatible with the envisaged future supply systems in the medium term;
- designing new supply systems for the long term, in harmony with the ethical demand for global ecological, social, and economic sustainability and respecting the governing principles of the biosphere.

In order to do this efficiently, an orientation grid (a "mental map") can be helpful to guide research, politics, and entrepreneurial activity.

The sustainability discussion in agriculture has so far developed in a rather casual and informal manner. There is some risk of failing to see the wood for being too fascinated by the trees. Therefore some general "guidelines" should be established. A narrowing "grid" for evaluation is therefore proposed. Accepting intergenerational and global solidarity as overriding principles implies that human supply systems should be designed in such a way as to be practicable for all people at all times.

In order to come up with practical management rules, more specific guidelines should be derived from this very general imperative. A constraint is that the biosystem has to maintain itself in balance, such that material flows are integrated by recycling mechanisms and driven mainly by solar energy. A set of general rules for sustainable action can be derived from this starting point. They are listed in figure 9.1.

A second essential guideline can be deduced from further discernible characteristics of the ecosystem to which humans are adapted. It may be called "respect for the governing principles of the biosphere" (fig. 9.2). These governing principles are characteristics of the ecosystem earth that cannot be altered by humans. They constitute boundary conditions for human action, as noted below.

The above broad principles imply that ecological principles have to be respected even more firmly than the social rules that have been developed within the past 200 years, if we are to give future generations a fair chance. The market mechanism should be acknowl-

In principle the mode of action should be practicable for an infinite period – only then is it really sustainable

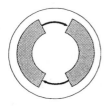

Anthropogenic material flows have to be digestible to the biosphere (locally and globally) as regards their quality and their quantity – especially with respect to the central recycling system of the soil

Σ Mat.Fl = Σ Dig.Cap.
(local & global)

Anthropogenic material flows should not change the magnitude of the global material buffer stocks, in order not to change dynamic equilibria to which the biosphere (i.e. also humans) is adapted

All supply strategies have to be site oriented, incorporating the demand for biodiversity and harmonious landscapes

Because planning activities always have to use simplification, which may turn out to be inadequate, strategies should be reversible

Fig. 9.1 **Basic rules for sustainable action**

edged as the best proven vehicle for economic development. It can encourage human creativity and foster a multitude of options and flexible interactions. But its benefits can be steered towards the commonweal only if it is directed to operate within the domain allowed by ecological (and social) constraints. Therefore the World Trade Organization (WTO), regional trade agreements, supranational institutions, and national constitutions should take into account the principles of sustainable action.

In view of the conflict between present-day economic pressures and expected future conditions it would be unwise to attempt instant change. The best strategy is to put the unavoidable rules definitely into force, to "send a message," but to "turn them on" gradually, so

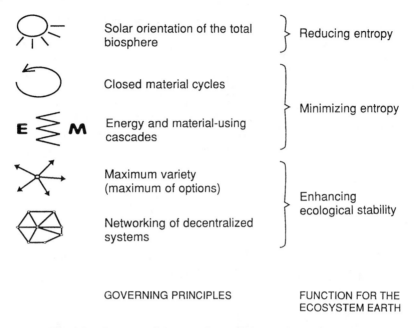

Fig. 9.2 **The essential governing principles of the biosphere**

as to discourage new investment in unsustainable technologies. It is important to provide for a long transition (depreciation) period, in order to avoid unnecessary destruction of capital that has been invested according to the old rules of the game. The basic rules can be easily cast in a normative form usable for national and international negotiation and legislation (Wohlmeyer 1994).

Public and private management in agriculture in industrialized countries is confronted by the political dilemma of present surpluses and looming future shortages. Present surpluses are a consequence of cheap fossil fuels and inappropriate agricultural subsidies and price supports that raise food prices in the industrialized countries, while doing nothing to increase the purchasing power of the world's poor and undernourished people. This mismatch suggests a different bridging strategy to prevent present market forces from driving marginal farmers out of production. Such a bridging strategy should also have the effect of alleviating pressure for unsustainable cost-reduction strategies.

My proposed bridging strategy is demand oriented. It is based on the observation that a sustainable economy for the long term cannot be founded on fossil fuels and raw materials. In order to relieve present agricultural surpluses in the industrialized countries while preserving production capacity that will be needed in the future, a decisive move towards the use of biomass in the intermediate term to substitute for petrochemical products and fossil fuels would make sense (see also chap. 6 in this volume).

Needless to say, both cost considerations and established economic institutions will resist rapid change. Nevertheless, in the first phase, the edible parts of plants can be used both as chemical feedstocks and as liquid (oil or alcohol) fuels. Parallel to this, the use of the non-edible parts of plants as feedstocks (e.g. by cellulose hydrolysis) will have to be brought towards industrial maturity. The latter approach would enable agriculture and industry to switch flexibly from edible to non-edible raw materials and so respond to the increasing demand for food[20] as well as for circular-oriented organic chemicals and for CO_2-neutral organic fuels. One could call this the food $\rightarrow$ non-food $\rightarrow$ food strategy.

Nevertheless, this scheme by itself will not be sufficient. If the industrial (non-food) market is to be developed, heavy subsidies will be necessary at first, because fossil fuels and fossil raw materials are still available at low cost ("plundering value"). Therefore, a taxation system on non-renewable raw materials, bringing their real cost up to their replacement value, would have to be an accompanying measure.

But even this "green taxation" measure has to be supplemented in order to achieve a balanced social situation. If the markets were cleared of food surpluses by the above means, food prices would go up to the marginal costs of production in disadvantaged areas. Thus, agriculturally "advantaged" regions (such as France and the United States) would harvest large differential gains. This would cause higher consumer prices for foodstuffs and higher bridging subsidies for the infant industry strategy in the realms of renewable organic chemicals and primary energy carriers.

Both of these features would be difficult to accept in the long run. Thus it might be necessary to introduce an additional economic instrument. *Compensatory payments* may have to be given to farmers in marginal areas. Such payments might be inversely proportional to the quality of soil and climate, and possibly other factors.[21] Such a package of measures would ensure that consumers pay the lowest possible prices that can be ecologically justified, while minimizing the need for "infant industry" support for chemicals and fuels based on biomass. But the play of market forces would not be excluded. Farmers in disadvantaged areas would get a fair chance, but would have to compete in the market. Thus this combination of measures can claim to be probably the most economical way to meet the basic aims of agro-eco-restructuring and of long-term food security.

To summarize this section, industrial agriculture has turned out to be unsustainable within a few decades. Thus there is growing (if not yet widespread) consensus that a regression to basic patterns of proven systems and their modernization is inevitable (OECD 1992). Traditional farming systems are the result of long and complex human experience. Therefore their basic design should be used as a starting point in order to develop more productive and less laborious production systems that will endure.

This is the more understandable if one keeps in mind that the testing periods of agricultural systems are much longer than the periods over which industrial entrepreneurs can depreciate their investments or over which they have to react to fundamental market changes. The mismatch of time-frames explains why the usual short-term industrial management horizons and practices are so inappropriate to agriculture. But it also explains why the regression to proven systems in agro-eco-restructuring is also feasible from the economic point of view. Organic agricultural practices, as described above, have evolved from ancient proven systems and make use of their insights – as modified by current scientific knowledge. Therefore relevant research and advisory services should be intensified.

In order to characterize sustainable production systems in concrete terms, and to provide tools for cost and price determination, general and regional (site-oriented) Codes of Best Management Practices[22] will have to be established.[23] These codes should be understood as obligatory minimum standards for ecologically sound production. Among other things, these "Best Management Practices" will be needed to calculate ecological "break-even" prices for the purposes of dealing with systems competition in international trade. In order to claim to be consistent with sustainability they must adhere to the general ecological limitations noted previously in this chapter. They must reflect long-term past experience as manifested in proven systems and the insights of pragmatic organic agriculture, i.e. a concept that defines agriculture as the enduring synergistic management of biosystems to meet human demand.

This broad definition can be opened out to yield more specific

guidelines by introducing the following major characteristics of sustainable agro-systems:
- cautious use of all natural synergisms possible at the specific site;
- the saving of energy and material inputs by using biological aids and more human labour;
- reliance on a high degree of biodiversity in order to achieve ecological stability, flexibility, and the availability of a multitude of usable synergisms;
- conservative use of other vital parts of the environment such as water, air, genetic information (soil life, wild plants, and animals);
- linkages with other sectors of the economy in a revolving management of material flows;
- embeddedness in harmonious landscapes, fostering their amenities and conserving their biological carrying capacity.

These characteristics can be reduced further to three central themes:
1. Cutting inputs of energy and non-renewable materials and using all available natural synergisms.
2. "Networking" in a complementary partnership with all other sectors of the economy as a supplier of foodstuffs, raw materials, and energy on the one hand and as the recycler of organic wastes (in biologically harmless qualities and quantities) on the other.
3. Protecting other vital parts of the environment, such as air, soil, water, and biodiversity and embedding agricultural activities in the landscape without overtaxing its biological carrying capacity or harming its natural amenities. This vision of harmonious, multifunctional landscapes is shown in figure 9.3.

Being confronted with short-term-oriented (myopic) market forces, which can usually not take account of environmental concerns and future shortages, and with systems competition between sustainable and unsustainable agro-systems, agricultural politics has to try to encourage traditional and new "islands of sustainability" in an unsustainable world economy (Wohlmeyer and Steinmüller 1993). Rules of fair competition should enable them to comply with the overriding imperatives of ecological balance, as well as with ecological, social, and cultural factors unique to each site.

Aspiring to this aim, the instruments should be chosen in such a way as to take advantage of market forces as far as possible. It is the philosophy of giving as much freedom as is possible and of using as much regulation as is necessary that should determine the policy mix. The desired strategy should also recognize that the right of self-determination towards sustainability and the right of long-term

301

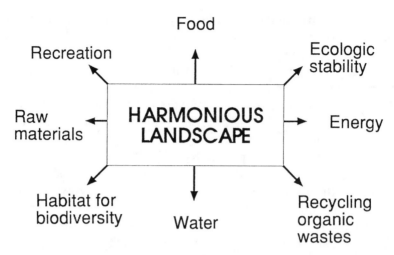

Fig. 9.3 **The vision: Agriculture and forestry embedded in harmonious landscapes supplying water, food and fodder, organic raw materials, and organic primary energy carriers for virtually unlimited time**

food security are derivatives of the norms laid down in the General Declaration of Human Rights.

These guiding thoughts have led me to propose a 12-level core concept to ensure sustainable agriculture and optimal world trade (see fig. 9.4). The proposed policy mix starts from the definition of obligatory minimum standards of ecologically sound production (see the previous section) and ends with international arbitration in the event of dispute.

The intermediate steps (levels) introduce the missing instruments for fair supply-side price bargaining, for demand-side removal of surpluses, and for ensuring a competitive position for disadvantaged regions and farms. They also integrate with already existing measures, such as payments for activities that do not produce a service that can be marketed but are necessary for (and desired by) the public, and temporary assistance within regional development programmes. By these means the core concept tries to ensure transparent and fair competition, incorporates the "bridging" strategy as explained earlier, gives disadvantaged areas and development a chance, and, last but not least, addresses the issue of ecologically necessary price levels for agricultural products. This topic, unfortunately, seems to be taboo for nearly all mainstream neo-classical agricultural economists.

12. Agreed arbitration in the event of a difference of opinion

s

11. Control by an international group of experts and by a joint standing committee of WTO, FAO, UNCTAD, and UNEP

s

10. Temporary assistance within the framework of regional development programmes for disadvantaged areas

s

9. Payments for non-marketable performance (especially ensuring environmental safety, water supplies, and biodiversity, and shaping and husbanding harmonious landscapes) according to published standards

s

8. Removal of general surplus and subsidized exports by directing national production surpassing present food needs towards the non-food sector (regrowing raw materials and primary energy carriers)

s

7. Compensations levies to ensure fair competition with world market supplies produced under lower standards of environmental and social protection and under more favourable eco-topical conditions

s

6. Equalization payments in inverse proportion to the quality of the soil and proportionate to geographical aggravations (especially inclination and climate)

s

5. Market orders to ensure cost covering prices plus a fair profit for the main goods produced in advantaged areas of the state concerned

s

4. Total costs calculation for the main products produced in the most effective way within the boundary conditions defined in (1), (2), and (3)

s

3. Determining site-oriented optimum farm size (sustainable workloads being the limiting factor)

s

2. Adaptation of these general standards to local conditions (eco-topical sustainability)

s

1. Definition of minimum standards for ecologically sound production

Fig. 9.4 A 12-strata core concept to ensure sustainable agriculture and optimal world trade

Final remarks

The main aims for strategic planning towards worldwide sustainability in agriculture can be summarized in ten guiding principles:

1. The agricultural system, embedded in the overall economic system, must be consistent with a scenario reducing the input of oil, gas, and coal per service unit to the order of one-tenth of present consumption.[24]
2. Simultaneously, it is essential for the long-term future of agriculture and forestry to achieve a high level of productivity per unit land area.
3. A feasible transition strategy must be devised to bridge the gap between the present surpluses, due to subsidies and high levels of resource inputs, and the anticipated future shortages of agricultural products.
4. In view of probable social and political turbulence arising from growing inequities, access to food should be recognized as a basic human right.
5. Apart from the guarantee of food availability, the fulfilment of other basic human needs, such as clean water, clean air, and functioning harmonious landscapes, should be integrated into long-term agricultural strategies.
6. Because ecologically sustainable agriculture is, in the long run, possible only within an ecologically sustainable economic system, a broader overall ecological strategy is needed. In this, agriculture and forestry are the indispensable source of all organic material flows.
7. The main future food supply pattern will have to consist of viable localized agricultural systems that are site adjusted, biodiverse, capable of utilizing all natural synergisms, and requiring therefore only low energy and material inputs. Thus, the best pathway to long-term human survival appears to be just the proven small-scale and mixed agricultural and forestry system that has been severely undercut by short-term interests and policies in the OECD (OECD 1991) and the WTO (GATT) as well as in the European Union.[25]
8. The agricultural strategy should be globally applicable but locally and individually adjustable.
9. The effective division of agriculture and forestry into mixed and labour-intensive small-scale farming in the densely populated developing countries on the one hand, and fully mechanized energy/material-intensive large-scale farming in the industrialized nations, on the other, is neither ecologically nor socially sustainable (Austria 1992). This is because the developing countries follow the example of the industrialized nations in choosing

their strategies. It is thus necessary, irrespective of the great variety in ecotopes and cultures, to strive for a common global scheme.

10. Finally, assurance of an adequate future food supply also calls for the maintenance of agriculture in marginally productive areas.

It seems that the conventional view of world agricultural development is paradoxical. Thanks in part to unsustainable high-input/high-output industrial agriculture, people are leaving the countryside and flocking to the cities. It is then argued that exactly this type of labour-saving agriculture is necessary to feed the urban agglomerations.

In my view, the sustainable future world will have to consist of a variety of diverse agricultural production systems embedded in cautiously husbanded landscapes. The essential rules of design will have to be global, but the details will vary according to local conditions. Differences in climate, soil type, topography, and cultural preferences will lead to a bouquet of solutions. Nevertheless they will have to respect the governing principles of the biosphere.

Fair-trading rules to cope with competition from unsustainable high-input systems will have to regulate the exchange of goods and services in such a way that the exchange is beneficial to a maximum of people both now and in the distant future. Therefore scope has to be given to allow for the internalization of the costs of respecting global and local ecological conditions, as well as of local cultural and social achievements. Yet this needs to be consistent with the basic rules of free international trade.

If world trade culture – especially within the World Trade Organization – does not adapt to these imperatives and still adheres to inappropriate theories of traditional trade that do not incorporate ecological and social aims and limitations, our economic system is on track to a general disaster. It is especially in the realm of agriculture that the dangers are most evident. Agriculture is the industry nearest to nature. Thus it should be seen as the tip of the ecological iceberg, which our titanic civilization is approaching with increasing speed.

This Cassandran judgement should not be mistaken for a tactical exaggeration. The traditional economic paradigm is already cracking from not being able to cope with rising structural unemployment, unfinanceable social services, loss of tax base, inability to finance growing environmental repair costs, unfinanceable general budgets, and unsustainable international systems competition. This situation will deteriorate further if the neo-classical dogma of unconditional free trade and capital transfer is not modified. Thus the apparent problems and necessary solutions for the agricultural sector could be eye-openers and pacemakers for general eco-restructuring. The other sectors of the economy could learn, from the industry nearest to nature, how nature has to be obeyed in order to be commanded.

Notes

1. Data in this paragraph are taken from Heilig (1995), tables 3 and 4.
2. Brown's scenario is analogous to the so-called energy crisis of 1973–1974. See Brown (1994, 1995).
3. Deposition consists of nitrates resulting from neutralization reactions between alkaline ammonia (volatilized from animal urine and manure) and nitric or sulphuric acids produced by atmospheric oxidation of NOx and SOx. The end results of these acid–alkali reactions are ammonium sulphate and ammonium nitrate, which dissolve in rainwater and fertilize the soil.
4. The crop yield per unit of fertilizer input is anomalously low for North Africa and the Middle East, but the explanation for this is almost certainly related to water scarcity. That is to say, yield could be increased sharply without more fertilizer input if more water were available.
5. This is roughly consistent with other estimates. For example, the US National Academy of Sciences estimated global N_2O output for 1988 at 1.5 MMT.
6. The rate of deforestation in the Amazon has apparently slowed down since the late 1980s, thanks to the withdrawal of subsidies to cattle-ranchers.
7. The Greek myth of Erysichton illustrates this. The prince plunders the sacred grove of Demeter, the goddess of agricultural fertility, and is punished by insatiable hunger. He ends up eating his own limbs, i.e. autoconsumption.
8. The underestimation is mainly due to the fact that the services rendered by agriculture in the common interest are not reflected in market prices (e.g. landscape amenity, biodiversity, drinking water supplies).
9. One of the most striking examples is the calculations of the costs of climate change done by Nordhaus (1991), which should be compared with the calculations and estimations by Hohmeyer and Gärtner (1992).
10. This was officially done in the Uruguay Round of the General Agreement on Tariffs and Trade.
11. Such as, for example, those adopted by World Food Summit (13–17 November 1996).
12. The present developments in South-East Asia (see Editor's Note) run in the opposite direction, thus aggravating the future situation.
13. Also excluding the food risks of climate change.
14. The above-reported 16 million ha include deteriorated grassland.
15. One is reminded of the outcry by J. M. Keynes in a similar economic environment in 1933: "Or again, we have until recently conceived it a moral duty to ruin the tillers of the soil and destroy the age-long human traditions attendant on husbandry if we could get a loaf of bread thereby a tenth of a penny cheaper. There was nothing which it was not our duty to sacrifice to this Moloch and Mammon in one; for we faithfully believed that the worship of these monsters would overcome the evil of poverty and lead the next generation safely and comfortably, on the back of compound interest, into economic peace" (Keynes 1933).
16. In particular, direct payments to farmers as long as they are not linked to production, income safety-net arrangements, set-aside programmes, and pension schemes; payment for environmentally friendly behaviour and landscape husbanding; research, quality control, and information.

17. For this section I am very much indebted to Dr. Thomas Lindenthal, Institute for Organic Agriculture at the Agricultural University of Vienna, who provided a wealth of essential information and literature.
18. Personal observation on various farms.
19. Personal information, 1996.
20. At present there is enormous need (more than 800 million people hungry) but not sufficient demand. Demand will increase when all world citizens get a comparable chance for adequate nutrition.
21. China is now about to abandon its mountain farmers for short-term reasons. By doing so it is destroying a major human capital for the future.
22. See also OECD (1992). The *Codex Alimentarius* should serve as an example. It continuously defines the best manufacturing practices for foodstuffs and codifies them.
23. The present endeavours of the OECD to establish a set of Agri-Environmental Indicators (AEI) are along these lines.
24. In a sustainable economy the use of fossil raw materials and primary energy carriers is admissible only to the extent that it is compensated by the natural deposition of CO_2 (especially in the form of calcification and sedimentation in the oceans) (Factor Ten Club 1994).
25. "The generally high price of Austrian farm products is, in particular, due to the fact that the domestic agriculture is small-structured. The available agricultural area is smaller, the animal stock per farm is smaller, and the specialization is less advanced than in the EU" (Austria 1992, p. 131).

References

Austria (1992) *Report on the Situation in Austrian Agriculture*. Vienna: Austrian Federal Ministry of Agriculture and Forestry.

Avery, D. (1995) The world's rising food productivity. In: J. L Simon, *The State of Humanity*, pp. 376–393. Cambridge, MA: Blackwell.

Ayres, Robert U., Leslie W. Ayres, and Albert Hahn (1995) *Industrial Metabolism of Selected Toxic Organic Chemicals*. Final Report, Contract 402302/94-4239. Fontainebleau, France: INSEAD Centre for the Management of Environmental Resources, 17 March.

Bakker, T. M. (1985) *Eten van eigen Bodem, een Modelstudie*. The Hague: LEI.

Barney, Gerald (Study Director) (1980) *The Global 2000 Report to the President*. Technical Report, vol. 2. Washington D.C.: Council on Environmental Quality/US Department of State.

Bechmann, A. et al. (1992) *Landwirtschaft 2000: Ist flächendeckende ökologische Landwirtschaft finanzierbar? Szenario für die Umstellungskosten der Landwirtschaft in Deutschland*. Hamburg: Greenpeace.

Berardi, G. M. (1977) Organic and conventional wheat production: Examination of energy and economics. *Agro-Ecosystems* 4: 367–376.

Beyer, L. et al. (1989) Humuskörper und mikrobielle Aktivität von schleswig-holsteinischen Parabraunerden. *Mitteilung der Deutschen Bodenkundlichen Gesellschaft* 59(I): 299–302.

Brandhuber, R. and U. Hege (1992) Tiefenuntersuchungen auf Nitrat unter Ackerschlägen des ökologischen Landbaus. *Bayerisches Landwirtschaftliches Jahrbuch* 69: 111–119.

Brown, L. (1994) Feeding China. *Worldwatch*, September/October.

—— (1995) *Who Will Feed China? Wake up Call for a Small Planet.* New York: W. W. Norton.

CE (Council of Europe) (1995) *Pan-European Biological and Landscape Diversity Strategy.* Environment for Europe, Council of Ministers, Sofia, Bulgaria, 23–25 October (adopted as an official conference policy statement).

Constant, Kurt Michael and William F. Sheldrick (1992) *World Nitrogen Survey.* World Bank Technical Paper 174. Washington D.C.: World Bank, Asia Technical Department.

Diez, T. (1991) Vergleichende Bodenuntersuchungen von konventionell und alternativ bewirtschafteten Betriebsschlägen - 2. *Mitteilung. Bayerisches Landwirtschaftliches Jahrbuch* **68**: 409–443.

Factor Ten Club (1994) *Carnoules Declaration.* Wuppertal, Germany: Factor Ten Club, October (Chairman, F. Schmidt-Bleek).

FAO (Food and Agriculture Organization of the United Nations) (1993) *The State of Food and Agriculture 1993.* FAO Agricultural Series 26. Rome: FAO.

FAT (1994) *Berichte über biologisch bewirtschaftete Betriebe 1994: Ergebnisse der zentralen Auswertung von Buchhaltungsdaten.* Tänikon, Switzerland: Eidg. Forschungsanst. für Betriebswirtschaft und Landtechnik.

GATT (General Agreement on Tariffs and Trade) (1994) *The Results of the Uruguay Round of Multilateral Trade Negotiations.* Geneva: Secretariat of GATT.

Gehlen, P. (1987) Bodenchemische, bodenbiologische und bodenphysikalische Untersuchungen konventionell und biologisch bewirtschafteter Acker-, Gemüse-, Obst- und Weinbauflächen. Ph.D. thesis, University of Bonn, Germany.

Granstedt, A. (1990) Kann die schwedische Landwirtschaft ohne Mineraldünger arbeiten? *Lebende Erde*, no. 4.

Haas, G. and U. Köpke (1994) Vergleich der Klimarelevanz ökologischer und konventioneller Landbewirtschaftung. In: *Studienprogramm Landwirtschaft der Enquete-Kommission: Schutz der Erdatmosphäre.* Bonn: Economica Verlag.

Harrington, L. (1992) Measuring sustainability. In: W. Hiemstra, et al. (eds.), *Let Farmers Judge: Experiences in Assessing the Sustainability of Agriculture*, pp. 2–16. London: Intermediate Technology Publications.

Heilig, Gerhard (1995) Neglected dimensions of global land-use change: Reflections and data. *Population and Development Review* **20**(4). Reprinted in IIASA RR-95-3, April 1995.

Henze, A. (1980) Zur Sicherung der Nahrungsmittelversorgung in der Bundesrepublik. *Agrarwissenschaft* **29**.

Hiemstra, W. et al. (eds.) (1992) *Let Farmers Judge: Experiences in Assessing the Sustainability of Agriculture.* London: Intermediate Technology Publications.

Hohmeyer, O. and M. Gärtner (1992) *The Cost of Climate Change: A Rough Estimate of Orders of Magnitude.* Report to the Commission of the European Communities, DG XII, Brussels.

Huq, Saleemul (1994) Patterns and prospects of global industrialization: A developing country perspective. In: Robert H. Socolow, C. J. Andrews, F. G. Berkhout, and V. M. Thomas (eds.), *Industrial Ecology and Global Change.* Cambridge: Cambridge University Press.

Isermann K. et al. (1994) *Lösungsansätze und Lösungsaussichten für eine hinsichtlich des Nährstoffhaushaltes Nachhaltige Landwirtschaft in Deutschland bis zum*

Jahre 2005. Studie für die Akademie für Technikfolgenabschäatzung, Baden-Würtemberg, Germany.

ISOE (Institut für sozialökologische Forschung) (1995) *Aktionsplan für eine nachhaltige Entwicklung der Niederlande*. Frankfurt: ISOE.

Jansen, L. A. (1993) Sustainable development: A challenge to technology. In: *Proceedings of the International Symposium: Sustainability, Where Do We Stand?* Graz, Austria: Technical University of Graz.

Kettunen, L. (1986) Self-sufficiency of agriculture in Finland in 1970–1983. *Journal of Agricultural Science in Finland* **58**.

Keynes, John Maynard (1933) On national self-sufficiency. *New Statesman and Nation*, 15 July: 66.

Lampkin, N. (1990) *Organic Farming*. Ipswich, Suffolk: Farming Press Books.

Lindenthal T., R. Vogl, and J. Hess (1996) *Forschung im ökologischen Landbau*. Soderausgabe des Förderungsdienst (es 2c), Bundesministerium für Land- und Forstwirtschaft, Germany.

Lockeretz, W. R. et al. (1976) *Organic and Conventional Crop Production in the Corn Belt: A Comparison of Economic Performance and Energy Use for Selected Farms*. St. Louis, MO: Center for the Biology of Natural Systems, Washington University.

Mäder P. (1993) Effekt langjähriger biologischer und konventioneller Bewirtschaftung auf das Bodenleben. In: U. Zerger (ed.), *Forschung im ökologischen Landbau*. SOL Sonderausgabe **42**: 271–278.

Maidl, F. X. et al. (1988) Vergleichende Untersuchungen ausgewählter Parameter der Bodenfruchtbarkeit auf konventionell und alternativ bewirtschafteten Standorten. *Landwirtschaftliche Forschung* **41**(3–4): 231–245.

Meyer, A. (1989) *Produktion von biologischen Nahrungsmitteln in der Geminde Riehen*. Oberwil, Switzerland: Forschungsinstitut für biologischen Landbau.

Netherlands Scientific Council for Government Policy (1992) *Reports to the Government No. 42: Ground for Choices. Four Perspectives for the Rural Areas in the European Community*.

Nordhaus, William D. (1991) To slow or not to slow: The economics of the greenhouse effect. *Economic Journal* **101**: 920–937.

OECD (Organization for Economic Cooperation and Development) (1991) *National Report for Austria, 1991/92*. Paris: OECD Publications.

——— (1992) *Agents for Change*. Summary Report from the OECD Workshop on Sustainable Agriculture, Technology and Practices, February 11–13, 1992. Paris: OECD Publications.

——— (1993) *What Future for Our Countryside? A Rural Development Policy*. Paris: OECD Publications.

Pimentel, D. et al. (1994) Natural resources and an optimum human population. *Population and the Environment* **15**(5): 347–369.

Radtke, R. (ed.) (1995) *Sustainable Agriculture: A Selection of Handbooks for Practitioners*, 2nd revised edn. Stuttgart: Bread of the World.

Reganold, J. P. et al. (1987) Long-term effects of organic and conventional farming on soil erosion. *Nature* **330**: 370–372.

Rist, S. et al. (1989) *Möglichkeiten und Grenzen des biologischen Landbaus im Kanton Zug*. Konzeptstudie. Oberwil, Switzerland: Forschungsinstitut für biologischen Landbau.

Scheller, E. (1991) Die Düngungspraxis im ökologischen Landbau – unverantwortlich oder wissenschaftlich fundiert? *Ökologie und Landbau* **78**: 12–15.

———— (1993) *Wissenschaftliche Grundlagen zum Verständnis der Düngungspraxis im ökologischen Landbau: Aktive Nährstoffmobilisierung und ihre Rahmenbedingungen.* Dipperz, Germany: Selbstverlag E. Scheller.

Schmidheiny, Stephen (1992) Food and agriculture. In: Stephen Schmidheiny with the Business Council for Sustainable Development (eds.), *Changing Course: A Global Business Perspective on Development and the Environment*, chap. 9. Cambridge, MA: MIT Press.

Simon, J. L. (1995) *The State of Humanity*. Cambridge, MA: Blackwell.

Sinabel, F. (1991) Regional solutions for global energy problems. Austrian Association for Agricultural Research, Vienna.

Smil, V. (1993) Unpublished mimeo.

———— (1996) Is there enough Chinese food? A review of L. Brown's *Who Will Feed China? New York Review of Books*, February: 32–34.

Tyler, P. (1993) China's water is drying up. *New York Times*, December.

Unger E. (1989) Bodenchemische Kennwerte konventionell und organisch-biologisch wirtschaftender Landwirtschaftsbetriebe in Erlauftal Niederösterreich. Diplomarbeit, Institut für Bodenforschung und Baugeologie, Universität für Bodenkultur, Vienna.

USDA (United States Department of Agriculture) (1980) *Report and Recommendations on Organic Farming.* Washington D.C.: USDA.

USNRC (National Academy of Sciences/National Research Council Board on Agriculture) (1989) *Alternative Agriculture.* Washington D.C.: National Academy Press.

Walker, David (1979) *Energy, Plants and Man.* Chichester, Sussex: Packard Publishing.

Weber, P. (1995) Protecting oceanic fisheries and jobs. In: Lester R. Brown et al. (eds.), *State of the World, 1995.* New York: W. W. Norton.

Wohlmeyer, Heinrich (1994) Zur Rezeption der ökologischen Vorgaben in Gesellschaft und Gesetzgebung. In: Enrique H. Prat and Peter Lang (eds.), *Kurswechsel oder Untergang.* Frankfurt am Main: Europäischer Verlag der Wissenschaften.

Wohlmeyer, Heinrich and Horst Steinmüller (1993) First results from Austria on regional "islands of sustainability." In: *Sustainability – Where Do We Stand?* Graz: Institute for Process Technology, Technical University Graz.

WRI (World Resources Institute) (1990) *World Resources 1990–91.* New York: Oxford University Press, in collaboration with UNEP and UNDP.

———— (1994) *World Resources 1994–95.* New York: Oxford University Press, in collaboration with UNEP and UNDP.

10

The restructuring of tropical land-use systems

Gilberto C. Gallopín

Introduction

Rural land use in the tropics is dominated by agriculture (used here in its broad sense to include forestry, animal production, and other related topics). Rural land use, and particularly agriculture, represents perhaps the most intense and intimate link between society and nature (Turner et al. 1993). The dynamics of ecosystems, and the fact that they respond in an active, rather than a passive, way to human actions, are particularly visible in the tropics. Agricultural activities have been, of necessity, more aware of the ecological or natural resources dynamics, opportunities, and limitations than have industrial activities. However, this does not mean that integration was (or is) a basic characteristic of the activity. On the contrary, the prevailing conceptualization is vertical, by product or crop, with specified priorities and policies, as if the production situations were ecologically, economically, and socially homogeneous (Girt 1990).

Eco-restructuring in general, and more so in the case of tropical agriculture, will have to involve much more than marginal improvements and mitigating measures recognized by many orthodox economists and politicians. Eco-restructuring is, or should be, about the deep changes required to advance towards sustainable development.

In moving towards sustainable agriculture, three partially over-lapping degrees of progress can be distinguished: efficiency changes, substitution changes, and fundamental redesign changes (MacRae et al. 1990).

Efficiency changes progress towards sustainability by reducing inputs for the same output, increasing output for the same input, and/ or reducing wastes (spot rather than whole-field applications of pesticides, avoidance of overfertilization, efficiency of water use, etc.). The advantages that efficiency increases provide towards sustainability (and often also towards economic gains) are generally accepted. However, maximizing efficiency can be a dead-end path if the system being made more efficient is intrinsically unsustainable (White et al. 1994). Besides, efficiency gains can be offset by increases in the total volume of the activity if it grows faster than efficiency.

Substitution changes can increase sustainability by replacing limited or environmentally damaging inputs with healthier, or less limited, alternatives. Substitution changes may involve replacing herbicides with mechanical weed control, or using legumes to replace fertilization with inorganic nitrogen.

Redesign changes are more fundamental and involve whole production systems. In agriculture, the emphasis would be on cropping systems and farming systems as a whole. In some cases, even whole landscape systems should be redesigned. Redesign changes are likely also to incorporate efficiency and substitution changes. For example, changing from a monocultural grain production system to a multi-year crop rotation system can involve numerous substitution and efficiency effects.

The general approaches of efficiency, substitution, and redesign changes apply to agriculture as well as to industry and services. However, there is a major difference between agricultural and industrial eco-restructuring. Although modern agriculture is in many senses becoming similar to an industrial activity, it is still fundamentally based upon the management of agricultural ecosystems, including living and non-living components. The functioning of those ecosystems under management depends upon (and affects) larger ecological cycles and processes, and also depends upon their own internal biogeochemical dynamics and capacity of response. This is particularly true in the case of the tropical agro-ecosystems, and in reference to complex agro-forestry production systems that mimic many of the features of natural ecosystems. The capacity of living systems for spontaneous behaviour and unexpected changes makes eco-restructuring in agriculture potentially more complex than in industry.

Models of rural development

Different approaches to rural development, including land use, have been applied in tropical regions.[1] Although the specific examples used here will mostly draw from the Latin American experience, some of the lessons have wider applicability.

Historically, the concept of **agricultural development** included the sum of the efforts directed towards the growth and diversification of production and towards increases in productivity. The conceptual base of agricultural development was essentially technical, mostly associated with yield increases through the Green Revolution, the expansion of the physical capital, and the creation of an institutional context coherent with the requirements of a continuously increasing agricultural output.

The concept of **rural development** arose as a response to the realization that agricultural development, as applied, did not lead to an overall improvement in the living standards of rural people and did not "trickle down" to the poor. Rural development was associated with a set of actions (including improvement in production systems, the availability of credit facilities for commercialization of harvesting, and the expansion of the physical infrastructure) specifically directed towards poor rural producers.

Different approaches to rural development were tried in Latin America. From the mid-1950s to the early 1960s, the United Nations promoted the **community development** approach, directed mainly at the integration of rural communities (particularly the indigenous people) in the national socio-economic context, the utilization of their potential for development through education, social organization, and social action, and participation. The strong dependence upon external financing and foreign experts, the failure to pursue rapid increases in production (to avoid conflicts with national agricultural policies), and the political struggles associated with the empowerment of communities in some countries seem to be among the major factors that contributed to the abandonment of this model.

In the 1960s **agrarian reform** was considered by many experts (and governments) to be the major instrument to lead to new rural structures that would be stable, efficient, and participative and result in a quantum leap in production and equity. The results have been mixed. The reform was concretely applied to no more than 20 per cent of appropriable land; today, Latin America is still the region of the world with the highest concentration of land ownership. The impacts on production were also non-conclusive: in some countries the impacts were positive, in others negative. Sustainability of the natural resource base and relations between the social changes triggered and the available technological package and credit, technical assistance, and training were neglected.

The prevailing approach during the 1970s was that of **agricultural modernization**, which led to economic concentration and the expulsion of labour, which is still happening in many countries of the region. Large and medium agricultural production was integrated into the national economy, as well as becoming more dependent on the market. Strong processes of proletarization, social differentiation, and recomposition affected, and still affect, the peasant economies.

The concept of **integrated rural development** (IRD) emerged in the early 1970s, and is still in use. It implies the definition of multiple goals: increases in production and productivity, social improvement, and physical capital formation. It also involved attempts to integrate action on different factors, institutional coordination, and strong participation by the beneficiaries. The approach was conceived as an integral state intervention, specifically targeting poor rural producers. Many of the projects operated at the micro level, in isolation. By the end of the 1970s, the need to link IRD projects with an explicit national policy coherent with national and sectoral development strategies gained political support. During the 1980s (officially known as "the lost decade" for development in Latin America), the economic crisis and recession led to the application of structural adjustment policies, including severe reductions in public expenditure. This also strongly affected IRD projects, in particular because they require substantial and sustained investments with long maturation periods. The impacts of the adjustment process upon the theoretical basis of IRD, as well as dissatisfaction with the results achieved in terms of the total rural economy and society, led to new analytical proposals in the late 1980s. These emphasized the need to focus on less complex projects, directed at a narrower target population, and to look for technical solutions that are economically viable for poor farmers and allow increases in production and income within the context of current macroeconomic and agricultural policies.

314

During the 1980s, a more integrated approach, "**social forestry**," started to be implemented as a response to the problems generated in ecologically fragile areas with high demographic pressures and a high incidence of poverty. A number of successful experiments exist. These projects emphasize the active participation of small and medium farmers in the design, implementation, and control of the project; the goals of the project are defined by the community; the projects integrate many relevant components (such as crops and farm animals associated with trees and other woody plants, small industries, marketing, training, agro-forestry, social organization of the population); the concept of the sustainability of the productive system is incorporated in the design of the projects as a prerequisite for rural development; and the projects explicitly attempt to reach synergy between the resources of the community (land, labour, appropriate traditional technologies, and organization). In general, they are not intensive in financial resources per person or per hectare.

In general in Latin America (although less so in the case of IRD and social forestry projects) the generic policies for rural development had few explicit linkages with macroeconomic policies (particularly with those defining urban–rural exchange relations) and with public investment. They also suffered from a lack of complementarity with the policy instruments applied to foster agricultural modernization. They concentrated too much on the productive aspects, without addressing the issue of the sustainability of production, and sometimes resulted in increased environmental degradation. They did not address the linkages between international agricultural trade and the degradation of natural resources within prevailing economic patterns. They were too much influenced by economic criteria and by the institutional policies of the international funding agencies. And, finally, they were often biased towards expensive and unconnected projects, which ended when the external financial resources were exhausted.

The need for integrated solutions in tropical land use

Tropical agriculture is not limited to the humid tropics; it also includes dry zones. However, it is in the humid tropics that the major challenges for eco-restructuring lie.

Humid tropic conditions are found over nearly 50 per cent of the tropical land mass and 20 per cent of the earth's total land surface –

an area of about 3 billion hectares. Tropical Central and South America contain about 45 per cent of the world's humid tropics, Africa about 30 per cent, and Asia about 25 per cent. As many as 62 countries are located partly or entirely within the humid tropics (NRC 1993).

Land transformation in temperate zones (such as Northern Europe) from its natural state to its present intensive agriculture and land use occurred over thousands of years. Changes in the tropics are occurring at a much faster rate; in some cases, areas are completely transformed and often degraded beyond economically feasible restoration within one generation.

Sustainable land use in the humid tropics will require an approach that recognizes the characteristic cultural and biological diversity of these lands, respects their complex ecological processes, involves local people at all stages of the development process, and promotes cooperation among biologists, agricultural scientists, and social scientists. The easing of rigid disciplinary boundaries is of special importance in the humid tropics.

Most public sector agricultural research and development programmes in the humid tropics have in the past used a commodity-oriented approach, aiming to maximize the production of cereals and a limited number of root and pulse crops. This approach has led to striking increases in food production in areas with good soil and water resources. However, by focusing attention on particular crops and agro-ecosystem components, it has tended to neglect the range of physical and biotic interactions that influence crop production, the ecological impacts of intensive production practices, and broader social and economic aspects.

This commodity-oriented approach has also ignored lessons from the performance of traditional agricultural systems. Many traditional resource management techniques and systems, often dismissed as primitive, are highly sophisticated and well suited to the opportunities and limitations facing farmers in the tropics. Their durability, adaptability, diversity, and resilience often provide critical insights into the sustainable management of all tropical agro-ecosystems. Although many of these systems have been deeply modified or abandoned owing to economic, cultural, and social pressures, some could, with modification, contribute significantly to the sustainability and productivity of agriculture in many tropical countries (NRC 1993; Gallopín et al. 1991).

Agricultural systems and techniques that have evolved from

316

ancient times to meet the special environmental conditions of the humid tropics include the paddy rice of South-East Asia, terrace, mound, and drained field systems, raised bed systems (such as the *chinampas* of Mexico and Central America), and a variety of agro-forestry, shifting cultivation, home garden, and natural forest systems. Although diverse in their adaptations, these systems share common elements, such as high retention of essential nutrients, maintenance of vegetative cover, high diversity of crops and crop varieties, complex spatial and temporal cropping patterns, and the integration of domestic and wild animals into the system (NRC 1993). Many of the required activities are highly knowledge intensive, even if based on empirical knowledge. This diversified holistic, empirical knowledge, or **socio-diversity** as it is sometimes referred to, is being lost in the tropics as fast as, and often faster than, biodiversity. This is a precious resource receiving insufficient attention.

It is generally agreed that sustainable agriculture typically will require more information, more and better trained labour, and more diverse management skills per unit of production than conventional farming. This is because diversification into each additional crop and additional animal species requires additional and different skills. A diversified farm requires better production management and a different kind of labour resource than a similar-sized farm growing only one or two crops. This is one of the major limiting factors (Pesek 1994). In the case of integrated pest management (IPM), based on sound scientific principles, it is argued that, when problems arise in its practice, they are usually associated with the large amount of knowledge and expertise needed to develop, implement, and improve an IPM programme and with a tendency to rely too heavily on strategies developed from inadequate knowledge and without sufficient consideration of all the consequences of their use (Funderburk and Higley 1994). It is also recognized that sustainable agriculture must be based in large part on site-specific information and knowledge (White et al. 1994). It seems ironic that modern agriculture in many cases has lost (and, in the tropics, is still losing) site-specific skills for managing complex agro-ecosystems in its quest for standardization and commoditization, and that the same skill factor (albeit with the incorporation of modern scientific knowledge) is limiting the transition to sustainable agriculture.

Although traditional knowledge is not a panacea, it could contribute much to sustainable agriculture when combined with modern scientific knowledge, as will be discussed later.

Table 10.1 **Summary of the three major types of agriculture**

	Industrial	Green Revolution	Resource poor
Main locations	Industrialized countries and specialized enclaves in the third world	Irrigated and stable rainfall, high-potential areas in the third world	Rain-fed areas, hinterlands, most of sub-Saharan Africa, India, Burma, Bangladesh, Indo-China
Main climatic zone	Temperate	Tropical	Tropical
Major type of farmer	Highly capitalized farms and plantations	Large and small farmers	Smallholders
Use of external inputs	Very high	High	Low
Farming systems, relatively:	Simple	Simple	Complex
Environmental diversity, relatively:	Uniform	Uniform	Diverse
Production stability	Moderate risk	Moderate risk	High risk
Current production as percentage of sustainable production	Far too high	Near the limit	Low
Priority for production	Reduce production	Maintain production	Raise production

Source: Chambers et al. (1989).

Tropical agriculture includes two of the three major types of agriculture (see table 10.1). These two types can be illustrated by the following extreme situations.[2]

- **The robust and fertile tropical agro-ecosystems.** These are characterized by relative homogeneity of the natural resource base. A realistic production objective in those agro-ecosystems may be to maximize yields subject to environmental constraints. The major inputs for production are chemical and genetic. Because these are mostly appropriable technologies, the private sector might undertake a large portion of the research effort, with the state playing a subsidiary and regulatory role. Ecological unsustainability is mainly reflected in the overuse of agro-chemicals (generating pollution), inadequate water management (leading to salinization and alkalinization), genetic erosion, and overexploitation (leading to loss of soil fertility). Production has a relatively stable market. One of the major economic instruments for regulation is the pricing policy.

Appropriate measures for moving towards sustainability include solving the basic genetic problems, managing crop rotations, establishing regulatory policies for the use of inputs, using integrated pest and nutrient management, etc. An economic objective should be the internalization of the real costs by producers. In terms of organizational requirements, a stimulus to private enterprises and horizontal cooperation between producers are particularly relevant.

In other words, owing to the essentially commercial nature of the activity, these agro-ecosystems can be made sustainable through adjustments optimizing the functioning of the system.

- **The fragile and resource-poor tropical agro-ecosystems.** A common feature is their great heterogeneity in terms of the natural resource base. A major objective is to reduce risk and sustain productive capacity. This requires a new technological pattern for the management of diversity and heterogeneity. Information and management are more important for production than agricultural inputs. These technologies are not easily appropriable by the private sector. This highlights the need for a strong role for public institutions and civil society (non-governmental organizations, unions, cooperatives, etc.). The major negative impact upon natural resources is degradation and physical destruction. Integrated approaches are essential here. Some policy problems are related to the fact that the market for the products is practically unknown and often unstable. One major economic policy instrument is the discount rate. The development of this technological pattern requires horizontal cooperation between international and national agricultural research centres but also vertical coordination involving the political decision makers, the makers of technology, and the agricultural producers.

This differentiation between two extreme situations illustrates the point that there is no single technological pattern for sustainable tropical agriculture, but rather a constellation of patterns corresponding to different agro-ecological situations. Furthermore, the role of integrated approaches, although important in all types of agriculture, becomes absolutely essential in the case of fragile, resource-poor, and heterogeneous tropical agro-ecosystems.

Where resources and inputs are scarce and crop failure might be fatal, diverse and complex cropping systems dominated by long-lived plants are appropriate. However, the very attributes that make forest mimics attractive – recycling of nutrients, freedom from dependence on large inputs of agro-chemicals, reduced risk, and effective use of available resources – seem to have biological costs that are incompatible with high yield. A plant's photosynthetic energy may be allocated either to harvestable products or to the ecological functions that sustain complex ecosystems, but not to both simultaneously (Ewel 1986). On the other hand, the development of new technologies (particularly biotechnology) may change the picture drastically, by allowing the making of useful food and non-food products from the biomass that is now considered non-harvestable.

The above-ground net primary productivity of natural ecosystems (biomass production per hectare per year) may be used as a rough indicator of the aggregated potential supply of ecological resources provided by an ecosystem. A study for Latin America (Gómez and Gallopín 1995) compares estimated natural above-ground net primary productivity with estimated potential yields of rain-fed agriculture in the same area. Tropical ecosystems tend to cluster in two groups, both with high potential agricultural yield: the first (including a number of savanna types and dry and open tropical forests) has relatively low net ecological productivity, and the second has much higher net primary productivity (this includes the tropical lowland and montane moist forests, mangrove forests, tropical deltas, and Amazonian forests). In a sense, agricultural food production in the first group has a comparative advantage, because it allows high agricultural yields in relation to natural ecological productivity. In the second group, the reverse is true. This comparison between ecological productivity and potential agricultural yields suggests that tropical savannas and grasslands should be the priority for classical agriculture, whereas tropical and subtropical forests (although they too have good agricultural potential under suitable technologies) would be best considered (from the productive viewpoint) as areas for the development of new eco-technologies allowing the tapping of the enormous natural biomass.

The need for integrated solutions to tropical land use is not limited to agriculture in fragile, resource-poor ecosystems. On the one hand, many interlinkages exist among the components of all tropical farming systems or types (Beets 1990). On the other hand, at a broader resolution level, the interlinkages between economic, social, and ecological factors in the unsustainability of land use are also clearly visible (fig. 10.1).

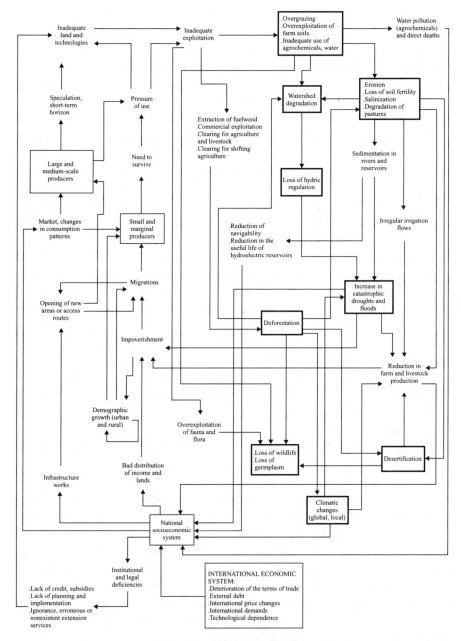

Fig. 10.1 **Interlinkages between ecological, economic, and social factors in tropical land use in Latin America (Source: Gallopín et al. 1991)**

As discussed above, the search for new technologies and production systems (contributing to the *availability* of sustainable solutions) in the tropics requires a high degree of integration. Beyond the issue of availability, that of the *replicability* of solutions is crucial. To ensure that sustainable agricultural technologies are adopted and generalized it is clearly necessary to take a broad view including social, economic, and cultural aspects in an integrated manner. Examples of a framework for comparing the attributes and potential contributions to the sustainability of land-use systems in the humid tropics appear in tables 10.2, 10.3, and 10.4 (NRC 1993).

Table 10.2 indicates a number of biophysical attributes directly associated with ecological sustainability, including the nutrient cycling capacity (understood as the capacity to cycle nutrients from the soil to economically useful plants or animals and replenish them without significant losses to the environment), the capacity of the system to conserve soil and water, the resistance of the system to pests and diseases (defined as its natural ability to maintain pests and diseases below economic threshold levels), the level of biological diversity within the system (referring to the diversity of plant and crop species, which, in turn, fosters diversity of flora and fauna both above and below ground), and the carbon flux and storage capacity of the system. Together, these attributes help to characterize the relative complexity, efficiency, and environmental impacts of the various land uses.

In terms of the total set of biophysical attributes considered, and assuming the best technologies available or under experimentation, the forest reserves rank highest, followed by the mixed tree systems (also known as forest or home gardens and mixed tree orchards), the regenerating and secondary forests, natural forest management, and modified forests. Intensive cropping, low-intensity shifting cultivation, and cattle-ranching rank lowest.

This is in direct contrast with the ranking of land uses according to social attributes (table 10.3): the highest values correspond to intensive cropping in both resource-rich and resource-poor areas, and agro-pastoral systems, and the lowest to regenerating and secondary forests, and forest reserves. Only mixed tree systems rank high in both biophysical and social attributes.

Table 10.3 shows the social attributes considered. Health and nutritional benefits (to farms and their local communities) reflect the capacity of a system to offset problems associated with intensive agro-chemical use, heavy metal contamination, degraded water

Table 10.2 **Comparison of the biophysical attributes of land-use systems in the humid tropics**

Land-use system	Nutrient cycling capacity			Soil and water conservation capacity			Stability toward pests and diseases			Biodiversity level			Carbon storage		
Biophysical attributes															
	L	M	H	L	M	H	L	M	H	L	M	H	L	M	H
Intensive cropping: high-resource areas[a]		X[c]	X[d]		X		X	O		X			X		
Intensive cropping: low-resource areas	X	O		X	O		X	O		X	O		X		
Low-intensity shifting cultivation		X		X	O		X				X		X	O	
Agro-pastoral systems		X			X	O		X			O			X	
Cattle-ranching	X[b]			X	O			X		X	O[e]		X	O	
Agro-forestry		X			X			X		X	O			X	
Mixed tree systems			X		X	O		X			X			X	O
Perennial tree crop plantations			X		X	O	X	O						X	
Plantation forestry			X		X	O	X							X	O
Regenerating and secondary forests			X		X	O		X			X			X	O
Natural forest management			X			X		X			X			X	O
Modified forests			X			X		X			X				X
Forest reserves			X			X			X			X			X

Source: modified from NRC (1993), pp. 140–141.

Note: The letters L (low), M (moderate), and H (high) refer to the level at which a given land use would reflect a given attribute. In this assessment, "X" denotes results using the best widely available technologies for each land-use system. "O" connotes the results of applying the best technologies currently under limited-location research or documentation. The systems could have the characteristics denoted by "O" given continued short-term (5–10-year period) research and extension.

a. Those areas having fertile soils with little slope and few, if any, restrictions on agricultural land use. They have adequate rainfall or irrigation during much of the year for crop growth.

b. High efficiency of recycling but low levels of nutrient removal through harvesting.

c. Present technologies may develop high flow with high crop production, but they often involve high nutrient loss. Future technologies hold promise for greater containment and efficiency.

d. Lowland, flooded rice production has both high nutrient flow and very high efficiency of recycling and of nutrient containment.

e. Assumes diversity of plant species under well-managed grazing systems, which may include tree species in silvipastoral systems.

323

Table 10.3 **Comparison of the social attributes of land-use systems in the humid tropics**

| | Social attributes | | | | | | | | |
| | Health and nutritional benefits | | | Cultural and communal viability | | | Political acceptability | | |
Land-use system	L	M	H	L	M	H	L	M	H
Intensive cropping: high-resource areas		X	O			X			X
Intensive cropping: low-resource areas		X	O	X	O		X	O	
Low-intensity shifting cultivation			X	X			X		
Agro-pastoral systems		X	O	X	O		X		O
Cattle-ranching	X	O		X	O				X
Agro-forestry			X	X	O		X	O	
Mixed tree systems	X	O		X	O		X		O
Perennial tree crop plantations	X			X					X
Plantation forestry	X			X					X
Regenerating and secondary forests	X			X			X		
Natural forest management	X			X	O		X		O
Modified forests	X	O		X			X		
Forest reserves	X			X			X		

Source: modified from NRC (1993), pp. 140–141.
Note: The letters L, M, H, X, and O are defined in table 10.2.

resources, high disease vector populations, and other public health concerns, as well as the capacity to provide local people with a diversity of food products at adequate levels. Cultural and communal viability indicates the capacity of production systems to be adapted to local cultural traditions and to enhance community structures, making optimum use of local resources and encouraging acceptable levels of local equity. The final social attribute is political acceptability, here taken as the system being politically desirable at levels above the local community (country, region, province, state, or national level).

Finally, table 10.4 shows the ranking of land-use systems according to three economic attributes. The first is the level of external inputs (such as fertilizer and equipment) required to maintain optimal production. These levels may not be environmentally sustainable in the long term. The second and third attributes are the amount of employment and income generated per land unit. The ranking according to economic attributes is fairly similar to the one based on social attributes, with the highest values given to intensive cropping in high-resource areas, followed by perennial tree crop plantations.

Table 10.4 **Comparison of the economic attributes of land-use systems in the humid tropics**

Land-use system	Economic attributes								
	Required external inputs			Employment per land unit			Income		
	L	M	H	L	M	H	L	M	H
Intensive cropping: high-resource areas			X			X			X
Intensive cropping: low-resource areas		X			X	O	X	O	
Low-intensity shifting cultivation		X				X		X	
Agro-pastoral systems		X			X	O		X	
Cattle-ranching		X		X				X	
Agro-forestry		X		X	O		X	O	
Mixed tree systems	X	O		X	O		X	O	
Perennial tree crop plantations			X[a]	X					X
Plantation forestry		X	X[a]	X				X	
Regenerating and secondary forests	X			X			X		
Natural forest management		X		X				X	
Modified forests	X	O		X			X		
Forest reserves	X			X			X		

Source: modified from NRC (1993), pp. 140–141.
Note: The letters L, M, H, X, and O are defined in table 10.2.
a. Includes capital investment for establishment.

Regenerating and secondary forests, forest reserves, modified forests, and cattle-ranching have the lowest ranks.

However, if one gives the highest ranking to the lowest levels of required external inputs (given that lower inputs are better than higher, both economically and environmentally), then the highest-ranking land-use systems are intensive cropping in both high- and low-resource areas, low-intensive shifting cultivation, and agro-pastoral systems, while the lowest ranking become cattle-ranching, plantation forestry, regenerating and secondary forests, modified forests, and forest reserves.

Comparing the three types of attributes indicates that there is no single "best" land-use system for the humid tropics. Each system entails positive and negative attributes that must be assessed in the context of local ecological, social, and economic opportunities and limitations. Different systems may be sustainable in different places, ecologies, and cultures.

But perhaps more than the kind of land-use system adopted, access to the best available technologies may be the strongest factor affect-

325

ing progress towards sustainability. In the case of the Latin American tropics, for instance, technologies exist for the sustainable management of many agro-ecosystems, but these are not generally used (Gallopín and Winograd 1995). Prevailing land use is generally environmentally unsustainable and economically inefficient.

Agriculture is a strongly regulated social activity and very much dependent upon the laws and policies established to govern it (White et al. 1994). It is clear that, in most cases, policies and institutions are greater determinants of agricultural methods of production than the availability of technologies. This is true even in industrial countries such as the United States, where the National Research Council Committee concluded that their laws and policies governing agriculture, especially their commodity policies, are among the major culprits interfering with alternative methods of production (NRC 1989). This is clearly shown on the left side of figure 10.1, where the major determinants of unsustainable exploitation of the land are indicated as the use of inadequate (or marginal) land and inadequate technologies (due to speculation and short-term planning horizons on the one hand, and to needs for survival associated with demographic growth and poverty, on the other), changes in the market and in consumption patterns, and institutional and legal deficiencies. Most of these factors are amenable to improvement through policy.

Strategic issues

One significant background fact is that the world is currently moving through a period of extraordinary turbulence reflecting the genesis and intensification of deep changes associated with the current techno-economic revolution, led by micro-electronics and accompanied by a constellation of developments based upon new, science-intensive technologies (biotechnology, new materials, new sources of energy, etc.) (Herrera 1986). This situation implies that sustainable land use must aim not only at preserving and maintaining the ecological base for development and habitability, but also at increasing the social and ecological capacity to cope with change and the ability to retain and enlarge the available options in the face of a natural and social world in permanent transformation. Sustainable land use in a rapidly changing world requires the capacity to confront many different types of change at the same time, without compromising the social, economic, and ecological sources of renewal, as well as to reduce vulnerability and retain or enlarge the range of available options.

Thus, the concept of sustainable land use cannot mean merely perpetuation. The central question is what is to be sustained and what is to be changed. Approaching sustainable land use, and sustainable development, requires (Gallopín et al. 1989): (1) getting rid of accumulated rigidities and impediments; (2) identifying and protecting the accumulated foundations of knowledge and experience that are important as a basis upon which to build; (3) sustaining the social and natural foundations for adaptation and renewal, and identifying and enhancing the lost renewal capacity needed; (4) stimulating innovation, experimentation, and social creativity.

For sustainable land use, the issues of **technological pluralism** (complementary use of traditional, "modern," and high technology) and **technological blending** (constructive integration of high technology into existing technologies, such as using biotechnology to improve the yield and pest resistance of traditional crops – thus increasing efficiency and substituting for pesticides – or applying advanced ecological theory to redesign production systems based on shifting cultivation to improve sustainability) assume paramount importance, requiring new forms of organization and an integral strategy for technological development and diffusion. The upgrading of traditional technology and empirical knowledge will become especially important for the medium- and small-scale sectors of rural areas. Many traditional technologies are already better adapted to local conditions and ecological cycles than the expanding "modern" technology. Technological blending could improve yields and avoid some of the limitations of traditional techniques. Such technological integration could reduce conflicts, promote self-sustainable technological innovation, be easily absorbed and adapted to local situations, and favour social, cultural, economic, and environmental sustainability. Special emphasis should be allocated to developing systems of production for the already altered ecosystems, including "neo-ecosystems" generated by human activities. Strategies should be developed for choosing areas for protection involving large-scale ecological functions and processes.

A general criterion is the maintenance of **productive pluralism**, with the coexistence of different major types of agriculture integrated through subnational, national, and regional policies. An example of different, coexisting, types appears in table 10.5. Structural reforms and technological innovations directed to the transformation of the present subsistence agricultural sector into an efficient and sustainable peasant agriculture will be required. New forms of high-technology diversified agriculture should be developed, directed to the selective

327

Table 10.5 **Major types of sustainable rural systems proposed for Latin America**

Agriculture	Meat production	Forestry	Fisheries
1. *Modern, capital-intensive agriculture.* Located on land with higher comparative ecological advantages (fertile and stable soils, optimal climate, good irrigation potential). Not necessarily in the form of large monocultures. It includes diversified crops, biological control of pests, crop rotation, and soil conservation.	1. *Modern intensive livestock-raising.* Capital-intensive animal husbandry, in herds or in barns, and intensive raising of wildlife with high food or commercial value.	1. *Integrated forestry.* Carried out by companies and cooperatives linking scattered households. Based on the sustainable management of natural and altered forests, mainly in the tropical rainforest zone, and including the rational use of most species (not just a few, as is the current practice). The products, for domestic consumption and export, include timber, hardboard, paper pulp, wood flour for animal feed, chemicals, raw materials for the plastics industry, fertilizers, soaps, charcoal, fuelwood, and hunting and fishing products.	1. *Intensive marine industrial fishing.* Confined to open seas. Managed by companies or large cooperatives. Mainly directed to domestic consumption and export, exploiting a diversity of species.
2. *Peasant agriculture.* Requires the implementation of structural reforms and technological innovations. Production directed to satisfying local food requirements as well as yielding cash products of high unit value made possible by special opportunities provided by local ecological conditions. Multi-purpose integrated or mixed farming widely adopted. Mainly	2. *Extensive livestock-raising.* Implies a modernization and rationalization of the current extensive ranching, and includes the harvesting and use of native species and wildlife management. Most current subsistence and nomadic pastoralism would be transformed into this activity or, alternatively, into peasant agriculture.	2. *Recollection forestry.* An artisan forestry, socially organized and provided with scientific research inputs;	2. *Modern marine artisan fishing.* In the coastal zones. Implies rescuing and improving existing techniques, using many species. Requires research and technical assistance (mainly to reduce post-harvest losses). Produce directed to domestic consumption (assuming changes in the current patterns of consumption) and export.
	3. *Modern and high-technology wildlife management and harvesting.* Implies the management, domestication, and harvesting of wildlife in captivity, semi-captivity, or wilderness, for the production		3. *Marine aquaculture.* In the coastal zones, estuaries, and fishponds. Implies setting priorities for the manage-

labour intensive, as well as intensive in technologies appropriate for diversified and small-scale production. Technological blending very significant.

3. *High-technology diversified agriculture*. Directed to the selective exploitation of local genetic resources for food, medicine, industry, etc. Implies the development of new, efficient technologies for diversified ecosystems.

4. *Indigenous farming systems*. By respecting cultural diversity, indigenous communities can maintain their lifestyles and integrated production systems if they so choose.

of meat, fur, fine wool, skins, and hides for domestic consumption and for export. Major candidates are chamelids, capybara, otter, alligator. Under good management, they can produce higher economic yields than cattle.

mostly located in the forests, savannas, and shrubby semideserts. Complements peasant agriculture, with communal organization of zones of extraction. Products, depending on the local ecology, could include palm sprouts, rubber, mushrooms, nuts, and palms.

3. *Productive plantations*. Run by companies or cooperatives in tropical rain forests and dry tropical and subtropical forests with scientific research inputs regarding local fast-growing species. Mainly for the production of paper, fuelwood, charcoal, and timber.

4. *Protective reforestation*. Important for watershed and highland protection; directed to restoring ecological regulation of floods and reducing erosion and the silting of reservoirs.

ment of local species and the protection of estuaries as breeding grounds. Production for domestic consumption and export.

4. *Modern freshwater artisan fishing*. Similar to its marine counterpart, but directed essentially to domestic and local consumption.

5. *Freshwater aquaculture*. In dams, fishponds, etc. Similar to its marine counterpart. Directed to domestic consumption and export.

Source: Gallopín et al. (1995).

exploitation of local genetic resources for food, medicine, industry, etc. It will imply the development of technologies for a new efficient recollection agriculture in diversified ecosystems, as well as new ranching and wildlife management systems, viewing ecological diversity, heterogeneity, variability, and singularities as resources rather than as hindrances or constraints. Forestry should emphasize the revalorization of the forests as multi-purpose producers (wood, energy, wildlife, special products, ecological functions). This will require deep changes in storage and commercialization systems. Today, market and consumer demand are geared to guaranteeing uniformity in products. This has favoured the dominance of monocropping, which is highly vulnerable to pests and genetic erosion. The challenge is now to ensure uniformity in quality and delivery at the consumer level while managing and even nurturing variability at the production system level. This implies a completely different approach to the whole system of production/distribution of agricultural produce.

Eco-restructuring for peasant agriculture in Latin America: An illustration

The case of peasant agriculture is a good illustration of the potential role of technical change for sustainable development if integrated with socio-economic policies. Peasant agriculture (including here much of so-called subsistence agriculture) is important in terms of the number of people involved, the intense environmental pressures it generates in many countries of the region, and the concentration of rural poverty.

The problem cannot be solved through technological fixes. An integral strategy for the transformation of the current subsistence agriculture into a sustainable and profitable peasant agriculture would need to include efforts in (a) facilitating access to the means of production, (b) eco-restructuring of the national economies and of the marketing and distribution systems, (c) community empowerment, as well as (d) research and development.

The strategy proposed here might be labelled Utopian by some readers. However, one should consider that technical innovation and diffusion have already occurred in the past few decades on a greater scale than implied in this section. Many remote areas are already being connected through radio, TV, and telephone networks, and communication costs are fast declining. The next decade or two will almost certainly involve tremendous additional technological change. The need to address the fact that fundamental, rather than incremental, changes in policy and values are required to move towards sustainable development is increasingly obvious.

Facilitating access to the means of production
The means of production include not only the land, agricultural inputs, capital, and technology but also (and this is likely to become increasingly important) information and knowledge. In the initial stages, the availability and redistribution of land for use through community management will be a key element, together with strategies for the restoration and rehabilitation of ecologically degraded lands. An agriculture under ecological management could in many cases lower requirements for material and energy inputs. Access to appropriate technology, and the stimulation of the social creativity to improve on it, should be supported. Finally, access to information in rural communities may be greatly improved through telematic networks connecting communal nodes. This includes quick access to information about the prices of products and inputs, the monitoring of weather conditions, of the condition of crops, and of erosion, meteorological forecasts, and the anticipation of natural disasters, besides programmes of education and capacity-building (local and at a distance). The same telematic networks could also be used to collect information about the state of the agro-ecosystems and of the population to facilitate regional and national planning.

Eco-restructuring of the national economies and of the marketing and distribution systems
Eco-restructuring of the national economies and marketing systems implies a redesign in order to benefit from technological and productive pluralism. This represents an important theoretical and organizational challenge. Many traits of the current economic systems rest on the homogenization of both production (e.g. monocultures) and consumption, which has often generated serious environmental problems and increased vulnerability to pests. Productive and distributive systems must be restructured in such a way that they will operate efficiently in situations where rural products are highly diversified (particularly in the tropics) and where the production of a given agricultural commodity is based on myriad dispersed exploitations, distributed in time and space. The new technologies, used within new forms of interlinked but decentralized social organizations, make pos-

331

sible sophisticated productive and distributive management making full use of variability and heterogeneity as assets rather than constraints. It will also be necessary to develop mechanisms for the articulation of large-scale, homogeneous agricultural production (which will continue to exist, directed particularly to urban consumption and agro-industry and to export) with diversified small-scale production (thus minimizing or reversing the expulsion of rural labour to marginal land).

A proportion of the diversified rural production would be used for self-consumption by the peasant populations, contributing to a balanced diet. The marketable surplus would be composed in large part of food or industrial crops of high unit value made possible by local germplasm and ecological conditions; many of these products would not have competition at the international level. Active exploration and measures to open up new national and international markets will be necessary. Peasant agriculture will increasingly focus on the ecological comparative advantages rather than on the comparative advantage of cheap labour (the latter, besides often being associated with low standards of living, is rapidly losing importance at the world level).

Community empowerment

Creative programmes to improve the living conditions of the peasant populations will be essential. The role of the new communication system is essential here, in synergy with the fostering of social participation and communal self-reliance. Access to health, housing, and education services should be improved, as well as access to the means for family planning. Technological advances, in a participative and decentralized context, can open up huge opportunities for the discovery of new, flexible, and adaptive solutions to the traditional liabilities of rural populations, while respecting their cultural identity. Support for the peasant populations will in many cases require the implementation of financial systems capable of managing thousands of small loans and investments, rather than only a few massive investments, as is typical of the majority of the national and international agencies for rural development and financing.

Research and development

A strong push to scientific and technological research will be required, directed to improving yields and the profitability of agricultural systems based (as appropriate) on traditional, modern, or even completely new systems and making use of local cultural and ecological comparative advantages. The systematic and comparative study of the potential of the regional germplasm is a priority area of research. Another priority is the implementation of an annotated catalogue or database of the traditional and modern technologies used in the region and, whenever possible, those that were used in the past. Such a catalogue should include the social and ecological conditions to which these technologies are adapted, their degree of environmental sustainability and social suitability, the type of products and their possible yields, and the major economic, social, cultural, political, or ecological constraints on their wide utilization. Comparison with other regions of comparable ecology could be of great utility (for instance between the technologies used in the tropical moist forests of South America and in the forests of other regions with ancient agricultural traditions, such as South-East Asia, or between the semi-arid American and African regions). On the basis of the comparative analysis of the relative advantages of the different technologies, it should be possible to select a menu of technologies as a basis for the development of suitable solutions for each ecological zone and socio-cultural realm, improving them on the basis of technological, ecological, and social research. These would help the development of diversified production, adapted to the different local conditions but integrated through regional, national, and international systems of capacity-building, information, transport, storage, and distribution.

The improvement of crop varieties through biotechnology and the relaxation of environmental constraints through the use of agro-technology, biotechnology, and informatics could include, for instance: the selection or creation of nitrogen-fixing or phosphorus-concentrating bacterial strains, which are easy to reproduce and have little environmental impact; the application of biological pest control; genetic manipulation to increase crop resistance to pests or drought; and social and anthropological research directed at improving the cultural and social suitability of production systems and the quality of the information and capacity-building systems. New technologies such as informatics and telematics could play a crucial role. For instance, serious attention should be given to the possibility of facilitating access to microcomputers and expert systems by local communities, to aid fertilizer and irrigation dosage, pest control, the management and administration of complex agro-ecosystems, medical diagnosis, education, etc.

The current level of technological development would make it possible to keep costs within a reasonable level, provided a decentralized and collective design is adopted, with computers run by community-based rural units and linked through telecommunication networks. The research requirements for the success of this strategy are significant. It suffices to consider the challenge represented by the need to develop efficient software for rural populations who are often illiterate or, as is the case with some peasant communities in Latin America, have a culture based on magical thinking, distant from Western logic. This would require new modes of research and interaction, interdisciplinary teams that include participation by local farmers (participatory research), the development of sophisticated forms of iconic communication, and the simultaneous utilization of alternative cultural paradigms. Regarding hardware, it will be necessary to develop inexpensive but very robust equipment, of low obsolescence and easy to update.

Ecological research in combination with anthropological research, making use both of the empirical knowledge accumulated by the peasant cultures of the region and of modern science, would allow sophisticated new forms of ecosystem management. The sequence and localization of human activities and of the germplasm would allow effective management of the local biogeochemical cycles – for instance, crops grown in a temporal sequence designed to regenerate their own nutrients, in a spatial mosaic designed so as to benefit from diversity and heterogeneity in order to minimize the growth of pest populations, and in a vertical architecture (such as multi-strata agriculture) allowing fuller use of resources.

The net result of such a strategy directly focused on peasant agriculture (upon which millions of people depend) would be an improvement in the rural quality of life, an associated decrease in the migratory flows to the urban centres, an important decrease in ecological degradation, and the utilization of an economic potential that is currently barely tapped.

Concluding remarks

The quest for sustainable development in the present historical context poses new, deep challenges to the ways we define problems, identify solutions, and implement actions. This reflects directly upon the issues of the feasibility of sustainable development and of capacity-building for sustainable development.

The prevailing mind-set in development and other areas is showing critical inadequacies. Indeed, in a number of cases, the very success of classical compartmentalized approaches has led to the aggravation of the environmental and developmental problems addressed. Even the language and metaphors we use may be hindering discussions about sustainable development.[3] Of more immediate concern, the present historical context and dynamics exhibit major differences from those of the past few decades.

The need for a change in direction was officially recognized at the Earth Summit at Rio de Janeiro in June 1992. However, the new direction is not yet clearly defined; moreover, most of the discussions and recommendations are still quite compartmentalized. Sustainable development requires: the integration of economic, social, cultural, political, and ecological factors; the constructive articulation of top–down approaches to development with bottom–up or grass-roots initiatives; the simultaneous consideration of local and global dimensions and of the way they interact; and a broadening of the space- and time-horizons to accommodate the need for intragenerational as well as intergenerational equity.

All of this has direct implications for capacity-building. The question of what kind of capacity is needed to foster sustainable development and to implement Agenda 21 and other necessary initiatives in a practical and relevant way must be addressed. Capacity-building certainly cannot be limited to the transfer of knowledge and skills from the North to the South.

Many aspects of what is called capacity-building involve traditional activities such as reinforcing institutions, developing skills, education, and training for science, technology and decision-making, the transfer of technology, mostly in reference to the South where these elements are critically scarce. However, capacity-building for sustainable development, in a world marked by a technological, economic, and political revolution and global interdependence, must be based upon the capacity for learning to learn, to cope with change and knowledge gaps, to combine different viewpoints and aspirations constructively, to tackle interlinkages and complexity, to integrate rational thinking with emotional experience, to transform knowledge into wisdom. It is very likely that this will require new kinds of institutions and new institutional mechanisms. This type of capacity still needs to be developed, both in the South and in the North. Although external financial support will be required in the South, the basic challenge holds globally, and the cross-fertilization between different experiences could result in powerful synergies.

Agriculture will represent one of the most important activities in the new path, and it will have to be conceived of in a much broader sense than now. Agriculture will have to become more than a food or an industrial crop production activity; it will have to encompass the stewardship of the earth's resources. The sustainable and increased production of food and the sustainable management of the renewable natural resources need to be integrated and complement each other in such a way as to meet the needs of present and future generations while preserving and even enhancing environmental quality. Using the power, flexibility, and understanding offered by the new and emerging technologies and scientific developments, blended when appropriate with traditional technologies, agriculture will eventually become synonymous with sustainable and productive management of *eco-resources*, which will include not only the soil, plant and animal varieties, and water, but biodiversity (in its double function of economic resource and basic ecological regulator), ecological functions and services such as watershed and climate regulation, chemical cycling, etc.

Notes

1. This overview is based on Lopez Cordovez (1993).
2. I am indebted to Dr. Filemón Torres for his inputs.
3. For instance, "development" is often described as a permanent increase (usually of GNP); expressions such as "target," "optimal path," or "trajectory" resonate with ballistic analogies. The word "sustainability" suggests reaching a state of constancy, preserving an existing situation. Therefore the phrase "sustainable development" intuitively sounds contradictory. The argument here is not that sustainable development is inherently contradictory (I believe it is not) but that the wording and conceptualization we use are not well suited to the new concepts being generated.

References

Beets, W. C. (1990) *Raising and Sustaining Productivity of Smallholder Farming Systems in the Tropics*. Alkmaar, the Netherlands: AgBé Publishing.

Chambers, R., A. Pacey, and L. A. Thrupp (eds.) (1989) *Farmers First*. London: ITP.

Ewel, J. J. (1986) Designing agricultural systems for the humid tropics. *Annual Review of Ecology and Systematics* **17**: 245–271.

Funderburk, J. E. and L. G. Higley (1994) Management of arthropod pests. In: J. L. Hatfield and D. L. Karlen (eds.), *Sustainable Agricultural Systems*, pp. 199–228. Boca Raton, FL: Lewis Publisher.

Gallopín, G. C. and M. Winograd (1995) Ecological prospective for tropical Latin America. In T. Nishizawa and J. I. Uitto (eds.), *The Fragile Tropics of Latin America: Sustainable Management of Changing Environments*, pp. 13–44. Tokyo: United Nations University Press.

Gallopín, G. C., P. Gutman, and H. Maletta (1989) *Global Impoverishment, Sustainable Development and the Environment.* Report to the International Development Research Centre, 3 March.

Gallopín, G. C., M. Winograd, and I. A. Gómez (1991) *Ambiente y Desarrollo en América Latina y el Caribe: Problemas, Oportunidades, y Prioridades.* S. C. Bariloche, Argentina: Grupo de Análisis de Sistemas Ecológicos.

Gallopín, G. C., I. A. Gómez, A. Pérez, and M. Winograd (eds.) (1995) *El Futuro Ecológico de un Continente. Una Visión Prospectiva para la América Latina.* Mexico, D.F.: Fondo de Cultura Económica.

Girt, J. (1990) *The Sustainable Development of Agricultures in Latin America and the Caribbean: Strategic Recommendations.* Report to the Instituto Interamericano de Cooperación para la Agricultura (IICA), San José, Costa Rica.

Gómez, I. A. and G. C. Gallopín (1995) Oferta Ecológica en la América Latina: Productividad y producción de los grandes ecosistemas terrestres. In: G. C. Gallopín, I. A. Gómez, A. Pérez, and M. Winograd (eds.), *El Futuro Ecológico de un Continente. Una Visión Prospectiva para la América Latina,* vol. 3, pp. 445–498. Mexico, D.F.: Fondo de Cultura Económica.

Herrera, A. O. (1986) The new technological wave and the developing countries: Problems and options. In: E. MacLeod (ed.), *Technology and the Human Prospects,* pp. 140–153. London: Frances Pinter.

Lopez Cordovez, L. (1993) *Lineamientos conceptuales para el desarrollo rural sostenible y equitativo.* San José, Costa Rica: Instituto Interamericano de Cooperación para la Agricultura (IICA).

MacRae, R. J., S. B. Hill, J. Henning, and A. J. Bentley (1990) Policies, programs, and regulations to support the transition to sustainable agriculture in Canada. *American Journal of Alternative Agriculture* 5(2): 76–92.

NRC (National Research Council) (1989) *Report on Alternative Agriculture.* Washington D.C.: National Academy Press.

——— (1993) *Sustainable Agriculture and the Environment in the Humid Tropics.* Washington D.C.: National Academy Press.

Pesek, J. (1994) Historical perspective. In J. L. Hatfield and D. L. Karlen (eds.), *Sustainable Agricultural Systems,* pp. 1–19. Boca Raton, FL: Lewis Publisher.

Turner II, B. L., R. H. Moss, and D. L. Skole (eds.) (1993) *Relating Land Use and Global Land-Cover Change.* IGBP Report No. 34 and HDP Report No. 5. Stockholm: IGBP/HDP.

White, D. C., J. B. Braden, and R. H. Hornbaker (1994) Economics of sustainable agriculture. In J. L. Hatfield and D. L. Karlen (eds.), *Sustainable Agricultural Systems,* pp. 229–260. Boca Raton, FL: Lewis Publisher.

11

The restructuring of transport, logistics, trade, and industrial space use

Paul M. Weaver

Introduction

The transport sector is a major contributor to environmental change. Apart from the land-take and materials-use implications of building transport infrastructures and machinery, which are considerable, environmental stress is imposed by the pollution implications of transport energy use. Part of the eco-restructuring agenda must therefore be to reduce the environmental disturbance caused per unit of transport, which is mostly a function of the characteristics of different transport modes and of modal splits, and to reduce the volume of transport.

The issues involved are complex partly because of the systemic interlinkages between production and consumption patterns, the characteristics of transportation technologies, the characteristics of other technologies that can substitute for physical transportation, and the prevailing incentive structures that give rise to patterns of land use and technological, logistical, and transportation choices. Geographical differences between countries in size, shape, topography, resource endowment, state of development, and socio-economic conditions also complicate analysis. So do differences in the structure of different firms and industries and the locations of different types of manufacturing activities. Above all, the key factors influencing transportation – those that affect both the scale and structure of transportation demand and the ways in which these are met – are dynamic. This systemic complexity means that there is need for broad and dynamic analysis of the linkages between transportation and sustainability.

This chapter is necessarily restricted to a partial analysis. None the less, the insights it gives are motivated by what I consider to be of special relevance for transportation policy at the start of an eco-restructuring agenda. It focuses on the already industrialized countries, where transport and related arrangements pose the greatest environmental burden and are most in need of restructuring. It focuses on options and measures to reduce the volume of freight transport in the near to mid term, which are investigated in relation to other possibilities for reducing environmental impacts in the longer term, including major changes in transportation technology, although these are not themselves explored here in any detail. Within the scope that this identifies, the chapter explores those options that provide greatest room and flexibility for effecting near-term change. These include the reorganization of production and logistics arrangements, technological and organizational adaptations within the confines of existing knowledge, mode-switching even within the context of the road freight transport category,[1] and physical goods transportation substitution possibilities.

The chapter also look at the dynamics of freight transportation, at the factors affecting developments, and at how these might be influenced. Because much of the scope for reducing freight volumes hinges on changing the nature of existing relationships and trends between freight transport, logistics (the ways in which companies organize the movement and storage of goods in the supply chain to consumers), and patterns of industrial and economic space use, the chapter looks at these together. Patterns of land use and freight transport in Western industrialized societies have co-evolved under market conditions where natural resource productivity has never been a priority, where road-building has been publicly financed, and where levels of (demand-led) road provision have been economically and environmentally excessive. Under these conditions, current (profit-maximizing) land-use and transport patterns represent an excessive use of transport. Although there is no necessary link between market liberalization and transport volumes, deregulation and shifts toward free trade have contributed to an internationalization – in some cases a globalization – of economic activities, which, in practice, has added significantly to freight tonne-kilometres. For this reason, developments affecting international trade and/or the relationship between internationalized economic activities and freight transport volumes are of interest because they may help or hinder progress toward eco-restructuring.

The choices made over the substance and coverage of the chapter in respect to the wider debate on transport and sustainability are due to my view of the importance of the transportation sector generally as regards policies and measures to usher in a restructuring of our economies and societies. Certainly, it is conceivable that much of the concern over the sustainability of current transport arrangements would be reduced were a competitively priced transportation technology based upon a renewable energy source to become available; for example, a technology based upon the solar-derived, hydrogen-based carriers that earlier chapters in this book suggest may ultimately be feasible. However, such technologies are unlikely to become available within the next 50 years. More importantly, their development will come about only in the context of appropriate incentives. In the near term, then, reducing the environmental impact of transport will depend mostly upon reducing transport volumes and increasing transport efficiency; i.e. cutting out or substituting for transport that can be avoided, undertaking remaining movement so that this does least environmental damage, and making most productive use of this remaining movement. This suggests that the preference should be for policy instruments that will stimulate these changes and simultaneously provide incentives for the longer-term development of fundamentally more sustainable transportation technologies. A lead taken along these lines within the industrialized countries would also signal an important message for caution over the extent of public road provision to countries now rapidly building their transportation infrastructures.

The significance of freight transport

Although the transport sector as a whole is receiving attention in the environment–development and eco-restructuring discussion – in particular, in respect to the future of private passenger transport – the discussion has tended to focus on the central role of the car and on urban settings. It is true that Western industrial societies and their cities can be characterized as autocentric. It is also true that in terms of perhaps the most topical environmental policy concern on the international agenda – climatic change – the contribution of the automobile to carbon emissions and the build-up of atmospheric concentrations of greenhouse gases is greater than that of freight transport. None the less, the relative importance of the two – cars and trucks – must be considered in terms of the significance of the sector as a whole in commercial energy use and its overall contribution to anthropogenic carbon emissions.

Transport energy use accounts for more than one-quarter of worldwide commercial energy consumption (Grübler 1993). Moreover, with an average growth rate of 2.7 per cent per annum between 1971 and 1990, transportation energy demand is the fastest-growing energy end-use category (IEA 1993a,b). Passenger travel accounts for 60 per cent of transport energy use, and freight movement for the remaining 40 per cent (Nakicenovic 1993). Transport energy use accounts for almost 30 per cent of all energy end-use-related anthropogenic carbon dioxide (CO_2) emissions (OECD 1995). Since anthropogenic CO_2 emissions currently amount to 26 billion tonnes annually, of which 80 per cent are energy related, transport is responsible for around 7.5 billion tonnes of CO_2 per annum. Passenger cars account for just less than half of this (around 3.6 billion tonnes) and goods vehicles for about one-third (*c.* 2.4 billion tonnes). Other vehicles account for the rest.

Although the freight share of CO_2 emissions is less than the passenger car share, the freight share is increasing. Moreover, at least in respect to most OECD countries, the energy intensity of goods transport is increasing owing to shifts to faster modes (Schipper and Meyers 1992). The Second Assessment Report of the Intergovernmental Panel on Climate Change (IPCC) has discussed this development in some detail and has analysed the reasons for it in respect to geographical differences between countries and to the types of trucks involved. "In countries where services and light industry are growing faster than heavy industry, the share of small trucks and vans in road freight is increasing. The energy intensity of light trucks is high compared with large trucks. Along with general increase in the power-to-weight ratios of goods vehicles, these developments offset and in some cases outweigh the benefits of improving engine and vehicle technology" (IPCC 1996, pp. 690–691). The two noteworthy points are that transportation energy intensity tends to be lower in countries where a high proportion of goods traffic is made up of bulk materials or primary commodities than in more industrialized and diversified economies, and that improvements in vehicle technology have partly been used to increase vehicle performance rather than to reduce energy use. Both contribute to the increasing energy intensity of goods transportation within the OECD countries.

Freight transport is therefore absolutely significant *in its own right* as a source of pollution and a target for eco-restructuring attention. Perhaps most important is to compare freight CO_2 emissions with those of industry. Industrial activity as a whole accounts for just less than 35 per cent of all anthropogenic carbon emissions; i.e. around 9 billion tonnes of CO_2 per annum. The contribution by freight transport is therefore equivalent to more than a quarter of all industrial CO_2 emissions. Moreover, the freight contribution is greater than that of any single industrial sector and is increasing. It is responsible for 10 times the energy-related CO_2 emissions of the cement industry (although only just over twice that industry's overall CO_2 emissions), eight times those of the pulp and paper industry, and twice those of the steel industry.

As well as contributing to carbon emissions, freight transport is associated with other pollutants. These include nitrogen dioxide (NO_2) and sulphur dioxide (SO_2). NO_2, like CO_2, is a greenhouse gas – though more than 200 times more potent than CO_2 in terms of radiative forcing. Both NO_2 and SO_2 contribute to environmental acidification. Carbon monoxide (CO) and nitrogen oxides (NOx), both of which are also emitted, have reaction products that add to these effects. The quantities of these emissions have recently been estimated as 2.1 g of CO and 1.85 g of NOx per tonne-kilometre (ECMT 1995). Noise pollution and accident fatalities were also included in the ECMT (European Conference of Ministers of Transport) study and are important because, although not directly relevant to globally or regionally threatening environmental change, they, too, represent costs that remain to be fully internalized within fuel, road, and transport prices. Another cost of transportation is the time cost of delays caused by congestion. Internalization of the costs associated with these externalities would contribute to reducing freight transport volumes and so, also, to eco-restructuring.

Viewed against the backdrop of the role that freight transport currently plays in environmental change, its relative neglect within the eco-restructuring discussion is surprising. Transport is usually considered in terms of passenger transport and car use, in respect to which discussions have focused heavily on technological opportunities for reducing unit impacts. These have centred around the need for energy efficiency improvements and for low-carbon or carbon-free energy carriers as replacements for fossil fuels. Work has also looked at public alternatives to private transport (train, metro, bus, tram, light railway, etc.) and at how modal shifts might be encouraged. In terms of demand management, there has been some discussion of the technological opportunities to substitute for passenger travel; for example, by using telecommunications for remote working, teleshopping, and home entertainment.

Relatively little has been done, however, to examine the relationships between patterns of space use and passenger transport demand; for example, the links between a greater mixing of land uses (residential, recreational, retail, office, etc.) or between the scale of provision of services (large centralized schools, hospitals, and shops versus small-scale facilities serving local neighbourhoods) and auto use. This omission is significant in respect to the parallels that exist between passenger transport (which is widely studied in the debate) and freight transport (which is not), because considerable potential for demand reduction in the freight sector could lie in reorganizing spatial divisions of labour and logistics to reduce transport intensities at the product level.

Several important issues in respect to past and future trends in the development of freight transport are, thus, raised:

- What factors and trends have been important in the past patterns of freight transport growth and development?
- What is the current level and structure of production of freight transport ?
- What factors and trends are shaping future developments in freight transport volumes and patterns?
- How much scope is there for reducing freight volumes?
- How might this scope be taken up?
- How would the space-use, logistics, transport, and trade patterns of a sustainable society and economy differ from today's patterns?

The remainder of this chapter is devoted to these questions and is structured around them. The discussion centres mostly on industrialized countries because these face the task of shifting from deeply embedded and unsustainable land-use patterns and reducing their transport dependence. Many of the examples and data given reflect European Union (EU) experience. None the less, these are believed to be representative for other industrialized countries. Inferences can be drawn for developing countries, especially in respect to opportunities for avoiding heavy investments in infrastructures that imply long-term commitments of environmental (and also economic) resources to potentially unproductive or low-productivity uses.

Past growth and patterns of freight transport development

Present-day patterns of transport, logistics, and land use are the still-evolving outcome of a century-long – and still ongoing – process of industrial development. Consistent features of the trajectory have been its exploitation of:
- volume production and consumption as a metric and target for economic growth,
- cost reduction via productivity improvements as an engine for growth,
- scale economies and comparative advantage for total factor productivity gains,
- energy/materials/capital to substitute for labour (for labour productivity gains).

Development has followed an energy- and materials-intensive production regime based heavily upon the one-time conversion of natural (environmental) capital stock to current income. The generated income has been used to develop different forms of "man-made" capital appropriate to the continuation of the trajectory and to provide for high levels of current consumption.[2]

Within this trajectory, the most important factors in shaping the evolving geography of economic activities have been: deregulation and the liberalization of markets; improvements in transport infrastructures/technology; the maintenance of low transport and energy prices; and developments in logistics and in information technologies. Competition and the search for profits have been the major dynamic forces. The major constraints have been some (usually weak) restrictions on land development and land use.

Market liberalization and deregulation

Liberalization has taken place within countries, between pairs or groups of countries, and at the global level, affecting both tariff and non-tariff barriers in respect to markets in factors, goods, and services. All factors (save labour) have been affected. The freeing-up of capital markets has been particularly comprehensive. The process began immediately after the end of World War II in an attempt to stimulate economic growth and prosperity at the world level and avoid a repeat of the depression that had accompanied inter-war protectionism. Some changes were agreed bilaterally among major trading partners, but the major multilateral mechanism for liberalizing world trade has been the General Agreement on Tariffs and Trade (GATT) process, which started in 1947 and culminated in the Uruguay Round of negotiations and Marrakesh agreements. The development of regional trading blocs has also been a significant – in the case of West European countries, perhaps *the most significant* – development in the post-war liberalization process. Blocs now include the European Union, the North American Free Trade Area, the Association of South-East Asian Nations, and Mercosul.

By way of illustrating the removal of tariff barriers, there is no better example than the passenger car. The contrast between tariff levels during the highly protectionist period of the 1920s and 1930s and those of the 1970s and 1980s is stark. During the inter-war period each European country separately determined its tariff level. The average across the major European car-producing nations in the 1930s was around 45 per cent of customs value. In the case of France and Italy, tariffs were in the range 47–74 per cent and 101–111 per cent, respectively. Japan also had a highly protected market. Its tariff level in 1940 was 70 per cent. By the early 1980s, the situation was completely different. The EU countries had harmonized on a tariff structure within a range to 10.5 per cent of customs value. Tariffs in the United States and Japan were minimal to non-existent (Altschuler et al. 1984).

The impact of deregulation and trade liberalization on transport demand arises through three principal effects: the exploitation of comparative advantage; the exploitation of scale economies; and the expansion of markets. In respect to the first two, the removal of barriers increases geographical specialization and concentration of production. Comparative advantage is particularly important for inter-industry trade, whereas exploitation of scale economies or experience is particularly important for intra-industry trade. In respect to the third, falling import barriers, lower product prices, higher per capita consumption, and access to wider markets lead to increases in the average distance between points of production and points of consumption (Gabel 1994).

As barriers to factor mobility have been reduced or removed, the world economy has become steadily internationalized. Together with accompanying technological, institutional, and organizational innovations, this has allowed economic activities to be restructured through a series of "spatial fixes" (Harvey 1982). As the spatial framework has expanded, entrepreneurs have been free to engineer the most profitable business arrangements under the prevailing new conditions. Harvey argues that, through these, a long-threatened growth crisis has been repeatedly postponed. Each new spatial fix has brought higher factor productivities and has permitted growth to continue within the context of the same mass-production/mass-consumption model.

Transport improvement, supply, and cost

Governments have taken responsibility for infrastructure provision and have used infrastructure development in macroeconomic policy, employment creation, regional development, and defence strategy as well as in transport policy. Governments have typically taken a supply-expansion rather than a demand-side management approach to balancing demand and supply. More important, they have catered for "anticipated" demands. A result has been the considerable extension and improvement of road infrastructures. Within OECD-Europe, for example, the motorway network length has almost tripled since 1970. Within the OECD group as a whole, motorway network length in 1993 stood at 150,266 km. This represents a 34 per cent increase since 1980. The average motorway network density within the OECD is currently 0.44 km/100 km^2; within some European countries (Belgium and the Netherlands) it is more than 5.5 km/100 km^2. Coupled with progress in truck technology, motorway development has significantly improved average speeds and journey times. The truck fleet has grown by more than 50 per cent since 1980. In 1993, there were more than 98 million goods vehicles in service within OECD countries. Within some countries of the EU (e.g. France, Italy, and the Netherlands), the fleet size has doubled since 1980.

Transport and energy prices

Meanwhile, markets in respect to energy, land, and transport have been so constructed as to externalize many costs. The environmental costs of energy use in terms of depletion and pollution have not been factored into energy prices, which have in any case been low and either stagnating or reducing in real terms over the past decade. Diesel and petrol prices to consumers were lower in 1993 than in 1985 in several countries (e.g. the United States). This reflects depressed oil prices, which have only partly been offset by increases in the percentage share of taxes in consumer prices. Neither are the environmental and social costs of land-take factored into user charges for roads, ports, or airports. As with all public subsidies, the benefits are available to be privatized while the costs are socialized. This has provided strong incentives for businesses to increase the use of transport and to make logistics a key aspect of technological choice in respect to strategies for rationalization, marketing, and competitiveness. Part of the low cost of transport has been passed on to consumers in the form of transport-intensive goods and services with prices lower than would have been possible without the subsidies.

Positive feedbacks mean that many of these distortions are self-reinforcing. Subsidy has favoured high levels of mobility and low-density land-use patterns. High dependence on mobility has been important, in turn, as a justification for further infrastructure provision, particularly because of the inherent biases toward provision within the benefit–cost and discounting methodologies used by government agencies for investment appraisal.

Developments in logistics

Particularly since the 1980s (although the start of the development can be traced back to the 1970s) the function of logistics within business operations and competitive strategy has changed. Key drivers have been shifts in consumer markets, with less brand loyalty and greater competition among producers. This has elevated the importance of customer service – including product availability, delivery lead-times, reliability of deliveries, etc. – within the competitive process and led to shifts in approaches to business management and logistics. A related development has seen logistics reorganization being used to secure reductions in inventory and warehousing costs. Facilitating developments have been deregulation and privatization and rapid advances in information technologies.

Change has followed a three-stage development (Cooper 1995). In the 1970s, companies began to bring together transport, warehousing, and inventory management at the firm level (integrated distribution). The concept was then extended beyond the boundaries of the firm so that the whole materials chain from the sourcing of raw materials to the final consumption of finished products was integrated (channel integration). By the early 1990s, a third phase has seen operations becoming integrated across national boundaries (geographical integra-

347

tion), which, as well as enabling the promotion of new product strategies, offers companies the opportunity to reap scale economies in purchasing, manufacturing, warehousing, and transport. By regionalizing warehouses, firms are able to rationalize and reduce inventory. A parallel development upstream in the supply chain has been a growing emphasis on "focused factories," where companies select factories to specialize in producing parts of the product range rather than its entirety. Focused factories invariably serve more than one country.

Information technology

An equally important development, from the perspective of truck-traffic generation, has been the growing importance of information technology in logistics management. Whereas inventory holding levels used to be greater than strictly necessary to compensate for deficiencies of information, transparency in the supply chain by virtue of information technology means that it is increasingly possible to reduce levels of inventory (Cooper 1995). Accurate and timely information on stock holdings and whereabouts increasingly encompasses stock on trucks. Together with a more responsive transport service, remaining inventory can be concentrated at a smaller number of strategic locations. Firms have been able profitably to trade off higher transport operating costs against (much) lower warehousing costs.

Within Europe, the lead companies in the integration process are those in the automotive and business equipment sectors together with some retailers (e.g. IKEA and Benetton). Bosch-Siemens, for example, has recently consolidated its Scandinavian warehousing operations – formerly based upon distribution centres in Finland, Norway, and Sweden – into one site in southern Sweden. Unilever (household products) and Ciba-Geigy (pharmaceuticals) are leaders in the focused factory approach. As well as implying higher transport demands and more international transport, these developments depend heavily upon road freight, which is much better suited to meet the new demands of users than competing modes. An important consequence has been the generation of higher levels of road freight activity through increases in average haulage length.

Spatial and transport outcomes

The most important spatial-economic outcomes of these developments and their implications for transport have been:

- increasing geographical specialization and concentration in production,
- growing separation of points in value-adding chains,
- increasing distance between points of production and points of consumption,
- internationalization of economic activities and of transport,
- growing transport volumes,
- increasing average haulage distances,
- shifts to faster modes.

In terms of the transport implications, the most significant effect has been rapid growth in the volume of truck-kilometres. In 1993, the OECD truck fleet travelled a total of 1,823 billion kilometres. This represents a 68 per cent increase over the 1980 kilometrage. Truck movements on important international corridor routes such as the Rhine and Danube valleys and through sensitive Alpine passes have become particularly problematic.

Part of the overall growth in truck-kilometres is attributable to increases in average haulage length. Within the EU, the average haulage length of goods (all commodities) transported by road grew by more than 20 per cent in the 10 years to 1990. Some of the growth has also come from mode shifts. Competition favours the use of flexible, direct, and fast modes of transport. Truck and air have gained relative to slower and less direct modes. Rail, in particular, has lost out. Not only is the rail share of total tonne-kilometrage reducing, but rail has experienced absolute reductions in freight-tonne kilometres. Studies of German freight transport have shown that the threshold of substitution between slower modes and truck occurs at value densities of little more than DM 1–2/kg. Truck dominates the value range from this to the DM 100/kg level (all figures in 1987 DM), which encompasses most consumer products including autos and domestic electrical (white) goods. Above DM 100/kg, air freight becomes dominant (Grübler 1988).

International trade has grown consistently and has outpaced the growth in real world product. No EU country now imports less than 30 per cent of its total GNP.

Competition and profit-maximizing behaviours have been the critical driving force behind these impacts. Together, these have constituted a powerful imperative to cut costs, expand market presence, and respond quickly to demand.

Evidence is rife of bizarre transportation consequences (Whitelegg 1994). Freight transport surveys have shown that, to take advantage of cost differences between countries, some products are shipped long distances in the process of adding value, ultimately only to arrive back at their point of origin. Prawns landed in Hamburg and destined to be sold in the German market have been found in transport to and from Poland, where they are cooked and peeled. Most West European household pot plants, wherever grown, are sold at auctions held in the Netherlands from where they are trucked to final market, sometimes even to places where they were originally grown. In both these cases, it is the same (not just an equivalent) product that is being transported in both directions. Even low value-density commodities and products have to be transported into foreign markets at risk of their producers losing overall market share. At the high value-density end of the market, there are even more questionable, but apparently profitable and cost-effective, goods movements. An example is the case of the Cadillac Allante. The car body is manufactured in Italy. But the car is assembled and sold in the United States. The body is transported over 5,000 km by air from Turin to Detroit (Grübler and Nowotny 1990).

There is evidence that transport intensities at the national level (measured as tonne-kilometres per unit GNP) may now have peaked in some OECD countries and even have begun to decline. This is the result of higher average specific values (value/kg) of cargo and is likely to reflect changes in the structure of economic activity within countries – including the offloading of environmentally damaging aspects of production to other countries. It is unlikely, therefore, to be a reliable indicator of shifts to or away from transport dependence. Time-series of product-specific transport intensities would be better indicators but these are not routinely calculated. In an exceptional (and exemplary) study aimed at establishing transport intensity at the product level, Böge has used lifecycle methods to trace all the inputs used in the manufacture of a single pot of strawberry yoghurt emanating from a production plant in southern Germany (Böge 1993, 1995).

The study includes all inputs involved in the manufacture of the product and its packaging; e.g. strawberries, sugar, milk, glass containers, cardboard and paper labels, and aluminium container lids. The transport requirement associated with producing the inputs, bringing these to the production plant in southern Germany, and distributing the final product to consumers is summarized over the life cycle on a unit product basis. Böge expresses the transport intensity in terms that enable it to be considered – and possibly listed – like any other "ingredient" on the label of the product. Each 150g straw-berry yoghurt was found to have required the equivalent of more than 9 metres of truck movement. Every tonne of yoghurt sold accounts for more than 600 truck-kilometres. In respect to overall sales of yoghurt – a seemingly simple, healthy, and "natural" product marketed in massive quantities – the implied daily, weekly, or annual transport requirement is enormous. Production from the single plant studied, which serves mostly local markets, gives rise to 24,000 truck-kilometres annually.

Future developments affecting freight volumes and patterns

As concerns reducing the environmental impact of the freight trans-port sector, virtually all present trends point in entirely the wrong direction. Freight volumes (measured in tonne-kilometres) are in-creasing not decreasing. Moreover, the growth in freight volumes is now attributable almost entirely to increases in the distance that goods are transported – reflecting greater separation between points in the value-adding chain – rather than to increases in the quantity of goods transported. What is worse, transport volume per capita tends to increase as societies become more affluent and, even though trans-port intensity (measured per unit of GDP) is beginning to fall in the most affluent societies, the decrease is more than offset by increases in GDP per capita. What matters from an environmental standpoint is that freight transport volumes and energy intensities are increasing in absolute terms.

The trends at international level are also bad. Most developing countries – assisted by Western advisers and consultants, by various international agencies, and by development banks – have develop-ment strategies that are heavily based upon providing physical infra-structures to facilitate industrialization on the Western model. If successful, these would lead to their joining the industrialized West in having economies and societies that are transport intensive and fossil-fuel dependent. Shachar points out that this convergence of indus-trialized and developing countries on the same mobility patterns and fossil-energy-based economies is one of the main reasons – if not the main reason – for our moving away from sustainability at the global level (Shachar 1991).

There is also reason for concern over the effects of further liberal-ization of world markets as a result of the Marrakesh agreements that concluded the final, Uruguay Round of the General Agreement on

Tariffs and Trade negotiations in April 1994. Although, in principle, trade liberalization is not inconsistent with environmental protection (because measures in respect to both have a common goal in securing efficient resource allocations), the sequencing of measures is important. Although it has been pointed out that both liberalization and environmental protection policies have broadly equal claims to priority – in that barriers to free trade and environmental externalities are both alleged to cause similar allocation distortions (Repetto 1993)[3] – progress toward free trade is being made more rapidly than progress toward internalizing environmental externalities. Moreover, the nature of the two distortions is fundamentally different in that tariff and non-tariff restrictions have the effect of restricting the spatial range of economic operations, both production related and marketing. In so doing, they act to limit the distortions in resource allocations – especially the excessive use of transport – that arise from market imperfections and subsidies.

Gabel (1994) has analysed the likely effects of further liberalization on freight transport, addressing the impacts arising from several different linkages. Liberalization within the transport sector itself will increase competition and lower the prices charged by operators. Liberalization within other sectors – specifically agricultural commodities, chemicals, petroleum, coal, steel, metals, and automobiles – presents considerable scope for trade expansion because these have traditionally been tightly protected at national level and are transport intensive. Liberalization of the transport equipment and energy industries will likely lead to reductions in the costs of inputs relevant to the supply of transport services and therefore to reductions in transport costs. Increased geographical specialization and concentration of production will increase average haulage lengths. Inter-industry trade is more likely to increase average transport distance than intra-industry trade because the source of trade gains – factor differences and comparative advantage – is geographically determined (Gabel 1994, p. 164). The impact of economic growth and increases in per capita income is complex. Of several, partially offsetting effects, that with the greatest environmental significance is likely to be the continuing displacement of bulk commodities by lower lot sizes with higher value-to-weight ratios. Although qualifying his analysis in several ways, Gabel concludes: "In summary, virtually all of the changes anticipated to accrue from trade liberalisation will probably increase transport output" and "may lead to a shift in the mode of transport to road and air" (Gabel 1994, pp. 169 and 170).

Results from studies aimed at projecting the impact of recent EU liberalization and deregulation show similar results (e.g. Venables and Smith 1988; Gabel and Röller 1993). Based on an econometric model, Gabel and Röller forecast impacts on international transport movements of the complete elimination of internal (non-tariff) trade barriers (but not elimination of the EU common external tariff). Elimination of non-tariff barriers was found likely to increase aggregate trade volumes in all industries. Estimates of increase ranged from 16 per cent for pharmaceuticals to 133 per cent for electrical machinery. In every industry, the percentage increase in intra-EU trade volume was estimated to be larger than the aggregate, suggesting some displacement of imports from non-EU countries. In tonne-kilometre or truck-kilometre terms, the effect of eliminating non-tariff barriers is to increase international road haulage by 38 per cent. The results confirm the expectations of an EU Task Force, which had predicted that shifts toward liberalization and deregulation might increase trans-frontier truck traffic by 30–50 per cent (CEC 1989).[4]

The scope for reducing freight volumes

There are many different feasible mechanisms by which to reduce the environmental impact of freight transport. The focus here is on the potential to reduce emissions by reducing the transport intensity of products (mostly through changes in the spatial division of labour) and by increasing the efficiency of use of existing modes – both within the context of existing infrastructural constraints.

Reducing the transport intensity of products

The scope for reducing the transport intensity of final products lies in several possible adjustments. One is to reduce the number of transport-intensive components that products embody. Another is to reduce the average length of individual transport movements. This can be done by obtaining raw materials and components locally, serving local markets, reversing current trends in logistics, and revising networking arrangements in respect to contractors and subcontractors in the value-adding chain. Finally, there is also scope to reduce the number of times that the same materials are transported during the process of adding value.

Reductions in the number of transport-intensive components and ingredients can be achieved by substitution. This is particularly important in the food industry because of the high quantities of food products now involved in long-distance transport and the high level of substitutability among foods and ingredients. This would imply greater reliance on local/regional produce and on produce in season.

Some physical goods movement can be substituted altogether by using the possibilities provided by flexible technologies and informatics. The possibility exists for information about the design of components embodied within complex products that are manufactured at a distance from the market to be provided with the product or transmitted electronically as need arises. In the event, say, of the product breaking down, a local parts manufacturer is thus able to obtain component design details and make a replacement part rather than having to order and ship this in from a distance.

Similarly, telecommunications can substitute for information-rich but formerly transport-intensive products and services. Just as fax and electronic mail can substitute for conventional mail, similar substitutions can be made in respect to whole industrial sectors. In the newspaper publications industry, for example, a combination of telecommunications and flexible printing plant could do away completely with the need to transport newsprint physically over long distances. It also provides a potentially improved customer service in the form of a greater choice of simultaneously published editions.

The long-distance shipping of goods between world regions could increasingly be replaced by capital flows by encouraging direct foreign investment as an alternative to trade. The attractiveness of direct foreign investment increases with the level of competition in non-standardized products and with the rapidity of market change. Moves toward the strengthening of regional trading blocs (such as the EU) could help in this direction.

Changing the spatial structure of inter-firm supply networks (the number and relative location of contractors and subcontractors) is important because these needlessly increase the transport intensity of final products. Strutynski (1995) argues that such traffic-generating arrangements are currently promoted by EU programmes aimed at integrating European economies, technology transfer, and increasing international marketing opportunities. Only international projects are promoted. Thus he says that: "It is easier to establish co-operation between enterprises in Northern Hesse and the North of Spain than between two neighbouring enterprises, for example in Baunatal and Kassel" (Strutynski 1995, p. 39).

Strutynski argues that there is scope for lean production to contribute to reductions in inter-firm freight transport *if* reductions in the number of direct suppliers are accompanied by reductions also in average transport distances between them. This depends upon regional concentration of production and supply relations. In a theoretical example based upon German conditions, he contrasts the transport implications of two different inter-firm supply structures. Both are geared toward producing an identical final product. The first represents a traditional relationship between final assembler and several suppliers in which all suppliers deliver directly to the assembler. The second represents a relationship based upon cooperation among suppliers organized into regional value-adding networks. The effect is that more value is added *within* the region before any components are transported long-haul. Only a small number of high value-density components are finally transported to the assembler. In his example, Strutynski (1995) demonstrates a theoretical 70 per cent reduction potential in total supply distance.

Increasing the efficiency of use of existing modes

Average loading ratios for trucks in Europe are typically 75–85 per cent (ECMT 1995). Empty truck movements account for approximately 1.5 per cent of all domestic freight traffic within countries of the EU. Prior to deregulation and the creation of the Single Market in 1992, one-third of trucks making international journeys on EU roads had empty back-hauls. Of trucks crossing the Dutch–German border, 30 per cent were empty (Gabel 1994). Although all these data are for the immediate pre-1992 situation, moves to phase out permits and restrictions on cabotage post-1992 were not anticipated to improve loading ratios. Surveys of hauliers undertaken before 1992 show the main causes of low loading factors to be related not to restrictions but rather to problems in arranging suitable backloads – for example, a lack of information on backload opportunities and problems of backload incompatibility (CEC 1989). Broadly similar loading ratios are likely to apply currently.

The problem of low loading factors is linked to operators' incentives. Some operators prefer to operate large vehicles because this maximizes flexibility and reduces average costs. As size restrictions have been relaxed, the average truck size of some operators' fleets has increased.[5] Once equipped with large vehicles, hauliers use these even with small loads (Zuckerman 1991).[6] The difference between actual and theoretically feasible loading factors implies scope for efficiency gains equivalent to 25 per cent of total kilometrage. While this may not be realizable owing to practical problems of special-ization and backloading, these constraints are themselves related to the overall paradigm of which scale economies, long-haul transport, and specialization of transport are part. Packaging is also part of this paradigm and part of the problem. Goods for final sale are trans-ported together with often bulky packaging. This reduces weight-to-volume ratios and increases truck-kilometres. The scope for efficiency gains is therefore a function not only of truck loading ratios but also of weight–volume ratios.

Taking up the potential

In principle, the geography of economic activities and the spatial division of labour represent the outcome of *choices* about the use of transport system improvements and low transport costs. However, choice is contextually constrained. Competitive forces and prevailing relative prices have made a business necessity out of moving mate-rials and goods (often repeatedly) between different points in value-adding chains. To the extent that profit-maximizing arrangements differ from those that would be environmentally optimal, this differ-ence arises from the ways in which markets have been constructed (legally, institutionally, and fiscally) and how this affects relative prices. A conclusion now widely drawn is that the social and envi-ronmental costs of transport services and energy should be included within their prices.

While recognizing the problems involved, an important element of strategy in eco-restructuring must be to take up the opportunities created even by apparently negative developments and trends. Growing traffic volumes represent a negative development. But the projected growth in traffic under conditions of already congested infrastructure is now focusing policy makers' attention on the need for demand-side management. Similarly, progress toward and actual experience with free trade have highlighted the trade-distorting impli-cations both of the underpricing of environmental resources and of differences in national policies toward environmental protection. As a result, the issues are growing in political importance. They are shifting from being purely domestic policy items to a central position on agendas concerned with the topography of the "playing field" for international competition. This gives them a much higher political priority.

Environmental protection – whether by harmonization of standards or by the use of compensatory mechanisms that would factor differences in national standards into the terms of trade – is now an agenda item for the newly formed World Trade Organization, the successor to the GATT. Differences in national policies affecting transport and energy prices within EU member states are causing these to come under critical scrutiny in ways and to a degree almost unthinkable within a purely national framework. At the same time, these differences are highlighting that the sources of distortions are often linked to policy interventions through subsidies and tax differentials and that fiscal regimes often bear no clear link to third-party costs (Gabel 1994). As a result, work is under way to elaborate basic principles for transport and energy pricing from the standpoint of economic theory and optimal resource allocation.

In this respect it is interesting that, although freight transport prices are consistently predicted to fall within the EU as a result of deregulation and the creation of the Single Market, expectations on longer-term price changes are more varied. In respect to recent questionnaire surveys (e.g. Byrne 1990), substantial disagreement among respondents was found reflecting different views on the likelihood and severity of environmental legislation. Many of those approached in a Delphi study on the European outlook anticipated price increases in the longer term as transport operators are made to pay for environmental damage and bear the full costs of infrastructure use. Theirs was the prevailing view. The study concluded that road transport prices would rise by 17 per cent in real terms between 1991 and 2001. A further conclusion was that price rises in the road freight sector would be significantly above those for other modes. The predicted rise for rail was 9 per cent (Cooper 1995). A report by the Council of Logistics Management (CLM 1993) similarly foresees that the shallow fall in prices associated with the Single Market will be followed by a sharp rise in the late 1990s, continuing on beyond the year 2000.

A recent ECMT study has calculated the price corrections that might be needed to internalize some of the more significant environmental externalities of the transport sector (ECMT 1995). The external costs of road and rail freight transport were assessed across four categories of externalities (accidents, noise, local pollution, and greenhouse effects). Results were expressed as ranges, reflecting different assumptions made about loadings. For road freight, total externalities were 18–30 Ecu per 1,000 tonne-kilometres. For rail freight, total externalities were 4.0–7.5 Ecu per 1,000 tonne-kilometres. The lower level for rail freight is associated with lower externalities across all categories, but especially for accidents. The road freight externalities equate to 0.29–0.38 Ecu per truck-kilometre. Were these costs to be factored into fuel prices (and on the assumption of an average fuel consumption of 35 litres/100 km for trucks), they would constitute a tax equivalent to 0.7–1.1 Ecu per litre. All of these figures are calculated for operating externalities only and do not include costs associated with infrastructure provision.

As a precursor or supplement to fiscal measures aimed generally at transport and energy, several truck-specific actions have been proposed. To correct the distortions that arise from the off-loading of warehousing and inventory costs, for example, Zuckerman (1991) proposes the use of a tax based upon a combination of weight and distance criteria, which would reduce reliance on distant suppliers and increase the attractiveness of local suppliers. Alternatively, a tax based upon weight and volume would address the packaging problem, discouraging manufacturers from inefficient and wasteful packaging. A combined weight–volume–distance tax could be designed to encourage truckers to make shorter runs, consolidate their own loads, and share space with other truckers. The net effect would be fewer vehicle-kilometres (Zuckerman 1991, p. 142).

There is need to institute new controls on trucks and to enforce both these and existing controls strictly. Data suggest that existing controls – many of them relevant to environmental impact – are frequently ignored. On British dual carriageways, surveys show that 92 per cent of articulated truck drivers exceed speed limits. Over 20 per cent of trucks fail annual inspections carried out under Department of Transport requirements, suggesting that these are inadequately maintained during the year. Calculations show that operators' potential cost savings in breaking regulations (for example, loading limits) are many times higher than the fines faced if caught. Technology now exists to enable automatic spot checks to be made as trucks pass sensors in the road bed. These would allow more systematic checking of speeds and loadings. In association with increased penalties, stricter enforcement of regulations would ensure higher compliance and greater environmental protection.

Part of the needed approach would be to reduce institutionalized support to processes and decisions that lead to increased transport demands. Road programmes have already been substantially cut back in many industrialized societies. None the less, land-use planning processes that might be expected to preserve green sites and prevent decentralization are consistently prejudiced by efforts to attract investment and enterprise into regions. Land-use planning processes need to be more fully linked into the overall effort to secure sustainable development and restrictions placed on developments likely to generate extra traffic. Such restrictions, once enacted, need to be more rigorously enforced through strengthened public enquiry and appeal procedures.

Another important aspect is to focus on consumers. By providing information on the transport intensity of different products, consumers would be empowered to make informed decisions. Studies such as that exemplified by Böge could be used as the basis for product labelling schemes.

Conclusion

Although it is not possible to specify in abstract which patterns of land use, trade, logistics, and transport would offer greatest scope for reducing environmental stresses, shifts toward sustainable societies and economies would most likely involve:
- less physical movement,
- less emphasis on physical transportation infrastructures,
- substitution of information and capital flows for physical goods movement,
- greater mixing of land uses,
- less specialization and concentration in production,
- smaller-scale installations and use of flexible technologies to emphasize economies of scope over economies of scale,
- decentralization of production,
- greater reliance on local resources,
- greater serving of local markets,
- new networking arrangements among contractors/subcontractors,
- more sensitivity in matching activities and locations so as not to overreach local environmental capacities.

The flexibility for spatial and sectoral shifting – even within the framework set by the inertia of sunk costs and market contestability – is considerable. However, the signs are not positive that these opportunities will automatically be taken up. Finding geographical and logistics arrangements that are less resource intensive and defining the market conditions under which these would be consistent with profit maximization is therefore a central concern for eco-restructuring. In this regard, spatial indicators could be important diagnostics in eco-restructuring processes. A reconfiguration of the market framework is necessary to provide the incentive/disincentive structure for change. Although it may not be politically possible in the short term to internalize all currently externalized social and environmental costs into environmental resource prices, it is important to begin that process soon and to target some sectors for early action. A combination of gradually increasing motorway tolls and fuel taxes, together with specific regulatory actions targeted at trucks and aimed at securing speed, loading, and environmental performance standards, would constitute an important start.

International agreement on a harmonized resource taxation system is unlikely. This implies that a way must be found to reconcile the need for individual countries or blocs to act independently to tax resource use without jeopardizing the competitiveness of their own industry in either domestic markets (*vis-à-vis* imports) or in export markets (*vis-à-vis* competing exporters). Maintaining a level playing field for international competition depends upon taxing imports on entry on the basis of their resource intensity and exempting exports from resource taxes using rebates, again based upon resource intensity. Such a solution would allow independent, incremental action by the lead countries. None the less, this would still depend first upon reforming the GATT agreement (Weaver 1995).

Because of interlinkages between freight transport and all other economic activities, actions targeted at freight transport (and at truck transport specifically) would have important knock-on effects.[7] Together with the energy sector, transport is privileged in this respect. Against the backdrop of industrialized countries' obligations under the Framework Convention on Climate Change and responsibility to take the lead in eco-restructuring, the fact that transport energy use is increasing faster within these countries than within the developing world is salutary. It is indicative that this is a lifestyle issue – a reflection of conspicuous over-consumption in the context of distorted incentives. This makes it all the more important for policy to focus on freight transport. It is a critical and potential swing sector in eco-restructuring.

Acknowledgements

I am grateful to Gilberto Gallopín, Walther Manshard, Ray Hudson, and Michael Taylor for editorial comments on an earlier draft. Friedrich Schmidt-Bleek alerted me to relevant work at the Wuppertal Institute and Eric Britton to relevant work of EcoPlan International. Landis Gabel provided helpful information on deregulation, market liberalization, and freight transport. Thanks are due also to two anonymous reviewers whose suggestions for improvement were most helpful.

Notes

1. A possibility that arises from the very differentiated nature of truck transport, which involves vehicles of different sizes, weight–power ratios, and resource productivity.
2. Judged on an economic growth criterion, impressive progress has been made under the regime. Between 1950 and 1990, real ($ adjusted) gross world product increased five-fold from US$3.8 trillion to US$18.8 trillion. On a sustainability criterion, we can be less sanguine because more rapid growth equates with more rapid conversion of environmental capital and higher rates of environmental change.
3. Both are alleged to cost 1–2 per cent of GDP in countries lightly affected by distortions and 3–5 per cent of GDP in countries with severe distortions (Repetto 1993).
4. A prediction that prompted the Task Force to single out transportation as the sector through which liberalization of the internal EU market would have its greatest environmental impact.
5. EU truck limits now allow truck lengths of 16.5 m, widths of 2.5 m, and gross weights of 40–50 tonnes.
6. The situation is actually even more complex than this suggests. Although some operators have increased their average truck size, the overall tendency recently has been for a shift in many OECD countries away from medium-sized trucks toward very large trucks for bulk freight and small trucks for retail distribution and high-value goods. Much of the recent growth has also been concentrated in small trucks. The environmental downside here is that these have relatively low energy efficiency per freight tonne (compared with large trucks (IPCC 1996, p. 691). Overall, it seems that the shift from medium-sized to large and small trucks has reduced overall transportation energy efficiency.
7. I have already focused heavily on the significance of distance – and the need to overcome distance – in contributing to environmental impacts. But distance has more significance than is immediately apparent in the shift toward sustainability. In respect to future sustainable societies and economies, distance is also important as: (i) a factor in the ecological viability of recycling; and (ii) a factor in the viability of service-driven business plans. As to the latter, proximity to the market will be more important as businesses shift from strategies based upon selling goods (the service delivery machinery) to those based upon selling services. Radical increases in resource productivity will depend upon such shifts (Ayres and Schmidt-Bleek 1993).

References

Altschuler, A., M. Anderson, D. Jones, D. Roos, and J. Womack (1984) *The Future of the Automobile*. London: Allen & Unwin.

Ayres, R. U. and F. Schmidt-Bleek (1993) *Toward a Universal Measure of Environmental Disturbance Potential*. CMER/INSEAD Working Paper. Fontainebleau, France: INSEAD.

Böge, S. (1993) Spatial effects of road freight traffic: Analysing the transport chains of goods and materials. *Informationen zum Raumentwicklung* 5(6): 351–362.

―――― (1995) The well-travelled yoghurt pot: Lessons for new freight transport policies and regional production. *World Transport Policy and Practice* **1**(1): 7–11.

Byrne, S. (1990) *European Shippers Survey*. London: G.E. Informations Systems.

CEC (Commission of the European Communities) (1989) *1992: The Environmental Dimension*. Report of the Task Force on the Environment and the Internal Market. Brussels: CEC.

CLM (Council of Logistics Management) (1993) *Reconfiguring European Logistics Systems*. Oak Brook, IL: CLM.

Cooper, J. (1995) *Transforming the Structure of the Freight Transport Sector*. UK contribution to a Round Table of the European Conference of Ministers of Transport, ECMT Round Table 99. Paris: OECD/ECMT, pp. 89–147.

ECMT (1995) *Report of the Task Force on the Social Costs of Transport*. Paris: ECMT/OECD.

Gabel, H. L. (1994) The environmental effects of trade in the transport sector. In: *The Environmental Effects of Trade*, pp. 153–170. Paris: OECD.

Gabel, H. L. and L.-H. Röller (1993) Trade liberalisation, transportation, and the environment. *The Energy Journal* **13**(3).

Grübler, A. (1988) *The Rise and Fall of Transport Infrastructures: Dynamics of Evolution and Technological Change in Transport*. Heidelberg: Physica Verlag.

―――― (1993) The transportation sector: Growing demand and emissions. Paper presented at the Seminar on Population and Natural Resources, TERI, New Delhi, India, September–October.

Grübler, A. and H. Nowotny (1990) Toward the fifth Kondratiev upswing: Elements of an emerging new growth phase and possible development trajectories. *International Journal of Technology Management* **5**(4).

Harvey, D. (1982) *The Limits to Capital*. Oxford: Blackwell.

IEA (International Energy Agency) (1993a) *Energy Statistics and Balances for OECD Countries 1960–1991*. Paris: OECD.

―――― (1993b) *Energy Statistics and Balances for Non-OECD Countries 1971–1991*. Paris: OECD.

IPCC (Intergovernmental Panel on Climate Change) (1996) *Second Assessment Report*. Geneva: IPCC.

Nakicenovic, N. (1993) Long-term strategies for mitigating global warming. *Energy* **18**(5): 401–609.

OECD (1995) *Global Warming: Economic Dimensions and Policy Responses*. Paris: OECD.

Repetto, R. (1993) Trade and environment policies: Achieving complementarities and avoiding conflicts. *WRI Issues and Ideas*, July. Washington D.C.: WRI.

Schipper, L. and S. Meyers (1992) *Energy Efficiency and Human Activity*. Cambridge: Cambridge University Press.

Shachar, A. (1991) Notes on the spatial organisation of society and sustainable development. Unpublished conference paper presented at the Abisko Workshop on Pragmatism and Effective Policy Making for Environment and Development, Abisko, Sweden, May.

Strutynski, P. (1995) A new approach to reducing road freight transport. *World Transport Policy and Practice* **1**(1): 37–40.

Venables, A. and A. Smith (1988) Completing the internal market in the European

Community: Some industry simulations. *European Economic Review* **32**(7): 1501–1525.

Weaver, P. M. (1995) Implementing change. A resource paper prepared for the Factor 10 Club meeting, Carnoules, France, September. Working Paper, Wuppertal Institute.

Whitelegg, J. (1994) *Driven to Destruction: Absurd Freight Movement and European Road Building*. London: Greenpeace.

Zuckerman, W. (1991) *End of the Road*. Post Mills, VT: Chelsea Green.

12

National and international policy instruments and institutions for eco-restructuring

Mikoto Usui

Introduction

The search for a viable path to a sustainable future must be hinged upon a wide array of complex problem sets, including not only the technological issues related to global climate, preservation of bio-diversity, and other natural/ecological constraints to the cohabitation of billions of world citizens, but also the very art of cohabitation in an ever-shifting hierarchy of political, economic, and social issues. The notion of eco-restructuring goes a few steps further than the UN Conference on Environment and Development's Rio Declaration and Agenda 21. It necessarily includes an element of "futurology," leading us into a wide range of possibilistic explorations. Experience shows, however, that, apart from a listing of possible technological breakthroughs, the futurology has been notoriously incompetent at dovetailing social breakthrough scenarios into a feasible policy package with concrete instruments and institutional devices. What difference would it make then, if, instead of a wholly original new World Order, we look for just a plausibly reconstituted version of the existing order?

We have had some way to come to back away from the carefree altar of "limitless economic growth." With the advent of an "ecotopian" challenge there is a still further distance to establish a satisfactory methodology to win the hearts and minds of accountants and bankers. As a paradigm of sustainable resource management has begun to emerge as something technically manageable in the vein of pragmatic gradualism, the hill has already got slippery enough. This technical paradigm is loaded with such buzzwords as impact assessment, risk management, energy efficiency, renewable resource/conservation strategies, population stabilization, a Global Commons law for oceans, atmosphere, climate, and biodiversity, etc. Some visionaries, such as Sagasti and Colby (1993), see a paradigm of eco-development looming in the further distance, however. It seeks not only to integrate society and the environment in accordance with longer-term economic and ecological goals, but also to restructure international society to the principles of equity and popular participation.

Given the prolonged world recession, coupled with a complex re-ordering of international security arrangements in the post–Cold War world, the process of following up on the UNCED agreements has seemed already to enjoy a much lower priority than was originally hoped. And yet it has been just visible enough to augur the beginning of a new process of international "learning by doing."

The discussion in this chapter purports, rather modestly, to build on the lessons being gained from past experience in taking up the challenge of sustainable development. A systematic assessment of all the relevant component instruments and related law-making processes would have been a much larger undertaking than was possible in the context of this book. In the following I attempt only selectively to highlight certain controversial aspects of the subject at hand.

I start, first, with an issue related to international environmental institutions. Features of the historical process of international environmental treaty-making will be examined, particularly with regard to changing practices of national sovereignty in the collective management of global common-pool resources. One important, rather hard-learned, lesson will be that the best strategy should be to start with, and build on, "small agreements," rather than to aim for a quantum-jump solution.

I then turn to the issues related to the designing and packaging of policy instruments for tackling environmental problems. I look into the recent trend towards the market-based approach in national environmental policy in OECD countries, the evolving knowledge base for the carbon tax, and then the art of policy packaging for neutralizing the power of special interest groups (particularly transnational corporations) tending to impede the negotiation process for new environmental agreements. Whereas the economists' typical advice is to "get the prices right," political scientists are concerned with how to "get institutional incentives right."

This is followed by an assessment of the North–South income-redistributional implications of joint implementation, or North–South partnerships, towards eco-development. The distributive bargaining over the twin issue of the transfer of financial and technological resources has long served as a natural common front for the South ever since the 1950s, but it is in conjunction with global environmental agendas such as climate change and biodiversity that Southerners have gained enormous bargaining power just by a threat of inaction or free-riding. Reference will be made to international incentive schemes such as the Global Environmental Facility and the trade-related aspects of international environmental regimes.

Then I try to step onto the scene within the developing world, particularly to see how an "environmental enlightenment" of developing society has taken place in conjunction with international development cooperation. The process has coincided with a spate of decentralization, mass participation, democratization, and "technology blending" at the grass-roots level. The latter trend may well be taken as a precondition for social breakthroughs toward eco-restructuring in the context of many developing societies.

The bottom–up approach is essential but is unlikely to be a sufficient condition for global eco-restructuring. So I dwell upon certain critical issues of science and technology for development. After examining briefly the question of technology transfer in the North–South context, I move on to shed light on a bias built into the world's science and technology community in that ever since the era of the Industrial Revolution the profession has succumbed to market mechanisms by responding sooner to the lucrative opportunities of urban mass markets than to the basic human needs of the people in disadvantaged regions. Attention will be drawn to some of the bolder propositions, contained in this book, that hint at possibilities for global engineering projects that would contribute to redressing the basic infrastructural conditions of currently energy-deficient and water-deficient regions.

Finally, I revert to the question of international institutions, searching for the image of a "third-generation world organization" or a United Nations renaissance. With the advent of a rapidly expanding universe of non-governmental organizations omnipresent in many aspects of international relations, and with an ever more muddled hierarchy of issues and organizations, we still need some sort of global focal point with a "switchboard" role for stimulating interactive thinking and planning among diverse actors, and thus enhancing humankind's capacity for collective learning.

Building on small agreements

The Convention Concerning the Use of White Lead in Paint (adopted in 1921 and enforced in 1923) marks the very beginning of the list of some 140 international environmental agreements (the UN Environmental Programme's International Register of Environmental Treaties now available through the Internet). These agreements have established rules for the use of the Antarctic, the exploitation of ocean resources, the protection of migratory and endangered wildlife, the abatement of pollution at sea and in the atmosphere, the management of watersheds, the control of pests and hazardous chemicals, the testing of nuclear weapons, the notification of nuclear accidents, and many other environmental problems that have trans-border complications. The number of signatory countries averages around 12 but varies from a minimum of 3 to a maximum of 161 (for the 1982 UN Law of the Sea Convention).

The pace of treaty-making has been accelerating. Taking as a divide the 1972 UN Conference on the Human Environment (UNCHE) at Stockholm, which propounded the notion of *Only One Earth*, the pace has increased from 1.2 treaties per year in the pre-UNCHE decades to some 4.2 per year during the subsequent two decades. Distinguishing the treaties concerned with the management of commons outside national control from those dealing with within-border or territorial resources, the proportion of the former grew from some 50 per cent before 1973 to nearly 70 per cent during the period since 1973. Moreover, countries have seemed to demonstrate a willingness to subordinate national controls to the requirements of international agreements. The proportion of treaties that regulate only extra-territorial activities has fallen from 44 per cent before 1973 to 15 per cent since 1973, with those calling for internal controls to internationally agreed standards and criteria rising to 85 per cent.

In spite of the "tragedy of the commons" thesis of rational choice theorists (Olson 1965; Hardin 1968), this may signify that humankind's willingness to assume collective responsibility for the manage-

367

ment of common-pool resources has increased, if not radically, and that the exigency of deepening interdependence has begun to erode the concept of the national sovereign state.

This does not presage, however, anything like an increased visibility of a Global Government. Empowerment of a supranational authority for treaty enforcement has occurred only twice so far (for the conventions on high seas fisheries and living resources of 1952 and 1958). And, in most of the cases in which supranational authorities are involved to assist national governments in treaty implementation, their role has been limited to collecting information and conducting research. This is in spite of the fact that the majority of conventions concerned with air pollution, water pollution, marine dumping, and natural resource conservation do not stop at mere *coordination* of national policies but involve *collaboration games* in which countries have conflicting interests and solutions entail real distributional costs (Haas and Sundgren 1993).

After long debates among ecological scientists, economists, and the policy community, a broad consensus seems to be emerging that the best strategy is to start with "small agreements" and build on their ratchet effects, rather than to struggle for a big, sweeping (and eternally elusive) agreement. One of the important lessons learned from the decade-long "marathon" of the Law of the Sea negotiations is that "to create a universally inclusive process with respect to both issues and participants, together with the requirements for consensus on an overall package deal" can be "a very serious time-consuming mistake" (Sebenius 1993, p. 198). The reason is that the ultimate results of such a heroic endeavour can easily be held hostage to the most reluctant parties on the most difficult issues.

"The process is the policy" was a strategy adopted by Maurice Strong for managing the UNCHE with the vast agenda of "human environment." It has since become a shared password in multilateral environmental diplomacy (Herter, Jr. and Binder 1993). The new pattern of interactive planning emerging in that process is roughly as follows.

First, a framework convention is instituted. It defines a commonly shared perception of the problems at issue and sets forth a set of principles and norms to be observed in tackling those problems. This is a precondition for subsequent, more specific rule-making protocols. The process provides enough time for laggard states to become motivated to reassess their respective national interests relative to others. It also allows time for the leading coalitions of interest groups and non-governmental organizations (NGOs) to generate public pressure against resistant institutions and governments. It thus paves the way for protocols and concurrent national and international regulatory activities.

This technique was first developed by UNEP's Regional Seas Programme for the Mediterranean in 1975, followed by the subsequent nine regional programmes (Haas 1990). A similar approach was adopted for the Long-Range Transboundary Air Pollution (LRTAP) Convention in Europe (1979) as well as the Vienna Convention to protect the stratospheric ozone layer (1985).

In the process of preparing for the Framework Convention on Climate Change (1992), debates continued for some time among the press and the scientific community as well as within the International Panel on Climate Change (IPCC), formed in 1988. These debates, which still continue, have gradually shifted from their initial focus. At first the issue was whether the available data sets and the existing climate models were really robust enough to base policy on. Now the question at issue is nearer to a matter of strategy: how fast must the level of carbon dioxide emissions be reduced to combat effectively the ongoing degradation of the global atmosphere at the lowest economic cost? The issue has spawned a growing number of global policy scenarios and simulation models (the Edmonds–Reilly model, the OECD–GREEN model, the Whalley–Wigle model, the Japanese CGER–AIM model, etc.). Conceivable options vary greatly. At one extreme is the approach that just puts a new policy structure into place and leaves aside the question of the uncertainty of costs and benefits. At the other extreme is a comprehensive, stringent, and universalized approach whose benefits might be more certain except that its realization would be politically impossible.

The currently considered target of stabilizing the annual emission of greenhouse gases at the 1990 level by the year 2000 would help slow the pace of global warming by just 20 years or so even if the developing countries and the former socialist economies joined the move. The grace period provided by this target (if it were met) would be no more than five years if the latter groups of countries did not join the protocol! This is due to the long residence time of trace gases in the atmosphere (170 years for N_2O, 100 years for CO_2, and so on). To stabilize the density of these gases in the atmosphere and thus really stop global warming would require a drastic cut in current emissions, say by as much as 50 per cent within 100 years (e.g. Matsuoka and Morita 1992). So we need to hurry up with both technological and social breakthroughs.

That might sound a very relaxed long-term agenda when ecologists keep warning that even a minor change in temperature is likely to have potentially significant impacts on a regional and local basis. But political scientists' reflective cynicism retorts that humankind has not yet learned enough to make any big systemic change in international political systems before a catastrophic signal becomes really palpable (Mathews 1989; also Cooper 1994, esp. p. 73).

"Looking for small agreements" is not escapist chicanery. On the contrary it is the basis for progressive, pragmatic wisdom. A grand paradigm of global eco-restructuring would remain just an act of hubris without consciously sustained gradualist efforts. The process is akin to climbing up a slippery hill that is, itself, a heap of older, but not yet discarded, paradigms to be followed by newer, increasingly more demanding, ones.

Economic policy instruments and mechanisms

In the forward planning for global eco-restructuring, policy designers are faced with the difficult task of determining an optimal mix and sequencing of various policy instruments. The most crucial of all is that national communities are sufficiently convinced of the urgency of the problem and the feasibility of solutions to accept particular targets. Then a plausible policy package ought to include appropriate counteractive tax cuts and other institutional incentives to cope with a host of distributional issues arising with the introduction of any new policy instruments – regulatory or market based. It is also important that the timing of introduction is coordinated internationally so as to minimize perturbative impacts on international trade. Furthermore, the notion of a "social net" must be internationalized so as to enable joint implementation with third world people.

In the next section, I first grapple with the economist's perspective, giving heed to the polluter-pays principle and also to the precautionary principle. I then move on to discuss the question of incentives that are crucial in steering the political process of policy-making toward a judicial blending of public and private initiatives. The question of equity will be dealt with in the section on "International Distributional Implications."

Regulatory vs. market-based measures

A report issued by the OECD working group on Taxation and Environment (OECD 1993a) affirms the merits of economic instruments in environmental policy, particularly taxation schemes that affect the very framework of competitive markets.

Economic instruments, as normally defined, are market based in the sense that they influence indirectly the quantitative supply and demand decisions through altered cost–price relations. They keep the market price-cleared and let those polluters with the lowest abatement costs select themselves in response to the signal provided by a pollution surcharge or tax. Environmental taxes and surcharges are meant to cover the social costs not reflected in private costs and benefits. They normally take the form of specific taxes to be levied on each unit of pollution identified (e.g. on the basis of the carbon content of fuels in the case of the carbon tax), thus serving as an incentive to reduce pollution (carbon dioxide emissions) as they increase the polluters' marginal cost of production.

Subsidies (grants, soft loans, and tax allowances or reliefs) provide a similar incentive on the basis of each unit of pollution abatement being effected. In practice, however, most subsidies tend to be paid not in relation to abatement but rather to encourage the development or use of environmentally friendlier technological alternatives. This is apparently not compatible with the "polluter-pays" principle. Yet, most specific taxes or charges that are expected to have incentive effects towards environmental protection have been instituted primarily as a revenue-raising instrument earmarked to finance environment-related public expenditures, including subsidies.

Tradable permits function as a price-based instrument, although the size of the permit market is administered as a quantity-based regulatory measure. This approach (currently practised only in the United States on an experimental scale) can guarantee a quantitative reduction in pollution but leaves uncertain the cost of emission controls to individual polluters. The argument over the plausibility of this approach relative to taxes and charges often stresses the contrast in this respect, because taxes and charges leave the quantitative abatement effect uncertain while fixing the cost to the polluters.

Broader definitions of the market-based approach would include enforcement incentives such as performance bonds (refundable upon assured compliance) and non-compliance fines.

These economic instruments are often contrasted to regulatory instruments, which refer to direct controls through quotas or bans in conformity with legislated standards and enforceable through administrative sanctions and/or litigation. The two mechanisms can in theory be used to equivalent effect. But in practice there are important differences.

Regulatory controls are often preferred by policy authorities on the ground that the effects of regulation are more certain than those of taxes and other economic instruments. Individuals and business firms, too, tend to prefer regulations to the extent that they make planning easier. An often-voiced objection to taxation is that the public revenues derived therefrom may be misappropriated or used directly or indirectly for other unspecified purposes. Besides, industry is familiar with the ways of influencing regulatory processes (which are always susceptible to some special exceptions) through lobbying and negotiation. US environmentalists used to object that the use of market mechanisms (in the form of tradable permits) implied "putting the environment up for sale."

Academic literature abounds with the controversy over regulatory versus market-based measures. Much of it hinges on the notion of "efficiency," i.e. the need to find a balance between the (social) costs of pollution and the costs of restricting pollution. One key argument (mostly among economists) in favour of market-based approaches to environmental policy is related to the information cost of regulatory controls. Different firms have different technologies, some incurring much higher costs in pollution abatement than others to a given emission standard. Similarly, the costs to individual households of reducing their use of particular polluting products vary owing to differences in taste and other circumstances. An efficient regulatory policy would require extensive information on those individual differences in abatement cost in order to ensure that abatement measures concentrate where reductions in pollution can be achieved at least cost. A regulation requiring all polluters to restrict emissions to the same extent would then be more costly than a market-based instrument aimed at the same overall impact (see, for example, Barbier et al. 1994, pp. 178–183).

Interesting as it is academically, this sort of argument does not seem to carry decisive weight in guiding the actual process of public choice between regulatory and market-based policy instruments. For example, in the case of local environmental problems, such as water pollution and waste disposal, the assimilative capacity of the environment may vary from one locality to another. Then a straightforward tax per unit of pollutant emitted may imply that firms in areas of low pollution are charged more than the value of the damage they inflict on the environment. Unless the tax rate is differentiated geographically with adequate information on the assimilative capacity of the environment, it cannot claim to be more efficient than the regulatory alternative.

Indeed, bureaucratic solutions that require the regulators to become too closely identified with firm-by-firm interests may be vulnerable to so-called "regulatory capture." However, market-based instruments are not without similar drawbacks. There is the risk that even "green" subsidies become an indirect or disguised protection to the industries considered. For that reason, the polluter-pays principle, as adopted by the OECD, is based on a baseline of zero subsidy as the most readily identifiable rule (OECD 1991).

In the case of global environmental problems, such as climate change and biodiversity, the question of "threshold values" for ecosystem parameters (i.e. the limits beyond which ecosystems are likely to collapse) complicates the design of appropriate policies. This is certainly a more serious matter than the information cost. The burden of "green" taxes would fall quickly upon consumers in general rather than upon the polluters immediately responsible for eco-degradation. Under uncertainty, people become suspicious that taxes and other economic instruments might not prove effective in countering ecological degradation. If the thresholds are not well known, or if the likely damage is uncertain, regulatory controls, too, can become vulnerable to the suspicion that they might produce more than adequate abatement effects at unnecessary cost to producers and final consumers. In such circumstances, pressure may emerge for deferring any substantial environmental policy change (be it for a new tax or a regulatory standard) in favour of "further studies and research" for greater certainty. This could easily gain political legitimacy on the ground that the expected economic efficiency loss be minimized.

True, both regulatory and market-based approaches require enforcement, which in turn requires effective monitoring systems and administrative and legal apparatuses to ensure compliance. The relative effectiveness of alternative policy instruments depends very much on the institutional effectiveness of the tax authority and environmental authority in each country in managing the process of enactment, enforcement, and compliance. The recently growing emphasis on the use of market-based instruments seems to stem from the reflection that these have in fact been long underutilized in environmental policy.

Even countries relatively more advanced in environmental policy, such as Sweden and the Netherlands, have relied mainly on instruments of the command-and-control type, coupled with a variety of specific-purpose taxes for raising revenues for environment-related subsidies and public expenditures. The environmental taxes introduced in the Swedish tax reform of 1990/91 included carbon dioxide and sulphur taxes on fossil fuels, chosen explicitly for their incentive effects rather than their revenue effects. The US feedstock tax on petroleum and chemical industries serves simply as a revenue source for Superfund operations, and none of the many bills proposing various environmental taxes submitted to the Congress has yet reached the level of support needed for enactment (as in many other countries).

The spate of policy assessments in favour of market-based measures in recent years in OECD countries may well be seen to be contingent on the continuing trend towards "smaller government" with a reformed fiscal package. Various existing taxes for revenue-raising purposes with or without environmental objectives may be re-consolidated into a new environmental policy package, such that there may be an opportunity for tax and subsidy cuts elsewhere. The Swedish case may provide a useful model for an extensive package deal that involves simultaneous adjustments of both fiscal and environmental schemes (OECD 1993b).

An outlook on the eco-tax

Proponents of the precautionary principle argue that a first necessary step should be to ensure that the current unsustainable market economy be redirected towards, if not immediately onto, an eco-development path. Knowledge of the social costs of crossing ecological thresholds is crucial for a societal decision on whether a specific limit should be imposed on economic activity. The determination of boundaries to the resilience of the whole complexity of ecosystems is itself a complex – and perhaps intractable – object of study. Hence, a precautionary decision would necessarily involve an ethical judgement concerning a margin of safety on our continued use of natural capital.

The ethical element seems to weigh even heavier in the case of the conservation of biodiversity than in the case of climate control.

The value of biodiversity needs to be established, not just in terms of personal preference. The ultimate decision cannot be based on whether every living entity is worth preserving "in its own right." It must be based on more fundamental scientific criteria, especially with regard to the essential role of biodiversity in assuring the resilience of ecosystems on which our economic activities depend. Biodiversity loss is unusual with respect to both the range of people affected (local, national, and international) and the degree to which it encompasses both unilateral and bilateral externalities. Ecological functions and resilience are sensitive to the mix of species, and a change in the mix can potentially have irreversible consequences. The interrelationships between biodiversity, ecosystem resilience, and the threshold effects of degradation thus remain an important challenge to ecological economics (Barbier et al. 1994).

In the spirit of the Slippery Hill strategy, the first piece of wisdom is, in the context of climate change policy, to put some moderate-scale policy into place concentrating on fossil fuel combustion. An example of such a policy might be a carbon (fossil fuel) tax that would reduce carbon dioxide (CO_2) by 20 per cent and inadvertently reduce sulphur dioxide (SO_2) emissions by 21 per cent and nitrogen oxides (NOx) by 14 per cent (Barrett 1991, p. 68). This would satisfy at least part of the conditions for "efficient" policy. Major sources would automatically be provided with incentives to reduce the marginal unit of net emissions to the point where the cost of doing so equals the emission charge avoided.

Economists are still ill at ease in predicting the power of a carbon tax. The large number of estimates thus far published (Nordhaus 1992, Cline 1992, 1993, Edmonds and Reilly 1983, Ferriter 1993, Manne and Richels 1992, Amano 1992, etc.) are not quite comparable one to another in regard to the modelling structure, the context, and the basic assumptions adopted. Broad agreement exists among mainstream econometric modellers that the higher the tax rate the greater the economic cost in terms of loss of potential GNP growth (Dean and Hoeller 1992). There is also agreement that the feedback effect through technological innovation can make the power of the tax greater in the long run than in the short run (although it is difficult to predict the pace of such innovations). Others (mostly non-economists, some represented in this volume) favour the so-called "double dividend" argument: that is, there are many unexploited opportunities to reduce both energy consumption and energy costs, whence, rather than cutting economic growth, the opposite might occur.

375

In designing an aggressive action programme to reduce emissions by one-third from the baseline, Cline (1992, 1993) allowed for a milder first phase with a cutback of 10–15 per cent during the first decade. Manne and Richels (1992) also suggested a cutback by some 12 per cent by the year 2000. The "optimal" cutback emerging from Nordhaus (1992) pointed to the order of 9 per cent by 1995. It is a relief to see a good degree of convergence emerging at least about the first-decade proposals.

The difficulty of determining the power of a tax lies among others in estimating the likely magnitude of the "double dividend" effect of the carbon tax on energy efficiency and substitution technologies. Closer dialogue between technologists and economists may in time dissolve this source of difficulty. Another, possibly less tractable, difficulty relates to the volatility of energy markets in responding to new taxes and other disturbances. Certainly energy markets are complex in terms of the structures of the demand for and supply of the mix of more, or less, substitutable fuel mixes. Their supply systems are dynamically linked to massive capital investments. And their demand systems are heterogeneous from sector to sector and from region to region. They interact with institutional rigidities. Resistance to change is particularly strong on the part of the notoriously conservative automotive transportation and petroleum refining/distribution sectors.

Although OECD countries already have some experience with various policy measures for energy systems management, further learning by doing is needed before the international community is equipped with a consensual knowledge base robust enough to tackle the steep path toward eco-development. The use of any policy instrument has differential effects on different individuals and countries. Even if the overall benefit of introducing a small carbon tax is very small, its short-term distributional implications can generate politically obstructive forces. The time has come for OECD countries, even if limited for the time being to certain "leading coalition" members, to carry through the first-stage socio-political experiments with a modest eco-tax system. (The Scandinavian countries have already started to do so.)

Much greater uncertainty remains from the perspective of the third world. The scenarios based on a target of stabilization of greenhouse gas (GHG) emissions at 1990 levels point to the need for a significant break between what is happening today (doubling energy demand every decade) and what is desirable (doubling only over 30 years,

1990–2020) (Churchill 1993). Much of future energy demand growth is likely to arise from the relatively price-insensitive transportation and heavy industry sectors. Once the capital investments are made, energy demand is locked in for many decades thereafter.

On the other hand, there is greater scope in the third world for improving management systems at both micro and macro levels. This is especially true of the existing, grossly inefficient, public utility sectors. Such basic institutional reforms, coupled with an accelerated transfer of cleaner and more economical technologies from industrial countries, would have a substantial cost-reducing effect. Yet there is a strong suspicion that a reduced energy cost might lead to a higher pace of energy demand growth in developing countries than otherwise (Churchill 1993).

Carbon taxes are likely to have the greatest effect on coal use (coal is the most carbon-intensive fossil fuel). Thus, measures for opening up access to liquefied natural gas (LNG) and other less carbon-intensive energy sources, and building the necessary infrastructure such as gas pipelines, would be essential in countries such as China and India (which are among the world top 10 carbon dioxide emitters). Indeed the initial first-decade CO_2 abatement effort may have to concentrate in the industrial countries. A more global response will be needed in subsequent decades, including developing regions. But, first, a consensual, politically palatable knowledge base must be developed for assessing the benefits and costs of GHG abatement in developing countries.

Transnational corporations' responses to new environmental agreements: How to "get the incentives right"

The link between causes and effects is often so far removed in space or in time that social and private interests can diverge widely even within a country. The costs and benefits of an environmental regulation fall differently upon different groups. Mancur Olson (1965) pointed out the classical problem of under-provision of public goods: when benefits from a public good are distributed over many people, each of whose contribution is small relative to the total cost of provision, the good will not be supplied in optimal quantity, unless institutional arrangements exist that induce incentives to provide it. The reverse side of this argument runs that public goods may be provided even in the absence of such a political institution, if a small "privileged" group can benefit from providing the goods. George Stigler (1971) elaborated the latter side of the argument in the context of cartel theory and regulation.

The classical Olsonian situation is thus such that the benefits of a regulation are diffused whereas its costs are concentrated on a few (as is the case with regulations on emissions of pollutants for cleaner air and water, and those on habitat destruction for biodiversity conservation). This is contrasted with the so-called Stiglerian situation in which regulatory benefits are concentrated on a few privileged actors while costs are diffused over many. When the benefits of a new regulation for the management of common-pool resources (such as the environment) are concentrated on those firms that are in possession of relevant new environmental technologies that can promise quasi-monopoly rents, such firms will be willing to coalesce with the environmentalists pressing for the regulation. A classical Stiglerian illustration is offered by the Montreal Protocol (1987). Its successful adoption only two years after the signing of a framework convention in Vienna (1985) can be said to be due to the concordance of economic incentives, political values, and scientific knowledge (Oye and Maxwell 1995).

Leading producers of chlorofluorocarbons (CFCs), particularly DuPont, followed by ICI, came to recognize incentives to support the Montreal Protocol for the protection of the ozone layer by the time the framework convention was signed in Vienna in 1985. During the decade prior to that, their research on CFC substitutes, initiated in the mid-1970s, had been discontinued on account of the lack of a market, and they had opted to impede the agreement-making process. In 1986, DuPont, having suffered over-capacity since the 1977 US ban on CFC use in aerosols, proposed an international agreement to limit worldwide CFC production to the then existing level. For a while the Montreal negotiation heard debates in which it sounded as though the critical issue was which companies were going to gain an advantage over which others (according to Mustafa Tolba, then the UNEP Executive Director). By 1988, ICI announced its intention to join DuPont in a rapid commercialization of CFC substitutes, prompting the UK and EC commitment to the eventual phase-out of CFCs.

Other examples of Stiglerian solutions can be seen with such regulations as:
- banning the use of leaded gasoline (for higher-profit production of unleaded gasoline);

- restricting the sale of DDT (to prompt a shift from the cheap, easy-to-produce chemical towards safer, more difficult-to-produce substitutes);
- requiring recyclable packaging (suspected of creating a barrier to non-German firms' entry in the German market);
- requiring special procedures and techniques for the handling and disposal of medical wastes (in favour of large waste-disposal firms equipped with special technologies);
- banning the sale of "immature" lobsters in the US market (aimed at raising a barrier to the entry of Canadian lobsters, which attain sexual maturity at a smaller size in cold waters);
- restricting development zones through strict environmental impact assessment (with rents accruing to the owners of previously developed properties at the expense of new developers).

In the Olsonian situation, there is no natural coincidence of business interests with the common good. So, in the absence of subsidies or compensatory payments, those who are the first to be affected by a regulation are likely to be the first to get organized to overturn the regulatory move. In this context, the slow progress on automotive emission regulations in the United States may well be contrasted with the relatively quick adoption of an even more stringent NOx standard (0.25 ppm) in Japan (in 1978).

In the United States, in spite of the adoption of the Amendment of the Clean Air Act as early as 1970, polarized debates have long remained unsettled between the Environmental Protection Agency (EPA), the National Academy of Sciences (NAS), and the automobile industry. Meanwhile, in Japan, the initial coalition of the automobile industry and the Ministry of Trade and Industry resisting the Environment Agency's proposal to adopt the 1970 US Clean Air Act Amendment standards was coaxed away by a skilfully managed incentives package. The Ministry of Finance agreed to reduce motor vehicle purchase taxes and ownership taxes for passenger cars that met the 1975–1978 emission standards. And the Ministry of Transport adopted less demanding test procedures for those cars (Oye and Maxwell 1995).

However, a great deal of care must be exercised to ensure that a policy package is both reasonably efficient and fair. In coping with the Olsonian situation, a general compensatory scheme for all those likely to be affected by regulation would be just too expensive. Besides, compensatory offers do not always reduce the intensity of opposition because, at times, an expectation of greater compensation might just intensify anti-regulatory lobbying. On the other hand, selective compensation aimed at only major burden-sharers in order to drive wedges into anti-regulatory coalitions may be less expensive but is problematic from the standpoint of fairness. A similar problem arises with the Stiglerian solution. The Montreal Protocol did in fact put minor, technologically less advanced producers at a disadvantage. The global ban envisaged at the London revision to the Protocol (1990) required compensation to developing countries in the form of a multilateral special fund to provide financial assistance to their phase-out efforts.

By the same token, the ideological shift toward privatization and market-based approaches, now increasingly widely shared in the international community, does not on its own guarantee an efficient and fair industry–government partnership towards sustainable development.

Indeed, there now exist numerous international business NGOs (BINGOs) adorned with their own "environmental charters" (e.g. the Coalition of Environmentally Responsible Economies, CERES; the Business Council for Sustainable Development, BCSD; the International Chamber of Commerce, ICC; the International Federation of Consulting Engineering, FIDIC; Alliance Internationale de Tourisme; etc.), along with national industrial confederations such as Keidanren (Federation of Economic Organization) in Japan, the Confederation of British Industry (CBI) in the United Kingdom, and Bundesverband der Deutschen Industrie (BDI) in Germany. However, the BCSD, which contributed an enlightening set of success stories – *Changing Course* (Schmidheiny 1992) – to the 1992 UN Conference on the Environment and Development (UNCED), draws only on private personal membership. The ICC is known for its ambiguous stance at global environmental forums. Reportedly, it persistently interfered in the drafting of Agenda 21 so as to minimize reference to "transnational corporations" in terms of the allocation of responsibility (Gleckman 1995).

All too often industry proclaims a "self-regulatory" strategy. This is somewhat of a facade, usually consisting of (a) promising "good business practice," (b) pacifying external pressures, and (c) lobbying for favourable governmental incentive measures. The first component stresses a truism that the creation of new markets and improved corporate images (with intra-firm environmental charters and self-audit practices) contribute to increased profits. The pacification strategy includes lobbying to delay domestic and international regulatory accords, and guarding consumers against aggressive media. The third component is aimed at settling on a looser regulation than any new tax and justifying specific subsidization and R&D subventions. A recent UNCTAD survey on industry's environmental "self-regulation" concluded that industry commitments still fall short of the provisions of Agenda 21 in the areas of reporting and public disclosure as well as full-cost accounting (UNCTAD 1995).

It is too early to judge yet whether a Stiglerian situation is emerging that is mature enough to propel the protocol-making phase of the global "climate change" regime. A survey study issued by the United Nations on the implications of international environmental law for transnational corporations maintains the hope, on the basis of historical experience, that non-binding instruments, such as intergovernmental declarations, codes of conduct, and guidelines, can be pointers towards future binding international legal instruments. This hope can be sustained as long as those instruments (binding or non-binding) affect the norms being shared and sooner or later put the states that are parties to them under an obligation to incorporate into their national laws appropriate legislation giving effect to their international legal obligations (United Nations 1993).

The emerging norms are being translated into a series of institutional mechanisms to facilitate market mechanisms to internalize social environmental costs. They include among others:
- public pricing of previously free goods (e.g. waste disposal services);
- national and corporate accounting systems that incorporate social environmental costs in budget forecasts;
- an eco-labelling system that encourages a shift in consumers' preferences towards environment-friendly products;
- a civil liability system that punishes environment- and health-unfriendly products and practices;
- a mandated requirement for manufacturers to be responsible for resource preservation over the full life cycle of their products;
- institutionalization of environmental assessment that discourages environmentally unfriendly regional development projects.

Added to these is a more general proposition that includes:
- a reform of national tax systems that is "incentive compatible," with taxes and charges on the use of non-renewable resources rather than on incomes and profits; and
- value-oriented science, technology, and education programmes that enhance the general public's awareness of the requisites of

381

planetary governance, and stimulate research and development for generating new seeds of technology that are of value as (both national and global) public goods.

In order to make the market itself self-correcting, with self-regulation and self-reporting on the part of industry, a great deal of institutional innovation will be needed so that the state, consumers, and workers can intervene effectively to prompt the internalization of environmental and natural resource costs into market prices. In both Olsonian and Stiglerian situations, reconciliation and, still better, coalition formation between public environmental interests and private self-interests may be a requisite for climbing up the ever-steeper hill toward the long-term goal of eco-development. There is still a lot of room for further research on the art of designing incentive-compatible regulatory systems that are efficient, fair, and welfare enhancing.

International distributional implications

In the North–South context, both equity and efficiency criteria would demand greater heed to the problem of judicial blending of private and public initiatives. In fact the twin issues of the transfer of financial and technological resources have long hovered high above the muddled hierarchy of issues connected with Agenda 21. The bargaining over these issues has served as a natural front for the South in both the pre- and the post-UNCED processes of multilateral negotiation. At first sight the issues may sound purely distributive. Yet there remains much scope for exploring further improved instruments of international management and incentives.

Leaving aside domestic transfer issues, the question of who collects the tax bears critically upon international finance issues. There are conceivably three alternative ways of administering taxation. First, if a *production tax* were collected from the producers of fossil fuels, the oil exporters (or multinational oil companies) would see an opportunity for earning substantially more per unit of fuel, while all other countries would be worse off. If the extra rents accruing to the oil exporters could be easily taxed away, this scheme would arguably be the most efficient administratively, because the number of producing entities is comparatively small.

Secondly, if the tax were collected by individual consuming countries in the form of a national *consumption tax*, the oil exporters would be worse off. They would thus be likely to stand as a blocking coalition against a carbon tax protocol. The consuming countries would have to tackle a number of vexing domestic distributional issues (which would prompt the automotive and energy service industries to join the blocking coalition). The consuming countries might as a whole enjoy a positive terms-of-trade effect (a decrease in the import price of oil relative to their export prices). But such a benefit would tend to be only thinly distributed over the general public, who might resist, if not the carbon tax protocol as such, a reallocation of the tax revenues for international compensatory purposes.

The third option is a *global tax*, to be collected directly by a supranational authority. In this case the international community would have a new opportunity for international income redistribution. The revenue could be recycled according to different criteria, e.g. on an equal per capita basis, or on some more complex formula reflecting an individual country's historical fuel use ("natural debt") combined with its ability to pay (e.g. per capita GNP). Certainly low-income countries would favour such a *global Keynesian* proposition. In reality, however, owing to Northerners' persistent rearguard action, the global tax notion has been safely obscured by piggybacking it onto the familiar agenda of the target ratio between official development assistance (ODA) and GNP (now 0.7 per cent for OECD donors).

The scale of income transfer from high-income countries to low-income countries could easily become several times larger than the current total ODA were an eco-tax conceived in a globally administered scheme. For example, Whalley and Wigle (1989) provide a sense of how (a) high-income, (b) low-income, and (c) oil-exporting country groups would be affected by different schemes of tax collection. In order to reduce global CO_2 emissions by 50 per cent in 2005 (or 20 per cent below the 1988 level), a national consumption tax would result in the three groups paying (a) US$67 billion, (b) US$121 billion, and (c) US$108 billion per year, respectively. If low-income countries were given a moratorium, high-income countries would have to pay a much higher share (the US$121 billion is equivalent to 1.15 per cent of the high-income countries' GNP). If, instead, a global tax were collected and redistributed on an equal per capita basis, the net payment of the high-income countries would amount to US$253 billion (2.4 per cent of their GNP) whereas low-income countries would have a net revenue of US$94 billion.

A simultaneous equilibrium solution for nine regions has been

Table 12.1   **A scenario of the world CO$_2$ emission permits market, 2000**

	Domestic surcharge (US$/tC)	CO$_2$ balance (million tC)	Net payment (−)/ receipt (+) (US$ billion)
Deficit regions			
North America	150	514	−111.0
Russia, Eastern Europe	104	401	−86.0
OECD Pacific	119	66	−36.0
OECD Europe	60	157	−34.0
Middle East	45	33	−7.0
Surplus regions			
South-East Asia	0	967	+208.0
Africa	0	265	+57.0
Latin America	0	15	+3.0
China	0	3	+0.7

Note: Total between-region transactions amount to 1.3 billion tC. The world emission permits market is cleared at US$215/tC in the simulation.

derived, assuming a combination of energy taxes and global tradable emission permits to stabilize global CO$_2$ emissions at 5 billion metric tons of carbon (tC) by the year 2000 (Yamaji et al. 1991). This exercise gave rise to the order of international resource transfer as shown in table 12.1.

The negotiations on global climate change, unlike those on local and regional environmental agreements, are concerned essentially with how to allocate "sacrifices" without corresponding immediately tangible economic benefits. The scenario in table 12.1 is not meant to be prescriptive but, rather, demonstrates how intractably difficult the equity issue can be in the allocation of responsibilities for planetary governance. The sharp asymmetry between the deficit and the surplus regions would foretell the difficulty of aiming for anything like a universal code of conduct and action plan. Those who find themselves legitimately in a position to put a higher priority on economic development than on environmental sustainability may enhance their bargaining power just by a threat of inaction or "free-riding."

The so-called "Group of 77" (the traditional coalition of all the developing countries in multilateral negotiation forums) is no longer united. It is suffering increased internal economic polarization, and new coalition blocs are emerging in global environmental negotiations that cut across the traditional divide between the North and the

South: there is a group dependent on coal-fired energy; another group with a relatively high commitment to nuclear energy; a third group of island and low-lying countries vulnerable to sealevel rises; a group dependent on forestry resources, partially overlapping with a group dependent on eco-tourism; a group whose economic subsistence is already threatened by desertification and recurrent natural disasters; and so forth.

Poor countries in the Sahel, for instance, would be preoccupied with getting greater international assistance for sustainable agriculture and even for an unprecedented kind and scale of innovations in the application of science and technology (which will be discussed later). The countries with established eco-tourist industries and large animals (mostly in Africa) see an opportunity for securing conservation compensation. Those urged to preserve rain forests for carbon sinks and biodiversity wish to be assured of a fair share in international transfers to cover their forgone economic benefits from logging and land-clearing.

Economists argue, albeit mainly on account of cost-effectiveness, that the incentives to protect existing forests and to reforest, for instance, might be easily financed from the proceeds from other protocols such as a small carbon tax scheme. So the easiest way to win international agreement at this stage might be a small carbon tax scheme (even of experimental significance) combined with a credit scheme for carbon sinks. Such a combination could have the dual effect of stimulating energy efficiency and forestry preservation (Barrett 1990).

In spite of the diversity of developing country interests, the issue of financial resources, combined with considerations of international equity, has generated a relatively common front for the South. Thus the broad pledge to the "Earth Charter" at the UNCED in Rio is only the beginning of a possibly decades-long, decathlon-like procession of international negotiations over diverse specific protocols. As mentioned above, the bargaining is purely distributive in nature at least for the time being. (This could change several decades hence if Southerners' continued inaction resulted in eventual catastrophe becoming more obvious).

It appears that Northerners' skilful resistance to financial sacrifice has so far been successful in guarding their neo-liberalist tradition by housing the Global Environmental Facility (GEF) in the World Bank (with joint administration by UNEP and the United Nations Development Programme, UNDP). So far their concession has been an

385

only marginal increase in its funding scale, even though faster than expected progress has been achieved toward a democratization of its political governance mechanism through the newly instituted Participants' Assembly.

The GEF administration has pioneered the so-called principle of "incremental cost financing" for joint implementation. This principle was endorsed in the recent formulation of the International Convention on Biological Diversity (ICBD). It implies that developed country signatories have an obligation to provide new and additional financial resources to those developing countries that are willing to implement globally beneficial conservation of natural capital, over and above the national benefits of doing so.

The thrust of this principle is that developing countries will not undertake additional conservation on behalf of the global community unless developed countries offer financial compensation for them to do so. This principle may be applicable to various other treaties and protocols concerned with protecting the stratospheric ozone layer, reducing GHG emissions, reducing acid precipitation, minimizing the risk of radioactive fallout, preventing waterways pollution, preventing the spread of pests and disease, and even preserving the world cultural heritage. The concept of incremental cost is itself a difficult one, especially when linked to incremental global environmental benefits. The analysis is difficult at best, with numerical results often being unreliable. Moreover, although the analytical issues are clearly separate from financing strategy issues, a strategy may be implicit in the way incremental cost is calculated (King 1993).

"Debt-for-nature swaps" represent another collective arrangement for transferring *development rights* from indebted developing countries to international environmental NGOs. Such swap deals are ad hoc, and subject to rather high transaction costs. Besides, an important discrepancy tends to arise between the values of the transferred development rights (linked to the conservation of ecological resources) and the actual costs of forgone development opportunities (which rise with a higher rate of discount in the secondary markets for debts).

A serious investigation of the issues and policy options for a sustainable trade regime is, as yet, in its infancy. Barbier and Rauscher (1994) examine, with their theoretical model, the effect of timber trade interventions on the incentives for timber exporters to conserve their forests. Trade interventions, through import bans, taxes, and quantity restrictions, could lead to reductions in the long-run equilibrium of the forest stock and thus be counter-productive if such interventions worsened timber exporters' terms of trade. (This would be the case if importers had an elasticity of marginal utility larger than unity with respect to imported natural goods.) This readily reconfirms that international market regulations ought not just to penalize resource use indiscriminately but to provide at the same time appropriate incentives for improved investment in eco-conservation. Barbier et al. (1994) also demonstrate that an important incentive to further investment in sustainable resource management would be to open international markets for the products of sustainable management rather than to restrict access to those markets.

Natural capital consists of multi-layered common-pool resources. Its loss generates externalities at local, national, and international levels. A pool of diverse genetic materials is able to generate new medicines, crops, and chemicals and also new biotechnologies and technologies for gene transfers. Diverse ecosystems such as forests, oceans, wetlands, migratory animals and fish, coastal environments, etc., along with the impacts of climate change, are interdependent. When they are disturbed, the consequences can have multiplier effects across regions and across different ecosystems. Developing countries are generally more important than industrial countries in terms of approaches to the incentive problem. They are, after all, the custodians of much of the world's remaining biodiversity and natural environments that are globally important common-pool resources.

A good case may be made for establishing an international system of legal rights over the genetic information content of natural biotic resources. The Instituto Nacional de Biodiversidad in Costa Rica attempts to collect, codify, and market genetic information from domestically available bio-samples in order to generate financial resources that will support conservation efforts (Aylward et al. 1993). Although this experiment has been commercially geared from the outset, it presents a good case for extending the regime of Trade-Related Intellectual Property Rights to address the issue of property rights associated with the potentially useful genetic information contained in biodiversity.

Developed country delegates have recently come to express a preference for a flexible, and somewhat noncommittal, notion of a "coalition of resources" rather than the creation of any more new special funds for multilateral cooperation. But, as more and more new conventions and protocols enter serious multilateral and mini-lateral negotiations in the coming years, it is likely that opportunities for cross-sectoral issue linkage will become broader and more tangible. A coalition of resources, if meant just as a facade now, may sooner or later have to evolve into something more real than just a Pandora's box .

A precondition for social breakthroughs in the context of developing societies

The long-term goal of eco-development calls for social breakthroughs that, in turn, must build on conscious, value-oriented responses at local, national, and international levels. This will involve complex bargaining and leveraging among a variety of contending, and hitherto not very well coordinated, actors. Important actors include not only the states and established international organizations, but also a myriad of NGOs, both international and local, and market-driven business entities.

Even more importantly, a leading role in the negotiation between humans and nature must be played by the *"epistemic community"* – policy analysts or "action" intellectuals, individual or institutional, who are more responsive than mere academic intellectuals to current major agendas of political importance. The Winter 1992 issue of *International Organization* was devoted to a serious reflection on the roles of the epistemic community in international negotiations. This is the community that can offer scientific diagnoses of the problems at issue and construct a set of alternative policy action proposals in a politically palatable form.

Some sceptics warn that the much-vaunted epistemic community might be a result, rather than a motor, of international negotiations, noting that scientists' transnational coalitions are formed more often in response to existing national coalitions than in advance of them (Haas 1992). This impression may hold especially in the process of a politicized international economic negotiation such as negotiations for the GATS ("trade in services") in the Uruguay Round. Drake and Nicolaïdis (1992), in examining the GATS process, distinguish two tiers of epistemic community: the "first tier" is often drawn from governmental or leading business organizations with direct interests in new policy alternatives and related political bargaining, while the "second tier" includes neutral academics, scientists, and lawyers whose stakes are more purely intellectual or a matter of professional entrepreneurship. It would be safe to say that the second-tier epistemic community tends to play a more active role than the first tier in many of the prolonged pre-negotiation phases of environmental agreement-making. Although both tiers actively engage in interest articulation at the national level, the second-tier members seem to be particularly quick in diffusing their policy advice transnationally through scientific bodies and other international organizations, so that their transnational links enhance their power to exert pressure toward a redefinition of state interests. One finds a similar picture when looking back on the history of North–South interactions on issues of environment and development.

True, the 1972 UN Conference on the Human Environment, proposed by Sweden and backed by the World Bank and many other OECD members, was received by most developing countries with indifference and partial hostility. But it should be recalled that the first systematic attempt to document the environmental consequences of development projects was the 1968 conference held by the US Conservation Foundation at Airline House, near Washington, D.C. The proceedings of this conference were published as *The Careless Technology* (Farvar and Milton 1972). Maurice Strong devoted a substantial part of the pre-negotiation phase of the Stockholm Conference to the problems facing the third world. The Conference thus succeeded in ushering in the issue of environmental planning and management as a respectable, if still minor, part of development cooperation in subsequent years.

By 1977–1978 explicit environmental assessment procedures, as proposed by the National Environmental Protection Act (NEPA), were incorporated into the US Foreign Assistance Act. A study by the International Institute for Environment and Development (IIED, the predecessor of today's World Resources Institute), published as *Banking on the Biosphere* (Stein and Johnson 1979), led to a further improvement in World Bank practices and to its Declaration of Environmental Policies and Procedures in 1980. By that time more than 120 governments in developed and developing countries had created environmental ministries or agencies, bringing the "Age of Innocence" to an end.

The following decade may well be characterized as "the beginning of an age of Environmental Enlightenment" in the context of international development cooperation (Runnals 1991). The 1980s witnessed an expansion of direct assistance to developing countries in the environmental domain. The decade also saw the growing involvement of environmental NGOs in developmental cooperation, although this phase was still largely focused on mitigating the side-effects of growth. Human resource development and training became an important part of the ODA project portfolio, including efforts at strengthening environmental agencies, legislation, and related policy research capabilities in the developing countries. Some donors have come to provide increased funds both to their own environmental NGOs with overseas activities and to local NGOs in the recipient countries.

These modest steps have penetrated slowly, but steadily, into the transition to sustainable development – an integrative notion whereby development and environment are interwoven increasingly with issues of societal dynamics such as good governance, decentralization, civil participation, and democratization. Such a broad issue linkage owes much to the changed international political environment. But at least a good part of the pressure in this direction seems to have arisen from the efforts of environmental policy analysts within the developing countries.

They have advanced the notion that, to influence the behaviour of the mass of non-specific actors, economic incentive schemes can be far more effective than a project-specific "command-and-control" approach. This notion gave rise for a while to a vogue for the neo-institutionalist ideology of "getting prices right." But more recently it has evolved into a broader, more integrative ideology of "institutional sustainability." It stresses a rule- and convention-oriented, rather than the traditional role- or task-oriented, approach to institutional development (Goldsmith 1992).

An ample illustration of this trend can be found in a series of country reports assembled for a meeting of developing country experts on environmental management, organized by the OECD Development Centre in October 1990 (Erocal 1991). In Africa, the World Bank's National Environmental Action Plans (NEAPs) have generated a number of country environmental studies (for Burkina Faso, Ghana, Guinea, Lesotho, Madagascar, Mauritius, Rwanda, etc.). The technical scope of these studies includes not only information systems, public awareness and education, and economic policy linkages but also issues of institutional dynamics. As an instrument for change, the NEAP process involved local NGOs and partnership arrangements between them and international NGOs (Arensberg 1991).

On the Asian scene, the Philippines has witnessed rapidly surging professional NGO forces, which are authorized, under the recently instituted Local Government Code, to function like local development councils, public awards committees, and school and health boards. In Thailand, where the rapidly depleting natural resource base has aggravated the political alienation of the rural peasantry, the 1987–1991 Plan put an emphasis on decentralization of natural resource management to local and provincial levels and promoting a sense of ownership and participation among local citizens. Here, too, NGOs have become increasingly active in mobilizing financial and technical resources for environmental management, as well as lobbying for improved government policy (Phamtumvanit and Lamont 1991). In Latin America, international technical assistance on environmental measures has a history of more than 25 years. Failures of planning (due to lack of finance, basic databases and monitoring systems, political authority, etc.) have led to a growing emphasis on regionally decentralized, multi-institutional approaches. During the 1970s incipient environmental movements at the grass-roots level existed only in Brazil, Mexico, and Venezuela. They expanded rapidly to most Latin American countries during the 1980s. In Brazil, for example, the number of activist environmental groups operating for more than one year grew from some 400 in 1985 to nearly 1,300 in 1992 (Rogers 1991; Viola 1997).

These stories testify to the growing awareness of the necessity for decentralization and mass participation in grappling with local environmental problems. The pace of institutional adaptation in that direction varies from country to country, and from region to region, but is increasing almost everywhere, cross-feeding on the upsurge of movements toward democratization and privatization in the post–Cold War international environment. This may not quite be the harbinger of a new lifestyle or a post-modern paradigm – which is much talked about in industrial societies. But it perhaps constitutes an important aspect of what we look upon as the "Fourth Wave of Democratization." In the third world context, this may well constitute a precondition for a real future social breakthrough toward global eco-restructuring.

Issues of science and technology for development

The transfer of technology

In multilateral diplomacy, the transfer of ecologically friendly technologies to developing countries and related domestic capability-building is indeed an agenda item of the utmost importance – especially during the first decade or so while these countries are allowed a sort of grace period before their fuller participation in the emerging conventions and protocols. Most developed country technologists contend that newly emerging technologies and related R&D have little to do with developing societies, where most of the environmental problems can be addressed with conventional technologies. Developed country diplomats still appear rather touchy about the issue of technology transfer, which all too often gets confused with that of financial resource transfer. In the UNCED process, the entire text on the subject remained "bracketed" throughout the final preparatory sessions. Contentious issues included the terms of technology transfer, intellectual property rights, and access to privately owned technologies.

The defensive argument on the part of the donor community (particularly the United States) is usually two-fold. First, most new environmentally sound technologies are locked up within private firms, with governments having very limited access to them. Secondly, subsidization of newer, "good" technologies would be less efficient because it is at variance with the polluter-pays principle, leaving older, "bad" technologies no more costly than before.

How to achieve a judicial blending of public and private resources for the transfer of environmentally sound technologies is still an unresolved issue. The lack of truly effective demand for newer environmental technologies in the developing world markets of today seriously limits private sector initiatives. Even politically negotiated markets (for ODA funding) are more readily open to a lot more conventional power plants than to fewer cleaner but costlier plants. Having learned a hard lesson in that way, many donors are now trying to shift their focus in international technological cooperation towards more energy-efficient, hence more economical, energy technologies. As a first avenue towards innovative mechanisms for promoting access to newer and better technologies, the UN Commission on Sustainable Development (UNCSD) urges governments to focus on "the transfer of environmentally sound technologies that are publicly owned or in the public domain" (ECOSOC E/1993/25/ Add.1, para. 46).

Another, and it is hoped much wider, avenue points to long-term technological cooperation and partnership between holders of environmentally sound technologies and their potential users. This was a line stressed by Stephen Schmidheiny in his address to the UNCED at Rio, supported by his book, *Changing Course: A Global Business Perspective on Development and the Environment* (1992). As warned above, however, Stiglerian solutions on a global scale are scarcely visible yet.

The burden of international public policy-making in this direction may readily fall within the purview of the new World Trade Organization (WTO), as it grapples with a "Green Round." Coupled with international coordination on major economic instruments such as eco-taxes, regulatory arrangements for international trade (as has actually been demonstrated in the endangered species regime – Young 1989) should be able to offer a more realistic framework for institutional innovation toward public–private partnerships.

The UN Commission on Science and Technology for Development (UNCSTD) has been reorganized (so as to absorb its formerly separate advisory body) only as a sop to G77 members after the battle over the United Nations' organizational slimming. The formal parallelism between the UNCSD and the UNCSTD, the latter claiming an independent role *vis-à-vis* the former, is both awkward and unfortunate. Indeed, it may have added further to the apathy to technology agendas on the part of most developed countries. But both Commissions having moved well into their fully operative phase, a subtle but interesting pattern of division of labour seems to be emerging between them.

In the UNCSTD (on which I happen to serve as a national delegate), with about half of its members drawn from scientific and policy research professions, the focus tends to shift towards issues of longer-term significance that require more studies and experimental research than in the more politically charged UNCSD. The 1994/95 intersessional work of the UNCSTD included such topics as "Science and Technology for Women in Development" and "Science and Technology for the Basic Needs of the Poor" in poorer societies. This is, to say the least, a challenging amalgam of the social- and the technological-breakthrough agendas in the context of development cooperation.

A built-in bias of the science and technology community

From the perspective of users of science and technology (S&T), one can discern two coordinates in relation to S&T. One measures the extent of standardization or orientation to the mass market, as opposed to "privateness" or closeness to human individual's life space; the other measures the degree of cost effectiveness or profitability in competitive markets (see fig. 12.1). Here, the two axes are

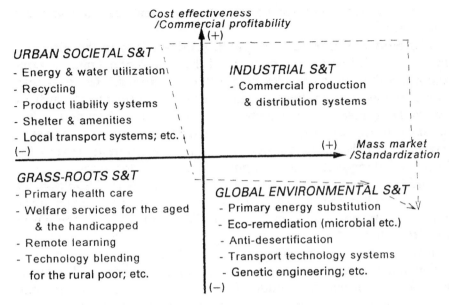

Fig. 12.1 **Four domains of science and technology (Source: adapted from an exploratory study initiated in the Institute for Science & Technology Policy Research, Japan – Kakizaki et al. 1994)**

forced to run orthogonally, although they are conventionally treated as being non-orthogonal, almost overlapping, from the perspective of producers or technology suppliers. In fact the latter perspective tends to concentrate in one of the four quadrants, *Industrial S&T*. My intention here is to bring into relief a bias that has long been built into the world's science and technology community.

As shown in figure 12.1, *Industrial S&T* has extended a limited distance into the north-western quadrant, *Urban Societal S&T*, which concerns the provision of basic utilities and urban infrastructural services. Here science and technology have come to address the innovation potentials in decentralized systems for energy, water, sewage, waste disposal, and recycling. Both hardware and institutional software need to be adapted to locality-specific natural and economic conditions, but a good degree of blending of private and public initiatives is feasible because the existing systems have historically evolved adjacent to industrial production systems.

In the urban societal domain, the initiative for innovation should preferably come from end-users of the technology systems. However, public utilities and transport authorities, imbued with the legacy of heavy capital investment, tend to be notoriously conservative. Household consumers, apart from those actively organized into advocacy NGOs, are not very sensitive to benefits and costs that are thinly spread over them, and are generally the last to get organized for policy change under normal parliamentary democracy. Much more has been said than done about the need for reinstating end-users' sovereignty in the application of science and technology.

Industrial S&T has also stretched out a bit into the south-eastern quadrant, *Global Environmental S&T*. This domain seeks applications as universal as those of Industrial S&T, with major agendas concerned with primary energy substitution, anti-desertification, microbial remediation of soil and water, disaster prevention, weather watching, etc. The unfilled gap between private and social costs in this domain justifies public policy intervention to foster basic and applied research among actors within the Industrial S&T domain as well, at least in its pre-commercial phases.

In the remaining quadrant, *Grass-roots S&T*, efforts are directed to more humanized applications of S&T, such as highly decentralized niches of health care for the aged and the handicapped, remote-village education, and other welfare activities at the grass-roots level. In most developed countries such efforts are seen as an integral part of the "social net" policy, and as such somewhat delinked from the Industrial S&T community. Nevertheless there is great scope for new scientific and technological inputs in this domain.

Ironically, this Grass-roots S&T domain has received greater attention in developing societies, particularly in the context of international development cooperation, if not so much in the S&T community as such. The concept of "technology blending" has gained currency gradually since the early 1980s. The concept originated from a recognition that the benefits of science and technology had not trickled down to the rural and urban poor. Compared with the earlier movements of intermediate technology and appropriate technology, the notion of technology blending is weighted towards an injection of selected elements (rather than pre-packaged systems) of emerging new technologies into the traditional ways of doing things. It has been geared rather consciously to the basic developmental needs of relatively underprivileged segments of developing society. The elements of new technology that have proved useful for such purposes range from micro-electronics and telecommunication technologies to new-energy technologies and advanced biotechnologies.

A panel of the UN Advisory Committee on Science & Technology for Development (UNACSTD) held at the Rice Research Institute, Los Banos, in 1982 looked upon the integration of newly emerging and traditional technologies as a "new frontier" in technology application in developing society (Weizsacker et al. 1983). The Advisory Committee's recommendation to compile a "portfolio of experiments and projects" on technology blending resulted in a first extensive state-of-the-art review by the ILO Technology and Employment Branch (ILO 1984).

Technology blending is intended not just for possibilistic scenario-writing, but as an actual improvement in traditional technologies in use in terms of unit cost of production, factor productivity, and output quality. Examples include:

– micro-electronics for crop planning, livestock monitoring, irrigation control, and farm management; electronic load control for micro-hydroelectric power generation and community saw-mills for rural development;
– symbiotic nitrogen fixation for food production and preservation, single cell protein to animal feed, bio-pesticides and other bio-technologies being experimented in several developing countries;
– telecommunications for distance learning and rural education;
– photovoltaics for irrigation pumps and refrigerators in rural hospitals; etc.

However, such technological innovations need to go hand in hand with social institutional innovations. Complementary changes must evolve simultaneously in marketing systems, consumer acceptance, and training and education systems, as well as in the overall policy environment affecting industrial structure. There is thus a need for *institutional blending* in order to stimulate technology blending, as well as to ensure an ever-broader market for it (Bhalla 1995, chap. 3). Unfortunately, most "developmental NGOs" tend to be rather ill equipped with managerial and commercial skills for productive undertakings. There is a need for supplemental inputs from private entrepreneurs and public technological institutions, which in turn requires an enabling policy environment for blending public with private initiatives, rural with urban economies, and small with large enterprises.

A bolder notion of science & technology for basic needs

Both great need and large scope exist for more serious policy research on the conditions and policy instruments for the development and diffusion of alternative technology systems in the "non-industrial" domains. An example of such systems for the north-west quadrant might be a "total system" approach employing unconventional mixes of alternative energy systems for decentralized communities (wind and solar energy, tidal, mini-hydro or LNG power plants, etc.), combined with co-generation and "cascade" systems to minimize energy waste. Innovations in this direction, as well as in the Grass-roots S&T domain, would have to assume a greater emphasis on the socio-organizational and economic dimensions of technology diffusion.

The bottom–up approach is essential but is by no means a sufficient condition for global eco-restructuring. The world's science and technology community has not only been guilty of the bias of "technological determinism" in grappling with societal problems, but its major outputs have tended to respond sooner to signals from lucrative urban markets than to basic human needs in underprivileged regions. There is no way to change the ethical foundation of the science and technology community overnight. So, a bolder exploration into science and technology for the basic human needs of the poor ought to be extended to the south-east quadrant (Global Environmental S&T) as well.

In fact, some of the avenues for primary energy substitution suggested in this book seem to open up opportunities of particular interest to currently energy-deficient and water-deficient parts of the developing world. Among others, the potential of combining solar energy and hydrogen energy with hydropower energy – all so-called "clean" energy sources – would invite attention in a broader, possibly interregional, perspective.

According to the World Resources Institute's survey (1992), only 14 per cent of the world total hydropower potential (some 2 million GWh out of 15 million GWh) has actually been developed into use. The rate of development is still very low in developing regions: 3.3 per cent in Africa, 9.4 per cent in developing Asia, and 10 per cent in Latin America (and also only 5.8 per cent in the former USSR). Leaving aside many environmentalists' objections to large hydropower projects (owing to village dislocation and habitat destruction), the potential of hydropower has been seriously deflated not only by the geographically uneven distribution of water resources but also by the seasonal instability of hydropower supply, with much of the existing capacity being wasted in rainy seasons.

To resolve this problem, an attractive option might be to utilize

397

(cheap) surplus hydropower during rainy seasons for the mass production of ultra-pure solar cells. This could also be coupled with the production of hydrogen (for fuel cells), based on electrolysis of water using photovoltaic electricity. Many energy experts expect hydrogen to become the chief energy "carrier" in the future, replacing both natural gas and liquid hydrocarbon fuels. Remarkable progress is being made in the complementary technologies to make energy storable and safely transportable even between distant regions (see Yamaguchi 1994; and chaps. 5 and 7 in this volume).

The probably century-long transition phase towards a hydrogen-based energy system is likely to be driven by an era of natural gas and methane. This intermediate phase will familiarize society with innovative gas-handling infrastructures, liquefaction technologies, and cryogenic storage. It will give rise to an interesting, albeit somewhat controversial, scenario that would be of particular interest to developing regions.

During this transitional phase (possibly lasting for about half a century), even the developed world might come to utilize biomass as a primary energy source with a wide range of new energy carriers. Today, biomass accounts for a negligible proportion of energy consumption in the developed economies. But the proportion amounts to 38 per cent in the developing world. Several experimental projects have been going on in India, Tanzania, etc., aimed at high-rate methanization for electricity generation as an option for environment-friendly extra energy supply. Some 100 million hectares of land could possibly be taken out of farming in the United States and Europe if agricultural surpluses and subsidies were really brought under control. In the developing world, especially in sub-Saharan Africa and South America, potential croplands are nearly three times larger than those currently in use (according to a 1991 FAO estimate), and some 1,000 million hectares might be left as surplus cropland even after allowing for a 50 per cent increase in future food requirements. (Regrettably China is excluded from this scenario.)

Although the surplus land is mostly "degraded" (in the form of logged forests, deforested watersheds, and semi-desertified drylands), Grainger (1988) estimates that some 750 million hectares would be suitable for reforestation. An appropriate sequence of planting could restore the soil condition of these degraded lands. Thus, Johansson et al. (1992) draw our attention to a "potential not yet well understood by most people." That is, plantation biomass in sub-Saharan Africa and South America could make a substantial contribution to the world's primary energy substitution path without serious conflict with food security. Countries in these regions (with China excluded) would then become major economic powers as large-scale exporters of bio-fuels as the biomass age sets in.

Heinrich Wohlmeyer (chap. 9 in this volume) complements this scenario by his thesis that biomass plantation would offer a good "bridging" strategy to conserve an enduring productive capacity even for marginal lands as the world moves from the present phase of food surplus to a possible future phase of food shortage. Growing non-food plants (for biomass energy, natural chemistry, and bio-technology) would help sustain the productive condition of disadvantaged lands during the food surplus phase, if farmers in these lands received compensatory grants in inverse proportion to the quality of the soil and climate.

Preaching socio-political reformation at micro levels (decentralization of public service authorities, blending of public services with markets and grass-roots organizations, and so on), fashionable as it is today, is not the only avenue for technology blending for the poor. There is scope for bolder global-scale schemes of international cooperation for technology blending in addressing the basic infrastructural conditions in the currently water-deficient and energy-deficient developing regions. Controversial as they may be, the long-term scenarios mentioned above suggest attractive ideas that are worthy of further technical and institutional feasibility studies under the aegis of a GEF-like multilateral facility. Certainly a "design-in" type participation of the science community of the developing countries would be desirable for such studies from the outset. It is to be hoped that the challenge in this direction may sooner or later make inroads into the multilateral agendas of sustainable development, given due pressure from the engineering consultancy communities for development cooperation.

A future United Nations system

Both the advent of a post-bipolar world order of security and an ideological institutionalization of sustainable development have been synchronized with the call for a renaissance of the United Nations system. That call has been obscured for some time amid the budgetary crisis that has been building since the mid-1980s. In parallel there has been an increasingly conscious search for a vision of a "third-generation world organization" (the term used by Maurice Bertrand

1989). A vision of functions does not immediately overlap with a vision of due organizational forms, however.

With the fiftieth anniversary of the United Nations, the long-overdue "rethink" of how to retrofit the existing complex array of multilateral organizations into a more coherent mechanism for global governance has begun to gather momentum. Much of the attention has so far been focused on the UN peace-keeping and peace-making operations. Although these can claim to be an integral part of global eco-restructuring, the techno-economic developmental arms of the UN machinery continue to decline.

Boutros Boutros-Ghali's staff reforms up to 1995 were still mainly confined to a "rationalization" of the United Nations proper, i.e. part of the secretariat for the high-level policy organs linked to the General Assembly and the Security Council. This part is dedicated to the upkeep of the most "diffuse" and universal regime for global governance. Some dramatic cuts may be foreseen in the administration of the now much overstretched technical cooperation machinery (a substantial number of Specialized Agencies, Funds, and Programmes). But the decisions to that effect remain largely decentralized or even fragmented. (These action arms of the system account altogether for about half of the dwindling total system budget of about US$5 billion per annum.)

The issue of how better to link the UN action machinery with the World Bank and the International Monetary Fund (IMF) remains unresolved. An earlier suggestion (by Bertrand 1987) to reintegrate the muddled hierarchy into a "13-Commissioners" system (including the IMF and the World Bank) to be overseen by the Secretary-General made way for a slightly more moderate Nordic proposal for a high-level body to govern the two-thirds of the UN system budget being spent on development cooperation. The recently initiated UNDP policy centred on "national execution" and a decentralized "programme approach" (UNDP 1990) seems to be serving as an initial shock strategy – a sort of "meta-policy" to de-institutionalize some of the major nodes of organizational resistance to change. However, the call for a better-coordinated, and budgetarily tightened up, "unitary" United Nations system (voiced mostly by the developed countries struggling with their own budget deficits) fails to acknowledge a crucial fact: that the grossly muddled hierarchy of international institutions just mirrors the reality of international relations.

As things stand, our collective learning effort is likely to be directed, in the classical functionalist tradition, mainly to less contentious sector-specific approaches. This means focusing individually on such subjects as industrial energy use, automobile emissions, agricultural practice, clean coal technology, carbon sinks, sustainable forestry management, watershed management, population growth, etc. Familiar cross-sectoral issues such as technology transfer and global sustainable development will be kept hovering to enhance the scope of "diffuse reciprocity" in multilateral agreement-making through opportunities for cross-sectoral and intertemporal issue linkages.

We need to muster a better hybrid than we have had so far between multilateralism, regionalism, bilateralism, and minilateralism. A better understanding is needed of how the virtues of one can be synergized with those of another, and the weakness of one rectified by the merits of another. Synergized bilateral or minilateral approaches would be essential particularly for accommodating the needs of big "problem regions" such as China and the economies in transition. Secret pacts and side agreements that undercut multilateralism will have to be discouraged through a central depository system of of agreements, pacts, and codes. Such a central bridgehead for multilateralization of national and regional initiatives must be combined with a mandate to analyse their impacts on the third parties and to trigger complementary or remedial negotiation processes for advancing a consensus and common standards on difficult issues.

Indeed, this is precisely the kind of task that the UN Commission on Sustainable Development is expected to fulfil. And this happens to be the only new organizational device that the global community has managed to create through the long UNCED process.

A *regime* is a process whereby countries seek governing arrangements that affect the pattern of interdependence and mediate among their different values, goals, and ideologies. An *organization* is a legal entity having offices, personnel, equipment, and budgets. Whereas many international organizations are explicitly linked to specific regimes, most UN Specialized Agencies are rather of the "free-standing" type, being geared to technical action to preset objectives rather than to steer interest articulation and regime-building. And there are many regimes that operate in the absence of central organizations to administer them. Such anarchical arrangements may help to sidestep a range of classical problems associated with the rubric of non-market failures: organizational paralysis, underfunding, co-optation, intrusiveness, and bureaucratization, to which no magic solution seems to exist yet (Young 1989, pp. 32–44).

The developed market economies tend to be generally resistant to "hard" international arrangements of the command-and-control type. The developing countries, in contrast, generally stand in favour of such arrangements, because they are in a position to benefit from the regime-generated rules without sharing the full cost. Indeed, the evolving new regimes for sustainable development may promise more attractive options for international resource transfer, as we have seen earlier, if international organizations (new or existing) are allowed to intervene to collect environmental rents in the name of humanity's common heritage (see above). This is not a new idea. It was once vehemently invoked in the form of an International Seabed Authority in the Law of the Sea negotiation. A similar idea, though on a more modest scale, materialized also with the commission created under CRAMRA (Convention for the Regulation of Antarctic Mineral Resource Activities). However, it is likely that, for the foreseeable future, major donors will continue to resist the idea of international organizations being entrusted with sizeable revenue sources that they can control on their own (Young 1993, p. 259). This tide of thought (which reflects a sort of "neo-realist" benevolence, coupled with the post-modernist preference for bottom–up multilateralism) points emphatically to a coordination and switchboard-type role for the CSD rather than to any pre-fixed blueprint for an organizational hierarchy to govern a number of specific environmental regimes that are evolving.

Haas et al. (1993) suggest, by way of the most general lessons to be drawn from past experience in international environmental negotiations, the principle of "three Cs": (i) to "increase governmental Concern", (ii) to "enhance the Contractual environment," and (iii) to "increase national Capacity."

The first "C" refers to the organizational ability to generate a complex network of international organizations, governments, NGOs, mass media, and industry groups, which can exert public pressure on laggard countries and interests. This includes open procedures for agenda-setting through which weaker states, as well as laggard states, are enabled to put their concerns in ways that cannot be ignored by the international community. It also allows for ways in which other issues of concern to them can be linked to the agenda at hand.

The second "C" refers to the ability to make and keep agreements. Means of doing this include information-sharing and bargaining forums that help reduce the transaction costs of negotiating agreements. Monitoring and verification are essential, particularly when we move from norms to rules, that is, laying the necessary groundwork for effective protocols on the basis of the shared problem diagnoses and behavioural norms.

The third "C" – capacity-building – stems from the need to help create domestic administrative and technological capacity and to transfer resources to weaker states. It also includes the creation of international networks that serve as catalysts and facilitators on a continual basis.

The desired switchboard-type role for a third-generation global institution would imply a renewed focus on the first and second Cs in particular. It will be important in these phases to help create and nurture leading coalitions among like-minded states, relevant "epistemic" communities, and advocacy NGOs. These phases do not seem to require a large administrative bureaucracy, albeit they do imply a need for a high staff quality for servicing the politically charged negotiation dynamics. Action-oriented capacity-building programmes may prove instrumental in enhancing the rule-making climate if they are strategically tied to the function of those first two Cs. (The third C-function becomes even more crucial in implementing the signed agreements that usually come with a prescription of complementary action agendas. And full-scale capacity-building actions must be "participatory" on a broader front, involving myriad actors such as bilateral donors, action NGOs, business communities, and the world's citizenry in general.)

Thus, a renaissance of the United Nations system is not likely to be conditioned by any clearer hierarchy of issues and organizations than the existing one at least for the time being. Although some functions are not readily covered, there is no shortage of international environmental organizations today. There seems to be ample room for piggybacking on existing organizations or sharing organizational arrangements for regime formation and maintenance (Young 1993).

So, let us hope that the Commission for Sustainable Development can get into gear towards a new turning point in humankind's art of organizational learning and institutional innovation for planetary governance. How it will manage the task for the coming years is thus a subject of the utmost interest.

The UN system is only a single facet of the formal and organized dimension of global governance. After all, global governance is a process of interactive thinking and planning among diverse actors, encompassing both governmental and non-governmental actors. It operates both at the level of individual behaviour and at the level of political aggregates in the form of national and international laws. No matter whether we are entering a new world order or just struggling with a partial reconstitution of the old one, we can more or less confidently sense the direction in which changes are occurring. We are witnessing both the globalization of national economies and the fragmentation of societies into ethnic, religious, and political subgroups. Amidst these contradictory trends (which are a natural consequence of the very dyad of modernization – *social differentiation* and *integration*), we witness an increasing willingness of citizens and local autonomies to coalesce on public and international issues.

That is to say, the very concept of the sovereign nation-state has begun to erode. Its sovereignty can no longer be defined in isolation. In many fields there is no real alternative to interactive decision-making and joint problem-solving arrangements with other states. National territory has to be reconceived in terms of trading regimes and common market-like arrangements for sharing different values and resources. And the nation's people, too, need to be redefined more in line with the requirements of inter-ethnic, inter-cultural cohabitation. Regionalism and localism need to be seen as being both the consequences of enhanced human freedom and the conditions for integration. Then many of a country's domestic political issues will have to be increasingly intertwined with those being faced in other countries.

References

Amano, Akihiro (ed.) (1992) *Global Warming and Economic Growth*. CGER-I1001-92. Centre for Global Environmental Research, Tokyo (in Japanese).

Arensberg, Walter (1991) Country environmental studies: A framework for action. In Denizhan Erocal (ed.), *Environmental Management in Developing Countries*, pp. 275–296. *Paris*: OECD Development Centre.

Aylward, T., J. Echeverria, L. Fendt, and E. B. Barbier (1993) *The Economic Value of Species Information and Its Role in Biodiversity Convention: Case Studies of Costa Rica's National Biodiversity Institute and Pharmaceutical Prospecting*. A report to the Swedish International Development Authority. London: Environmental Economics Centre.

Barbier, E. B., J. C. Burges, and C. Folke (1994) *Paradise Lost? Ecological Economics of Biodiversity.* London: Earthscan.

Barbier, E. B. and M. Rauscher (1994) Trade, tropical deforestation and policy interventions. *Environmental and Resource Economics* **4**(1): 75–94.

Barrett, Scott (1990) The problem of global environmental protection. *Oxford Review of Economic Policy* **6**: 68–79.

———— (1991) Economic instruments for climate change policy. In: OECD, *Response to Climate Change: Selected Economic Issues*, pp. 51–108. Paris: OECD.

Bertrand, Maurice (1987) The role of the United Nations in the economic and social field. *Journal of Development Planning*, no. 17.

———— (1989) *The Third Generation World Organization.* Dordrecht: Martinus-Nijhoff.

Bhalla, Ajit S. (1995) *Facing the Technological Challenge: Essays on Third World Perspective.* London: Macmillan (esp. Chapter 3: "Concept and practice of technology blending").

Churchill, Anthony A. (1993) The developing world: The new energy consumer. Paper presented at the United Nations University Conference on Global Environment, Energy and Economic Development, Tokyo, 25–27 October.

Cline, William R. (1992) *The Economics of Global Warming*, Washington D.C.: Institute for International Economics.

———— (1993) Modelling economically efficient abatement of greenhouse gases. Paper submitted to the United Nations University Conference on Global Environment, Energy and Economic Development, Tokyo, 25–27 October.

Cooper, Richard N. (1994) *Environment and Resource Policies for the World Economy.* Washington D.C.: The Brookings Institution.

Dean, Andrew and Peter Hoeller (1992) *Cost of Reducing CO_2 Emissions: Evidence from Six Global Models.* OECD Economic Department Working Papers No. 122. Paris: OECD.

Drake, William J. and Kalypso Nicolaïdis (1992) Ideas, interests and institutionalization: "Trade in services" and the Uruguay Round. *International Organization* **46**(1): 37–100.

Edmonds, J. and J. Reilly (1983) Global energy and CO_2 to the year 2050. *Energy Journal* **4**: 21–47.

Erocal, Denizhan (ed.) (1991) *Environmental Management in Developing Countries.* Paris: OECD Development Centre.

Farvar, M. Taghi and John P. Milton (1972) *The Careless Technology: Ecology and International Development.* New York: Natural History Press.

Ferriter, John P. (1993) Effects of CO_2 reduction policies on energy markets. OECD/IEA paper presented at the United Nations University Conference on the Global Environment, Energy and Economic Development, Tokyo, 25–27 October.

Gleckman, Harris (1995) Transnational corporations' strategic responses to sustainable development. In: Fridtjof Nansen Institute, *Green Globe Yearbook 1995*, pp. 93–106. Oxford: Oxford University Press.

Goldsmith, Arthur A. (1992) Institutions and planned socioeconomic change: Four approaches. *Public Administration Review* **52**(6): 582–587.

Grainger, A. (1988) Estimating areas of degraded tropical lands requiring replenishment of forest cover. *International Treecrops Journal* **5**(1–2).

Haas, Peter M. (1990) *Saving the Mediterranean: The Politics of International Environmental Cooperation.* New York: Columbia University Press.

405

———— (1992) Introduction: Epistemic communities and international policy coordination. *International Organization* **46**(1).

Haas, Peter and Jan Sundgren (1993) Evolving international environmental law: Changing practices of national sovereignty. In Nazli Choucri (ed.), *Global Accord: Environmental Challenges and International Responses*, chap. 12. Cambridge, MA: MIT Press.

Haas, Peter M., Robert O. Keohane, and Marc A. Levy (eds.) (1993) *Institutions for the Earth: Sources for Effective International Environmental Protection*. Cambridge, MA: MIT Press.

Hardin, Garret (1968) The tragedy of the commons. *Science* **163**, 13 December.

Herter, Jr., Christian A. and Jill E. Binder (1993) *The Role of the Secretariat in Multilateral Negotiation: The Case of Maurice Strong and the 1972 UN Conference on the Human Environment*. FPI Case Studies No. 21, SAIS. Washington D.C.: Johns Hopkins University.

ILO (International Labour Organization) (1984) *Blending of New and Traditional Technologies: A Portfolio of Experiment and Projects*. Document submitted to the 4th session of the UN Advisory Committee on Science and Technology for Development, New York, February 1984. Geneva: ILO, January.

Johansson, T. B., A. K. N. Reddy, and R. H. Williams (eds.) (1992) *Renewable Energy: Sources for Fuel and Electricity*. Washington D.C.: Island Press.

Kakizaki, F., K. Matsubara, and K. Gonda (1994) A study on the policy for the development and diffusion of "social science and technology." Report presented at the Annual Conference of the Japan Society for Science Policy and Research Management (Session 2C7), Tokyo, 29–30 October (in Japanese).

King, Ken (1993) *The Incremental Costs of Global Environmental Benefits*. Global Environment Facility Working Paper No. 5. Washington D.C.: GEF Administrator.

Manne, Alan S. and Richard G. Richels (1992) *Buying Greenhouse Insurance: The Economic Case of CO_2 Emissions Limits*. Cambridge, MA: MIT Press.

Matsuoka, Y. and T. Morita (1992) Models for forecasting global warming. *Keisoku to Seigyo [Measurement and Control]*, **31**(5): 577–585 (in Japanese).

Mathews, J. T. (1989) Redefining security. *Foreign Affairs* **68** (Spring): 162–177.

Nordhaus, William D. (1992) An optimal transition path for controlling greenhouse gases. *Science* **258**, 20 November.

OECD (1991) *Environmental Policy: How to Apply Economic Instruments*. Paris: OECD.

———— (1993a) *Taxation and Environment: Complementary Policies*. Paris: OECD.

———— (1993b) *Taxation and Environment: Four Case Studies*. Paris: OECD.

Olson, Mancur (1965) *The Logic of Collective Action*. Cambridge, MA: Harvard University Press.

Oye, Kenneth A. and James H. Maxwell (1995) Self-interest and environmental management. In: Robert O. Keohane and Elinor Ostrom (eds.), *Local Commons and Global Interdependence*, chap. 8. London: Sage Publications.

Phamtumvanit, Dhira and Lamont, Juliet (1991) Thailand's experience with environmental planning. In: Denizhan Erocal (ed.), *Environmental Management in Developing Countries*, pp. 297–310. Paris: OECD Development Centre.

Rogers, Kirk P. (1991) Strengthening government capacity for environmental planning in Latin America. In: Denizhan Erocal (ed.), *Environmental Management in Developing Countries*, pp. 323–340. Paris: OECD Development Centre.

Runnals, David (1991) Environmental management or management for sustainable development? In: Denizhan Erocal (ed.), *Environmental Management in Developing Countries*, pp. 25–45. Paris: OECD Development Centre.

Sagasti, Francisco R. and Michael E. Colby (1993) Eco-development and perspectives on global change from developing countries. In: Nazli Choucri (ed.), *Global Accord: Environmental Challenges and International Responses*, chap. 5. Cambridge, MA: MIT Press.

Schmidheiny, Stephen, with the Business Council for Sustainable Development (1992) *Changing Course: A Global Business Perspective on Development and the Environment.* Cambridge, MA: MIT Press.

Sebenius, James K. (1993) The Law of the Sea Conference: Lessons for negotiations to control global warming. In: Gunnar Sjöstedt (ed.), *International Environmental Negotiation*, chap. 11. Newbury Park, CA: Sage Publications (for IIASA).

Stein, Robert E. and Brian Johnson (1979) *Banking on the Biosphere.* Lexington, MA: Lexington Books.

Stigler, George (1971) The economic theory of regulation. *Bell Journal of Economics* **2**: 3–21.

UNCTAD (United Nations Conference on Trade and Development) (1995) *Self-Regulation of Environmental Management.* New York: United Nations.

UNDP (United Nations Development Programme) (1990) *Government Execution: Report of the Administrator to the Governing Council.* DP/1990/33. New York, 4 May.

United Nations (1993) *International Environmental Law: Emerging Trend and Implications for Transnational Corporations.* Environment Series No. 3, Department of Economic and Social Development. New York: United Nations.

Viola, Eduardo J. (1997) The environmental movement in Brazil: Institutionalization, sustainable development and crisis of governance since 1987. In: Gordon J. MacDonald, Daniel L. Nielson, and Marc A. Stern (eds.), *Latin American Environmental Policy in International Perspective*, pp. 88–110. Boulder, CO: Westview Press.

Weizsacker, E. U. von, M. S. Swaminathan, and A. Lemma (1983) *New Frontiers in Technology Application: Integration of Emerging and Traditional Technologies.* Dublin: Tycooly International Publishing.

Whalley, J. and R. Wigle (1989) *Cutting CO_2 Emissions: The Effects of Alternative Policy Approaches.* University of Western Ontario, Dept. of Economics, September.

World Resources Institute (1992) *World Resources 1992–93.* London: Oxford University Press.

Yamaguchi, Masashi (1994) Energy barter through the utilization of hydropower. Paper presented at the 30th Anniversary on The Roles of Development Consultants Towards the 21st Century, ECFA (Engineering Consulting Firm Association of Japan), Tokyo, 16 June.

Yamaji, Kenji, K. Nagano, H. Yamamoto, and K. Okada (1991) An analysis of the CO_2 emission controlling policy based on marketable emission rights. *Proceedings of the 7th Conference on the Energy System and Economy*, Japan Energy and Resources Society, Tokyo (in Japanese).

Young, Oran R. (1989) *International Cooperation: Building Regimes for Natural Resources and the Environment.* Ithaca, NY: Cornell University Press.

——— (1993) Perspectives on international organization. In: Gunnar Sjöstedt (ed.), *International Environmental Negotiation*, chap. 13. Newbury Park, CA: Sage Publications (for IIASA).

Contributors

Robert U. Ayres
Sandoz Professor of Management and
the Environment, INSEAD,
Fontainebleau, France

Faye Duchin
Dean, School of Humanities and Social
Sciences, Rensselaer Polytechnic
Institute, Troy, NY, USA

Paolo Frankl
Centre for the Management of
Environmental Resources, INSEAD,
Fontainebleau, France (formerly of the
Dipartimento di Meccanica e
Aeronautica, Università di Roma I
"La Sapienza," Rome, Italy)

Gilberto C. Gallopín
Director, Systems and Sustainable
Development Programme, Stockholm
Environment Institute, Stockholm,
Sweden

Walter Manshard
Institute for Geography, University of
Freiburg, Freiburg, Germany

Anton Moser
Institute of Biotechnology, Technical
University Graz, Austria

Hans-Holger Rogner
Section Head, Planning and Economic
Studies Section, International Atomic
Agency, Vienna, Austria

Kalpana Rohatgi
Department of Biology, Marquette
University, Milwaukee, WI, USA

Pradeep Rohatgi
Materials Department, College of
Engineering and Applied Sciences,
University of Wisconsin-Milwaukee, WI,
USA

Mikoto Usui
Professor of International Development
and Political Economics, College of
Cross-Cultural Communication and
Business, Shukutoku University, Japan

Paul M. Weaver
Director, Centre for Eco-efficiency,
Enterprise and Economy, Universities of
Durham and Portsmouth, UK

Robert H. Williams
Center for Energy and Environmental
Studies, Princeton University, Princeton,
NJ, USA

Heinrich Wohlmeyer
President, Austrian Association for
Agricultural Research, Vienna, Austria

Index

acidification, 342; of soil, 25, 26, 31, 59–60; of water, 31, 59–60
agrarian reform, 313–14
agricultural trade policy, 289
agriculture: and biotechnology, 80; in China, 277–78; balance with forestry of, 282, 304; definition of, 300; eco-restructuring of, 312–13; economic role of, 284; education for sustainability in, 282, 291, 317; emissions from, 280–82; and food production, 276–79; industrial, 283, 284, 285, 300; mixed, 285, 290, 291, 304; modernization of, 314; "no till," 282; organic, 290–95; peasant, 284, 330, 332; policies governing, 326; productivity of, 18–19, 278, 284–90, 291; reform of, 32; role of, 284, 336; surpluses in, 298, 299; sustainability of, 283, 284, 286–87, 296, 300, 303–305; technological status of, 78; traditional, 91–92, 316–17; tropical, 311, 315; types of, 318
agro-ecosystems: tropical, 318–20; sustainable, 300–305

air freight, 349
air pollution, 69–70, 113–14
aircraft industry, 123, 131–32, 133
allelopathy, 86
alloys: eutectic, 131; high-temperature, 123–26
aluminium, 111, 118, 267
ammonia emissions, 280, 281
Austria, organic farming in, 293–94
automobiles, 34–35, 132–33, 273, 341, 342, 345. *See also* fuel cell vehicles
automotive industry, 118, 126, 128, 132–33, 379

Bakara Agricultural College, 290
Best Management Practices, Codes of, 300
bio-catalysts, 83
bio-leaching, 87
bio-pesticides, 83–86
biodiversity, 8, 61–62, 103, 107, 322, 374–75
biofertilizers, 93–94
biogas systems, 80

biological control agents, 83–87

Biological Diversity, International Convention on, 61, 62, 386

biomass, 159, 162, 163, 164, 185, 203–204, 208–209, 211, 213; as animal feed, 282, 299; as energy source, 162–63, 182, 398–99; as material for polymers, 272

biopol, 89

biopolymers, 88–89

bioprocessing, 81–82, 103

biosphere: divisions of, 56; management of interactions with the, 73–74; stability of, 27–31, 305

biotechnology, 19, 62, 79–82, 85–98, 105–106, 273, 333

bridging strategies, 298–99, 304, 399

Brundtland Commission. *See* World Commission on Environment and Development (WCED)

building-integrated photovoltaic systems, 232–33, 238–39, 242–43, 246, 247, 249, 251

cadmium, 23, 115

capacity-building, 335

carbon, 15, 29, 159, 166–67, 322

carbon cycle, 28–29, 30

carbon dioxide: atmospheric concentration of, 169, 180, 181; changes in levels of, 66, 369; consumption of, 281–82; disposal of, 169, 187–90, 191, 193, 202, 211; emissions of, 167, 169, 180–81, 283, 341, 342; sequestration of, 169, 184–87, 192–93, 202, 205–210, 211

carbon dioxide fertilization, 9

carbon sinks, 385

carbon taxes, 203, 205, 208, 371, 375–76, 377, 385. *See also* taxes

carbon/hydrogen ratio, 170–71

carbon/oxygen cycle, 12

carrying capacity, global, 18–19

catalytic energy conversion, 164

cellulose, 88–89

ceramics, 126–28, 132, 145

channel integration, 347

chaos, 30

chemicals: production of, 23–27; toxic emissions from, 23–24

China: agriculture in, 277–78; groundwater shortages in, 278; integrated bioprocessing in, 97; population growth in, 277

chlorofluorocarbons (CFCs), 7, 17, 27, 59, 378

clean technology, 39, 110, 114

climate change, 17, 31, 57–60, 149–50, 341; development of agreements on, 369–70; Framework Convention on, 57, 150; Intergovernmental Panel on, 58

coal, 166, 170, 181, 208, 377

commodities, biomass-based, 98–102

community development, 313

comparative advantage, 345

compatibility constraints, 151–52, 252

compensation schemes, 299–300, 379–80

competition, 73, 263, 301, 349

Convention on Biological Diversity, 61, 62

cryogenic fuels, 168

crystalline silicon technology, 227, 247

DDT, 26, 281, 379

"debt-for-nature" swaps, 386

decarbonization, 169–71, 182–84, 211–12

deforestation, 19, 69, 282–83

degradability, 271–72

demand-side management, 154

dematerialization, 110, 114–15, 128, 169

denitrification, 87–88, 280–81

design for environment (DFE), 39, 110, 114

developing countries: agriculture in, 285; and biotechnology, 90; energy demand in, 244, 248; and environmental management, 376–77, 384–85, 386; population growth in, 262–63; and sustainable development, 171–73, 390

development, strategies for, 41–42, 351, 390

dioxins, 24

direct foreign investment, 354

discount rates, 319

distribution, integrated, 347
distribution systems, 331–32
Dutch elm disease, 62, 105

earth system, 30–31, 57
East Europe, diffusion of photovoltaic technology in, 249, 250
eco-principles, 90
eco-restructuring, 35, 66, 67, 158, 260, 273–74, 293, 311, 364
eco-technology, 78, 81, 106
eco-villages, 97
economic blocs, 263
economic growth: factor inputs for, 261–62; and sustainability, 13–14, 36–37, 109, 172–73
economic instruments, 371
economic modelling, 260
ecosystems, industrial, 96–97
efficiency: agricultural, 312; energy, 34, 37–38, 163–64, 294; "second-law", 37, 39; transport, 349–50, 355–56
effluent taxes, 43
electric motors, special-purpose, 142–45
electric power, 34, 160, 161, 181, 244
electric-powered vehicles, 34–35, 145
electrochemical technology, 164
emission reduction, 32, 150, 181, 182, 353, 369–70
"end-of-pipe" treatment, 109, 113
energy: currencies for, 153, 154, 160, 162; demand for, 377; efficiency of, 34, 37–38, 163–64, 294; policies for, 152, 157, 174–76; prices of, 152, 346–47; sources of, 3, 4, 35, 161–63; substitutions of, 166–69, 397–98
energy sector, function of, 153
energy service palette, 162–63
energy services, 153, 154, 162
energy systems: decarbonization of, 169–71; eco-restructuring of, 151, 158; efficiency of, 155–57; policies for, 397; reference, 150, 151; structure of, 152–54, 155; sustainable, 150–52, 159–160, 173, 253
entrepreneurs, 42, 346
environmental biotechnology, 80

environmental charters, 380
environmental costs, accounting for, 44, 171, 262, 305, 342, 346–47, 352, 356–57, 360, 381
environmental degradation, 171, 173
environmental disputes, 263–64
environmental impact, measures for, 12
environmental planning, 174, 388–91
environmental regulation, 4, 40, 43, 47, 71, 113, 372, 377–81
environmental resources: pricing of, 356; valuation and allocation of, 16–17
environmental services, 16–17
environmental taxes, 371, 372, 373, 374, 376, 381, 382–84
environmental threats: assessments of, 4–5, 6–7; public perceptions of, 13–14
enzymes, 83, 103
epistemic community, 388–89
erosion, 31, 279, 280, 282, 285, 294
ethanol, 93, 100
eutrophication, 15
exergy efficiency, 37, 39, 155–56
extractive industries, 56–57

ferrites, 142
ferromagnetism, 140–42
fertilizers, 279–81, 294
fisheries, 9, 32
food production, 276, 277, 279
food supply, 64, 283, 284, 288, 289, 293, 307
food technology, 80
forestry, 32, 276, 304, 330
fossil fuels, 32, 33, 36, 58, 98, 162, 166, 174, 267
Framework Convention on Climate Change, 57, 150
framework conventions, 368–69, 378
freight efficiency, 355–56
freight transport, 349–51, 357–58
freight volumes, 339, 349, 351
fuel cell vehicles, 185, 203, 204–207, 208–211, 213
fuel cells, 164, 183–84
fusion, 161, 169

gas liquefaction technology, 168
General Agreement on Tariffs and Trade (GATT), 264, 289, 345
genetic engineering, 89–90
genetically engineered organisms (GEOs), 79, 80, 89, 103–105
genome mapping, 90
geosphere, 56
Germany: nitrogen surplus on farm land, 295; organic agriculture in, 291–92
global economy, 263
Global Environmental Facility, 385–86
global environmental science and technology, 395
global governance, 399–400, 401–402, 403–404
global warming, 17, 46, 58, 62, 283, 369–70
globalization, 259–60, 263, 265, 339–40, 345–46, 404
gold, bio-leaching of, 87
governments, role of, 47, 48, 174
grain production, 276–77, 279–80, 293–94
grass-roots science and technology, 395
green revolution, 72, 278–79
"green" taxes, 40, 47, 299
greenhouse gases, 17, 31, 58, 149, 150, 167–68, 182, 185, 369, 377. *See also* ozone depletion
groundwater resources, 9, 18, 32, 278, 289. *See also* water

habitat preservation, 32
"half-way" technologies, 77–78
haulage distances, 349, 351, 352
health care, 79–80, 92
heavy metals, 25, 26, 31, 64, 113
hemp, 95
hormones, 80
human rights, 264, 302
hydrogen, 29, 159, 160–61, 162, 164, 175, 183, 185, 398; production of, 35, 181–82, 183, 184, 192–203, 204, 252, 253
hydrogen embrittlement, 214–15
hydrological cycle, 9, 12, 57–58
hydropower, 397–98

income transfer, 383–84
incremental cost financing, 386
India: bio-pesticide market in, 84; pesticide use in, 281; urbanization in, 277
indigenous technologies, 90–92
industrial biotechnology, 80–81
industrial ecosystems, 96–97
industrial ecology, 35, 66, 158, 260. *See also* eco-restructuring
industrial metabolism, 66, 67, 260. *See also* eco-restructuring
industrial science and technology, 394–95
industrialization, 3–4, 70–71, 171–73
information, agricultural, 331
information technology, 57, 273, 333–34, 348, 354
infrastructures, 151, 154, 157, 158, 346
inks, plant-based, 98, 100
institutional sustainability, 390
integrated distribution, 347
integrated resource planning, 154
integrated rural development, 314, 315
Intergovernmental Panel on Climate Change, 58
international agreements, 365, 367, 368–69, 402–403
International Insurance Pool, 58
international organizations, 73, 356–57, 399–401, 402, 403–404
inventory reductions, 348
"itai-itai" disease, 23

kairomones, 86

labour productivity, 32
land, as factor of wealth, 3, 4
land cover, 65–66
land use: changes in, 65, 66; ranking of systems of, 322–26; sustainability of, 285, 316, 320, 326–30; for transportation, 338, 343, 358–59; in West Africa, 68–69
landscape ecology, 57, 67–68
Latin America: environmental movements in, 391; peasant agriculture in, 330–34; rural development in, 313–14, 315

Law of the Sea Convention, 367, 368
leaching, 280, 285
lead, 26, 115
liberalization: economic, 261; market, 344–46; trade, 261, 339–40, 345, 351–52, 353
lithosphere, 64–65
logistics, transportation, 339, 347–48

magnets, 142, 145
Malthus, Thomas Robert, 4, 18, 288
manufacturing, 56; downstream consequences of, 39–40
market liberalization, 344–46
market mechanisms, 20, 46–47, 288, 296–97, 301, 366, 381
materials: ceramic, 126–28, 132; composite, 128–33; cycles, 66–67; electronic, 133–40; ferromagnetic, 140–42; high-temperature, 123–26; information-intensive, 145–47; matrix, 130, 131, 132; photovoltaic, 139–40; productivity of, 32–33, 67, 110, 114–16; semiconductor, 136; strength of, 129–30; substitution of, 115, 128, 131–32, 271, 273, 312; taxonomy of, 117; technology, 117–18
materials intensity per unit service (MIPS), 12, 32, 67, 290
matrix materials, 130, 131, 132
meat production, 277
mercury, 23, 24, 115
metallurgy, 117–18, 126
metals and metal ores, 111–13, 117
methane, 167–68, 169, 170, 175, 279, 281, 398
methanol, 184, 185
micro-organisms, 80, 103, 104
Minamata disease, 23
Montreal Protocol, 46, 59, 264, 378, 380

National Environmental Action Plans, 390
natural capital, 4, 387
natural gas, 167–68, 169, 170, 173, 175, 189–90, 193, 267, 398; as feedstock for hydrogen, 205–208
natural systems: disturbance of, 9, 67
Neem oil, 86

neo-Malthusianism, 16, 20, 33, 37, 113, 288
nitrogen, 14–15, 28, 29; fixation of, 80, 94, 105, 279; loss of, 87–88, 279, 280
nitrogen cycle, 12, 30
nitrogen efficiency, 295
nitrogen oxides, 24–25, 26, 59, 66, 342, 369
"no till" agriculture, 282
non-governmental organizations (NGOs), 380, 389–91
"non"-technologies, 77
nuclear power, 34, 161, 162, 169
nutrient cycles, 27, 294–95, 322
nutrient elements, 14–15

ocean currents, 12
oceans: food potential of, 286; storage of carbon dioxide in, 169, 187–88
oil, 95, 166
oilseed crops, 100–102
organic agriculture, 290–95
organic liquids, 145
Our Common Future. See World Commission on Environment and Development (WCED) report
oxides, 24–25
oxygen, 15, 28
ozone depletion, 17, 46, 59. *See also* greenhouse gases

parasites, 86
pathogens, 85–86
pest and disease resistance capacity, 322
pest management, integrated, 317
pesticides, 281; biological, 83–86
pests, migration of, 62, 105
petrochemical products, cost of, 95, 102
pheromones, 86
Philippines, NGOs in the, 390
phosphorus, 279, 282, 294
photosynthesis, 28, 282, 320
photovoltaic cells, 223–26, 229–33, 239–42, 245–46, 252–53
photovoltaic technology, 139–40, 145, 181–82, 226–29, 233–39, 246–52. *See also* solar energy
phyto-extraction, 87

phytoremediation, 86–87
pipelines, convertibility of, 211, 214–15
plant matter, for industrial materials, 95, 98–100
plastics, recycling of, 271–72, 273
pluralism, technological, 327
policy instruments: for technology systems, 396–97
political ecology, in West Africa, 71
"polluter-pays" principle, 371, 373
pollution: abatement, 372; accounting for, 262; air, 69–70, 113-14; chemical, 22–27; control of, 6–7, 113–14; as inhibitor of growth, 21–22; and sustainability, 8, 9
polymers, 89, 120, 271, 272
population growth, 151–52, 171, 262–63, 266, 287; in China, 277; stabilization of, 5, 18–21; in West Africa, 69
poverty, 72, 73
primary materials, changes in consumption patterns of, 267–70
productivity: agricultural, 18–19, 278, 284–90, 291; ecological, 320; materials, 32–33, 67, 110, 114–16; primary, 320; resource, 12, 15–16, 45
property rights, in biotic resources, 387

rabbits, introduction into Australia of, 62, 105
radiation balance, 12
rail freight, 349, 357–58
recycling, 3, 40–41, 45, 115, 264; efficiency of, 39; redesign for, 271, 272, 312
reforestation, 398
regulation, 4, 40, 43, 47, 113, 372, 377–81
remanufacturing, 41, 115. *See also* recycling
replicability, technological, 322
resilience, systems, 30–31
resources: non-renewable; 109–110; productivity of, 12, 15–16, 45; taxes on use of, 43, 360
respiration, aerobic, 28
rhizofiltration, 87
roads, 63–64, 339, 340, 346, 358
rural development, 313–15, 332
rural electrification, 241–42, 245–46, 249

saline aquifers, as reservoirs for carbon dioxide, 190–192, 211
scale economies, 348
science and technology, domains of, 393–95
sea lampreys, introduction into the Great Lakes, 105
sealevel rise, 58
"second-law" efficiency, 37, 39
self-regulation, 380–81
semiconductors, 133, 134
silicon scraps, 233, 234–36
social differentiation, 72
social forestry, 315
social welfare, 7, 261, 264
socio-diversity, 317
soil: acidification of, 25, 26, 31, 59–60; degradation of, 287; erosion of, 279; loss of, 287
soil and water conservation capacity, 322
soils, 63–64
"sol-gel" processing, 127–28
solar cells, 139, 140; production of, 398
solar electric home systems, 230–32
solar energy, 159, 161–62, 246, 253. *See also* photovoltaic technology
steel alloys, 118, 121
structural adjustment programmes (SAPs), 72–73
subsidies, 43, 371, 373; agricultural, 182, 298, 304; in transport, 347, 357
substitutability limits, 2, 7–8, 13
substitution, materials, 115, 128, 131–32, 271, 273, 312
sulphur, 29
sulphur cycle, 12
sulphur dioxide, 26, 59, 342
superconductors, 136, 139
sustainability: agricultural, 283, 284, 286–87, 296, 300, 303–305; criteria for, 7–8; definitions of, 7–8; ecological criterion for, 8; economic criterion for, 7–8; indicators of, 8–12; and industrialization, 3–4; institutional, 390; principles for achieving, 296; route to, 44–45, 106–107; technical conditions for, 31–39; use of term, 2

sustainable development: regimes for, 402; requirements for, 335–36

Sustainable Development, UN Commission on, 392, 393, 401

symbiosis, 263

synthetic fibres, 120–21

synthetic fuels, 181–82

systems, non-linear, 30–31

tariffs, 345

taxes: as regulatory mechanism, 372–74, 381; carbon, 203, 205, 208, 371, 375–76, 377, 385; consumption, 382–83; effluent, 43; global, 383; on production, 382; resource-based, 43, 44, 292, 299, 360, 374

technologies: advanced, 78; agricultural, 19–20, 325–26; availability of, 325–26, 331; blending of, 366, 395–96, 399; clean, 39, 110, 114; energy service, 154, 157, 164; "half-way", 77–78; impact of, 71–72, 265–67; indigenous, 90–92; life cycle of, 81; planning for, 396–99; projections on use of new, 33, 42–43, 266; replicability of, 322; solar energy, 159; substitutability of, 3, 4, 8, 13; traditional, 327, 333; transfer of, 173, 391–93

telecommunications, 259, 354

Thailand, NGOs in, 390–91

thermoplastics, 89

thin-film technology, 140, 227–29, 236, 247

Thomas, Lewis, 77

Toxic Release Inventory, 23–24

toxic wastes, 70, 113

toxicity, 26–27

toxification, 21–22

tradable permits, 43–44, 371, 372, 384

trade: barriers to, 264, 345, 353, 386–87; liberalization of, 261, 339–40, 345, 351–52, 353; policies, 305

trading blocs, 263, 345

traditional technologies, 327, 333

transistors, 133

transport infrastructure, 338, 343, 346

transport intensity, 350–51, 353–55, 359

transportation: automobiles and, 273; efficiency of, 349–50, 355–56; electric, 34, 35; energy intensity of, 341–42; factors affecting, 338–40; fuel cell use in, 183–84, 185; logistics of, 339, 347–48; policies for, 340; space used for, 338, 343, 358–59

treaties, environmental, 367–70, 378, 389

tropics, 60–61, 64–65, 315–26

truck transport: energy intensity of, 341; regulation of, 349, 358, 360; size of fleet, 346; taxes on, 358

UN Commission on Science and Technology for Development, 393

UN Commission on Sustainable Development, 392, 393, 401

UN Law of the Sea Convention, 367, 368

unemployment, 43, 45

United Nations, 399–400

United States of America: chemical emissions data from, 23–24; consumption of metals in, 111–13; energy use in, 38, 39, 294; environmental regulations in, 379; oil crops in, 100–102

urbanization: in Asia, 64; in China, 277, 278; in West Africa, 70, 71

Utility Photovoltaic Group, 243

volatilization, 20

vulnerability, 60–61

Waldsterben (forest die-back), 25, 60

waste emissions, reduction of, 109–110

waste management, 270–72

waste mining, 115–16

wastes, solid, 70

water: acidification of, 31, 59–60; consumption of, 62–63; denitrification of, 87–88; pollution of, 70; resources, 286, 289. *See also* groundwater resources

water–gas shift reaction, 211–12

West Africa: air pollution in, 69–70; environmental regulation in, 71; industrialization in, 70–71; land

resources in, 68–69; land zones in, 67–68; need for land-use policies in, 68–69; political conditions in, 68, 71; population growth in, 69; solid wastes in, 70; structural adjustment programmes and, 72–73; urbanization in, 70, 71; water pollution in, 70
Weterings & Opschoor taxonomy of sustainability indicators, 8–9

wind power, 34, 251
women, education and status of, 5, 21
wood, as a fuel source, 166
World Commission on Environment and Development (WCED) report, 4, 7, 36, 265, 274
World Trade Organization, 357, 393

zero-carbon energy system, 157–58